$ 22
mc

INSIGHT GUIDES

ROME
CITY GUIDE

www.insightguides.com/Italy

⊙ Walking Eye App

Your Insight Guide now includes a free app and eBook, dedicated to your chosen destination, all included for the same great price as before. They are available to download from the free Walking Eye container app in the App Store and Google Play. Simply download the Walking Eye container app to access the eBook and app dedicated to your purchased book. The app features an up-to-date A to Z of travel tips, information on events, activities and destination highlights, as well as hotel, restaurant and bar listings. See below for more information and how to download.

MULTIPLE DESTINATIONS AVAILABLE

Now that you've bought this book you can download the accompanying destination app and eBook for free. Inside the Walking Eye container app, you'll also find a whole range of other Insight Guides destination apps and eBooks, all available for purchase.

DEDICATED SEARCH OPTIONS

Use the different sections to browse the places of interest by category or region, or simply use the 'Around me' function to find places of interest nearby. You can then save your selected restaurants, bars and activities to your Favourites or share them with friends using email, Twitter and Facebook.

FREQUENTLY UPDATED LISTINGS

Restaurants, bars and hotels change all the time. To ensure you get the most out of your guide, the app features all of our favourites, as well as the latest openings, and is updated regularly. Simply update your app when you receive a notification to access the most current listings available.

Shopping in Oman still revolves around the traditional souks that can be found in every town in the country – most famously at Mutrah in Muscat, Salalah and Nizwa, which serve as showcases of traditional Omani craftsmanship and produce ranging from antique khanjars and Bedu jewellery to halwa, rose-water and frankincense. Muscat also boasts a number of modern malls, although these are rare elsewhere in the country.

TRAVEL TIPS & DESTINATION OVERVIEWS

The app also includes a complete A to Z of handy travel tips on everything from visa regulations to local etiquette. Plus, you'll find destination overviews on shopping, sport, the arts, local events, health, activities and more.

HOW TO DOWNLOAD THE WALKING EYE

Available on purchase of this guide only.

1. Visit our website: www.insightguides.com/walkingeye
2. Download the Walking Eye container app to your smartphone (this will give you access to both the destination app and the eBook)
3. Select the scanning module in the Walking Eye container app
4. Scan the QR code on this page – you will be asked to enter a verification word from the book as proof of purchase
5. Download your free destination app* and eBook for travel information on the go

* Other destination apps and eBooks are available for purchase separately or are free with the purchase of the Insight Guide book

HOW TO USE THIS BOOK

This book is carefully structured both to convey an understanding of the city and its culture and to guide readers through its attractions and activities:

◆ The Best Of section at the front of the book helps you to prioritize. The first spread contains all the Top Sights, while the Editor's Choice details unique experiences, the best buys or other recommendations.

◆ To understand Rome, you need to know something of its past. The city's history

and culture are described in authoritative essays written by specialists in their fields who have lived in and documented the city for many years.

◆ The Places section details all the attractions worth seeing. The main places of interest are coordinated by number with the maps.

◆ Each chapter includes lists of recommended shops, restaurants, bars and cafes.

◆ Photographs throughout the book are chosen not only to illustrate geography and

buildings, but also to convey the moods of the city and the life of its people.

◆ The Travel Tips section includes all the practical information you will need, divided into four key sections: transport, activities (including nightlife, events, tours and sports), an A–Z of practical tips and language.

◆ A detailed street atlas is included at the back of the book, with all hotels, restaurants, bars and cafes plotted for your convenience.

PLACES AND SIGHTS

Chapters are **colour-coded** for ease of use. Each neighbourhood has a designated colour corresponding to the orientation map on the inside front cover.

A locator map pinpoints the specific area covered in each chapter.

Margin tips provide extra snippets of information, whether it's a practical tip, a whimsical quote, an historical fact or advice on shopping and eating.

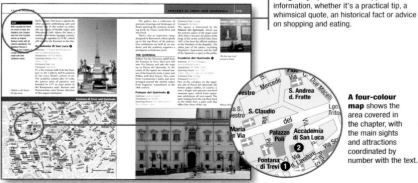

A four-colour map shows the area covered in the chapter, with the main sights and attractions coordinated by number with the text.

PHOTO FEATURES

Photo features offer visual coverage of major sights or unusual attractions. Where relevant, there is a map showing the location and essential information on opening times, entrance charges, transport and contact details.

The Essentials

Address: 100 Viale Vaticano; www.musei vaticani.va

Tel: 06-6988 3145

Opening Hours:
Mon–Sat 9am–6

SHOPPING AND RESTAURANT LISTINGS

Shopping listings provide details of the best shops in each area. **Restaurant listings** give the establishment's contact details, opening times and price category, followed by a useful review. Bars and cafés are also covered here. The coloured dot and grid reference refers to the atlas section at the back of the book.

Gelateria dei Gracchi
272 Via dei Gracchi
06-321 6668
www.gelateriadeigracchi.it
[p316, C2]

Owner Alberto is an artist with passion for ice-cream making and the recipes he follows are more than 100 years old. His *gelato* flavours are all-natural with real fruit and absolutely

TRAVEL TIPS

GETTING AROUND

From the Airport

From Fiumicino, there are frequent train services to the city every 15–30 minutes to Trastevere Station and every utes (every 15 minutes time) to Stazione T

Travel Tips provide all the practical knowledge you'll need before and during your trip: how to get there, getting around and what to do. The A–Z section is a handy summary of practical information, arranged alphabetically.

THE BEST OF ROME: TOP ATTRACTIONS

Here, at a glance, are the city's must-sees, from the iconic monuments of Ancient Rome to the vibrant squares of Campo de' Fiori and Trastevere, and the tranquil gardens of the Villa Borghese.

◁ **The Forum.** The majestic ruins of the the civic centre of Ancient Rome are best seen on a Sunday when the busy thoroughfare that cuts through the site is closed to traffic. See page 98.

▽ **Vatican Museums.** These merit a lifetime's study, but if you only have a few hours, be sure to include the Sistine Chapel in your tour of this vast repository of art. Michelangelo's breathtaking ceiling is a triumph of fresco painting. See page 148.

▽ **Colosseum.** A shadow of its marble-clad imperial days, but impressive nonetheless and, as a symbol of Rome, it remains one of the city's key sights. See page 92.

▷ **Spanish Steps.** All human life converges here, at the heart of Rome's main shopping district. See page 124.

△ **Capitoline Museums.** For a real insight into life in Ancient Rome, follow a tour of the Forum with a visit to this imposing collection of ancient art and Roman statuary. Among its most famous exhibits is the original bronze statue of a she-wolf suckling Romulus and Remus. See page 90.

▷ **Trevi Fountain.** When a voluptuous Anita Ekberg frolicked in here in Fellini's *La Dolce Vita*, she turned it into a Roman icon. Throw a coin in the water and enjoy an ice cream on the steps. See page 113.

▽ **Trastevere.** This old working-class district, across the Tiber from the centre, is now a trendy quarter full of boutiques, restaurants and wine bars. See page 201.

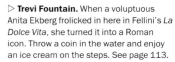

▽ **Villa Borghese.** This leafy spot is perfect for picnicking and home to two world-class museums. See page 185.

◁ **Pantheon.** The best-preserved of all Ancient Rome's buildings is Emperor Hadrian's perfectly proportioned temple. See page 153.

▽ **Piazza Navona.** Della Porta's masterpiece, the *Fountain of Neptune*, stands at the northern end of this elegant, enclosed square full of buskers, street performers, street artists and tourists. See page 156.

THE BEST OF ROME: EDITOR'S CHOICE

Unique attractions, festivals and events, top shops, pizzas and piazzas, church art, family outings ... here are our recommendations, plus some money-saving tips.

BEST VIEWS

The Gianicolo hill. Worlds away from the tightly packed streets of Trastevere and the chaos of the city below. See page 207.

Piazza Venezia. Fine views from the Vittoriano monument with the added advantage of excluding the hulking monument itself. See page 88.

Caffè Capitolino. Romantic views of terracotta rooftops and countless cupolas from the Capitoline Museum's pretty café. See page 89.

The Tabularium. Take in the Forum and the Palatine from a terrace in the ancient archive of Roman Law. See page 87.

Pincio Gardens. Views from the Villa Borghese Gardens stretch from Monte Mario to the Gianicolo and the piazza below. See page 187.

Michelangelo's Pietà.

Rome is for romantics.

BEST CHURCHES FOR ART

San Luigi dei Francesi. The dramatic paintings by Caravaggio in the Contarelli Chapel were the artist's first great religious works. See page 156.

Santa Maria in Trastevere. A pretty medieval church with spectacular mosaics on the facade and in the apse. See page 203.

Basilica di San Pietro. Michelangelo's tender and moving *Pietà* in St Peter's was completed when the artist was only 25 and remains one of his most famous works. See page 136.

San Pietro in Vincoli. This church houses another Michelangelo masterpiece, the restored statue of *Moses*. See page 237.

Santa Maria della Vittoria. So sensual is Bernini's famous sculpture of the *Ecstasy of St Teresa* that many suggest the rapture on her face is more than an expression of piety. See page 185.

Santa Prassede. The 9th-century church is filled with magnificent Byzantine mosaics. See page 236.

Santa Maria del Popolo. A treasure house of art, with paintings by Raphael and Pinturicchio, plus two impassioned Caravaggios. See page 121.

BEST GETAWAYS

Ostia Antica. Well-preserved ruins of an old Roman port town. See page 257.
Tivoli. See the sumptuous Villa d'Este and its fountain-filled garden, and the remains of Hadrian's magnificent villa. See page 263.
Etruscan tombs. Cerveteri is the most atmospheric of the many Etruscan necropolises outside Rome. See page 284.

Oasi di Ninfa. An enchanting English-style garden with medieval ruins. See page 269.
Beaches. Head for Ostia or Fregene, or to Lazio's southern coastal stretches. See page 260.
Castelli Romani. The hills south of Rome are a relaxing destination for a picnic and great wine. See page 271.

Hadrian's Villa.

Children of all ages will enjoy Castel Sant-Angelo.

BEST PIAZZAS

Piazza Navona. Baroque grandeur, spectacular fountains and lively atmosphere. See page 156.
Piazza Farnese. A welcome relief from the chaos of neighbouring Campo de' Fiori. See page 175.
Piazza Mattei. A small piazza with a playful fountain and trendy café. See page 172.
Piazza Santa Maria in Trastevere. This neighbourly square buzzes with activity round the clock but never seems crowded. See page 202.
Piazza San Pietro. Vast, colonnaded square designed by Bernini to accommodate those on the papal pilgrimage. See page 135.
Piazza del Campidoglio. For the beautifully elegant staircase designed by Michelangelo. See page 86.
Piazza di Spagna. A spectacular urban space, perfect for people-watching. See page 125.

ROME FOR FAMILIES

Villa Borghese Gardens. Laid out over rolling hills, this is the perfect city park for picnicking and relaxing. Attractions include museums, a zoo, a kids' playhouse, a boating lake and bikes for hire. See page 186.
Castel Sant'Angelo. Drawbridges, trapdoors, cannons, ditches and dungeons … everything but dragons in this ancient castle. See page 141.
Children's Museum. Explora is a delightful "playtown" where kids can touch, draw and play to their heart's content. See page 300.
Puppet shows. Free Punch and Judy shows on the Gianicolo hill. See page 206.
Coins in the fountain. A coin tossed in the Trevi Fountain is said to guarantee your return to Rome. See page 113.
A leisurely ride. The No. 116 electric bus weaves its way from Via Veneto to the Vatican. Lovely for sightseeing and a welcome relief for sore feet. See page 290.
Villa Torlonia park. Let your older kids (11–15) interact with technology or simulate the set of a TV programme at Technotown, then relax in the fairytale setting of the Casina delle Civette. See pages 193.

Nuns on Piazza San Pietro.

BEST BUYS

Ice cream. Head for Grom for colouring- and preservative-free ice cream made with organic ingredients. See page 165.
Valentino. Ready-to-wear from Rome's beloved designer. See page 126.
Shoes. From Fratelli Rossetti, a classic Italian footwear maker. See page 131.

Food. Two legendary delis for Roman specialities are Volpetti in Testaccio and well-stocked Castroni in Prati. See pages 216 and 142.
Jewellery. In New York there's Tiffany, in Paris there's Cartier, and in Rome there's Bulgari, where extravagant jewellery reigns supreme. Serious money. See page 131.

Fashion by Valentino.

ONLY IN ROME

Cat colonies. There are thousands of cats in Rome, many of them living wild among the ancient ruins. See page 171.
Priestly couture. Papal party gear, nuns' underwear, incense burners and more can be found in shops for religious garments and accessories on Via dei Cestari and Via di Santa Chiara. See page 154.
Cappuccino. Rome is full of atmospheric cafés serving excellent coffee. Piazza Rotonda and Piazza Farnese are prime spots, but the neighbourhood cafés frequented by locals are more fairly priced.
Catacombs. Three of the largest underground burial sites are to be found in the vicinity of the Appian Way. See page 250.
Made by monks. The potions and lotions, teas and preserves on sale at Ai Monasteri are all made by monks. See page 160.

Legendary Volpetti deli.

BEST FESTIVALS AND EVENTS

RomaEuropa. An experimental arts festival held every autumn.

Estate Romana. "Roman Summer" is the collective name for all the events held outdoors in parks, villas, monuments and ancient sites, from June to September.

Easter week. Torchlit processions and a huge open-air Mass in St Peter's Square. Plus chocolate and pastries galore.

Rome Film Fest. Rome's official film festival. Held at the Auditorium in October.

Il Natale di Roma. On 21 April Rome celebrates its founding with fireworks, music and other events.

Opera at Terme di Caracalla. Every summer, Rome's opera theatre moves outdoors for magnificent performances amid the ruins. For more about Rome's festivals see page 296.

Pizzas may have originated in Naples, but there are many excellent ones to be found all over Rome.

BEST PIZZAS

Dar Poeta. A special yeast-free dough is this Trastevere pizzeria's trademark. A local favourite. See page 211.

Formula Uno. The best and most down-to-earth pizzeria in the San Lorenzo university quarter, which is known as pizza central. See page 242.

Da Baffetto. A legendary pizza venue with fast-moving queues outside all night long. Brash but efficient service adds to the quintessential Roman experience. See page 164.

Napul'è. More than 40 types of authentic Neapolitan pizza. See page 145.

O' Pazzariello. A Neapolitan pizzeria with lots of ambience in a fairly small space. See page 165.

PizzaRé. Serves a huge range of crusty Neapolitan-style pizzas that are reliable and appetising. See page 133.

Ai Marni. Thin-crusted pizza baked to perfection in the heart of Trastevere. See page 211

Two of the many cats roaming the streets of Rome.

MONEY-SAVING TIPS

Free museums EU citizens under 18 and over 65 years old and all children under 6 get free entry to state and city museums.

Free churches All the basilicas and churches in Rome are free, including the Pantheon.

Settimana della Cultura Cultural Week is held all over Italy in late April or May, when entrance is free to all state-run museums and historical sites (log onto www.beniculturali.it for more details). See page 297.

Bus tours Buses in Rome are cheap and efficient. An army of small, electric buses (116, 117 and 119) wind their way through the most scenic parts of Rome where cars and "real" buses cannot venture. See page 290.

Cheap eats Anywhere marked *tavola calda*, where you can choose from well-stocked buffets, or *pizza al taglio*, where you can buy slices of pizza to enjoy on the steps of a nearby fountain or square.

House wine Order house wine instead of a bottle. It's more than decent and much cheaper.

Free Vatican Entrance to the Vatican Museums is free on the last Sunday of the month, but be prepared for long queues. See page 139.

"Roman Summer" events Most events that are part of the Estate Romana programme are usually fairly cheap (€10–20). See page 296.

Drinking water Once you've drunk your first bottle of water, refill it over and over again at one of the ever-running drinking fountains. Their water is healthy and fresh, and 100 percent free.

Aperitivo time on Via della Pace.

San Bartolomeo all'Isola church, on
Tiber Island.

THE ETERNAL CITY

Romantic, artistic, and rich with legends from yesterday and today – not only is Rome a feast for the eyes, it's also a living museum, breathing human history at every turn.

Few cities in the world manage to combine the eras as gracefully as Rome does. The glorious jumble of history and art we see today has been an ongoing construction site for more than 2,700 years. Layer upon layer, the Romans have built and rebuilt their city infinite times, always using the past as a foundation for the future.

A stroll in the streets of this truly "eternal" city is both a history lesson and a journey for the senses. The warm colours of the roofs and buildings blend perfectly with the Italian sunset, the scent of good food is a backdrop for the city's lively, loud soundtrack, and the diverse views offer the whole repertoire of western architecture, from the ancient columns of the Republic to the curved facades of the Baroque period, from the neoclassical perfection of the 1700s to the futuristic museums of today.

The iconic Fiat 500.

A flush of colour.

Rome changes slowly, but the 21st century has brought a waft of fresh air to the world's most ancient city, giving a much-needed facelift to many of the city's ancient sites and bringing changes in the dormant artistic and architectural scenes. Revamped galleries, new contemporary art spaces, a cinema festival and the creation of a superb music complex turned Rome into a modern city that stays true to its glorious past while facing the future with confidence. The revival of once forgotten neighbourhoods, such as Flaminio and EUR, further amplified the tourist offer, with major works of public architecture such as the Music Bridge that connects Flaminio with the Foro Italico, the Fuksas' "cloud" building, and the EUR's *Aquarium of the Mediterranean*, a see-through structure built under the water of an artificial lake.

While not a new Dolce Vita, there is a cinematic gloss to the emerging city, with eclectic festivals, a funky club scene, sleek cafés, boutique hotels and a more cosmopolitan air. Rome is an immense outdoor museum, but a simple walk in the centre can be enough to take in the atmosphere and understand the magic of one of the world's most enchanted cities.

Piazza di Spagna at dusk.

ROME AND THE ROMANS

Dubbed the Eternal City by poets and artists, Rome inspires the mind, appeals to the senses and captures the heart. With its combination of new and old and of peace and chaos, it is a city of charming contrasts.

Chaotic but compact, bewildering but walkable, beguiling but exhausting, the Eternal City sparks mixed feelings in both locals and visitors. Everybody ends up loving Rome, but one thing is certain: traffic is one of the city's distinctive features just as much as the Colosseum, and it is possibly the first thing any visitor will notice when stepping out of Termini Station. The public transport system, from the pointless metro to the overcrowded buses, is woefully inadequate with two metro lines going nowhere relevant for most visitors. The new metro line, running northwest to southeast, is not due for completion until 2020 at the earliest. Fear of damaging ancient sites and becoming mired in bureaucracy are why radical measures have never been contemplated before.

The Eternal City has shaken off its dusty toga and slipped into contemporary clothes. As the mayor says: "Rome dares to dream again".

For now, cynical Romans see a decent transport system as a gift to their grandchildren, much as straight roads were a gift to the Empire's grateful colonies. Until then, the locals will continue to fume in traffic jams, flit by on flimsy Vespas or rattle around in speedcrazed buses. For visitors, the good news is that, with stoicism, sturdy shoes and enough caffeine-fuelled café stops, Rome is still a heavenly walking city.

Comforting words on Piazza del Popolo.

Neighbourhoods

The locals jest that Rome is not for Romans: few Romans live in the historic centre any more. In the 1960s the tradesmen moved to the suburbs in search of comfortable apartments while the *centro storico* succumbed to gentrification; once-crumbling *palazzi* were snapped up by astute investors, from bankers to politicians. Yet individuals remain attached to their *rione* or neighbourhood: the original 14 date from the time of the Emperor Augustus, but have grown to 22, each with its own civic crest.

Outsiders often see Rome as devoted to Imperial posturing, whether of the ostentatious

Colosseum-Forum variety or Mussolini's self-aggrandising EUR district. Yet local neighbourhoods can be both cosmopolitan and homely, ranging from the formalised domesticity of Parioli, framed by embassies, to mellow Trastevere, louche yet intimate. Looming above Trastevere is the leafy, *fin de siècle* Gianicolo district, home to many expatriate newcomers.

Rome can be rough around the edges, but its lack of manicured perfection is part of its charm. The Esquilino area, around the Fascist-Modernist Termini Station, nicknamed "the dinosaur", is a case in point, as is Testaccio, the former meat-packing district that is, with Ostiense, the pulsating heart of clubland. Once dilapidated, these districts are being gentrified but retain their edginess, youthful spirit and multiethnic flavour. Rome is more cosmopolitan than at any time since the Empire, though hardly on the same scale.

Yet beyond its bustle and bravado, the Eternal City feels static, imprisoned by its past. Rome is *the* place for contemplating the passage of time and the vanity of human wishes. "Within a short time you forget everything; and everything forgets you," said Marcus Aurelius. The world-weary population has little inclination to relive the glory, decline and fall. Nonetheless, there is a residual melancholy and romantic nostalgia for both the grandeur of Imperial Rome and for the cultural and artistic creativity witnessed in the Renaissance, the two moments in history that still make the Romans extremely proud – without, however, having inspired any major creative revivals so far.

Shopping on the Campo de' Fiori.

The temporal and the spiritual

Novelist Alberto Moravia used to say: "Rome is an administrative city dominated by two institutions: the State and the Church." While an oversimplification, Rome *is* the meeting place of temporal and spiritual powers and, as the capital, lives and breathes politics. As for piety, the Vatican has traditionally been treated as a temporal power, as the corporate arm of the papacy. "Faith is made here but believed elsewhere," is the local dictum.

Essentially, the Romans are more ritualistic than religious, even if the death of John Paul II saw an outpouring of emotion that surprised cynical Rome-watchers.

At work, Romans have an inbuilt resistance to Milanese efficiency, schedules and short lunch breaks. Life is too Latin for a Protestant work ethic. Indeed, there are few qualms about playing the tourist at home, from eating an ice cream on Piazza Navona to tossing a coin in the Trevi Fountain, visiting the Vatican museums on a Vespa, lolling around the Villa Borghese Gardens, or peeking into the Pantheon while on a café crawl.

As the local saying goes: "*ce piace mangia bene ce piace poco lavorà*" – "we prefer eating

---

ALL ABOARD

For the cheapest, most chaotic tour through the time machine that is Rome, hop on the 87 bus, which runs from east to west, scoring a cross-section of the city's history. The route runs from bustling Piazza Cavour to the rural Via Appia Antica archaeological park. En route are swathes of the Imperial, Early Christian, Renaissance and Baroque city in all its glory, from the gladiatorial Colosseum to seductive Piazza Navona, the Tiber and the legendary Seven Hills of Rome. Flashing past your eyes is all Roman history, from monumentality to murder most foul.

To see Rome as Fellini saw it, ride the No. 3 tram, which Fellini claimed gave him inspiration.

Church attendance is waning; only a quarter of Italians attend Mass regularly.

Romans at play

Bar aficionados believe you can tell a lot about a Roman by his café of choice. Cardinals favour the upstanding Caffè San Pietro near the Vatican, while haunts such as Caffè Rosati on Piazza del Popolo are proud of being the place *not* to be seen – here, celebrity regulars unwind in a discreet Art Nouveau ambience.

Roman café owners proudly announce that "this was Fellini's favourite place", "Mastroianni's haunt", or that "Bertolucci prefers our pastries". Bar Canova, near Piazza del Popolo, was Fellini's second home: he came straight from his Oscar success to a party in the bar. The back room, where the visionary director held meetings, is now a Fellini shrine.

Yet the best bars compel a sentimental attachment that goes well beyond celebrity-worship: the journalist wife of former mayor Francesco Rutelli even dedicated a book to her local bar-owner in Caffè del Teatro Marcello.

Nightlife is less tribal than café culture, inspired by "*vivere e lascia vivere,*" a "live and let live" philosophy. Party-goers start late and finish

Romans ooze sophistication.

and drinking to working" – in theory, that is. In reality, however, lots of modern-day Romans would do anything to be able to work. The 2012 crisis produced unprecedented rates of unemployment as thousands of companies shut down, and a posto fisso, a permanent job, has become the number one dream of thousands of young Italians.

> As the writer Alberto Moravia said: "There are no Romans, only people from all parts of Italy who adopt Roman characteristics".

Italy is a family-based society, but most young Romans are cosmopolitan enough to at least wish they could contradict the mammoni stereotype, which generally describes Italians as unwilling to leave their mamma's home until they get married. Shortage of jobs and the extremely high rents, however, make it impossible for most Romans to leave their nest, and many just can't afford to say bye to mum until they are in their 40s, or even 50s.

late, with clubbers calling into a bar for a *cornetto* (sweet croissant) and cappuccino before heading home. San Lorenzo, a city within a city, is an erstwhile immigrant district that is now the heart of the main university quarter, around Via dei Volsci. By night, books are exchanged for bar crawls, with Happy Hour an excuse for wine-tasting, tapas bars, emerging bands and, bizarrely, even board games.

Clubland is centred on Testaccio and Via Ostiense, particularly since the Roma Tre university campus has revitalised the area, while the Ponte Milvio (Flaminio) neighbourhood houses a number of clubs and bars conceived to entertain a see-and-be-seen crowd, and often frequented by local starlets. More mellow visitors may feel more at home with Trastevere's arty ambience, and an evening spent in cool bars, listening to the Blues, followed by an *affogato* ice cream, drenched in liqueur.

High culture

As for high culture, Rome has seen a swathe of renovations and reopenings. The most radical project is The MAXXI, by Anglo-Iraqi architect Zaha Hadid, which saw former army barracks reborn as the National Museum of Contemporary Art. More traditional is the major refurbishment of the Palazzo Barberini and Gallery of Ancient Art, set in a palace designed by Borromini and Bernini, the founders of the Italian Baroque style. The museum's facelift also incorporated the placement of 200 additional paintings in the palazzo's newly acquired rooms, which formerly housed an exclusive club for army officers.

Another modern site is the Ara Pacis Museum, a steel, glass and marble structure

Roman caffè society.

designed to house a 2,000-year-old Altar of Peace that, ironically, was used for sacrifices. Created by Richard Meier, this is the first new public monument erected in the historic centre since Mussolini's day, and when first built it divided local opinion. Art critic Vittorio Sgarbi called it "an indecent cesspit", while others have praised it as an airy, accessible building that lets citizens see into the mindset of Emperor Augustus and Ancient Rome.

The Romans have a reputation for being artistic connoisseurs rather than creative

SUMMER NIGHTS

Estate Romana (Roman Summer) is the name of the umbrella festival promoting art shows and music, cinema, dance, museum, theatre and kids' events, which takes place from late June to August every year. Created more than 30 years ago, it was first intended to amuse the unlucky few who weren't able to escape the Rome heat and go away for the month of August as per Italian tradition.

But the times they are a-changin' and with the economy in a downturn, more people are unable to afford to close up shop and take a holiday. On the bright side, Estate Romana is getting more popular every year. The main venues are the city parks, hosting high-level concerts every night: there's a jazz festival in Villa Celimontana, world music in Villa Ada, opera in Terme di Caracalla, classical music and dance in Villa Adriana. On the Tiber Island, pavements are set up with an array of stands selling crafts, CDs, clothes, jewellery and food, and there's an open-air cinema. Other summer attractions include a swimming pool by the Colosseum, an outdoor gym in Flaminio, and a faux beach on the river below Castel Sant'Angelo. Get the programme at www.estateromana.comune.roma.it.

Easter concert performance at the Auditorium.

artists. As blasé sophisticates, they have seen it all before and bought the T-shirt. Yet despite their love of bread and circuses, contemporary citizens have cultivated a dynamic arts scene, with one of the most vibrant music venues in Italy. Much credit is due to the Auditorium Parco della Musica, Renzo Piano's theatrical space, where beetle-like pods create perfect acoustics in settings suitable for symphonies or soul, Rachmaninov or Lou Reed. Casa del Jazz, in the gardens of Villa Osio, a property confiscated from a Mafia boss, has grown into the city's major dedicated jazz venue, and, while the Rome Film Fest may not rival Venice's, it seeks to involve the Roman public rather than outsiders.

In trendy Testaccio, the Mattatoio, a former slaughterhouse, houses macro Future, a hip art museum. In the San Lorenzo area, near Termini Station, galleries in unconventional settings combine literary cafés with installations, photographic displays and performance art. Dotted around the city are concept stores and bookshops that double as bars and multimedia venues. Rome also playfully mixes art and entertainment: in eclectic club Brancaleone, crowds dance the night away before video art screenings, while the Literature Festival in May is housed amid the marvellous ruins of Maxentius' Basilica.

Party-goers start late and finish late.

Fashion parades

Rome is that rare thing – a city on the international shopping circuit that somehow manages to keep small shops in business. Svelte Romans saunter down Via del Corso and Via Condotti to window-shop for chic designer names. As for Roman brands, the leading lights are Valentino, renowned for his red-carpet style, Brioni, dresser to James Bond, and Fendi, displaying bespoke bags and politically incorrect furs in the gorgeous Palazzo Fendi at the foot of the Spanish Steps. More individualistic shopping awaits in the art galleries and workshops of Trastevere and the Borghetto Flaminio antiques market. Rome is full of *botteghe*, and many artisans' workshops will copy a marble bust on demand. Come nightfall and *aperitivo* time, the fashionistas emerge, to parade around lively Campo de' Fiori and the beguiling Piazza Navona area.

Set in stone

Despite all the surface glitz, there is no escaping the architecture, which assails one's senses around every corner. The Romans were arguably the greatest builders of antiquity, combining monumentality and utility with Greek grace and a sense of creation for eternity. The Pantheon remains an

Shopping on Via dei Condotti.

inspiration to contemporary architects, while down-to-earth football fans are equally struck by the Stadio Olimpico, Mussolini's Olympic

Carabinieri on duty.

Some pizzas are worth queuing for.

Stadium, which hosts the deadly rivals, Roma and Lazio.

For an architectural overview, the Crypta Balbi displays recent archaeological finds and traces the city's development from the pre-Imperial era to Early Christian and medieval times. While some city museums are unduly didactic, the theatrical streets are a revelation.

Given its cinematic glamour, Rome can't help resembling a film set. Memories of gladiatorial contests are inescapable, superimposed on scenes of Fellini-esque excess or *dolce vita* charm, a *Roman Holiday* with Gregory Peck and Audrey Hepburn. Not that Hepburn will suddenly hitch up her Givenchy skirt and hop on a Vespa – the *dolce vita* doesn't linger on, despite the retro sexiness of the city. Yet a certain sultriness does linger, combining with the ancient stones to ensure this Eternal City continues to appeal to all who visit.

EASTER IN ROME

Easter is a heartfelt Roman festival, when history and tradition merge with common piety and cheerful consumerism, and when the city is never more at ease with its Christian heritage. On Good Friday, the Pope retraces Christ's Via Crucis in a moving candlelit procession, ending in a huge open-air Mass on St Peter's Square on Easter Sunday. The Easter procession winds from the Colosseum to Monte Palatino, re-enacting the 14 Stations of the Cross, from Christ's death sentence to his entombment, with a prayer at each station. Thousands of pilgrims gather with torches to follow this solemn procession, which coincides with classical music concerts in many churches. Not that Roman festivals eschew gaiety and self-indulgence. The city's pastry shops display Easter eggs stuffed with tiny silver picture frames, toys or costume jewellery. Wealthier Romans instruct their favourite chocolatiers to encase treasured gifts in the eggs, ranging from engagement rings to car keys. The less devout, however, like to use the long Easter weekend as an excuse to go to the countryside or to spend a few days at the beach, as per the Italian saying "Natale con i tuoi, Pasqua con chi vuoi" ("Christmas with your family, Easter with your friends".)

DECISIVE DATES

The Roman Republic: 753–27 BC

753 BC
Traditional date when Rome is said to have been founded by Romulus, on 21 April.

c.600 BC
First parts of Forum built.

509 BC
Rome becomes a republic.

390 BC
Gauls sack Rome, but are then driven off.

264–146 BC
Punic Wars against Carthage: after its destruction in 146 BC Rome is the dominant power in the entire Mediterranean.

100 BC
Birth of Julius Caesar.

58–48 BC
Caesar conquers Gaul, invades Britain, then leads his army back into Italy,

The Capitoline Wolf at Musei Capitolini.

Dispute from the Stanza della Segnatura, one of the Raphael Rooms.

challenging the Senate. He defeats Pompey and is made dictator of Rome.

44 BC
Caesar assassinated.

31 BC
Octavian (Augustus) defeats Mark Antony and Cleopatra at the battle of Actium, in Greece.

The Roman Empire: 27 BC–AD 476

27 BC
Augustus declared Princeps or sole ruler, and founds the Empire. Peace is established and the arts flourish.

AD 14
Death of Augustus, to be succeeded by Tiberius.

AD 64
Great fire in Rome: Nero builds his Domus Aurea or Golden House. First major persecution of Christians.

69–79
Emperor Vespasian builds the Flavian Amphitheatre (Colosseum). In AD 81 the Arch of Titus is erected to commemorate the destruction of Jerusalem by Vespasian and his son and successor Titus.

98–117
The Roman Empire achieves its greatest extent under Emperor Trajan, after his conquests in Dacia (Romania), Persia and Arabia, extending from northern England to the Persian Gulf.

117–38
Hadrian builds walls to secure the Empire's borders against barbarian invasions.

161–80
Reign of Marcus Aurelius. His column, with reliefs showing his victories over Danubian tribes, stands in Rome's Piazza Colonna.

193–211
Septimius Severus leads campaigns against the Parthians, commemorated by a grand arch in the Forum.

284–305
Emperor Diocletian divides Empire into Western and Eastern halves. Intense persecution of Christians.

312
Constantine defeats his rival Maxentius at the

The Colonna di Marcus Aurelius.

Milvian Bridge, near Rome.

313
Edict of Milan establishes toleration of Christianity.

330
Constantinople made the new capital of the Empire.

395
Division of the Roman Empire made permanent.

410
Rome sacked by Visigoths.

476
Romulus Augustulus, last Western emperor, deposed by Ostrogoth leader Theodoric, who declares himself king of Italy.

Surviving: 476–1377
536–68
Rome and most of Italy recaptured by Eastern Empire, with a stronghold at Ravenna, but the Byzantine armies are overwhelmed by the Lombards.

590–604
Pope Gregory the Great protects Rome by making peace with the Lombards, and sends missionaries throughout Europe.

750s
Pepin, king of the Franks, aids Pope Stephen III, returns lands taken by the Lombards and lays the foundations of temporal sovereignty of the papacy.

A statue of Emperor Trajan.

800
Charlemagne is crowned Holy Roman Emperor by Pope Leo III in St Peter's.

962
Saxon King Otto I becomes Holy Roman Emperor.

1084
Rome is sacked twice, by Emperor Henry IV and by the Normans.

1309
Clement V moves the seat of the papacy to Avignon.

Papal Rome: 1377–1801
1377
Papacy returns to Rome under Gregory XI, but rival popes still contest the claims of his successors.

1417
Single papacy re-established in Rome, under Martin V.

1450s–1520s
Rome enjoys great prosperity during the High Renaissance. The popes

Map of Rome (c.1641) by Matthus Merian.

attract great artists, among them Bellini, Botticelli, Bramante, Donatello, Michelangelo and Raphael.

1527
Charles V's army sacks Rome.

1545–63
Council of Trent initiates the Counter-Reformation.

1585–90
Pope Sixtus V orders major public works in Rome, including the restoration of ancient aqueducts and fountains.

Detail from a fresco depicting the 1870 Bersaglieri Battalion assault against the papal army.

1626
Consecration of St Peter's.

1796–9
The French Revolutionary armies under Napoleon take Rome and make it a Republic. Pope Pius VI dies in exile in France in 1799.

1801
Pope Pius VII agrees a concordat with Napoleon in order to be allowed to return to Rome.

1811
Napoleon makes his baby son the king of Rome.

Rome in Italy: 1814–1945

1814–15
Papal States are restored to Pius VII by the Congress of Vienna.

1848–50
Pope Pius IX gives Papal States a constitution but refuses to support Italian unification and flees Rome. Radicals declare Roman Republic; Rome is besieged by French troops, who restore papal rule and protect Rome until 1870.

1870
French troops withdraw: Italian troops take over Rome, which is declared capital of the kingdom of Italy. The popes refuse to recognise the state and withdraw to the Vatican.

1871–1910
New Italian government undertakes massive building works in Rome, including the Tiber embankments.

1922
Mussolini marches on Rome and seizes power. More new building, with broad avenues and monuments, and suburbs around the city.

1929
Lateran Treaty: Church recognises the Italian state, which acknowledges the Vatican as an independent state with the Pope at its head.

1940
Italy enters World War II.

1943
Mussolini arrested; Allies land in southern Italy; Germans occupy the north.

1944
The Allies liberate Rome, on 4 June.

1945
Mussolini is killed by partisans.

Modern times
1946
After a referendum, Italy becomes a republic.

1957
The European Economic Community (now the European Union) is established by the Treaty of Rome; Italy is one of six founder members.

1960
La Dolce Vita is released, and Rome hosts the Olympics.

1962–5
Second Vatican Council.

1978
Cardinal Karol Wojtyla becomes the first Polish Pope, as John Paul II.

1981
Ali Agca tries to assassinate Pope John Paul II in St Peter's Square.

1993
Corruption scandals rock Italy, and national unity government formed. Francesco Rutelli becomes Rome's first directly elected mayor.

1994
Media magnate Silvio Berlusconi briefly becomes prime minister.

1995
Giulio Andreotti, seven times Italian prime minister, goes on trial for Mafia association.

1996
First left-wing government in Italian post-war history.

1998
Massimo D'Alema is first former Communist to head an Italian government.

2000
Millions flock to Rome for Holy Year celebrations, after a frenzy of restoration work. Centre-left government coalition falls.

2001
Berlusconi becomes prime minister for the second time.

2005
Pope John Paul II dies: Cardinal Joseph Ratzinger elected Pope Benedict XVI.

2006
Berlusconi loses power by the narrowest of margins to a centre-left coalition led by Romano Prodi.

2008
Berlusconi becomes prime minister for the third time and the Romans elect their first right-wing mayor, Gianni Alemanno.

2010
Berlusconi is investigated for an alleged sexual

The infamous former Prime Minister Silvio Berlusconi leaving office on 16 November 2011.

relationship with an underage dancer known as "Ruby the Heartstealer".

2011
In November, amid the European sovereign debt crisis, Berlusconi resigns from post. Four days later, former EU commissioner Mario Monti is sworn in at the head of a technocratic government supported by a bipartisan majority in Parliament.

2013
Pope Francis succeeds the resigning Pope Benedict XVI. Enrico Letta's centre-left Democratic Party (PD) and his Grand coalition win the general elections and Letta becomes PM.

2014
Matteo Renzi, the replaces Letta as PM and starts ambitious reforms.

2015
Hundreds of would-be migrants from North Africa drown in the Mediterranean while trying to reach Italy's shore. Sergio Mattarella is elected Italy's president.

Detail showing battle scenes on the
Column of Marcus Aurelius.

THE MAKING OF ROME

Emperors and popes, dictators and rebels, philosophers and barbarians, saints and sinners, from immense wealth to pillage and ruin – Romans really have seen it all.

Romulus and Remus, the twins famously suckled by a she-wolf, are not the only candidates for the title of founders of Rome. One account offered by Pliny the Elder was of a noblewoman who was surprised by a male organ rising from the ashes of a hearth. The resulting child became King Servius Tullius, builder of the first wall around Rome.

> Rome is the only great city that has a birthday – 21 April, Il Natale di Roma, the precise day when, according to Livy, Romulus founded the city back in 753 BC.

The Livy version

Implausible pregnancy is a feature of many of the legendary accounts, and this is no accident. Archaeology has unearthed evidence of scattered settlements in the Roman hills in 1200 BC, but these early Latins were culturally overshadowed by Etruscans and Greeks. Roman historians preferred a neat break with the past. Miraculous conception was just the ticket.

A large part of Livy's vast *History of Rome*, written in the 1st century BC, is devoted to weighing up theories on its origins, including that of the poet Virgil, who relished the idea of the Greek world as Rome's spiritual cradle. Aeneas, the hero of Virgil's *Aeneid*, is a survivor of the sacking of Troy who drifted to North Africa and was sent by the gods to found Rome. Livy added more divine intervention: King Numitor of Alba Longa, the city founded by Aeneas's son, Ascanius, was usurped,

The Etruscan art masterpiece, The Apollo of Veio.

Livy explains, by his brother Amulius, and Numitor's daughter Rhea Silvia hid in a cave. She was visited there by the war god Mars, who became the father of her twins Romulus and Remus. Doubting this unlikely story, Amulius had her thrown into the Tiber, while the twins were put in a basket and cast adrift to meet their fate. The basket was washed up below the Palatine Hill, and the babies' cries attracted a she-wolf, who suckled the boys until they were rescued by a shepherd. Mars later appeared to the twins and pointed them towards their glorious destiny. They founded Rome, wrote Livy, in 753 BC.

The rape of the Sabine women, as seen by David in the 1790s.

Relations between them then soured. Remus proposed a site on the Aventine, and the name Rema; Romulus demanded the Palatine and the name Roma. Remus ridiculed Romulus' new walls, jumping over them. Furious, Romulus killed his brother, and the walls were ritually anointed with his blood.

Again as Livy tells it, Rome's population grew fast, but with many more men than

THE STATUS OF WOMEN IN ROME

In Roman law men had absolute power over women – in theory. The head of a family or pater familias enjoyed total authority over all the women in it, and on marriage a woman simply passed from his authority to that of her husband. If she fell short of "virtue in all things" he could instantly divorce her, or punish her. Reality, though, often intervened. Wars sent high-born men away for years on end, leaving their wives in charge of their property, and created many wealthy widows, often with various lovers. At the start of the Empire, Augustus tried to re-establish old disciplines with fierce punishments for misbehaviour, but without much success: his own daughter Julia was soon exiled for adultery.

women. Romulus decided to lay on games so magnificent all the surrounding tribes were bound to attend. What they did not know was that their women would not be going home. This has been immortalised as the "rape of the Sabine women".

Republican virtues

Seven kings were said to have ruled Rome after Romulus. Most – despite the legends – were Etruscans, indicating that Rome was still subordinate to the older civilisation. The city's institutions took shape: the patrician class provided priests and judges, while plebeians took care of agriculture, cattle-breeding and trade.

Tensions were frequent between Etruscans and Romans. They came to a head over another notorious rape, of Lucretia, the virtuous wife of a Roman, Collatinus, by the degenerate son of Rome's Etruscan King Tarquinius Superbus. As Roman historians tell it, the populace rose up against the licentiousness of the Etruscan court, and drove Rome's last Etruscan king into exile. In 509 BC Lucius Junius Brutus, leader of the revolt, was elected one of the two Consuls who ruled Rome as it became a republic. An Etruscan

The Roman Senate in session.

across the Alps and almost brought Rome's progress to a dead stop, the Republic prospered and its Empire steadily grew, expanding into Spain and the banks of the Danube. With the final defeat of Carthage in 146 BC, Rome dominated the entire Mediterranean.

A mighty military machine was needed to control the conquered provinces, and successful generals became the most powerful figures in the state, with violent rivalries between them. In 91 BC two generals, Marius and Sulla, put down a revolt in several Italian cities, but then fought each other, and the unscrupulous Sulla took advantage of the situation to seize power and install Rome's first brief military dictatorship. The Roman Republic was dying.

Enter Caesar

The squabbles of the Roman elite continued after Sulla's death, but were interrupted by a vast slave revolt in 73 BC, led by the gladiator Spartacus. It was finally crushed by Crassus, which helped him become for a time the Empire's foremost general. From 59 BC he shared power in the First Triumvirate with Pompey and Julius Caesar, a brilliant commander who was about to conquer Gaul and

attempt to retake the city was seen off at the bridge across the Tiber by the hero Horatius.

The Roman Republic was tightly organised, above all for war – to which every Roman citizen had to contribute – but had no democracy. Only patricians could vote and sit in the Senate, to which the Consuls were responsible. In 494 BC the post of Tribune was created to protect plebeian interests, and from 450 BC the Twelve Tables of laws were displayed in the Forum, but the thousands of slaves had no rights at all.

Continental domination

Rome made little effort to develop an economic base: it simply lived on the proceeds of conquest. Against the backdrop of an invasion by the Gauls in 390 BC, when cackling geese sounded the alarm, as well as the wars with Carthage, when Hannibal led his elephants

> The Roman Republic stood out among its neighbours for its military organisation and belligerent belief in its right to conquer all comers.

Pan and a Maenad depicted on a ceramic bowl.

The satirist Juvenal said that Roman emperors ruled with "bread and circuses" – doling out free grain to the poor, and dazzling the masses with lavish spectacles and bloody gladiatorial combats.

lead his legions across the English Channel. While in Gaul, he made sure a generous share of his booty went back to the capital to buy political support, and the friendship between him and Pompey turned into bitter enmity. Caesar was forbidden to return to Italy, but in 49 BC he defied the Senate by crossing the River Rubicon with his army, with the aim of seizing power. Defeated by Caesar's legions in Greece, Pompey fled to Egypt, where he was killed by his former Egyptian friends. Caesar followed him, and lingered in Egypt, besotted by its young queen Cleopatra, with whom he had a son. When he returned to Rome, she accompanied him.

Caesar now had unchallenged power, and endeared himself to the people with a spectacular building programme. Rome still had Republicans determined to resist dictatorship,

The grape harvest, in a Roman mosaic.

Philosopher-emperor Marcus Aurelius.

however, and a band of senators led by Brutus cut Caesar down, on the Ides of March, 44 BC.

Gods and Empire

Caesar's murder did not lead to a restoration of the Republic but a new civil war, in which the conspirators were easily defeated by an alliance of Caesar's nephew and adopted son Octavian and Caesar's leading general, Mark Antony. These two, though, were also rivals, and became open enemies when Antony developed his passion for Cleopatra, which provided romantic interest for the next 13 years. After the two famous lovers committed suicide, Octavian, who took the name Augustus or "revered one", emerged as victor and – although the Senate remained in place, with little power – the first Roman emperor.

Cleopatra's expropriated treasure funded Augustus' transformation of Rome from "a city of brick into a city of marble". The Augustan Age was Rome's cultural apex, producing Virgil, Ovid and Livy. To end the political bickering of earlier years, Augustus gave Rome a much stronger civil service, which kept the Empire and its capital going throughout all the bizarre misbehaviour of his successors.

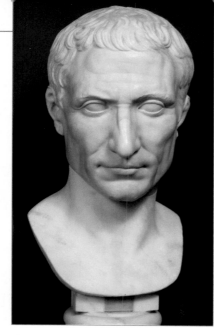

The noble head of Caesar.

imposed immense strains on the Empire. In 286, Emperor Diocletian decided ruling the Empire had become too big a job for one man, and divided it into two halves, Eastern and Western. After his death this led to more fighting between rival emperors, which ended, briefly, in 312 when Constantine the Great emerged as sole emperor. He, however, reaffirmed the division between East and West and moved his main capital to the shores of the Black Sea; to the city he gave his name, Constantinople. Rome, once the *caput mundi* or "head of the world", was left just a shadow of its former self.

Constantine's other world-changing decision was to grant tolerance to Christianity, which only recently had been fiercely persecuted. In 324, he effectively made it the state religion of the Empire. In Rome itself the new faith and old pagan traditions coexisted for decades, but Constantine's decisions established Christianity as the religion of the Western world. In Rome the first great churches were built; eventually Christianity and paganism fused, and images of ancient goddesses metamorphosed into the Christian Madonna.

Hard times

Rome was still the seat of the so-called Western emperors, who clung on, relying on armies of barbarian mercenaries. In 410, Emperor Honorius failed to pay the Visigoth leader Alaric, who sacked Rome, an event seen as the real end of the Roman Empire in the West.

Political collapse left a leadership vacuum increasingly filled by the new religion, and especially the bishop of Rome, the Pope – in contrast to the East, where Christian patriarchs

To reinforce his power (and ego) Augustus encouraged the worship of Julius Caesar and the rest of his family as gods, and this was taken to heart by his descendants, who literally believed they could do anything. Emperors such as Tiberius, Caligula and Nero acted like monsters at the pinnacle of society, rivalling each other in their decadence, gleefully related by the later writer Suetonius. Alongside Roman excess there was a strange devotion to formality; the Greek Plutarch wrote long treatises on morality and etiquette, including which subjects to discuss at dinner.

Honour was restored to the throne after the death of Nero in AD 68 by a succession of effective emperors, notably Trajan, Hadrian and the philosopher-emperor Marcus Aurelius, who between them led Rome to the height of its power in the second century AD. With over 1 million inhabitants, it was a city without equal anywhere in the world, attracting people from every part of its Empire and the known world.

Constantine and Christianity

Over the centuries, defending its vast possessions against a host of potential invaders

NERO'S DREAM HOME

Nero's extravagance was extraordinary even for one of the Caesars. After Rome's great fire in AD 64 – which many said he started – he seized 80 hectares (200 acres) of land by the Forum to build his Domus Aurea or "Golden House", with facades clad in gold, ivory and mother-of-pearl tiles, and fountains sprinkling perfumes. "At last," he said when it was finished amazingly quickly, "I can live like a human being." So hated was Nero, though, that demolition began immediately after his death in AD 68, and his artificial lake-bed was used as the site of the Colosseum, to entertain the masses.

were subordinate to the Byzantine emperors. In 452, Pope Leo I played a major part in buying off the hordes of Attila, the "Scourge of God", but he was unable to stop another sack of Rome, by the Vandals in 455. The city's essential aqueducts were no longer maintained, and Rome was partly abandoned.

> Around AD 100 Rome's population was well over 1 million; by AD 600 it had no more than 20,000 people, living among the ancient ruins and using them as a quarry.

Germanic tribes dominated Italy, and in 476 the Ostrogoth king Theodoric finally deposed Romulus Augustulus, theoretically the last Western Roman emperor. In the next century, the Byzantine emperor Justinian sought to restore the old Empire and succeeded in regaining control of most of Italy, but even then his governors ruled from Ravenna, not Rome, and they were unable to resist another Germanic invasion, by the Lombards. The popes left

Portrayal of a Roman orgy with dancer.

Ravenna and returned to Rome, installing themselves in the Castel Sant'Angelo.

A major part in building up the role of the papacy was played by Gregory the Great, pope from 590–604. Seized by the beauty of Anglo-Saxon youths in Rome's slave market, it is said, he was inspired to send missionaries to convert their country to Christianity. Missionary expeditions were also used across the Continent to assert papal authority over all the Christian communities of Western Europe, which until then had largely gone their own way.

Nostalgic Empire

The papacy's search for a Christian ruler to protect the Church focused on an alliance with the Frankish kings, sealed on Christmas Eve 800 when Pope Leo III crowned Charlemagne as Holy Roman Emperor in Rome. By this act Leo sought to make it clear that popes preceded emperors, but this was only the prelude to centuries of struggle for supremacy between the two. The "Holy Roman Empire" evoked the stability of the past, but it was never clear what the powers or role of this Empire were.

The founding of Constantinople, as depicted in a tapestry.

Ancient Rome's last great monument, the Arch of Constantine.

Rome was attacked by Muslim Saracens, in 846, and Romans fought Romans in political factions. Pope Gregory VII, elected in 1073, established many characteristic institutions of the Catholic Church, including the College of Cardinals and compulsory celibacy for priests. He also attempted to claw back authority over the Holy Roman Empire at the expense of Emperor Henry IV. He looked for new allies in the Normans, but this led to disaster (see box).

UNSUITABLE ALLIES

In his struggle with Emperor Henry IV, Pope Gregory VII lacked an army, so he tried to get Robert Guiscard, the ferocious Norman warrior-ruler of southern Italy, to support him. However, when Guiscard reached Rome in 1084 he found that its people had already surrendered to Henry, and instead of protecting the Pope, the Norman army (which included many Saracen mercenaries, indifferent to squabbles among Christians) set about sacking Rome, surpassing anything done by Goths or Vandals. Pope Gregory was blamed. Hated by Romans, he lived out his life in exile.

Popes frequently excommunicated rulers who displeased them, but this only encouraged disrespect for the papacy. In 1309 France imposed its own candidate as pope and even moved the papacy to Avignon, from where seven successive popes reigned in the papacy's "Babylonian captivity".

Return to splendour

The papacy returned to Rome in 1377, but this was just the prelude to the Great Schism, when there were two or even three popes at the same time. The papacy was only unified with the election in 1417 of Martin V, of the aristocratic Roman Colonna clan.

Rome was in a ruinous state, but the restored papacy enjoyed a new authority that enabled it to demand funds from across Europe, so immense wealth began to flow into the city. Pope Nicholas V (1447–55) is credited with bringing the Renaissance to Rome, founding the Vatican Library and first proposing the complete rebuilding of St Peter's, which was on the verge of collapse. Posterity

Mass of Pope Gregory the Great, from an 11th-century manuscript.

is indebted to the Renaissance popes for their lavish patronage of the arts, but it was viewed with suspicion at the time, as Northern Europeans suspected they were just Italian princes extending their power. Fears were reinforced by Machiavelli's *The Prince* of 1513, a study in political intrigue based on the life of Cesare Borgia, illegitimate son and soldier-henchman of the Spanish Pope Alexander VI (1492–1503). Stories circulated around Europe of the love of luxury and sexual pecadilloes of the popes, and one, Julius II (1503–13) – as well as being one of the greatest patrons of art and architecture – sought to end the papacy's dependency on untrustworthy monarchs by building up a large army of his own. Called "the warrior-pope", he launched a war against Venice, and played a full-blooded part in all the intrigues of Italian and foreign rulers for dominance in Italy.

Enormous wealth had also made Italy, and Rome, great prizes over which the European powers, especially France and Spain, fought for 60 years. In the 1520s Pope Clement VII mistakenly favoured the French against the mighty Emperor Charles V – then ruler of Spain and Austria – and in 1527 the emperor's army, which included many German Lutherans, took revenge in the infamous Sack of Rome. The Swiss Guard were killed to a man, "old nuns beaten with sticks, and young nuns raped and taken prisoner". This was the end of the papacy's pretentions to be an independent power. Clement vii, fortunate to be alive in his Castel Sant'Angelo refuge, was the first of a series of popes who threw in their lot with Charles V

Alaric and his Visigoths sack Rome.

and his Spanish successors. Artists who had fled Rome gradually drifted back, but with a changed spirit. Michelangelo's *Last Judgement* in the Sistine Chapel (1536) is said to reflect the sombre mood of the time.

Counter-Reformation

The shockwaves of the Reformation were soon felt in Rome. In 1545 Pope Paul III convened the Council of Trent to define the "Counter-Reformation", the Catholic Church's response to the crisis. A newly severe religious discipline was to be maintained, heretical ideas were to be stamped out, and militant new religious orders such as the Jesuits were encouraged to combat Protestantism. Art was required to have a far more emphatic religious message, seen in the growth of the Baroque.

In Rome, some saw an improvement in the social and religious climate. "Several popes in succession have been men of irreproachable lives", wrote Paolo Tiepolo, almost with surprise, in 1576, "hence all others are become better, or have at least assumed the appearance of being so… the whole city has become much more Christian-like in life and manners."

GOD'S BANKER

The richest man in Renaissance Rome was Agostino Chigi. He made a fortune trading in salt and alum (used in textile-dyeing), then made himself still richer by extending loans to several popes, to the point of being named Julius II's official treasurer. Dubbed Il Magnifico, he was a legendary bon vivant and art connoisseur; his mistress Imperia famed as Rome's most beautiful courtesan. In 1508 he had a dazzling villa built by the Tiber, with paintings by (among others) Giulio Romano, Perugino and Raphael, including The Triumph of Galatea. His heirs were less successful, and in 1580 the villa was sold to the Farnese clan, to become the Villa Farnesina.

Detail from Michelangelo's Last Judgement.

Nevertheless, while the extravagances of Renaissance Rome may have faded, the papacy remained hugely wealthy, and the popes were now able to dedicate more time and resources to Rome itself. This was the background to the extraordinary creativity that produced Baroque Rome, which perhaps marked the city visually even more than the High Renaissance. No longer a political power, Rome could still be a giant symbol of the glory of the Church. This could be kept up so long as the flow of wealth into Rome continued, but from around 1650 the papacy faced tighter times.

Napoleon upsets things

In 1796 Napoleon issued a proclamation: "Peoples of Italy, the French army comes to break your chains … we have no quarrel save with the tyrants who enslave you." After defeating the papal army, he demanded money and art treasures from the Vatican, and sovereignty over the Papal States. Pope Pius VI was bundled across the French border to Valence, but his successor, Pius VII, agreed to recognise Napoleon and crown him emperor in return for being allowed to return to Rome. Napoleon installed

his mother in a palace in Piazza Venezia, and married his scandalous sister Pauline to the Roman Prince Camillo Borghese, who reciprocated by selling him the Borghese art collection, for 13 million francs.

> The Medici Pope Leo X loved extravagant banquets. "God has given us the papacy," he said to his brother, "let us enjoy it."

Risorgimento

After Napoleon's fall, papal rule was restored at the Congress of Vienna in 1814–15, together with Austrian dominance over Italy. This was the background to the Risorgimento, the rise of modern Italian nationalism, and the liberal and nationalist conflagration that swept Europe in 1848. Pope Pius IX was perceived as a liberal reformer, but was also terrified of revolution.

As unrest grew in Rome, he fled to Naples in November 1848, and a Roman Republic was proclaimed, led by a "triumvirate" including the idealist Giuseppe Mazzini. France's new

Warrior-pope and art patron, Julius II.

Coronation of Pope Pius II, by Vecchietta.

their princes and united, not behind Mazzini's Republic but a kingdom of Italy under Victor Emmanuel II of Piedmont. The Pope meanwhile convened the First Vatican Council. It had just asserted the doctrine of Papal Infallibility when in 1870, after Napoleon III's downfall led to French withdrawal, an explosion rocked the old Aurelian Wall and the Italian army poured through the breach. The Pope barricaded himself in the Vatican, and Rome began to adjust to life after 11 centuries of papal rule.

The capital of united Italy

When Rome was proclaimed capital of united Italy in 1871 a third of its population, then about 200,000, were beggars. For decades the clerical elite had paid no attention to mundane

> *Garibaldi and Italian patriots called for "Rome o morte" – "Rome or death" – but the papacy bitterly resisted the city's incorporation into the new Italian nation.*

matters like drainage, at which the ancients excelled, and every flood on the Tiber cascaded through the Old City. The new state unleashed an unprecedented round of new building, as old *palazzi* were converted into ministries, wide new streets were laid out and giant edifices were put up to house government offices, while the poor were forced into shanty towns on the city's edge.

World War I was, for Italy, virtually a private fight against the Austro-Hungarian forces in the north, and Rome itself was not directly affected. Repercussions came later in the person of Benito Mussolini, the former editor of a socialist paper, who came out of the war "burning with patriotism and bursting with ambition, a *condottiere* of fortune... shrinking from no violence or brutality".

ruler, Napoleon III, however, needed Catholic support, and saw the restoration of the pope as a way to win it. Garibaldi (a key revolutionary figure) and his 4,000 red-shirted volunteers were no defence against French troops, but after resisting for months Garibaldi escaped with the remains of his band across Italy, to gain immortality.

Pius IX was protected by French troops for 20 years, while the Italian states threw off

---

THE ORIGINAL TOURISTS

After 1700 Rome and the papacy were no longer major players in European power politics. Instead, the city settled down into being the Continent's first great tourist attraction, as a "Grand Tour" of Italy and its ancient relics became an essential part of a Northern European gentleman's education. Writers such as Gibbon, Smollett, Goethe and Keats all wandered the ruins of Ancient Rome, pondering on its lost civilisation. Romans responded enthusiastically, and streets like Via Condotti were full of servants, guides and "artists' models" looking for tourist business.

Mussolini and Fascism

Mussolini named his black-shirted party after the *fasces*, the symbol of authority in Ancient Rome. In 1922 he marched on Rome, ostensibly to save Italy from Communism. With King Victor Emmanuel III nominally still on his throne, Mussolini pushed through sweeping

The Italian army ends papal rule, 1870.

In pursuit of his imperial dreams, Mussolini invaded Ethiopia and Albania. He took Italy into World War II in June 1940, when he felt sure Germany would win. But Fascist power proved to be made of straw, and one military disaster followed another. By July 1943 the Allies were preparing to invade Sicily. With the support of the king, senior generals had *Il Duce* arrested and Marshal Badoglio made head of government. Hitler, however, guessing the new government would make peace with the Allies, sent German troops into Italy and paratroops to rescue Mussolini, who became puppet ruler of a Fascist republic in the north.

The next two years of war devastated Italy, but Rome – after some Allied bombing in 1943 – was declared an "Open City", which would not be directly fought over by either side, a period captured in Rossellini's remarkable film *Rome, Open City*. Rome had no strategic value, but was a great symbolic prize. Rome was liberated on 4 June 1944, yet it was not until 28 April 1945

Caricature The Dancing Congress shows the sovereigns of Austria, Russia and Prussia at the Congress of Vienna.

changes in Italian society. He dreamed of creating a new Roman Empire, with Rome as its showpiece. Roads were bulldozed through the old centre to modernise the city and its traffic.

Pope Pius XI, a semi-recluse in the Vatican, warmed to the dictator as he restored the crucifix to schools and worked towards a treaty between the Vatican and the Italian state, formalised in the concordat of 1929.

FOOD FOR WARRIORS

In 1930 the Futurist artist and Fascist Filippo Marinetti launched a campaign against pasta, which, he said, made Italians fat, lazy and apathetic. It had not been part of the diet of the ancient Romans, it was said, when they had conquered Europe. Mussolini himself often said he wanted to make Italians tougher and more dynamic, less addicted to pleasure and more to combat and heroism, and for a time the campaign was taken up by the regime – which also wanted to lower Italy's dependence on imported wheat. Most Italians, though, ignored it, and remained as devoted to pasta as ever.

that Mussolini was captured, shot and hung from a lamp-post in Milan.

Slicing up the post-war cake

Conditions in Rome after the war were vividly portrayed in films of the era such as Vittorio de Sica's *Bicycle Thieves*. A common backdrop was the high-rise blocks that proliferated under Salvatore Rebecchini, mayor 1947–56. Property developers bribed bureaucrats, and empty spaces filled with illegal buildings.

> "All merely picturesque things are to be swept away," proclaimed Mussolini in his plans for Rome, "and must make room for the dignity, hygiene and beauty of the capital."

The 1957 Treaty of Rome spelt out a vision of a European Common Market, but Italian political life was blighted by strikes and instability. The Communists were the largest single party, but all other parties agreed they

Patriarch of Italian nationalism, Garibaldi.

The Tiber in the 18th century.

must be kept from power by any means; no other party was big enough to form a government, so the result was a run of short-lived coalitions. Nevertheless, Italy managed an economic miracle, and instead of being associated with poverty, Rome began to attract new waves of tourists with the image of *La Dolce Vita*, enshrined in another film, by Fellini, from 1960.

In 1978, the Polish cardinal Karol Wojtyla became the first non-Italian pope in 450 years, as John Paul II. He brought a new international prestige to the Vatican, but it was also damaged by irregularities in its finances, and in 1985 the government ended Catholicism's status as the state religion of Italy.

Modern times

Ever since 1945 the Christian Democrats had been the constant in every government coalition, but over the next decade their dominance disintegrated as the judicial system cracked down on organised crime. This campaign spread to the worlds of business and politics in 1992, under the name *mani pulite*

Mussolini holds forth.

Paul II, succeeded by German cardinal Joseph Ratzinger as Benedict XVI.

The 2008 financial crisis left Italy relatively unaffected thanks to a less internationalised banking system. However, once the sovereign debts crisis hit Europe (2011), Italy staggered under the weight of its uniquely high public debt. Involved in an endless series of sex-related wire taps, Berlusconi failed to convince his European partners he could redress the country. In November 2011 he stepped down to be replaced by Mario Monti and his technocratic government.

The year 2013 saw two important events in Rome. In an unprecedented move, Pope Benedict XVI resigned from his post and the papal conclave elected Argentinian Cardinal Jorge Mario Bergoglio as his successor, the first Jesuit pope and the first to be appointed from the Americas. The general election saw a Grand coalition led by Enrico Letta's Democratic Party (PD) assume power. Letta was replaced after a year by the PD's young and dynamic leader, Matteo Renzi. The new prime minister embarked on an ambitious programme of reform, including the drafting of a new electoral law and a radical revamp of the labour market. In 2015, Renzi appealed to the EU for more action on sea migration following the arrival of large numbers of migrants from war-torn countries in the Middle East and Africa on islands in the south of Italy, and the deaths of hundreds of would-be migrants who drowned whilst attempting to reach Italian shores.

(clean hands), and the system of corruption and kickbacks that had ruled post-war Italy began to crumble.

It seemed like an opportunity for a completely new beginning, but the hole left by the Christian Democrats on the right was filled by media mogul Silvio Berlusconi and his Forza Italia party. Bringing a new, brash, populist style to Italian politics, Berlusconi has been often accused of being more interested in solving his numerous judiciary cases than the country's structural problems. The centre-right leader briefly led the country for the first time in 1994. Berlusconi went on to win the 2001 election and become prime minister for the second time. His five-year tenure, Italy's longest-lived government since 1945, was followed in 2006 by the unstable cabinet of Romano Prodi.

Meanwhile, Berlusconi turned Forza Italia into the wider People of the Freedom (PoF) party and was elected again at the early election of March 2008. In 2005, another era of Rome ended with the death of Pope John

MAMMA MIA SILVIO!

Three-time prime minister Silvio Berlusconi will undoubtedly leave his mark on Italy's history. The rich and powerful owner of AC Milan football club and three TV channels, Il Cavaliere (The Knight), as he is nicknamed for his knighthood to the Order of Merit for Labour, chaired three G8 summits and always thought that most problems could be solved with a friendly pat on the shoulder. Accused of having tailored Italy's laws in order to overcome his many judicial problems, Berlusconi seemingly had the ability to understand his electors' feelings, although he was less appreciated by his international peers. He resigned in late 2011 amid the European sovereign debt crisis and a series of sex-related scandals.

The magnificent dome of St Peter's Basilica.

The Temple of Antoninus and Faustina
was converted to San Lorenzo in
Miranda in the 1100s.

ART AND ARCHITECTURE

Three great eras – the ancient city, the Renaissance and the Baroque – have largely defined Rome's visual identity, blending in an astonishingly harmonious mix, studded with masterpieces.

Walking through Rome's Centro Storico, one is frequently amazed by the sheer size and grandeur of the buildings crammed into narrow, winding streets. Rome has the kind of beauty that provokes passionate responses. It has also been a centre of power throughout its 2,700-year history, home to ancient emperors, then popes, and even Mussolini. Every era has left its mark.

A visible past

Romans' indifference to their extraordinary surroundings is nothing new. Rightly or wrongly, they have been blamed for mistreating their architectural heritage since ancient times. Emperor Maxentius (AD 306–12) accused contemporaries of tearing down "magnificent old buildings" to get material for new houses. Pope Pius II (1458–64) shuddered at people burning marble monuments to obtain lime.

Every corner seems to have something worth stopping to look at: a shady courtyard with a bubbling fountain, a Baroque facade above a street market, an obelisk blocking traffic in a way no modern planner would allow.

Goethe, visiting in the 1780s, complained that "what the barbarians left standing, modern architects have destroyed", and a century later the German historian Gregorovius thundered against the Piedmontese remodelling of the papal city. In the 20th century Alberto Moravia

St Peter's dome from Castel Sant'Angelo.

classified four-fifths of Rome "a disaster area of civic architecture". Yet these critics all stayed on in Rome, unable to desert it.

Locals' disregard has a natural explanation in overfamiliarity. Rome is a city standing on the shoulders of its predecessors, where layers of history run into each other. Materials have been taken from older buildings to make new ones, and buildings adapted to suit changing needs. Medieval churches rise from the remains of ancient houses; a Renaissance palace balances on top of the Theatre of Marcellus, next to 20th-century apartments. Even if buildings disappear, their shapes remain. A key feature of

Italian city life – the piazza – is a direct descendant of the ancient Forum.

First steps

Rome's first permanent civic buildings were erected in the Forum. Most of the area now called the Centro Storico was little-populated for centuries, and much of it kept empty as the Campus Martius, the training ground where Roman men kept themselves ever-ready for war. Wealthy families built villas on top of Rome's hills, especially the Palatine, Viminal and Esquiline, while the dip between them – only just west of the Forum – was the Subura, the great slum of ancient Rome.

Republican Rome, though, grew in a fairly haphazard fashion, with few of the monumental symmetries now associated with Roman cities, and little of the splendour its imperial role seemed to demand. Accordingly Julius Caesar was the first to set out on a programme to improve the city. Soon Rome was flaunting its wealth; under Caesar, 640 gladiators wore silver armour at the city's games.

Caesar's nephew, the emperor Augustus (27 BC–AD 14), liked to boast that he had found Rome made of brick and left it of marble. The urbanisation of the Campus Martius began, and was divided into *rioni* – the zones of central Rome that still exist today. Large parts of the Imperial Fora also date from these years.

The capital of the world

With over 1 million people – a size not reached by any other city for nearly 2,000

The arch of Septimius Severus.

years – Ancient Rome was closely packed, noisy and crowded. While the wealthy lived in elegant houses – relics of which many have survived – the Roman masses lived in insanitary *insulae* or apartment blocks of mud-bricks and timber, and fires, house collapses and epidemics were common. The *insulae* grew so rapidly and rose so high that after the fire of AD 64 destroyed the city centre, a decree of Nero limited their height to 20 metres (60ft).

In the wake of the fire, disagreement raged between those who wanted Rome's old alleys retained and Nero who wanted broad avenues on which to display monuments to himself. As has gone down in legend, it was also rumoured that Nero had started the fire himself, to clear space for his vast palace, the Domus Aurea or Golden House. More practically, though, Nero forbade the use of wooden ceilings and insisted on the provision of water buckets in houses.

Little of Nero's constructions remain because they were destroyed by his successors Vespasian (AD 69–79) and his sons Titus

---

THE FIRST FORUM

"Forum" is one of the most pervasive words the Romans have given to European languages. The marshy area below the Capitoline Hill was drained by Rome's Etruscan rulers as early as 600 BC, and served as a common space for every purpose – meeting up, buying and selling, settling disputes – and the site of the temple where the Vestal Virgins guarded the Sacred Flame, which ensured Rome's survival. Its grandeur grew with that of the city: around 180 BC the humblest market traders were driven out, and permanent law courts and trading halls were built. Later rulers added new Fora as monuments to themselves, but the original Forum remained the heart of the ancient city.

Trajan's Markets.

and Domitian. To win popularity and dissociate themselves from Nero they erected more democratic centres of enjoyment, among them the Colosseum, on land originally covered by Nero's private lake. Domitian's legacy was the stadium over which Piazza Navona was built.

One of Rome's greatest architects was Apollodorus of Damascus, master builder of Emperor Trajan (98–117), responsible for Trajan's Forum and the semicircular market behind it – a revolutionary idea, regarded as one of the wonders of ancient Rome, and still astonishingly well-preserved. Trajan also built a massive bath complex, on another part of the land that was once part of the Domus Aurea.

Rome's emperors built on until their last days – one of the last great monuments is the Arch of Constantine, completed only a few years before he left for Constantinople – but then centuries of construction came to a halt, and within decades much of the city was a ghost town. Few civic buildings survive from the centuries between the fall of the Empire and the Renaissance, but this was the time when Rome's major churches were founded, often incorporating parts of pagan temples. Defensive towers were also built, like

The Colosseum.

The spectacular apse mosaics of Santa Maria in Trastevere.

the Torre delle Milizie (1309), above Trajan's Market.

The great rebirth

A huge proportion of Rome's architectural gems date from the years between 1454 and 1670, when Rome was again one of Europe's great power centres, and at the heart of Renaissance and Baroque art and architecture.

PAPAL STREET PLANS

The Renaissance popes changed the face of Rome in many other ways as well as in their individual buildings and great monuments. Julius II (pope from 1503–1513) conceived Via Giulia, the first example of urban renewal since antiquity. Sixtus IV (1471–84), patron of the Sistine Chapel, commissioned the Ponte Sisto, the first new Tiber bridge in over 1,000 years. Leo X (1513–21) had Via di Ripetta created to link the Medici family palace and Porto di Ripetta, while another Medici pope, Clement VII (1523–34), commissioned Via del Babuino, thereby completing the Tridente or "Trident" of (today very fashionable) streets that, with Via del Corso, flow south from Piazza del Popolo.

The Renaissance – Rebirth – stemmed from a rediscovery of the ancient art and culture that had been abandoned after the Roman Empire fell in the 5th century. It began in Italy in the late 14th century and, over 150 years, swept across Europe, leading to fundamental changes in culture, intellectual life and the way people lived and saw their place in the world.

Christopher Columbus and Vasco da Gama discovered new countries and trade routes, and philosophers such as Erasmus reapplied the humanist philosophies of the ancients. While not yet questioning the supremacy of God, this attitude of enquiry encouraged a questioning of the dogma of the Catholic Church, which led ultimately to the birth of Protestantism.

In Italy, however, it was in art and architecture that the new movement was most visible – in the development of perspective, the more naturalistic presentation of subject matter and especially the human body, and the use of classical proportions and styles in building.

The Renaissance first developed in northern Italy, particularly Florence. Nevertheless, most

The Fountain of the Four Rivers, Piazza Navona.

great artists of the era came to Rome at some point, to study the classical lines of ancient relics, or carry out commissions for the popes.

Rome's own renaissance

In the mid-15th century, two factors aided the re-emergence of Rome as a cultural centre. First, the papacy of Nicholas V (1447–55) began a line of powerful popes with time, money and the desire to improve Rome's appearance. Secondly, the Italian League of 1455 ushered in a period of relative peace across Italy, leaving the popes free to occupy themselves with broader ambitions.

Many changes made in the ensuing 70 years still define the look of Rome today. Nicholas V believed Rome had to be made majestic again to be a worthy centre of the Christian world. Well educated, he was a patron of artists, craftsmen and scholars: advised by the architect Alberti, he was also the first to propose that Constantine's Basilica of St Peter – which was threatening to fall down in any case – should be demolished and replaced with a giant new focus for the Church. This suggestion would not be fully taken up until 1506, by Pope Julius

> The ruins of ancient Rome served later builders as a giant quarry for centuries, until many dwindled away to nothing.

II (1503–13), and work would go on for 120 years, but over the decades the new St Peter's incorporated contributions from nearly all the greatest masters of Renaissance painting, sculpture and architecture.

These same masters left their mark elsewhere in Rome: Bramante, Julius II's first choice as architect of the basilica, had earlier built the lovely Tempietto beside the church of San Pietro in Montorio on the Gianicolo, revolutionary in its use of classical form and considered the first true Renaissance building in Rome. Raphael, a later director of works at St Peter's, painted frescoes that can be seen in the Vatican and Villa Farnesina, and Michelangelo, who, aged over 70, designed St Peter's dome in the 1540s, had earlier painted the Sistine Chapel, sculpted the *Pietà* and, in 1536, designed the Campidoglio for Pope Paul III.

Artists continued to flock to Rome until the 1527 Sack, to work for the popes or the great families who vied for the papal throne – the Barberini, Borghese, Farnese, Pamphilj and

Michelangelo's staircase leading to the Campidoglio.

others. Dating from this time are churches such as Santa Maria del Popolo and Santa Maria della Pace, the *palazzi* on Via Giulia and of course great works of art, now mostly in the Vatican or the *palazzi* Barberini and Doria Pamphilj.

The popes left an indelible stamp on the layout of Rome after the Sack, too (see page 52). The greatest papal "planner" was Pope Sixtus V (1585–90). His network of streets built to link the city gates and improve access for pilgrims is still mostly intact: Via Felice (now Via Sistina, and other names) led straight to Santa Maria Maggiore and Santa Croce in Gerusalemme from Piazza del Popolo, one of four nodal points where obelisks were erected, with Santa Maria Maggiore, San Giovanni in Laterano and St Peter's.

City of the Baroque

In the latter part of the 16th century, creativity was curbed by papal decree, in response to the threat of Protestantism. The Council of Trent laid down guidelines for Church commissions: all art was to have an unmissable religious message. Realism was allowed, but there was to be no prettification, and emphasis had to be put on the suffering of martyrs to remind people of the infernal torments awaiting them if they

Bramante's Tempietto.

Grand stairway in the Palazzo Barberini.

> The object of Baroque painting and building was to give the onlooker a vivid image of both the horrors of hell and – more frequently – the joys of heaven.

offended the Church. Niccolò Pomarancio's gruesome frescoes of martyred saints in Santo Stefano Rotondo and Santi Nereo e Achilleo date from this time.

While the Renaissance was imported from Florence, Baroque style had its home in Rome. It may seem strange that the sombre images of the late 16th century should lead to the ornate Roman Baroque of the 17th, but both were provoked by the fear of Protestantism. Both sought to promote Catholicism, but while one used shock tactics, the other sought to dazzle.

Size and visual impact were the main themes explored in Baroque architecture: the aim of religious art and building was to exalt the greatness of the Church and create a foretaste of heaven, and to this end every kind of visual effect could be deployed. By the 1620s, extravagantly decorated churches with *trompe l'œil* ceiling paintings and gold-encrusted altars were thought more likely to keep people in the

Fresco by Annibale Carracci in the Palazzo Farnese.

Catholic fold than portrayals of suffering. The basic form of these buildings might still owe much to classical models, but now everything was highly decorated with statuary and reliefs.

It was no accident Rome's first major Baroque churches were built for the new religious orders of the Counter-Reformation: the great Jesuit churches such as Il Gesù (1568–75) and Sant'Ignazio de Loyola (1626–50), and the initially less ornate Chiesa Nuova (1575–99) of the Oratorians, founded by San Filippo Neri, loved in Rome for giving charity to the poor.

This was the age of Bernini and Borromini, whose facades grace streets and piazzas, and whose fountains and sculptures decorate Piazza Barberini and Piazza Navona, Ponte Sant'Angelo, Villa Borghese and the Vatican.

As well as exalting the Church, the Baroque could add grandeur to more earthly powers, and was eagerly taken up by great monarchs such as the Spanish Habsburgs and Louis XIV of France. Rome's great families were just as keen to demonstrate their wealth, by building massive city palaces and villas amid gardens. The Villa Borghese dates from this time, as do parts of Palazzo Doria Pamphilj, Villa Doria Pamphilj and the Palazzi di Montecitorio and Barberini. Once again artists flocked to Rome

to study and find patrons among its great families. Velázquez, Rubens and Poussin all worked here, and left major works in Rome.

After about 1660, however, funding dried up, and the papacy and Roman aristocracy had to moderate their designs. No era since the Baroque has marked the city so deeply. The monuments of Bernini, Borromini and their contemporaries remain, stunning pieces of work that create a cityscape that is as Roman as the Colosseum and the Forum.

THE DEMON CARAVAGGIO

Caravaggio (1571–1610) was the greatest artist working in Rome at the end of the 16th century, but his fame lasted only a decade. Despite Counter-Reformation injunctions to show the realities of suffering, his dramatic lifelike figures and earthy details, his saints with dirty fingernails, did not meet with the approval of many art patrons used to the reverence of a Raphael or a Michelangelo, while many in the Church found such naturalism blasphemous. Even more of a problem was his character: violent and argumentative, he had to flee Rome after killing a man in 1606. Trouble followed him to Naples, Sicily and Malta, and it has never been clear how he died.

BERNINI AND THE BAROQUE

The dominating figure in Roman Baroque, Bernini used the drama of false perspective and *trompe l'oeil* to create a style that later influenced European Baroque.

A self-portrait of Bernini.

Gianlorenzo Bernini (1598–1680) was at the forefront of Roman Baroque, pioneering spectacular effects.

Although more restrained than elsewhere in Europe, Roman Baroque is theatrical, bold and, at times, bombastic. Bernini's Rome is an open-air gallery of fountains and facades. Palaces and churches boast sweeping curves, majestic facades and theatrical vistas flanked by flights of steps. As a virtuoso sculptor, Bernini worked in broad brushstrokes, with illusionistic verve, often lending glamorous dynamism and animation to the stony stillness of portraiture. He was a showman renowned for his theatricality and technical brilliance.

Bernini's unique ability to capture, in marble, the essence of a narrative moment with a dramatic naturalistic realism, and his use of light as an important metaphorical device in the perception of religious subjects, found favour with a succession of popes, who commissioned many scenic sculptures and portraits. Even St Peter's is, in part, a Bernini creation, graced by two freestanding colonnades around the elliptical piazza leading to the basilica. For St Peter's interiors, Bernini also designed an enormous marble, bronze and gilt *baldacchino* (1623–24) standing over the papal altar. Other masterpieces include the witty design for an elephant to bear the obelisk of Santa Maria sopra Minerva and the graceful angels on Ponte Sant'Angelo. As for palaces, Palazzo Barberini (1629–33) heralded the Baroque style and was completed by Bernini, assisted by Borromini, who became his arch-rival.

Bernini's Sant'Andrea al Quirinale (1658–70) is a subtle tour de force inspired by Michelangelo's architectural feats.

Having worked for decades on the interior of the basilica, Bernini was commissioned to redesign St Peter's Square (1656–67). The colonnaded arms of the keyhole-shaped piazza reach out to Catholics in a symbolic embrace from the Mother Church, according to Bernini.

Bernini's obelisk-carrying elephant outside Santa Maria sopra Minerva church.

FRANCESCO BORROMINI

Borromini (1599–1667) made use of revolutionary, gravity-defying architectural forms. While Borromini lacked the confidence and all-round virtuosity of Bernini, his churches abound in visual trickery. His work is characterised by a sculptural quality, the alternation of convex and concave forms, and a conspicuous fondness for geometric designs as well as for subtle plays of light and shade.

San Carlo alle Quattro Fontane (see page 116) was Borromini's first solo commission. Based on an oval design, the ingenious church is notable for its illusionistic dome. The sinuous, seemingly swaying, walls inspired countless Baroque artists. His other masterpiece, Sant'Ivo alla Sapienza, dazzles the eye with its curved lines that make the building come alive.

In his time Borromini's genius was not fully recognised, partly because of his temperament (he was a depressive who eventually committed suicide) and his rivalry with Bernini, but he is now considered one of the great masters of Baroque.

Rome's loveliest Baroque square, Piazza Navona, is home to three fountains and other works by rival architects Bernini and Borromini. In the foreground is Bernini's Fontana del Moro. His sumptuous fountains vie for attention with Borromini's church of Sant'Agnese, with its striking interplay of towers, domes and facade.

In the church of Santa Maria della Vittoria is what many consider to be Bernini's sculptural masterpiece, The Ecstasy of St Teresa.

Apollo and Daphne, which is displayed with other Bernini masterpieces in the Galleria Borghese. This is Bernini's most famous sculpture. The magnificent, youthful work shows the nymph fleeing from the sun god.

Richard Meier's museum pavilion housing the ancient Ara Pacis altar.

THE SHAPE OF MODERN ROME

In a city that is regularly compared to a giant museum, the intrusion of modern streets, suburbs and rail lines has been condemned as vandalism. Rome's survival, though, has always depended on its ability to integrate past and future.

So pervasive is the past in Rome, that it's easy to think this represents the whole city. And yet Rome has grown vastly since 1700, and has never ceased to grow, build and adapt.

By the time of the death of Bernini in 1680 the extraordinary impetus behind the creation of Baroque Rome had visibly fallen away. Stylistically, rococo flourishes were added to the Baroque, but most of the city's architects lived on the legacy of the past.

Nevertheless, two of Rome's most famous, and most popular, sights date from this time. The Spanish Steps, built to link the French church of Trinità dei Monti with Piazza di Spagna, were completed in 1726, while Nicola Salvi's Trevi Fountain, designed for Pope Clement xii, was finished in 1762.

Modernity arrives

The changes brought by the 19th century were as much utilitarian as aesthetic. In 1856 Rome acquired its first railway line, to Frascati, and in 1862 the first part of Stazione Termini was built. These few novelties in sleepy papal Rome, however, were as nothing compared to the transformation that came after the city's incorporation into a united Italy in 1870.

The new state's rulers were modernisers, but found in their new capital a decaying, archaic city impassable to modern communications. Some needs could be met by recycling: Bernini's Palazzo di Montecitorio became Italy's Chamber of Deputies. Other changes were far more drastic. All-new, wide, un-Roman-looking avenues, such as Via Cavour,

Rome's first opera theatre.

Via Nazionale and Corso Vittorio Emanuele II, were cut through to "open up" the old centre and connect it to an expanded Termini Station. The new Italy wanted to add its own touches of grandeur to Rome to compete with those of the ancients and the popes, and did so in a bombastic style epitomised by the vast Vittorio Emanuele monument on Piazza Venezia.

Other developments included the creation of new residential areas such as that around Piazza Vittorio Emanuele (1886), and – one of the most positive – the building of the Lungotevere or Tiber embankment in the 1870s, which put a stop to Rome's disastrous floods.

Mussolini's Legacy

There is more to Roman architecture than ancient buildings and Baroque facades. Mussolini's Fascist regime has left a powerful imprint on the city as well.

Whole areas of Rome are dominated by massive, conspicuous buildings with facades of white rectangular columns against a plain white or reddish-brown background, adorned with statues of naked athletes and grim-faced women holding ears of corn or bunches of grapes. This style even continued – shorn of its more obvious ideo-

The Palazzo della Civiltà del Lavoro, EUR.

logical symbols – after World War II, when Mussolini's regime had collapsed.

In contrast to Hitler, whose taste in art and architecture was always backward-looking, Mussolini liked to show he was in touch with 20th-century trends, and his regime recruited some of Italy's most innovative modern architects for its schemes, notably Marcello Piacentini and Angiolo Mazzoni.

The style they came up with was a mix of austere Modernist functionalism and an evocation of Ancient Rome, with an added touch of the monumentalism that was a Fascist essential.

Some of the most striking examples are Piacentini's Città Universitaria and the rebuilt Stazione Termini, begun by Mazzoni in 1937 but only completed (with major changes) in 1950. Another is the building south of the Circus Maximus, now used by the United Nations Food and Agriculture Organization, originally intended as the administrative hub of the African Empire of which Mussolini dreamed. Piacentini also adapted the old Costanzi theatre to turn it into Rome's first opera theatre, the Teatro dell'Opera. He redesigned and moved the theatre's facade, embellished the interiors with stuccos and decorations, and added a tier of boxes. His large inscription praising Mussolini still stands above the stage today.

Reminder of the Fascist dictatorship

Some of Mussolini's projects involved not building but large-scale demolition. He wanted Italians to be more conscious of their Roman heritage, and so commissioned excavations of the Roman Fora. However, his interest was not academic, for he simultaneously destroyed a part of the Fora by driving Via dei Fori Imperiali through the middle of them, as a route to hold parades with the ancient ruins as an unbeatable backdrop. As a symbol of reconciliation between the Holy See and the Italian state, the construction of Via della Conciliazione into the Vatican involved demolishing the Spina, one of Rome's most celebrated historic streets.

However, the most prominent examples of Fascist architecture can be seen at the Foro Italico (see page 195) and the area in south Rome known as EUR (pronounced *ayoor*). The *Esposizione Universale di Roma* was to have been held in 1942, as a giant exhibition to mark 20 years of Fascist rule. The war prevented it from taking place, but building continued after 1945, and the EUR district is today a strange monument to Fascist taste (see page 220).

20th-century transformations

These innovations were detested by lovers of Old Rome, but they effectively created Rome as a modern city, around its ancient core. They also enabled Rome to accommodate a flood of immigrants from rural Italy, which had been gaining momentum ever since Unification. In 1922 Rome had about 800,000 people; by the end of World War II it would have 1.8 million.

The idea of building self-contained estates on the edge of Rome, the Agro Romano, was first mooted in 1907. Expansion had started before 1922, with the Art Nouveau Coppedè Quarter for the wealthy in the north of the city, and the engaging Garbatella workers' quarter south of Testaccio. Then Mussolini ushered in his own dramatic changes, to build a city fit to be the seat of his intended empire. He also decided Rome needed "living space and greatness", and began building the *borgate* (estates) of Prenestina, Pietralata and San Basilio. Depressing in form and materials, they soon became symbols of wretchedness.

Post-war, slums girdled Rome, while at the other end of the social scale the wealthy got planning permission to build on the Via Appia. Slum clearance began in 1976: older *borgate* were given lighting, power, mains water and bus routes, while others were replaced by supposedly exemplary new suburbs such as Tor Bella Monaca or Tor de' Cenci. However, these too developed the usual problems of poverty, poor services, unemployment and drugs.

Rome urgently needed to improve living standards and integrate its outer sprawl into the rest of the city by improving the inadequate transport system, but solutions to urban blight seemed lost in the tangle of local politics. Since 1993, the city authorities have initiated great city-wide improvements in services and a swathe of new building, and major improvements, can be seen today.

Modern architecture

Modern architecture was a rarely seen phenomenon in Rome until 2002, when the state-of-the-art Auditorium by Genoese architect Renzo Piano opened, spawning a wave of major architectural projects by big-name architects.

Superstar architect Richard Meier's design for the pavilion housing the Ara Pacis, an ancient Roman altar, proved controversial, but like it or loathe it, it's a major landmark on the cityscape. The futuristic MAXXI, Rome's contemporary art museum designed by Zaha Hadid, was built over converted army barracks in the Flaminio neighbourhood, known as the city's new music hub. In order to poetically connect music and sports, a bridge, the Ponte della Musica, now links the Flaminio district to the sports areas across the Tiber.

The southern EUR suburb is also undergoing a revival. A futuristic expo centre – a suspended, amorphous structure – was completed in 2006; the Aquarium under EUR's artificial lake is a see-through structure that allows a visual continuity with the lake's water, and a suspended cloud inside a congress building by Fuksas is currently under construction off Via Cristoforo Colombo.

As well as this wave of public building, there is a residential building boom. Rome's renaissance, it seems, is in full swing.

Termini station, one of the largest train stations in Europe.

NEW GALLERIES

The list of the city's innovative spaces dedicated to the arts is impressive. Apart from Zaha Hadid's MAXXI museum, the MACRO, Rome's other contemporary art museum, is now spread over two sites – one a converted Peroni brewery near Piazza Fiume, the other a converted slaughterhouse in Testaccio, whose ceilings still carry the old hooks where the animals used be hung. Rome's old power station is now home to the overspill of the Capitoline collection, and the contrast between the ancient statues and the 20th-century machinery is truly stunning. More centrally, the stables of the hilltop Quirinale Palace have been converted into a clean, crisp space for high-profile exhibitions.

ROME ON FILM

A city of unparalleled grandeur and soul-stirring beauty, Rome lends itself particularly well to cinematography and has been a backdrop for talented actors and directors ever since the birth of cinema.

Anita Ekberg exudes glamour and sex appeal in La Dolce Vita.

Italian cinema was born in Rome in 1905. The country's first feature, *La Presa di Roma* – a dramatic tale of the city's incorporation into Italy in 1870 – marked the beginning of the Eternal City's enduring love affair with celluloid.

The birth of Cinecittà

Mussolini saw film as the perfect propaganda vehicle for Fascism, and in a typical attempt to trump the Americans he built his own Hollywood-on-the-Tiber at Cinecittà, the largest film-making complex in Europe. Directors with the right ideological credentials were bankrolled by the regime, but created little of much merit. Nevertheless, some of Italy's greatest directors were meanwhile learning their trade at the studios, as second-unit directors or writers.

Neorealism

The fall of Fascism marked the emergence of one of the world's great film movements: neorealism, depicting the post-war conditions of ordinary people. Around the same time, the city that was born as Mussolini's film set ironically found fame with the Americans he was trying to outdo. In the 1950s good light, the pleasures of working in Italy and the renowned skills (but low costs) of its technicians brought Hollywood to Rome – turning Cinecittà into a household name for millions around the world.

For over a decade Cinecittà was synonymous with the epic – titles like *Quo Vadis* (1951), *Ben-Hur* (1959), Taylor and Burton's *Cleopatra* (1963) – but also made the film that launched a thousand tourist trips, *Roman Holiday* (1953). In its glory years the studios produced over 1,000 films.

> Rome's love affair with cinematography began in 1905, and it would appear that the Eternal City is destined to remain at the heart of Italian cinema.

International productions brought added glamour to Cinecittà, but its bread-and-butter was Italian commercial movie-making. Italians

Poster for Cinecittà's Burton and Taylor epic Cleopatra.

funeral; in a 50-year career he had appeared in over 100 films, including Fellini's 1953 classic *I Vitelloni*.

Cinecittà's comeback

Television production replaced cinema as Cinecittà's everyday business. Home-grown comedies still play well in Italy, but in recent years there have only been fleeting glimpses of Rome in films shown outside the country. An exception is *La Finestra di Fronte* (The Window Opposite, 2003), in which Turkish-born director Ferzan Ozpetek used his adopted city, setting the film in the Ghetto.

After years in the wilderness Cinecittà is back. In 2002, Martin Scorsese reconstructed entire blocks of 19th-century New York here for *Gangs of New York*. This heralded a slew of international productions including Mel Gibson's *The Passion of the Christ* (2004) and the lavish HBO/BBC series *Rome*. In 2012, Woody Allen paid yet another tribute to the city, with his *To Rome with Love*, while the internationally acclaimed Paolo Sorrentino's *The Great Beauty* (2013), also set in the Eternal City, won an Oscar for Best Foreign Language Film.

have always loved their comedy stars. Each city has its home-town clown: Naples is forever linked with Totò and Massimo Troisi, while Florence has Roberto Benigni. When Rome's chief jester, Alberto Sordi, died in 2003, over 80,000 people crammed the streets for his

Award-winning La Grande Bellezza *(The Great Beauty; 2013).*

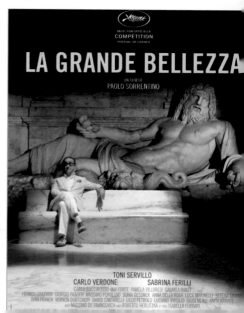

NEOREALISM

Stimulated by the desperate state of Italy at the end of the war, the *neorealismo* auteurs set out to record the life of ordinary people.

At their forefront was Roberto Rossellini, who began shooting *Rome, Open City* (1945), on the devastated streets around Via Prenestina even before the German troops departed.

The signature film of neorealism was Vittorio de Sica's *Bicycle Thieves* (1948). The story of a man and his son in the Rome slums was a huge international success. Other directors influenced by neorealism included Federico Fellini and, in the 1960s, Pier Paolo Pasolini, with his underworld of small-time thieves and desperate love. "We discovered our own country," said Fellini, "and its reality was so extraordinary we couldn't resist photographing it."

PANINI

SANDWICHES

FOOD AND DRINK

Whether it's a long Sunday lunch or a stop-off for an ice cream on an evening stroll, eating in Rome is a very social activity – and one with 2,000 years of tradition, customs and ingenuity behind it.

Culinary traditions run deep in Rome, reaching back to the ancient peoples who first populated the region. For centuries Romans have held firm against the influence of new ingredients, dishes and cooking techniques that have come as a result of Rome's contact with the rest of the world, as well as from the fads and fancies of the upper classes, emperors and popes.

> *Often, what might seem to be slow service is merely the Roman way of stretching a meal far into the night.*

The exotically spiced sauces, fancy game dishes and "delicacies" like fried parrots' tongues dressed with honey that delighted Roman emperors have faded into history, but something does remain from the high cuisine of the past: the unreserved pleasure with which Romans go to table. This is probably not the city to hunt down the top restaurants – few consider *la cucina romana* the best of Italy's regional cuisines – but Rome may well be one of Italy's most pleasurable cities in which to eat. Most restaurants plan on one seating per evening, so you will not be rushed, or pressured to leave.

Tradition and culinary trends

Take any two Italians and listen to their conversation. Sooner or later, it will veer towards food. Food is sacred to Italians and whether they are housewives, businessmen or politicians, they will always find a way to talk about

Pizza is a Roman staple; there are more pizzerias in the city than restaurants.

something they have eaten recently, or about what they would like to eat. The average Italian still looks at exotic cuisines with scepticism, preferring mamma's *pasta al sugo*. It is therefore not surprising that 95 percent of Rome's restaurants exclusively serve Italian or Roman cuisine, either traditional or "with a touch of creativity", which usually means taking the old recipes and adding one (Italian) ingredient or two. But Rome is a big, international city and international food is out there somewhere – if you know where to look. The Prati neighbourhood has a few good sushi places and a couple of Persian and Mexican options. For Chinese and Indian, the multi-ethnic Esquiline district is the place to go, while the Jewish ghetto, which mostly serves Roman-Jewish food, also has a couple of Middle Eastern and Israeli restaurants.

If Italians see food as a religion, fast food is considered pure heresy, and the rare McDonald's and Burger King restaurants available are mostly frequented by teenagers and foreigners. To contrast this, the Slow Food movement was created in northern Italy to promote healthy eating habits based on local, seasonal ingredients and a slower lifestyle, and these principles are now pervading the Roman eating trends, with more and more restaurants serving organic food made with selected ingredients that are hand-picked daily by the chefs at local markets.

La cucina romana

Quite a lot of the local cuisine involves offal, the so-called *quinto-quarto* (fifth quarter) of the animal. Long-time favourites include *rigatoni con pajata* (pasta with veal intestines) and *trippa alla romana* (tripe with tomato sauce, mint and pecorino), but you will find that most restaurants in the centre of town tend to avoid such specialities in favour of dishes from other parts of Italy that are more familiar to an international clientele, such as pasta with pesto sauce (from Genoa), risotto and polenta.

But you needn't eat innards to eat Roman. Every restaurant will have at least a few home-grown dishes, all sharing the frugality that

Olives are a common antipasto.

marks the region's food. *Spaghetti alla carbonara* (with bacon, egg and pecorino cheese), *cacio e pepe* (with pecorino and black pepper), *all'amatriciana* (with bacon or *guanciale* - cured pork jowl - and tomato), and *bucatini alla gricia* – Rome's own tube-shaped style of pasta with *guanciale* – all share an undeniable simplicity. Pasta even makes its way into Roman soups: *pasta e ceci* (chickpea soup flavoured with rosemary) and *broccoli e arzilla* (clear soup of broccoli and skate). *Gnocchi alla romana* (potato dumplings in a meat sauce) are traditionally prepared on Thursday, while *baccalà* (salt cod) is served on Friday.

> Romans may love a leisurely meal, but stopping for slices of pizza, a few scoops of ice cream or a shot of fruit and crushed ice is also an essential part of any passeggiata.

Nor is fish fussed over: clams tossed with spaghetti and olive oil become *spaghetti alle vongole*, and *pesce azzurro* (fish from the sea) is baked in the oven (*al forno*) or cooked on the grill (*ai ferri* or *alla griglia*). Two common meat dishes are *saltimbocca alla romana* (veal slices

APERITIVO HOUR

The Milan-born tradition of an early-evening *aperitivo* accompanied by buffets of savoury munchies has exploded onto the scene in Rome. Gone are the days of humble olives and nuts; opulent spreads now top the counters of even the tiniest bars from around 6 to 8pm every evening. Tramezzini sandwiches bursting with tuna, mozzarella and tomatoes, mini pizzas, focaccia sandwiches and omelette chunks left over from lunch grilled to a crispy finish and sliced up in quarters are typical. Fancier places offer pasta and rice dishes, salads, *bruschetta* and all manner of tempting *fritti* (deep-fried foods). Many bars advertise their *aperitivo* as "happy hour", and offer drink specials as well.

Pasta is served as a first course.

rolled with prosciutto and sage) and the arch-Roman *coda alla vaccinara* ("oxtail butcher's style", slow-braised in a garlic, pepper, tomato and celery sauce), but the meat to try is *abbacchio* (milk-fed lamb), which is usually roasted with herbs and garlic or served *alla scottadito* (as grilled chops).

> Romans are the undisputed masters of the artichoke. At restaurants throughout the city you will be able to try them prepared in several different traditional styles.

Greens on the side

Save room for vegetables, which abound in Rome's markets all year long and are usually served simply prepared, often steamed or blanched and then briefly sautéed. November to April is the season for another Roman speciality, artichokes, which can be served many different ways. Among them are *carciofi alla giudia* ("Jewish-style" and so typical of the Ghetto – deep-fried) and *carciofi alla romana* (stuffed with garlic and mint, and stewed).

A typical winter salad is *puntarelle*, made by shredding the stalks of locally grown chicory

and serving them with a lemon-anchovy dressing. Summer brings roasted peppers, aubergines and courgettes (zucchini) served in a variety of ways, and large tomatoes stuffed with herbs and rice, while in spring you'll see asparagus and *fave con pecorino* (raw broad beans with pecorino cheese).

Many Italians like to have just one main dish and finish a meal with a piece of fruit, then a coffee. Accordingly, appetisers and desserts get little attention in most Rome restaurants. A few common starters are melon or figs with prosciutto and *fiori di zucca* (deep-fried zucchini flowers filled with mozzarella and anchovies). Popular desserts are *torta di ricotta* (ricotta tart), *panna cotta* (eggless, firm creamy custard with a fruit sauce) and *tiramisù* (coffee trifle).

Find your wine

The local wines that still dominate the wine selections of most Roman restaurants – those from Frascati are the best-known – are nowadays much better than they used to be, but still pale in comparison with wines produced in other parts of Italy, which are now widely available in the capital. For a good wine, it's usually

Zucchini (courgette) flowers are either fried or stuffed with ricotta-based fillings.

Volpetti on Via Alessandro Volta is one of Rome's best delis.

Greens are often served as a side dish.

better to bypass the house wine and choose a non-local label.

Italians rarely drink without eating, but stopping by a bar for an early-evening aperitif with a snack has become one of fashionable Rome's biggest fads *(see box)*. Wine bars *(enoteche)* are also very popular. They have much better wine selections than most restaurants, and offer a great alternative to a restaurant meal, with a relaxed, easy-going atmosphere. Choose from usually about a dozen wines available by the glass (or from more than a thousand different labels by the bottle), and a great selection of high-quality cheeses, salami and other cured meats and smoked fish, as well as soups and salads, quiches and gratins, and sometimes home-made desserts.

Roman pizza

The Neapolitans are credited with inventing pizza, but Romans eat their fair share. There are more *pizzerie* than restaurants in town, and Romans have their own version of this staple dish: whereas a big Neapolitan pizza is made with a thick, softish dough and has a raised rim, a *pizza romana* is plate-sized, and rolled

The ever-popular gelato.

Accordingly, *gelaterie* are never far away and stay open late. Other treats that can be picked up from street vendors all over town are roasted chestnuts in the autumn and winter, and refreshing *grattachecca* (shaved ice with syrup) and watermelon wedges in summer.

Romans often stop at the local bar a couple of times a day, first for a breakfast of espresso or cappuccino and a *cornetto* (the Italian version of the croissant), then another espresso and perhaps a snack, such as a *panino* or *tramezzino* (small sandwiches) later in the day.

Pizza al taglio (by the slice) is also easy to find. Thicker than pizzeria pizza and topped with dozens of imaginative combinations, *pizza al taglio* is always sold by weight; an *etto* (100 grams) is a small portion. Many of the same shops also sell *supplì* (fried balls of rice and mozzarella), a classic Roman snack.

A good *alimentari*, or grocery shop, is worth visiting as this is where you'll find regional products from all over the country. The local cheese to try is *pecorino romano*, made from ewe's milk in big wheels, bathed in brine and aged for 18 months. A by-product is *ricotta di pecora*, brought in fresh from the farms and delicious on its own. A memorable sandwich can be made from *porchetta* (whole roasted pig, sliced to order), a speciality of the hill towns around Rome.

very thin and flat. Both kinds must be baked in a wood-burning stove (*forno a legna*). A night out at a pizzeria (few are open for lunch) is a quintessential Roman experience.

On the go

For Romans, *gelato* (ice cream) is not so much a dessert as an afternoon or after-dinner snack to accompany a leisurely stroll around town.

An espresso, the way to start the day and end a meal.

ICE CREAM HEAVEN

Romans have enjoyed ice cream since ancient times: Nero ate snow transported all the way from Vesuvius, mixed with fruit topping. But Italian gelato is different from its American cousin. By definition, it contains less fat and more sugar, and is often home-made, using natural ingredients. Most bars and cafés in Rome sell ice cream, although not all of this will be home-made. The better producers only use real fruit, or specialise in new flavours and combinations, such as basil, or rice and honey. Sicilian ice-cream shops are particularly popular and often sell *granita* (sometimes known as *cremolata*), consisting of crushed ice mixed with fruit, chocolate, or coffee.

SHOPPING

When it comes to shopping, Rome can hold its own against its famous northern rival, Milan. It has enough haute couture, chic boutiques, designer homeware and leatherware to satisfy the hungriest style vultures.

Rome teems with designer boutiques.

For years Rome has been vying with big brother Milan for status as a fashionista magnet. While history hawks and culture vultures perpetually head for the Eternal City, serious shopaholics are quick to name Milan

Now more than ever, Rome boasts a shopping scene for all tastes – from the seekers of chic to lovers of all things ornate and original.

as the hands-down fashion capital of Italy. The Roman shopping experience, however, is more individualistic and maybe more relaxed than its northern Italian equivalent, with a thriving market for high-quality hand-craftsmanship and a taste for small boutiques. Those looking for the big names in fashion won't be disappointed, with luxurious names like Armani, Prada, Gucci and Bulgari that set up shop in the prestigious Piazza di Spagna area.

Made in Rome

For the keen-eyed and eager shopper, there are unique purchases to be had, from that hand-cut leather jacket you've always dreamed of, to handwoven textiles and home-grown Roman designer wear. They may not be parading the catwalks yet, but these unique up-and-comers are worth seeking out. In a city that refuses to leave behind the values of solid craftsmanship, so intrinsic to the "Made in Italy" mark, a savvy shopper will delight in the objects on offer.

Be aware that the big guns of Italy don't necessarily cost less on their own soil. Those with an eye on the major labels would be wise to peruse price tags at home before landing in the capital. The outlets outside Rome, although cheaper, are a bit of a trek, so think twice about stocking up on your Prada, Fendi and Ferragamo.

The good news is that younger Roman labels like AVC (fabulous shoes; www.avcbyadrianacampanile.com) and Arsenale (a truly art gallery-esque women's boutique; www.patriziapieroni.it) are springing up, paving the way for fresh Roman fashion.

Well-made bags and other leather goods are good buys.

Shopping areas

Rome's shopping scene is often summed up by one glorious avenue: Via del Corso, the road stretching from Piazza del Popolo to Piazza Venezia. It is here that you'll find everything from the national and international retail stores, high- and lower-end labels, and all the books, music and trinkets you're after. Many turnoffs lead to Piazza di Spagna and, most famously, Via Condotti. This is where the real designer glitz resides – that and about 99 percent of the tourist masses. For a far more

GETTING AROUND

Getting from one area to another in Rome is easy. If you are staying in the city centre and are armed with a decent map, you can walk almost everywhere, and will definitely find it a more pleasant experience than trying to jam yourself onto one of the packed buses that chug through the traffic-choked city's central thoroughfares. Keep an eye out for the small electric buses that snake quietly through the city though, as they can provide welcome relief for tired feet. For the more outlying areas there is usually a handy bus or metro stop not too far away, to make it easier to carry your purchases home.

leisurely shopping experience, weave your way through the backstreets, starting from Piazza del Popolo. Be sure not to overlook the hip Via

> Rome is characterised by the olde-world values of artisan craftsmanship, artful design and good food, which define the shopping cityscape.

del Babuino. The entire triangle is referred to as Tridente.

The areas around Piazza Navona, the Pantheon and the Campo de' Fiori are teeming with boutiques and shops stocked with homeware, fabulous shoes and accessories, and not to mention some tempting delis and pampering perfumeries. Via del Governo Vecchio and Via dei Coronari are dedicated to the marvels of yesteryear, with famous vintage and second-hand shops and the best antique dealers in town. For an ultra-Roman experience, spend the afternoon trying on 1970s leather jackets and boho dresses, before re-fuelling at one of Via del Governo Vecchio's copious wine bars. Via dei Giubbonari and the surrounding tangle of streets are lined

Prada heels.

with small boutiques catering for a young and youthful crowd. Across Via Arenula, the ghetto is the place to go for Judaica items, while those looking for Christian religious goods such as church candles, priest garments and accessories can take a stroll in the alleys of the Borgo Pio area around the Vatican, or visit Via dei Cestari and Via di Santa Chiara, both in the Navona area.

The Vatican-Prati neighbourhood to the north is also home to shopping mega-street Via Cola di Rienzo. A slightly shorter jaunt than Via del Corso, this popular strip is lined with youthful retail chains, some great boutiques, and COIN, Rome's best department store. You'll also find some of the finest selections of speciality food and drink shops.

In the hilly side streets of Monti, art galleries, bric-a-brac shops and funky boutiques have turned this area into a very trendy hotspot, and an afternoon passeggiata in these quiet streets is a very relaxing experience. While in the more upscale area around Piazza Fiume and the beginning of Via Salaria, you'll find Rinascente department store (www.rinascente.it), and some retailers of pretty clothing, shoes and accessories.

On a rainy day, it may be a good idea to spend some time in one of Rome's malls or shopping centres – if you don't mind the crowds, that is. The Galleria Alberto Sordi (http://galleriaalberto sordi.it) on Via del Corso is pretty and central, but not on the big side. The lower level of Termini Station (www.romatermini.com) houses about 40 shops and is a good option for a few hours. Serious shoppers, however, should travel a bit and spend a day at one of the bigger malls,

A Trastevere artisan at work.

like Porta di Roma (www.galleriaportadiroma.it) at the very end of Via Salaria, EUROMA2 (www.euroma2.it) in EUR, or the outdoor shopping centre Parco Da Vinci (www.parcocommercialeda vinci.com), near Fiumicino airport.

If you feel you've outdone yourself, the streets around Termini Station and Santa Maria Maggiore are packed with shops selling suitcases, bags and backpacks of any kind.

When to hit the shops

Opening hours in Rome are a law unto themselves. What visitors find most surprising is the tendency for many shops to close for at least two hours at lunchtime and all of Monday morning. However, in highly commercial and touristy areas such as the Tridente, Via del Corso, the Trevi Fountain and Via Nazionale, most shops, especially the chain stores, department stores and high-fashion boutiques, now operate a so-called *orario continuato* (continuous opening hours), sometimes called the not-quite-English *orario no-stop*, both of which mean they do not close at lunch time, and may be open Monday morning.

The big names, chain stores and department stores in touristy and central areas are open on Sunday afternoons, in some cases on Sunday mornings, too. Another thing to remember

---

BEST BUYS

Rome is the place for quality rather than bargains, so its best buys tend to be at the luxury end of the market, principally in the form of designer clothes and accessories, antiques and objets d'art. That said, careful shoppers may still come away with affordable buys: attractive books on art and architecture, classic leather shoes and bags, striking kitchenware, herbalists' concoctions, distinctive marbled notepaper, leather-bound notebooks, old prints, market bric-a-brac, and a whole host of gourmet treats, all represent good value. If Rome is your only Italian stop, it may also be worth it to check out hand-crafted objects from other Italian regions, such as Venetian glass or Tuscan ceramics.

is that in July and August, as the heat starts to become oppressive, local and independent shops may close on Saturday afternoon, and most close for at least two weeks in August for their annual holiday.

Roman service

It won't be long before you experience a phenomenon well known to regular visitors to Rome – the unhelpful shop assistant. Although there are many exceptions, most notably the designer boutiques who are dependent on tourist trade, and the small independent stores, Roman retail staff are not known for polite customer service. Shop assistants may seem either too bored or too busy talking to pay you any attention. Don't take it personally – simply ask firmly for what you want and you'll find the assistants usually snap to attention.

Bargain-hunting

Discounts are not generally given in most types of stores, although you may be able to get one if you are making a large purchase, or you happen upon a small defect of manufacture. One exception is the many large *profumerie* (perfume and cosmetics stores) where most items are sold at a *prezzo scontato* (discount price). Another way of getting reliable bargains is the end-of-season sales *(saldi)*.

The two main sales periods start in early January, continuing into February (or as long as they've got anything left on the racks), and in mid-July, lasting until the end of August. At other times of the year, interesting deals can often be had at stores showing a *liquidazione* sign, which indicates a closing-down sale.

> As a general rule, it's next to impossible to return merchandise for a refund. By law, unused items may be exchanged on site, but ask what the store's exchange policies are, and be sure to keep the receipt.

The Fashion District outlets of Valmontone, 40km (25 miles) outside Rome, are definitely worth visiting for excellent deals and discounts. Among the stores represented are Gianfranco Ferre, Pierre Cardin, Calvin Klein Jeans, La Perla, Rosenthal, Bassetti, Adidas, Lotto and loads more. Trains leave hourly from Termini Station. Castel Romano hosts over 100 stores and offers up to a 70 percent discount on merchandise. Buses for Pomezia Via Pontina depart regularly from Metro B station Laurentina. Ask the driver to indicate the stop.

Don't underestimate the goods on offer at the open-air markets around town. For second-hand gems, Porta Portese, Via Sannio and Borghetto Flaminio are prime (see page 74).

Designer fakes

Another way to get your "designer" goods cheaply is to buy them from the street vendors who populate the city's most touristy thoroughfares and bridges. Of course, they are selling bags that only look like real Prada, Gucci, Fendi and Louis Vuitton numbers, often to an unsuspecting international clientele. Remember, though, that when you are given prices at a fraction of those of the original labels, the goods are definitely not the real thing, and that trade in counterfeit goods is actually illegal. It's not an unusual sight to see the sudden scattering of such vendors at the sight of a police car rolling by.

Retro homewares.

MARKETS IN ROME

Neighbourhood markets are an essential part of the Roman way of life. They are full of local colour and goods to bring back home.

Rome has about 150 official *mercati rionali* (neighbourhood markets), which run from Monday to Saturday, where there's generally an abundance of the freshest fruit and vegetables, as well as stalls selling meat, fish, cheeses, hams and spices, and others loaded with kitchenware, household linens, clothing and toys. In the past decades the city has gradually moved many of these open-air markets into closed structures, making it easier for the sellers to work under the pouring rain or boiling sun. The most recent of these is the Testaccio market, which was moved to a new location on Via Galvani in 2012.

Although supermarkets are competing hard, there are a number of reasons why the tradition of buying from markets will be hard to extinguish. In the city centre a lack of space dictates that the supermarkets that do exist are still comparatively small, and have no convenient parking spaces. Buying from markets is still often more convenient, both economically and in terms of location.

Also extremely important are the personalised service and human contact, as well as the possibility to touch, feel and inquire about every single item you are intending to buy. Many residents value this highly, and will spend time chatting to stallholders and other customers as they make their purchases. In the past, going to market was also an excuse to catch up on the latest gossip.

Markets, especially flea markets, also offer the opportunity to do some bargaining. Whether you go to buy or to browse, Rome's markets are worth visiting for their atmosphere alone.

Hand-painted crockery for sale.

The city's best-known food market is Campo de' Fiori. Here you will find everything from upmarket stalls selling exotic fruits and rare herbs at exorbitant prices to stalls where fresher-than-fresh produce on show is grown by the farmer who is serving you.

Another classic Roman market is held on Via Sannio, just behind the Basilica of San Giovanni in Laterano. This is the place to come for jeans, leather jackets, sports gear and shoes. There are also several stalls selling retro and second-hand clothes.

SOMETHING FOR EVERYONE

Pick up a 'replica' version of the local team's kit.

There's something poetic about market shopping. It may be the sky above your head, or the idea that whatever you are buying is, or at least feels, unique. The Eternal City is full of little markets, many of which specialise in very particular items. The flower market in the Trionfale neighbourhood only sells flowers and plants, and is open to the public on Tuesday mornings. The Mercato delle Stampe in Largo della Fontanella Borghese specializes in old books, ancient maps, scientific tables and decorative prints. The Nuovo Mercato Esquilino is the place to go for herbs and exotic spices. Vintage markets are often organised in music venues like the Micca (www.miccaclub.com) or Bar Necci (www.necci1924.com). But for all of the above and many more, however, it's always best to get up early on a Sunday morning and rummage through the sky-high piles of everything at Porta Portese.

Although supermarkets have sprung up all over Rome in recent years, most Romans still prefer to buy fresh produce from their local daily market.

Rome's biggest flea market is Porta Portese, held on Via Portuense and adjacent streets between Piazza Porta Portese and Via Ettore Rolli.

Find antiques and art at the Soffitta Sotto I Portici market in Piazza Augusto Imperatore.

Piazza della Rotunda and the Pantheon.

Morning light pours into St Peter's.

ORIENTATION

While getting lost amid the dizzying beauties of the Eternal City may sound romantic, understanding the different neighbourhoods is important in order to appreciate the city's history.

Rome is crammed with great sights. In no other city are the accumulated layers of history so evident. Every corner seems to lead to a famous monument, church or square. However, for first-time visitors trying to grapple with the layout of its seven hills, the city can seem confusing. The best way to orientate oneself is to look upon Via del Corso as a spine, with the leafy Villa Borghese quarter at the top, the archaeological zone at the bottom, the Centro Storico to the west, Piazza di Spagna to the east, and the Vatican and Trastevere on the far bank of the Tiber.

The main archaeological sites – namely the Capitol, Forum, Palatine and the Colosseum – reflect key episodes in the city's history and provide the foundation for layer upon layer of architectural styles.

Shopping for souvenirs.

What is referred to as the Centro Storico, or historic centre, is the dense centre of Rome contained in the great bend of the Tiber; this includes Piazza Navona and the Pantheon, and Campo de' Fiori and the Ghetto, areas that flourished in the Middle Ages and were further embellished by the architects of the Baroque era.

Rome sign.

Two of the most iconic landmarks of the Eternal City, the Trevi Fountain and the Spanish Steps, were built in the 1700s and are situated within the heart of Rome's shopping district. This area is known as the Trident as it is comprised between three streets, Via di Ripetta, Via del Corso and Via del Babuino, all departing from piazza del Popolo.

On the west bank of the Tiber are the Vatican and the authentic Trastevere district. In between stands the Janiculum Hill, with its sweeping views of the city.

Beyond the usual tourist routes are Villa Borghese, the Aventine and Testaccio, Monti and Esquilino, and the Appian Way, while for those who want to escape the noise and heat of the city, Rome's environs offer many day-trip opportunities.

Praised by the artists and writers of the past for its views, warm colours and the delightful scents pervading the streets, a trip to the Eternal City is a magnificent journey through time.

Rome

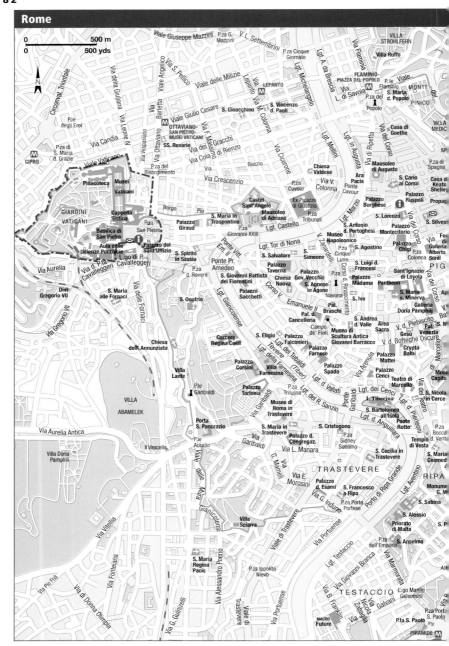

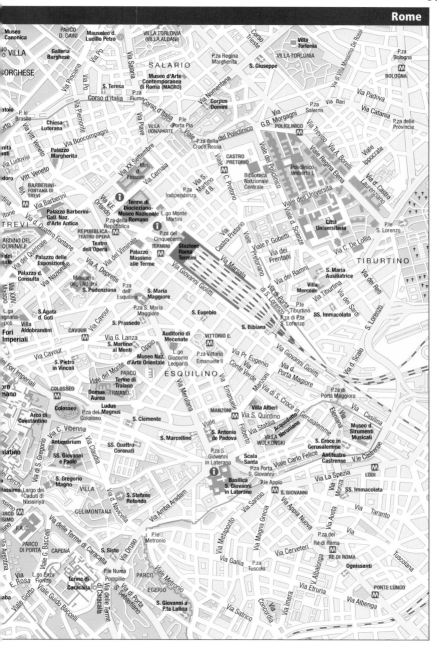

Michelangelo's staircase leads to the Campidoglio, watched over by the twin gods, Castor (pictured) and Pollux.

THE CAPITOLINE HILL

Capitoline Hill, the political power centre of the ancient world, beautified by Michelangelo's designs during the Renaissance, is now home to the world's oldest museums.

The Capitoline Hill started life as a fortified stronghold and later became the city's religious and political centre. As a 12th-century guidebook, *Mirabilia Romae (The Marvels of Rome)* stated: "The Capitol was the head of the world, where consuls and senators abode to govern the earth." At only 50 metres (150ft), it may be the lowest of the city's seven hills, but Rome was founded at its feet. During the Renaissance, it was glorified with the Piazza del Campidoglio, a harmonious square designed by Michelangelo, and second only to Piazza San Pietro in its architectural symmetry.

The twin crowns

In ancient times the hill looked quite different, with steep cliffs of porous tufa rock falling steeply on all sides of its twin crowns. On the southern crown, known as Campidoglio (the Capitol), stood the Tempio di Giove (Temple of Jupiter), which was the religious hub of the state. Originally the size of a football pitch, it was begun by the Etruscan kings and dedicated in 509 BC, the first year of the Republic. Behind its six-pillared, south-facing frontage a great anteroom led to the shrines of

three great gods – Jupiter, Juno and Minerva. Every New Year's Day, the consuls were inaugurated in a formal ceremony on the Capitol.

The triumphal processions followed Via Sacra, the holy road, coming up the hill from the Forum. Remnants of the basalt paving of this street can be seen quite clearly from Via di Monte Tarpeo. Anyone guilty of treason was thrown from the Rupe Tarpea (Tarpeian Rock), the Capitol's southern precipice. The other crown of the hill housed the temple to Juno Moneta, the goddess

Main Attractions
Santa Maria in Aracoeli
The Capitoline Museums
Mamertine Prison
Il Vittoriano Monument
Museo del Risorgimento
Museo di Palazzo Venezia

Piazza Venezia viewed from the steps of the Vittoriano monument.

The stairway to the entrance of Santa Maria in Aracoeli.

Statue of Marcus Aurelius in the Campidoglio.

who is supposed to have warned the Romans of an attack by Gauls in 390 BC by making her sacred geese honk. The mint also stood here, hence the word *moneta*, meaning money.

Santa Maria in Aracoeli ❶

Address: Scala dell'Arce Capitolina 14
Opening Hours: daily 9am–12.30pm, 2.30–5.30pm (3.30–6.30pm in summer)
Entrance Fee: free
Transport: see Musei Capitolini

The site of the ancient Temple of Juno Moneta is now occupied by the church of **Santa Maria in Aracoeli** (St Mary of the Altar in the Sky). The church hides behind a 13th-century brick facade, but its origins go back much further, as its ancient columns testify. Records from AD 574 mention a church on this site. The present church was built by Franciscans in around 1250. The interior features an ornate coffered ceiling dating from 1572–5 and a striking Cosmatesque

floor. This style of intricate, geometric polychrome patterns is named after Lorenzo Cosmati (1140–1210), its inventor. In the first chapel on the right are Renaissance frescoes by Pinturicchio depicting the life of St Bernard. The restoration of the Chapel of San Pasquale Baylon revealed beautiful 13th-century frescoes concealed behind 16th-century works. Steps lead down from the exit in the right transept to the level of the Piazza del Campidoglio.

PIAZZA DEL CAMPIDOGLIO

Between the hill's two peaks sits the **Piazza del Campidoglio** (Capitol Square). In ancient times it was the site of the Asylum, a sacred sanctuary that protected the persecuted, said to date back to the time of the founder of the city, Romulus. The magnificent square, its buildings and the broad staircase leading up to it were designed by Michelangelo for Pope Paul III, who wanted a majestic

Capitoline Hill and Ancient Rome

setting for the reception of the Holy Roman Emperor Charles V on his visit to Rome in 1536.

As it turned out, the square wasn't completed until the 17th century. Standing guard at the top of the **Cordonata**, as the staircase is known, are two imposing statues of Castor and Pollux. The piazza's centrepiece is a first-rate copy of an immense equestrian statue of Emperor Marcus Aurelius. The original is kept inside the Capitoline Museums.

Straight ahead is **the Palazzo Senatorio**. At the bottom of its double staircase is a fountain of Minerva flanked by two statues representing the Nile (left with the Sphinx) and the Tiber (right with the she-wolf).

The Musei Capitolini ❷

Address: Piazza del Campidoglio 1; http://en.museicapitolini.org
Telephone: 06-0608
Opening Times: daily 9.30am – 7.30pm

Entrance Fee: charge
Transport: 30, 40, 44, 46, 51, 60, 62, 63, 64, 70, 81, 83, 85, 87, 118, 130F, 160, 170, 492, ,628, 715, 716, 780, 781, 810, 916, C3, H

The two grand *palazzi* on either side of the square – Palazzo Nuovo (New Palace) and Palazzo dei Conservatori (Conservators' Palace) – house the oldest public museums in the world. The **Musei Capitolini** are entered via the Palazzo dei Conservatori, on the right of Michelangelo's Cordonata. Together they contain a rich collection of ancient sculpture, and late Renaissance and Baroque art (see page 90).

The two palaces are connected via a passage lined with artefacts that runs underneath the square. From here you can visit the **Tabularium**, Rome's ancient archive (from 78 BC). It was built around the even older Temple of Veiovis, and rose four storeys high, with 10 arches opening onto the Forum, although all but

EAT

Avoid the refreshment stands dotted around the major tourist sites unless you're absolutely desperate for a drink. They're overpriced and prey on thirsty tourists. If you don't want to be ripped off, it's worth stocking up on a supply of bottled mineral water from a grocery store, or take advantage of the water gushing out of the drinking fountains.

Fragments of a colossal statue of Constantine in the Palazzo dei Conservatori.

Tomb of the Unknown Soldier.

The Vittoriano monument.

three of them are now bricked up. Memorable views across the Roman Forum can be had from here.

Carcere Mamertino (Tullianum) ❸

Address: 1 Clivo Argentario; www.archeoroma.beniculturali.it
Telephone: 06-679 2902
Opening Times: daily summer 9am–7pm, winter 9am–5pm
Entrance Fee: charge
Transport: see Musei Capitolini

A road winds its way down from the left of the Palazzo Senatorio to the church of San Giuseppe dei Falegnami and the **Carcere Mamertino** (Mamertine Prison). Defeated kings and generals, having been paraded through the streets in their victor's triumphal march, were imprisoned here before being executed. A small chapel next to a spring commemorates St Peter, who is said to have been incarcerated here, and to have baptised his guards with water from a spring he miraculously created. From the prison, the road leads down to Via dei Fori Imperiali.

Piazza Venezia ❹

If all roads lead to Rome, then all roads in Rome seem to lead to Piazza Venezia, the hub of the city's road network since 1881.

Il Vittoriano (Altare della Patria) ❺

Address: Piazza Venezia
Opening Times: daily summer 9.30am–5.30pm, winter 9.30am–4.30pm
Entrance Fee: free
Transport: see Musei Capitolini

Compared to the grace and majesty of the Campidoglio, **Il Vittoriano**, which dominates the square and while is undeniably impressive, is a bombastic structure. Romans refer to it irreverently as the typewriter, the wedding cake or even Rome's false teeth. In the 19th century, a whole swathe of medieval streets was razed to make way for this hulking white monument erected in honour of Victor Emmanuel II of Savoy, the first king of the newly unified Italy. However, entrance is free and visitors can climb the steps (or pay €7 for the elevator ride; Mon–Thu 9.30am–6.30pm, Fri–Sun till 7.30pm)

for wonderful views of the city and welcome refreshments in the outdoor café behind it (see page 89).

Below the equestrian statue of Victor Emmanuel II is the tomb of the Unknown Soldier flanked by perpetually burning flames and two armed guards. The monument also has a permanent museum complex. **The Museo del Risorgimento** (www.risorgimento.it; daily 9.30am–6.30pm) recounts the history of the Risorgimento (literally "Resurrection"), a turbulent period of war and political wrangling that led to the reunification of Italy. However, few of the exhibits are labelled in English, and it's of limited appeal to those with only a passing interest in military history.

Around the back of the building is a space used for high-profile international exhibitions, while on the other side there's a museum focusing on Italian emigration (www.museo nazionaleemigrazione.it).

Palazzo Venezia ⑥

Address: 118 Via del Plebiscito; www.museopalazzovenezia.beniculturali.it
Telephone: 06-678 0131
Opening Times: Tue–Sun 8.30am–7.30pm

Entrance Fee: charge; free first Sun of each month
Transport: see Musei Capitolini

Although the Vittoriano is the most dominant, the **Palazzo di Venezia** is the most interesting building on this square. Built by Cardinal Balbo in 1455 and enlarged when he became Pope Paul II, it was later handed over to the Venetian ambassadors and then the Austrians until Mussolini decided it would make a perfect office. He addressed the crowds from its balcony, the very balcony from which Pope Paul II watched the races along the Corso.

This palace now holds the **Museo di Palazzo Venezia**, with displays of medieval paintings, sculptures and artefacts, terracotta models (some by Bernini), bronze sculptures, and glass, silver and ivory objects. A permanent collection of Renaissance arts and crafts is joined by regular exhibitions dedicated to various art movements.

Behind the palace is the church of **San Marco** (daily 7.30am–12.30pm, Mon–Sat 4–7pm; Sun until 7.30pm), with a lovely mosaic in its 9th-century apse. Outside the church stands the buxom **statue of Madama Lucrezia**, one of Rome's so-called "Talking Statues" (see page 163).

TIP

Some of the best views of the city can be seen from the cafés in the Palazzo dei Conservatori and the Vittoriano monument. Take the lift (€7) and spare your feet 196 steps.

RESTAURANTS, BARS AND CAFÉS

PRICE CATEGORIES

Price includes dinner and a half-bottle of house wine.
€€€€ = more than €60
€€€ = €40–60
€€ = €25–40
€ = under €25

Restaurants

The restaurants and bars in this area are very touristy and not really recommended, but we detail a few places worth visiting, as much for the views and atmosphere as for food and drink.
Vecchia Roma

18 Piazza Campitelli
06-686 4604
www.ristorantevecchiaroma.com
L & D Thu–Tue
€€€€ [p324, C4]
At Vecchia Roma you pay for the location, the service and some of the city's finest outdoor seating. The classic dishes are usually good, although occasionally only competent, and the wine is excellent. It's expensive for what you get, but memorable.

Bars and Cafés

The Ara Coelis Café
Behind the Vittoriano monument;

accessible from the Piazza del Campidoglio.
[p324, D3]
A great, if touristy, spot for a drink. Fine views of the Forum and the Roman skyline.
Caffè Capitolino
Top of Palazzo dei Conservatori, adjacent to Piazza Campidoglio
[p324, D4]
This caffè offers its clientele one of the most panoramic views in Rome. Outdoor seating under sunshades, on the so-called "Terrazza Caffarelli", is certainly expensive but delightful if it's not too hot. Inside, cafeteria-style service is cheaper.

THE CAPITOLINE MUSEUMS

The Capitoline Museums house a varied collection of artworks which constitute some of Rome's most admired treasures.

Divided between two palaces on either side of the Campidoglio, the Capitoline Museum collection is the oldest public collection of classical sculpture in the world – and the first-ever public museum. The first group of bronze sculptures were made over to the people of Rome by Sixtus IV in 1471, while the museum was officially inaugurated in 1734 by Pope Clement XII. Designed by Michelangelo as part of the restoration project for Piazza del Campidoglio, the two museum palaces were completed after his death. The Palazzo dei Conservatori's frescoed halls house the municipal offices of the Comune di Roma, while the museum contains a large sculpture collection and artworks by Caravaggio, Van Dyck and Tintoretto. Palazzo Nuovo is filled with row upon row of portrait busts of Roman emperors, while the first floor has some exquisite examples of Roman statuary. A visit to the museums begins in the Palazzo dei Conservatori (to the right of the Michelangelo staircase), where the ticket office and cloakrooms are. The two museums are connected via an art-lined underground passageway that takes you to the Tabularium (see page 87), which offers an excellent view of the Forum.

Detail from the vast frescoes decorating the Hall of the Orazie and Curiazi where the Public Council of Conservators convened. Painted by Mannerist Cavaliere d'Arpino (1595–1640), they illustrate the origins of Rome as told by the Roman historian Livy.

The Essentials

Address: Piazza del Campidoglio; www.museicapitolini.org
Tel: 06-0608
Opening Hours: daily 9.30am – 7.30pm
Entrance Fee: charge
Transport: 40, 62, 63, 64, 95, 170, plus many more

Sensual portrayal of St John the Baptist by Caravaggio.

A TOUR OF THE TREASURES

One of the most iconic exhibits in the Palazzo dei Conservatori is the original she-wolf wet-nursing Romulus and Remus, symbol of Rome. The wolf is Etruscan, dating from the 5th century BC, but the twins were added in the 15th century by Florentine artist Pollaiuolo. You can also get a good close-up view of the original equestrian statue of Marcus Aurelius (the one on the square is a copy) exhibited in a sky-lit room. Other highlights include a graceful 1st-century BC figure of a boy removing a thorn from his foot, an earlier Venus, a fine collection of Renaissance and Baroque paintings, and fragments of a huge statue of Constantine.

The central exhibit in the Hall of the Doves is the exquisitely crafted mosaic of drinking doves found in Hadrian's Villa at Tivoli. In the same room is another highly expressive 2nd-century mosaic of two Greek theatre masks, probably from an imperial villa on the Aventine hill.

The most famous pieces in the Palazzo Nuovo are the *Dying Gaul* – a beautifully evocative statue of a fatally wounded warrior, the voluptuous *Capitoline Venus*, the Mosaic of the Doves from Hadrian's villa, the 2nd-century mosaic of theatre masks, and the red marble *Satyr Resting*, a copy of an original by Praxiteles. In his novel *The Marble Faun*, Nathaniel Hawthorne describes this statue by writing: "It is impossible to gaze long at this stone image without conceiving a kindly sentiment towards it, as if its substance were warm to the touch, and imbued with actual life."

The Palazzo dei Conservatori and Palazzo Nuovo are linked by an underground tunnel which leads to the Tabularium, the ancient Roman State Record Office, erected in 78 BC. It affords fine views of the Forum.

The Rape of the Sabine Women by Pietro da Cortona. He was a contemporary of Bernini, and together they pioneered a true Baroque style, as illustrated by the movement, richness of colour and theatricality of this painting.

In the courtyard of the Palazzo Nuovo is a fountain which incorporates a 1st-century BC statue of a river god. Known as "Marforio", this is one of Rome's famous "talking statues", to which placards containing satirical comments on the events of the day were attached during the Renaissance.

THE GRIM GLORY OF THE COLOSSEUM

"While the Colosseum stands, Rome shall stand; when the Colosseum falls, Rome shall fall; when Rome falls the world shall fall," an old prophecy says.

The Colosseum is the city's most stirring sight, "a noble wreck in the ruinous perfection" in Byron's words. It was begun by Vespasian, inaugurated by his son Titus in AD 80, and completed by Domitian. This majestic amphitheatre could seat over 50,000 spectators who revelled in the spectacle of gladiators fighting to the death. On the arena's opening day, 5,000 animals were slaughtered. In AD 248, the millennium of the founding of Rome was celebrated here by gladiatorial contests. "Bread and circuses" was the judgement of Juvenal, the 1st-century poet, on the way the city's rulers kept the populace happy. The last gladiatorial fight took place in AD 439, while animal fights ended the following century, when the barbaric *munera* (blood sports) were made illegal. With the fall of the Empire, the Colosseum fell into disuse. During the Renaissance, the ruins were plundered of their valuable travertine to build churches and palaces. Quarrying was only halted by Pope Benedict XIV in the 18th century and the site dedicated to Christian martyrs.

Gladiators, named after the Roman sword, gladius, were mostly condemned criminals, prisoners of war or slaves. They were trained to fight then pitted against each other and against various exotic animals.

The Essentials

Address: Piazza del Colosseo; www.coop culture.it
Tel: 06-3996 7700
Opening Hours: daily 8.30am — one hour before sunset; ticket office shuts one hour before closing time
Entrance Fee: charge
Transport: Colosseo

Views from the higher tiers down to the arena show a maze of passageways normally hidden from view. The moveable wooden floor was covered in sand to soak up the blood. The subterranean section concealed the animal cages and sophisticated technical apparatus, from winches and mechanical lifts to ramps and trap doors.

Renaissance historians believed that ancient Roman arenas were sometimes flooded to stage mock naval battles, but there is scant evidence to suggest that such a display ever took place in the Colosseum.

ENTERTAINMENT FOR THE MASSES

Audience participation was part of the games.

Although supremely public, the Colosseum was a stratified affair. The podium, set on the lowest tier, was reserved exclusively for the Emperor, senators, magistrates and Vestal Virgins. Above them sat the bourgeoisie, with the lower orders restricted to the top tier, and the populace on wooden seats in the very top rows. Shortly before the games began, the Emperor and his followers would enter the amphitheatre, and spectators would show their reverence by clapping, cheering, and chanting their sovereign's honorifics.

A trumpet call started the games and spectacles began with cries of "Hail to the Emperor, those about to die salute thee". If a gladiator tried to retreat into the underground chamber, he was pushed forward with whips and red-hot irons. The gladiators mostly fought to the death. A wounded man could beg for mercy by lifting a finger of his left hand. If the crowd waved handkerchiefs, he was saved; thumbs down meant death. After the gladiators came the wild beasts, which were made to fight one another or human beings – armed or unarmed. The animals, mostly imported from Africa, included lions, elephants, giraffes, hyenas, hippos, wild horses and zebras.

The Colosseum is Rome's top tourist sight, and when floodlit at night it creates a wonderful spectacle. It has been used as an arena for crowd-pulling concerts – Andrea Bocelli sang here in 2009.

Men dressed in traditional Roman costumes stroll around the perimeter of the Colosseum – some indulge in light-hearted role-playing for the benefit of tourists, others will fleece you for a photo.

The Arch of Titus, the oldest triumphal arch in Rome.

ANCIENT ROME

Discover the places where Ancient Rome once thrived, declined and eventually fell. Here lie the remains of the Fora, the Palatine, and the Colosseum, resplendent testament to this ancient world.

By 7.30 in the morning, a traffic jam usually blocks the intersection of Via Labicana and Via dei Fori Imperiali, which leads to the Colosseum and the Appian Way. This boulevard, commissioned by Mussolini for the greater glory of the Fascist Empire, slices through the heart of Rome's ancient sites. Here, Nero built an artificial lake to grace his palace. Then the Flavians – in a bid to return the tyrant's palace to the people – built the Colosseum. The construction of Via dei Fori Imperiali in 1932 was a relatively recent attempt to use Ancient Rome's monuments to underwrite modern political ambition.

Bulldozers flattened one of the city's oldest medieval quarters to make way for the route, destroying ancient walls, imperial palaces, temples and arches, some dating from the 3rd century BC. Architects ignored the archaeological massacre. When *Il Duce* ordered the removal of a pile of stones near the Colosseum, nobody pointed out that they marked the Meta Sudans, an ancient spring. Ludwig Curtius, then director of the German Archaeological Institute, said: "It would have been easy while building the street to excavate those parts of the Fora of

Julius Caesar and of Trajan still lying underground, and to direct the road over them as a bridge, but the dictator, concerned only for his next demonstration of power, was in a hurry … "

Originally, Mussolini had hoped to excavate the Imperial Fora, which would have served as decoration alongside his new processional road, symbolically connecting his regime with the glory of Roman antiquity. If these plans had been followed, an archaeological park

21st-century centurion and friend.

Statue of Julius Caesar in front of his Foro di Cesare.

would have extended from the excavated Forum area to the ruins of the Baths of Caracalla and on to Via Appia Antica. But the project was never realised and the road became a major thoroughfare. It is unlikely that the ruins beneath it will ever come to light.

THE IMPERIAL FORA

Address: Via dei Fori Imperiali
Transport: Colosseo

The remains of the Fori Imperiali lie on either side and buried beneath the Via dei Fori Imperiali (not open to the public, visible from the road only), which is beautifully lit at night. As Rome grew in power, its population increased and the original Roman Forum was no longer big enough to serve the city's needs. The Imperial Fora were built by a succession of emperors from Caesar to Trajan.

The **Imperial Fora Visitor Centre** Ⓐ (daily 9.30am–7pm) is located on the Via dei Fori Imperiali between Via Cavour and the Colosseum metro stop. Inside you can find background information on the site and toilets.

Via dei Fori Imperiali.

Foro di Cesare

On the south side of the Via are the remnants of **Foro di Cesare** (Caesar's Forum) Ⓑ, the first Imperial Forum, built in 51 BC by Julius Caesar when the original became too small for Rome's increasing population. It was dedicated, still unfinished, in 46 BC and completed under Augustus (23 BC–AD 14). Following Hellenistic models, it was square and enclosed by pillars. On its western side stood the Temple of Venus Genetrix (look for three reconstructed columns), built as Caesar believed himself to be a descendant of the goddess.

Foro di Augusto

The **Foro di Augusto** (Forum of Augustus) Ⓒ across the street was built to celebrate the emperor's victory and revenge over the army of Cassius and Brutus, who had led the conspiracy to assassinate Julius Caesar, his adoptive father. In the centre stood the temple of the war god Mars Ultor (Mars the Avenger), and in the great apses of the square stood statues of the mythical ancestors of Augustus' family.

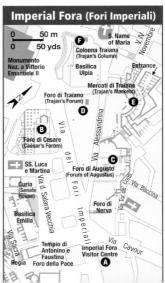

Imperial Fora (Fori Imperiali)

0 — 50 m
0 — 50 yds

Monumento Naz. a Vittorio Emanuele II

S. Name of Maria

Colonna Traiana (Trajan's Column) Ⓕ

Basilica Ulpia

Entrance

Mercati di Traiano (Trajan's Markets) Ⓔ

Foro di Traiano (Trajan's Forum) Ⓓ

Via Alessandrina

Foro di Cesare (Caesar's Forum) Ⓑ

Foro di Augusto (Forum of Augustus) Ⓒ

Via Baccina

SS. Luca e Martina

Foro di Nerva

Curia (Senate House)

Via d. Salara Vecchia

Basilica Emilia

Via Cavour

Via Sacra

Tempio di Antonino e Faustina

Imperial Fora Visitor Centre Ⓐ

Regia   Foro della Pace

Foro di Traiano and Trajan's Markets

The **Foro di Traiano** (Trajan's Forum) ❶ was a massive complex of temples, libraries and markets, surrounded by colonnades that outdid the other Fora in size and splendour. It was designed in AD 106 by Apollodorus of Damascus, the best architect of his time. Building it meant removing a small hill between the Quirinal and the Capitol. To the northwest, it was bound by the vast Basilica Ulpia, which had five naves. In its western apse, the Atrium Libertatis, slaves were liberated.

Emperor Trajan also commissioned his architect to build the **Mercati di Traiano** ❷ (Trajan's Markets; entrance 94 Via IV Novembre; tel: 06-0608; daily 9.30am–7.30pm; charge; www.mercatiditraiano. it), the ancient equivalent of a multi-storey shopping mall. Its remains stand behind the Forum on the slopes of the Quirinal, between two libraries. They reveal a complex system of streets on various levels, with shops, administrative offices and spaces reserved for the distribution of grain to the public.

While there is also a lower entrance, the upper one on Via IV Novembre offers the best view of this marvellously preserved testament to Roman daily life. You'll first enter the Great Hall, which was most likely the place for grain rations. From the adjoining terrace are good views down to the commercial spaces below, which would have held offices and shops. Nearby is Via Biberatica, which judging from its name (*bibere* means "to drink" in Latin) once housed bars for thirsty shoppers and businessmen. Today, the Mercati di Traiano site also hosts frequent modern art and photography exhibits.

The magnificent **Colonna Traiana** (Trajan's Column) ❸ was erected in AD 113 to celebrate Trajan's victory over the Dacians (inhabitants of today's Romania). The 40-metre (120ft) -high column is decorated with a spiral frieze of bas-reliefs depicting various phases of the Dacian campaigns (AD 101–2 and 105). Originally the reliefs were

TIP

The simplest way to reach the Forum is to take metro line B or one of the buses indicated to Colosseo or Piazza Venezia. The entrance to Trajan's Markets is only a 10-minute walk away from the Colosseum.

Trajan's Markets.

TIP

Before working your way around the Forum and trying to make sense of the ruins, it's a good idea to get an overview of the site. The best vantage point for this is the Tabularium (see page 87). You can also refer to the detailed map of the Roman Forum on page 98.

brightly painted and would have been visible from the balconies of the libraries. In AD 177, a golden urn containing the emperor's remains was buried under the column. The statue topping the column is of St Peter, commissioned by Pope Sixtus in 1587 to replace what was once a statue of Trajan.

THE FORO ROMANO ⑧

Address: Via dei Fori Imperiali; http://archeoroma.beniculturali.it
Telephone: 06-3996 7700
Opening Hours: daily 8.30am–one hour before sunset
Entrance Fee: charge, ticket also includes Palatine hill, Palatine Museum and Colosseum
Transport: Colosseo

The best place to begin a tour of the Foro Romano is at the main entrance on Via dei Fori Imperiali, roughly level with Via Cavour. Originally a marshy valley between the Capitoline and Palatine hills,

the area was drained by the Cloaca Maxima, the great sewer, and the site became a marketplace that developed into the religious, political and commercial centre of Republican Rome. By the time excavations began in the 18th century, most of the Forum was buried under rubble, and the place was known as Campo Vaccino (Cow Field), since it was used for grazing cattle.

Via Sacra

From the entrance a path leads down to the **Via Sacra** (the Sacred Way) Ⓐ, the oldest street in Rome, which once ran through the Forum from the Arch of Titus up to the Capitoline. Triumphal processions of victorious generals in horse-drawn chariots parading their prisoners and spoils of war, and followed by their soldiers, would pass along the street to the Temple of Jupiter on the Capitol, where they would make sacrifices to Jupiter, the supreme god.

Forum (Foro Romano)

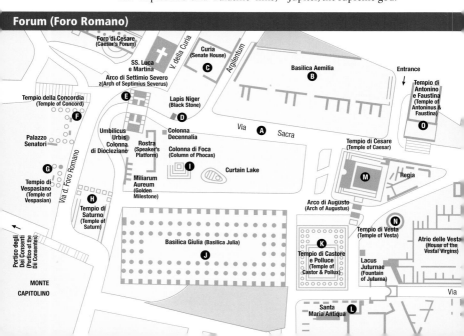

Walking westwards in the direction of the Capitoline, to the right stand the remains of the **Basilica Aemilia** , a massive assembly hall for politicians, businessmen and traders dating from the 2nd century BC. It was rebuilt by Augustus after a fire, and then again after another fire in 410, when Alaric and his Goths invaded the city during the conquest of Rome. You can still see the stains left by coins burnt into the floor. Until 1500, most of the hall was still standing, but Bramante, Rome's chief architect during the High Renaissance, used some of it to build Palazzo Torlonia in the Borgo quarter. On the steps, you can see the remains of a temple to Venus, nicknamed *Cloacina* because the small circular building marks the spot where the **Cloaca Maxima** (the city's main sewer built in the 1st century BC) emptied into the valley of the Forum.

Beyond the Basilica Aemilia is the **Curia** , the ancient Senate House that was the centre of political life in Republican Rome. In the Middle Ages, the Curia was consecrated as a church, but the current building, a replica of Diocletian's, dates from 1937. The bronze doors are copies of the originals, which were transferred in the 17th century to the Basilica of San Giovanni in Laterano (see page 225). In the cavernous inner hall (30 metres/90ft long, 20 metres/60ft wide, 20 metres/60ft high), the 300-strong Senate would gather to control the destiny of the Empire. In front of the Curia is the Comitium, where the Popular Assembly met.

Even older is the **Lapis Niger**  (Black Stone), a pavement of black marble laid to mark a sacred spot; according to legend, the tomb of Romulus, Rome's mythical founder. The remains of a monument from the 6th century BC have been excavated from under the Lapis Niger, and, while they do not prove the

Refreshment stands are a familiar sight.

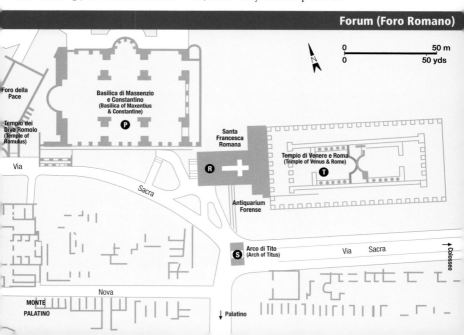

Forum (Foro Romano)

Foro della Pace

Tempio dei Divo Romolo (Temple of Romulus)

Basilica di Massenzio e Constantino (Basilica of Maxentius & Constantine) **P**

Via

Sacra

Nova

MONTE PALATINO

Santa Francesca Romana

R

Antiquarium Forense

Tempio di Venere e Roma (Temple of Venus & Rome) **T**

Arco di Tito (Arch of Titus) **S**

Via   Sacra

Colosseo

↓ Palatino

0   50 m
0   50 yds

existence of the grave, they are evidence that Romulus was already venerated in early Rome.

Arco di Settimio Severo

Behind looms the imposing **Arco di Settimio Severo** (Arch of Septimius Severus) **Ⓔ**. The triple arch is 25 metres (75ft) wide, 10 metres (30ft) deep and 20 metres (60ft) high. It was built in AD 203 to celebrate the 10th anniversary of the emperor's ascent to the throne. The reliefs on the arch depict the victorious campaigns Septimius Severus and his two sons, Geta and Caracalla, fought against the Arabs and the Parthians (in present-day Iran). In earlier years, the arch was topped by a statue of the emperor in a four-horse chariot.

Later, Caracalla had his brother murdered in the arms of their mother and then placed him under *damnatio memoriae* (exile from memory) by ordering the deletion from monuments of all references to Geta and replacing them with laudatory titles to himself. You can still see the chisel marks on the inscriptions, which were originally inlaid with metal.

Beside the arch is the **Umbilicus Urbis**, a navel-shaped piece of stone that marked the centre of the city.

Trajan's Column.

Carrera marble sculpture by modern artist Jiménez Deredia, on the Via Sacra.

Here, too, stood the **Miliarum Aureum**, a gilded bronze milestone that marked the start (or end) of all the Imperial roads connecting the main towns of the Empire to Rome. Beside it stood the **Rostra**, the speaker's platform moved here from the Comitium by Julius Caesar. It was

ROMAN DOMUS

On Clivio di Scauro, south of the Colosseum, and under the Basilica of Saints John and Paul on the Caelian Hill, 20 underground rooms dating from between the 2nd and 4th centuries AD were reopened to the public after extensive restoration work. A series of residences and private baths built in the 2nd century AD were transformed into a single, luxurious house *(domus)* a century later by a wealthy owner and decorated with frescoes. The Roman *Domus* is now open to tourists (tel: 06-7045 4544; www.caseromane.it; Thu–Mon 10am–1pm and 3–6pm; charge). Book in advance if you want a guided tour.

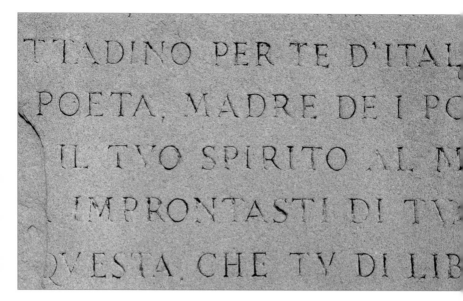

once decorated with the prows or beaks *(rostra)* of ships captured at the Battle of Actium in 31 BC. Trophies from Cleopatra's fleet are reputed to have been displayed here as well.

Behind, to the right, are the remains of the **Tempio della Concordia** ❻ (Temple of Concord), a reconstruction by the Emperor Tiberius (AD 14–37) of the sanctuary erected to mark the peace accord between the patricians and plebeians following the Class Wars of 367 BC.

Two temples

After their deaths, many emperors were automatically deified and had temples consecrated to them. All that remains of the **Tempio di Vespasiano** (Temple of Vespasian) ❼ (AD 69–79), erected by his sons Titus and Domitian (both of whom later became emperors)are the three Corinthian columns that rise up behind the Rostra.

In the northwestern corner of the Forum stands the **Tempio di**

Saturno ❽ (Temple of Saturn), which housed the Roman state treasury. All that remains of this, the most venerated temple of Republican Rome, consecrated in 498 BC, are eight Ionic columns on a podium. Saturn was god of agriculture and ruler of the mythical "Golden Age".

Stone inscription in the Roman Forum.

Arco di Settimio Severo.

Triumphant reliefs inside the Arch of Titus.

A detail from the Arco di Settimio Severo.

Painting the Foro di Traiano.

Each year in December the festival of Saturnalia was celebrated (see page 104).

Colonna di Foca and Colonna Decennalia

Heading eastwards now along the Via Sacra (with your back to the Capitol), to your left stands the Corinthian **Colonna di Foca** (Column of Phocas) ❶, the most recent of the classical monuments in the Roman Forum. This column was erected in 608 by Smaragdus, the Byzantine exarch (governor) for Italy, in honour of the Eastern Emperor Phocas who donated the Pantheon to the Church. Next to it, a bronze inscription commemorates one of the sponsors of the paving of the Forum, L. Naevius Surdinus, in the 1st decade BC. A fig tree, an olive tree and a vine, which used to grow here, together with a statue of Marsyas, symbolised Roman justice.

Between the Column of Phocas and the Rostra is the base of the **Colonna Decennalia**, raised in AD 303 to celebrate 10 years of rule by the two emperors Diocletian and

Maxentius. The relief on the base shows the *Souventaurilia*, the ceremonial state sacrifice of a boar, a ram and a bull.

Basilica Giulia

On the other side of the Via Sacra stood the **Basilica Giulia** . Started by Julius Caesar in 50 BC and completed by Augustus, it was originally the largest building in the Forum (101 metres/330ft long and 49 metres/160ft wide). All that remains of this two-storeyed, marble-faced structure are its pillared foundations. The basilica housed four courts of law, was the seat of the Roman office of weights and measures, and was a meeting place for bankers.

Tempio di Castore e Polluce

Heading in the direction of the Colosseum, you'll come to the three surviving columns of the **Tempio di Castore e Polluce** (Temple of Castor and Pollux) **K**, built in 448 BC to commemorate the decisive battle of Lake Regillus fought between Latins and Romans in 499 BC. The Romans believed victory was secured by the miraculous appearance of Castor and Pollux, Jupiter's twin sons, and built the temple in their honour. A block of marble from this temple was used by Michelangelo as the base for the equestrian statue of Marcus Aurelius he made for the Piazza del Campidoglio.

Behind the pillars is a small marble altar with reliefs of the heavenly twins, and the site of the **Lacus Juturnae** (Fountain of Juturna), the sacred well at which the Dioscuri (the collective name for Castor and Pollux) watered their horses after bringing news of the Roman victory.

On the other side of the temple, at the foot of the Palatine, is the oldest Christian structure in the Forum: the church of **Santa Maria Antiqua** **L** (closed to the public) was built in AD 365 on the site of a temple to Augustus.

Tempio di Cesare

A path leads away from the church entrance back past the temple of Castor and Pollux to the **Tempio di Cesare** (Temple of Caesar) **M**, which occupies the site where Caesar's corpse was cremated after his assassination on the Ides of March in 44 BC. So great was the grief of the

TIP

The Archaeologia Card (€27) is valid seven days and allows entrance to the Palazzo Massimo alle Terme, Palazzo Altemps, Crypta Balbi, Terme di Diocleziano, Colosseum, Foro Romano and Palatine Hill, Terme de Caracalla, Villa dei Quintili and the tomb of Cecilia Metella. It can be purchased at all of these sights, except the last two, or at the Rome Tourist Board at via Parigi 5.

Remains of the Temple of Saturn, and the three Corinthian columns of the Temple of Vespasian.

FACT

During the festival of Saturnalia, masters and their slaves briefly traded places; generous banquets were held and gifts exchanged. The festival originally lasted for one day only, but became so popular with the people that it later continued for a whole week. Scholars widely agree that Christmas was established around this time of year to coincide with the widespread pagan holiday.

A bust of the emperor Vespasian.

Basilica of Maxentius and Constantine.

people that they kept his funeral pyre burning for days. After the cremation, his ashes were washed with milk and wine and then buried. The temple was built on the site of the pyre by his adopted son, the emperor Augustus.

Behind the Temple of Caesar lie the remains of the walls of the **Regia**, the official residence of the Pontifex Maximus, the Chief Priest of Ancient Rome; the title is still held by the Pope today.

Tempio di Vesta

Directly opposite, 20 Corinthian columns surround the remains of the circular **Tempio di Vesta** (Temple of Vesta) , goddess of the hearth and patron of the state. Here the Vestal Virgins kept the eternal flame of Rome burning and watched over the sacred image of Minerva (daughter of Jupiter and Juno), saved, according to legend, from blazing Troy by Aeneas. The Vestals entered divine service as young girls and lived a chaste life for at least 30 years in the **House of the Vestal Virgins**, the rectangular structure next to the temple, a once luxurious building.

Tempio di Antonino e Faustina

Back near the main entrance of the Forum, a broad flight of steps leads up to the **Tempio di Antonino e**

VESPASIAN

Emperor Vespasian was one of ancient Rome's more successful rulers. His reign (AD 69–79) brought a welcome period of peace and prosperity to a city and an Empire in disarray following the death of Nero. Unlike his predecessors, he was never considered an excellent soldier, but was nevertheless respected by his people for his strong personality and strategic abilities.

Vespasian put to shame the extravagances of Roman nobles by the simplicity of his own life. In order to restore state finances after the disastrous extravagances of Nero (AD 54–68), he renewed old taxes and instituted new ones; one such tax was levied on urine, which was collected from public urinals. Urine was a useful raw material for producing ammonia and for dyeing wool, and Vespasian imposed this tax on all washermen. The Emperor was also known for his sense of humour: when asked by one of his sons how he could make money with such a malodorous substance, he replied *"Pecunia non olet"* – "money doesn't smell". These taxes helped finance the building of great public works, not least of which was the Colosseum. Nowadays, in the Italian language his name is synonymous with "urinal".

Faustina ⊙ (Temple of Antoninus and Faustina), built in AD 141 by the emperor in memory of his wife and converted to a church in the 12th century. It is the only Forum building that gives a real indication of just how monumental Roman temples were.

Basilica di Massenzio e Constantino

The eastern half of the Forum is dominated by the **Basilica di Massenzio e Constantino** (Basilica of Maxentius and Constantine) **❷**, a three-aisled basilica that was begun by Emperor Maxentius (306–12) and completed by his successor, Constantine (306–337). Only the northern nave remains. The central nave was crossed by cruciform vaults, each resting on eight side pillars, one of which has been outside the church of Santa Maria Maggiore since 1613.

Numerous Renaissance architects are said to have used its apse and arches as models, the most famous being Michelangelo, who studied its hexagonal coffered arches when designing the dome of St Peter's.

In the western apse, a **Colossus of Constantine** was discovered in 1487. Bits of the huge statue, including head, feet and hands, can be seen in the courtyard of Palazzo dei Conservatori.

Tempio di Romolo and Santa Francesca Romana

Next to the basilica is the circular **Tempio dei Divo Romolo** (Temple of Romulus) **❷**, dating from AD 309, which now forms the apse of the church of Santi Cosma e Damiano (daily 9am–1pm and 3–7pm), converted in the 6th century. Beneath the temple are the remains of tiny rooms believed to have been part of a brothel.

With its colourful brickwork, the Romanesque bell tower of the church of **Santa Francesca Romana** **❷**

(daily 10am–noon and 3–5pm) will have caught your eye. The present building is 13th century, though the facade was added in 1615. Francesca Romana is the patron saint of motorists, and on her festival day – 9 March – cars are parked as close as possible to the church to be blessed.

Arco di Tito

Beyond the church, marking the end of the Via Sacra, stands the majestic **Arco di Tito** (Arch of Titus) **⑤**, the oldest triumphal arch in Rome, built by Domitian to celebrate the capture of Jerusalem in AD 70 by his brother Titus and father Vespasian. Reliefs inside the arch show Titus in his chariot with Nike, goddess of victory, and the spoils of war, including a menorah, the ritual Jewish seven-branched candelabra, being carried in triumphal procession.

Tempio di Venere e Roma

Between the Arch of Titus and the Colosseum is the **Tempio di Venere e Roma** (Temple of Venus and Rome) **❼**, originally built by Hadrian (AD 117–38) and rebuilt by Maxentius in 307 after a fire. At 110

Dramatic remains of the Temple of Castor and Pollux.

View of the forum with detail of the Regia in the foreground.

FACT

During the Middle Ages, when the Forum was flooded and buried in rubble, the half of the Arch of Septimius Severus still above ground was used as a barber's shop.

by 53 metres (361 by 174ft), it was the largest temple in Rome and comprised two shrines placed opposite one another, surrounded by pillared halls in the Greek style. It is well documented that Hadrian was an ardent admirer of Greek culture.

PALATINE HILL ❾

Address: Palatine hill; http://archeo roma.beniculturali.it
Telephone: 06-3996 7700
Opening Hours: daily 8.30am–one hour before sunset
Entrance Fee: charge, ticket includes entry to Palatine Museum, Colosseum and Roman Forum
Transport: Colosseo

From the Arch of Titus the road goes up to the **Palatino**, where Rome's Imperial rulers lived in luxury. Legend holds that Romulus killed his twin brother Remus on the Palatine Hill before founding Rome here in 753 BC. Whatever the truth of this, archaeological remains do confirm the existence of a sheep-herding population whose simple homes were excavated on top of the hill. At the height of Roman opulence, the area offered a beautiful panorama of the city away from

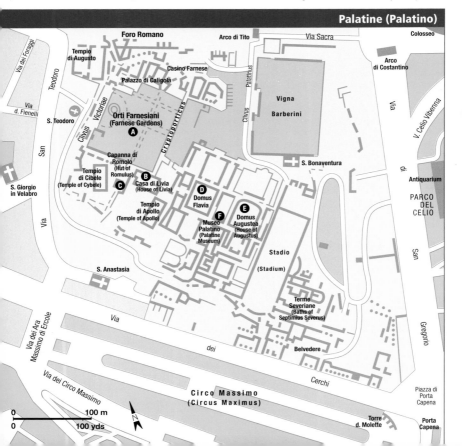

Palatine (Palatino)

the chaos below, and expansive villas packed the area. It wasn't until the 16th century that Cardinal Farnese recognised the value of the land and purchased most of it.

Orti Farnesiani

Paths and steps lead up to the **Orti Farnesiani** (Farnese Gardens) . These pleasure gardens were laid out in the 16th century for the cardinal, over the ruins of the Palace of Tiberius. They end at a viewing terrace with a fine panorama over the Forum. A subterranean vaulted passageway leads to the **Casa di Livia** ⒷB (guided tours only, in English Sat–Sun at 2pm, booking required; tel: 06 3996 7700; www. coopculture.it).

In the southwest corner of the hill, excavations have revealed the oldest traces of a settlement in the city (8th century BC). The story goes that the Iron Age hut known as the **Capanna di Romolo** (Hut of Romulus) Ⓒ was the dwelling of a shepherd who raised Romulus and Remus, after they were suckled by the wolf in a nearby cave.

Domus Flavia and Domus Augustana

South of the gardens lay the **Domus Flavia** (House of Flavia) Ⓓ, built by Emperor Domitian, who is said to have lined his throne room with

TIP

Underneath the Farnese Gardens is a long tunnel built by Nero, possibly a secret route to other parts of the Palatine. The tunnel is also a welcome escape from the blazing heat of the Roman summer. Relax in the shade as long as you can without blocking tourist traffic.

Temple of Antoninus and Faustina.

The Palatine hill.

EAT

You can take a picnic into the Forum/Palatine area. Officially, it's not allowed, but if you are discreet and tidy, and take your rubbish with you when you leave, there will be no problem.

mirrors in order to see approaching enemies from any angle. The room with a pattern traced on its floor was the courtyard; behind that was the dining room, and the room to the right was the nymphaeum, where diners retired for breaks during banquets.

Next to this palace was the **Domus Augustea** (House of Augustus; guided tours only, in English Sat–Sun at 2pm, booking required; tel: 06-3996 7700; www.coopculture.it) **E**, private residence of the emperor. The oval building next to it, the vast outline of which can be clearly discerned, was a stadium built for the emperor's private games. To the south are the impressive ruins of the **Arcate Severiane** (Arches of Septimius Severus).

Museo Palatino

The tall grey building sandwiched between the Domus Flavia and the Domus Augustana is the **Museo Palatino** **F** (Palatine Museum; tel: 06-3996 7700; www.coopculture.

it; daily 8.30am–one hour before sunset; charge, ticket includes entry to Palatine hill, the Colosseum and Roman Forum). Inside is a fine collection of artefacts found during the course of excavations on the site.

CIRCO MASSIMO ⑩

The remains of the Palatine palaces overlook the **Circo Massimo** (Circus Maximus), one of the oldest Roman arenas. Not much of this 6th-century BC stadium remains, but you can make out the track, which was used mainly for chariot races. There are traces of seating to the south (the tower is a medieval addition). In its heyday the arena held around 300,000 spectators, and not only hosted chariot races, but also staged sea battles, which required the pumping of gallons of water into the stadium space.

THE COLOSSEUM ⑪

Address: Piazza del Colosseo; www.coopculture.it
Telephone: 06-3996 7700

The defining image of Rome.

Opening Hours: daily 8.30am—one hour before sunset; night tours Mon and Thu—Sat 8.10pm
Entrance Fee: charge, ticket includes entry to Palatine hill, Palatine Museum and Forum
Transport: Colosseo

At the far end of the Roman Forum lie the remains of the majestic **Colosseum**, the most enduring symbol of Ancient Rome. Its monumental grandeur and violent history have enthralled and appalled visitors for over 2,000 years. Work on its construction began in AD 72 under Vespasian, who decided to build it on the site of Nero's artificial lake, and was completed by his son Titus. The vast amphitheatre measured 190 metres (570ft) long and 150 metres (450ft) wide, it had 80 entrances and could seat between 55,000 and 73,000 spectators. It opened in AD 80 with a three-month programme of games to satisfy a bloodthirsty audience. Christians fought lions, gladiators fought each other and wounded contestants lived or died according to the emperor's whim, expressed by the Imperial thumb, which pointed either up or down. Today, the walls of the various dungeons, cages and passageways, gruesome reminders of the centuries-long slaughter that took place here, can be seen through the caved-in floor of the arena.

The **Ludus Magnus**, the nearby training ground of the gladiators, was connected to the arena by a tunnel. The remains of seating for up to 3,000 people shows how much the public liked to watch gladiators learning the tricks of their trade.

Gladiatorial combat was banned by Honorius in AD 404, and over time the amphitheatre became a quarry supplying material for many of Rome's buildings, including Palazzo Venezia and St Peter's. In 1744, Benedict XIV consecrated the arena to the memory of Christian martyrs who died in it.

Between the Colosseum and the Palatine Hill is the **Arco di Constantino** (Arch of Constantine),

EAT

The organic food market on 74 Via di San Teodoro, near the Circo Massimo, is a great place to shop for local gourmet products. You can also buy a plate of hot pasta that you can eat in the beautiful cloister (Sat—Sun 9am—6pm).

A wonder of the world – inside the Colosseum.

An umbrella pine provides atmosphere but scant shade for the ruins of the Palatine hill.

The entrance to Domus Aurea.

built to commemorate Constantine I's victory over Maxentius at the Ponte Milvio in AD 312.

DOMUS AUREA ⑫

Address: 1 Viale della Domus Aurea; www.coopculture.it
Opening Hours: closed for restoration, guided tours only, Sat–Sun 9am–5pm, booking required; tel: 06 3996 7700
Transport: Colosseo

A short walk uphill from the Colosseum is **Domus Aurea** (Nero's Golden House). Work began here in AD 64 immediately after a fire had devastated a large chunk of Rome.

Made up of a series of pavilions surrounded by pastures, woods, vineyards and a small artificial lake (on which the Colosseum now stands), it originally extended from the Palatine to the Caelian and Oppian hills. The enormous complex was filled with Greek statues and monumental fountains.

According to the Latin biographer Suetonius, its vestibule was large enough to contain a statue of Nero 40 metres (120ft) high, and the house was covered in gold and decorated with precious gems and mother-of-pearl. There were dining rooms with ivory ceilings from which rotating panels showered guests with flowers, and fitted pipes sprinkled them with perfume. The palace had its own aqueducts to supply water for the fountains, and the baths could be filled with sea or sulphurous water, according to Nero's whim.

The main building was decorated with shiploads of plundered Greek works of art. But Nero did not have long to enjoy it. He committed suicide in AD 68 after he was condemned to death by the Senate.

Almost immediately the house began to be stripped, demolished or built on by his successors. In the early 16th century, frescoes belonging to the house were discovered by artists, including Raphael and Michelangelo, but no one linked these cave-like rooms to the emperor's outrageous abode until centuries later.

It is hard to get an idea of the opulence and size of the extraordinary 250-room mansion, built on an estate that covered a third of Ancient Rome; only the skylit Octagonal Hall gives any real idea of its former architectural grandeur. Some 30 rooms are usually open to the public, but structural problems forced the city to close the site for restoration in 2010. The reopening date hasn't yet been scheduled, but the city occasionally opens very limited portions of the monument for small group visits.

The Arco di Constantino, another triumphal arch built for the glory of the emperors.

Try to visit the Colosseum first thing in the morning, before the crowds build up.

RESTAURANTS, BARS AND CAFÉS

PRICE CATEGORIES

Price includes dinner and a half-bottle of house wine.
€€€€ = more than €60
€€€ = €40–60
€€ = €25–40
€ = under €25

The overpriced tourist restaurants around the Colosseum should be avoided, but if you wander eastwards into the huddle of streets behind it you'll find some good neighbourhood eateries.

Restaurants

Forum Pizzeria
34–38 Via San Giovanni in Laterano
06-7759 1158
L & D daily.
€ [p322, B2]
A large pizzeria serving delicious, thick-crusted pizzas from a wood-fired oven.

Ristorante Mario's
9 Piazza del Grillo
06-679 3725
L & D Tue–Sun.
€–€€ [p324, D3-E3]
Traditional Roman food (fish is their speciality) at affordable prices. Has a lovely pergola in the square outside.

Trattoria San Teodoro
49–51 Via dei Fienili
06-678 0933
www.st-teodoro.it
L & D daily (Sun closed in winter).
€€€€ [p324, D4]
Located in a tranquil piazza, this elegant restaurant offers traditional food centred on seasonal availability. Staples are fish carpaccios and home-made pasta.

Bars and Cafés

Coming Out
8 Via San Giovanni in Laterano
06-700 9871
www.comingout.it

[p322, B2]
This gay bar just across from the Colosseum, in an area known as "gay street", serves drinks until 2am. A lively scene ensures a faithful following, not just from the gay community.

Cristalli di Zucchero
Via di San Teodoro
06-6992 0945
www.cristallidizucchero.it
[p320, E2]
One of the finest bakeries in Rome. Indulge in a tray of mini pastries.

Oppio Caffè
72 Via delle Terme di Tito
06-474 5262
www.oppiocaffe.it
[p324, E4]
Hi-tech meets classical Rome: plexiglass and video screens contrast with ancient brickwork. Outside seating provides stunning views of the Colosseum. Open all day, with live music some nights. Aperitivo for €10–12 from 5.30–10pm.

The much-photographed Trevi Fountain.

FONTANA DI TREVI AND QUIRINALE

The Quirinal, Rome's highest hill, is synonymous with Italian politics. Its summit is crowned with the President's official residence and at its foot, hidden in the maze of narrow streets, is the Trevi Fountain, one of Rome's most iconic sights.

The Quirinal hill, the highest of Rome's seven classical hills, is crowned by the Piazza del Quirinale and the imposing presidential palace. Originally built as a papal residence, this palazzo has housed thirty popes, four kings and all the Italian presidents. The former papal stables, the Scuderie del Quirinale, are now an important museum and exhibition space. The Quirinal square is somewhat austere but the labyrinth of surrounding streets is well worth exploring.

Fontana di Trevi

A good place to begin a tour of the area is the **Fontana di Trevi** (Trevi Fountain; www.restaurofontanaditrevi. it) ❶, which rose to fame in Fellini's 1960 classic *La Dolce Vita* when blonde bombshell Anita Ekberg plunged provocatively into it for a midnight bathe. Nowadays, if you try to put a foot in the water, a whistle blast from the city police will stop you in your tracks. That, and a €170 fine.

However, no one will stop you from throwing a coin in the fountain (over your shoulder with your back to the fountain), an old custom said to ensure your return to the Eternal City. A restoration financed by the Fendi fashion house was completed in 2015 and the steps around the fountain are once again packed with tourists tossing coins, eating ice creams and taking endless photos.

The flamboyant rococo-style fountain was designed in 1762 by Nicola Salvi, "some sculptor of Bernini's school gone absolutely mad in marble" was Nathaniel Hawthorne's assessment. Its central figure is the sea god Neptune standing astride a giant shell drawn by winged horses

Guard outside the Quirinale Palace, official residence of the President of the Republic.

EAT

With arguably the finest ice cream in town, the Gelateria San Crispino near the Trevi Fountain serves up original flavours made with all-natural ingredients. The signature flavour, Il Gelato di San Crispino, is a basic Italian crema made with wild Sardinian honey.

led by Tritons. One horse is placid, the other agitated, symbolising calm and stormy seas. In the niches on either side are statues of Health (right) and Abundance (left). Above the latter, a marble relief shows Agrippa commissioning the aqueduct in 19 BC, which still supplies the fountain to this day.

Accademia di San Luca ②

Address: 77 Piazza dell'Accademia; www.accademiasanluca.eu
Telephone: 06-679 8850
Opening Hours: Mon–Sat 10am–7pm
Entrance Fee: free
Transport: Barberini

It's a five-minute walk from the fountain to the Galleria dell'Accademia di San Luca, Rome's school of art. The academy, named after St Luke, the patron saint of painters, was founded in 1577 to train artists in the Renaissance style. Bernini and Domenichino were former directors of this august institution.

Obelisk in the Piazza del Quirinale.

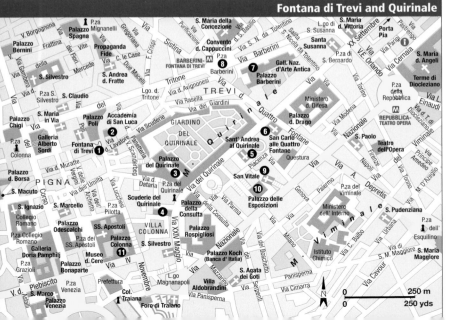

Fontana di Trevi and Quirinale

The gallery has a collection of portraits, drawings and landscapes of Rome spanning the centuries, including works by Titian, Guido Reni and Van Dyck.

There's also an impressive ramp, designed by Borromini, which spirals up to the top floors of the *palazzo*. Free exhibitions are held by art students, and the academy organises a prestigious architecture prize.

THE QUIRINAL

Follow Via San Vincenzo uphill from the Fontana di Trevi, then turn left into Via Dataria and take the steps up to Piazza del Quirinale. In the centre of the square are colossal statues of the heavenly twins, Castor and Pollux, with their horses. They came from Constantine's baths and were arranged around the obelisk (taken from Augustus' mausoleum) in the 18th century.

Palazzo del Quirinale ❸

Address: www.quirinale.it
Telephone: 06-46991
Opening Hours: Tue–Wed and Fri–Sun 9.30am–4pm

Entrance Fee: charge
Transport: Barberini

The square is dominated by the **Palazzo del Quirinale**, which was the summer palace of the popes until 1870, when it became the palace of the kings of the newly unified Italy. Since 1947, it has been the official residence of the President of the Republic. The oldest part of the palace, including Napoleon's Apartments and the Hall of the Tapestries, is open to the public.

Scuderie del Quirinale ❹

Address: 16 Via 24 Maggio; www.scuderiequirinale.it
Telephone: 06-3996 7500
Opening Hours: Sun–Thu 10am–8pm, Fri–Sat until 10.30pm
Entrance Fee: charge
Transport: Barberini

Part of the complex on the opposite side of Piazza del Quirinale, the former palace stables, or *scuderie*, is now a bright and spacious two-level museum space, which hosts important exhibitions all year-round. The stairs leading from the top floor back to the lobby have a glass wall that offers fine views of the city.

The best way to get around in Rome.

Palazzo del Quirinale.

FACT

Mental torment and genius often go hand in hand, as was the case for Borromini. The church of San Carlino was his first solo job, completed when the artist was just 35 years old. Borromini had hoped to be buried in the crypt's splendid funerary chapter, but his suicide put paid to that, and he was dumped in an unmarked grave at San Giovanni dei Fiorentini.

Across the square from the Quirinale Palace sits the sugary-white **Palazzo della Consulta**, which houses Italy's Supreme Court. The structure was built atop the ruins of Constantine's baths.

BAROQUE MASTERPIECES

Via del Quirinale runs along the southeast flank of the palace and, on the opposite side, passes two pretty parks (dotted with shaded benches if you need a rest), and two Baroque churches. **Sant'Andrea al Quirinale** ❺ (http://chiese.gesuiti.it; Tue–Sat 8am–noon, 2.30–6pm, Sun 9am–noon, 3–6pm) is the work of Bernini, whose genius is demonstrated in the elliptical plan, gilded dome and stucco work. Light from the clerestory windows illuminates the white-and-gold stucco work of the dome and the richly coloured inlaid marble of the walls and floor.

Further along is the tiny **San Carlo alle Quattro Fontane** ❻ (www.sancarlino.eu; Mon–Fri 10am–1pm, 3–6pm, Sat–Sun 10am–1pm) by Bernini's arch-rival, Borromini. It may be small (it is often referred to as San Carlino), but with its concave

The exquisite staircase inside Palazzo Barberini.

and convex surfaces it illustrates Borromini's ingenuity at creating the illusion of space in an awkwardly shaped site. His love for illusion and trompe l'œil is evident throughout the structure, most notably in the cloister, which is rectangular but appears octagonal.

The church gets its name, Alle Quattro Fontane, from the four Baroque fountains at each corner of the busy crossroads, placed here in 1593, which represent the Tiber, the Nile, Diana and Juno. From here, the highest point of the Quirinal Hill, you can look down towards the Trinità dei Monti obelisk in one direction and the Santa Maria Maggiore obelisk in the other.

Palazzo Barberini ❼

Address: 18 Via Barberini, entrance on 13 Via delle Quattro Fontane; http://galleriabarberini.beniculturali.it
Telephone: 06 4824184
Opening Hours: Tue–Sun 8.30am–7pm
Entrance Fee: charge
Transport: Barberini

From the Quirinal, Via delle Quattro Fontane leads to **Palazzo Barberini,**

MATTER OF WATER

Ancient Rome's water system still leaves us astonished today; with 11 aqueducts coming from up to 60 miles (97km) away, the city's uniquely clean and hydrated population had far more water per person than modern aqueducts can deliver. In order to introduce the newly built aqueducts to an impatient population, emperors and consuls liked to celebrate the water by building imposing fountains right at the end point of the aqueducts. These fountains were called *fontane mostra* (showing fountains) and one of the first ones, the Mostra dell'Acqua Giulia, can be viewed in the gardens of Piazza Vittorio Emanuele.

After the end of the Roman Empire in the 5th century AD, many of the existing aqueducts were destroyed by the barbarians, and the population was forced to rely on the Tiber for centuries. In the 1500s, the popes began restoring the water system and from then on took turns in improving, decorating and embellishing the existing *mostras*, providing us with masterpieces of beauty like the Fontanone on the Janiculum Hill and the Fountain of the Naiads in Piazza della Repubblica. The most famous *mostra*, however, remains the Trevi Fountain, built to celebrate the spring of the Acqua Vergine and renovated in the 1700s (see page 113).

the family palace of Pope Urban VIII (1623–44), built by three of Rome's most prominent 17th-century architects, Bernini, Borromini and Maderno. It houses the **Galleria Nazionale d'Arte Antica**, which displays works from the early Renaissance to the late Baroque, including *The Annunciation* by Lippi, canvases by Caravaggio, Raphael's celebrated *La Fornarina*, Pietro di Cosimo's *Maddalena*, a portrait of Henry VIII by Holbein and a fine ceiling fresco by da Cortona.

Bernini's fountains

In the **Piazza Barberini** ❽ are two Bernini fountains. The **Fontana del Tritone** (1632–7) features four dolphins supporting a shell on which the water-spouting Triton sits. The **Fontana delle Api** (Bee Fountain, 1641), on the north side of the square, features the ubiquitous bee, symbol of the powerful Barberini family. Running from the northwest of the piazza is Via Vittorio Veneto, the avenue rendered immortal in Fellini's film *La Dolce Vita* as the gathering place for the glitterati to see and be seen.

From here Via Barberini leads to Largo Santa Susanna and the church of **Santa Maria della Vittoria** (www. chiesasantamariavittoriaroma.it; daily 8.30am–noon, 3.30–6pm) home to Bernini's *Ecstasy of St Teresa*, another masterpiece of Baroque sculpture.

TIP

Not far from the Trevi Fountain, beneath the arthouse Trevi Cinema (www.fondazionecsc.it; sometimes screens films in English), is the fascinating Area Archeologica del Vicus Caprinus (www.archeo domani.com; Tue–Sun 11am–5.30pm, Sat–Sun 11am–7pm; charge). Here lie the remains of a 1st-century BC *caseggiato* – a communal Roman dwelling.

The Trevi Fountain looks best at night.

SHOPPING

The shop selection in this very central area can be a bit touristy, especially around the ever-crowded Trevi Fountain, while Via Nazionale offers many reliable chains as well as a few boutiques.

Accessories

Segue
160 Via Nazionale
06-678 3031
www.segue.it
The bag mecca by Benetton. This is the place for those hard and happy-coloured cases and matching carry-alls and carry-on bags.

Books

Feltrinelli International
84/86 Via V.E. Orlando
www.lafeltrinelli.it
The international branch of one of Italy's most important bookstore chains. The store is divided into various sections, each dedicated to a different language, with the English section the largest.

Clothing

Anteprima di Moda
38-39-40 Via delle Quattro Fontane
06-482 8445
www.anteprimadimoda.com
Elegant women's clothes and acces-
sories, with an eccentric touch. New romantic, contemporary, ethnic, gipsy chic and floral are just some of the styles featured.
Massimo Dutti
Galleria Alberto Sordi
www.massimodutti.com
Casual to elegant fashion chain for men and women with classic designs.

Department stores

La Rinascente
Galleria Alberto Sordi
www.rinascente.it
The most elegant of stores, with a vast range of goods, especially fashion for women and children. Also a large cosmetics section.

FACT

The Princess Isabella Apartment, the 15th-century wing of Palazzo Colonna, has been preserved in all its original majesty. Decorated with ornate frescoes by Bernardino di Betto (known as Pinturicchio), there are many notable works of art here, including some magnificent small paintings on copper by Jan Brueghel the Elder.

Fontana delle Api on Piazza Barberini.

Barberini Palace.

The end of Via XX Settembre is marked by **Porta Pia**, Michelangelo's last architectural work and an excellent example of the transition from High Renaissance to Baroque architecture. It is also the symbol of Italy's unification as on 20 September 1870 the Italian army made a breach in the gate and defeated the Pope's soldiers, putting an end to the Church's secular power.

VIA NAZIONALE

Running parallel to Via del Quirinale is Via Nazionale (laid in 1870 when Rome gained its new status as capital), which links Piazza della Repubblica with the Imperial Fora. Towards the southern end are **San Vitale** ❾, a church built in the 5th century and restored in the 15th century, and the **Palazzo delle Esposizioni** ❿ (194 Via Nazionale; www.palazzoesposizioni.it; tel: 06-3996 7500; Sun, Tue–Thu 10am–8pm, Fri–Sat until 10.30pm; charge).

It is hard to miss this massive 19th-century edifice. The neoclassical structure was designed in 1883 by Pio Piacentini to house the

Quadriennale d'Arte, a national art exhibition, and the first reactions were not very forthcoming: the Romans criticized the monumental entrance and the lack of windows on the facade (the rooms receive light

from the glass ceilings). Originally containing fine art, the Palazzo now houses a vibrant cultural centre with an important programme of exhibitions and events, covering art, music, photography, film and theatre. There's also a café, restaurant and gift shop. Its large bookstore focuses on art, design and architecture books, and is open until late.

Across the road are the impressive **Palazzo Koch**, headquarters of the Banca d'Italia, and the **Villa Aldobrandini**, behind which is a small public park (currently closed for restoration).

Palazzo Colonna ⑪

Address: 66 Piazza SS Apostoli, entrance on Via della Pilotta; www.galleriacolonna.it
Telephone: 06- 679 4638
Opening Hours: Sat 9am–1.15pm (last entry), guided tour in English at noon
Entrance Fee: charge
Transport: 40, 60, 64, 70, 117, 170, H

Via Nazionale curves around into Via IV Novembre (leading to Piazza Venezia), then passes Trajan's Markets and the Palazzo Colonna. The *palazzo* housed over 23 generations of the Colonna family, and represents a fascinating, if often juxtaposing, architectural panorama spanning four centuries (1300–1700). Inside is a charming art gallery, with richly vaulted, frescoed ceilings, one of which portrays Marcantonio Colonna's victory at the battle of Lepanto (1571). Artists represented here include Lorenzo Monoco, Veronese, Jacopo and Domenico Tintoretto, Pietro da Cortona and Guercino. Be sure to look out for Bronzino's gloriously sensuous *Venus and Cupid*, and Annibale Carracci's *Bean-Eater*, the gallery's most prized work. A new wing recently opened to the public includes the Chapel Hall and the Artemisia Tapestries Collection.

From the palace, Via della Pilotta leads back to the Trevi Fountain.

TIP.

The Palazzo del Quirinale, which was once the residence of the pope, is now the Italian president's home. Its marvellous gardens can only be visited once a year, on Republic Day (2 June), after the end of the military parade on Via dei Fori Imperiali. The queue is always long, so get there early.

RESTAURANTS, BARS AND CAFÉS

PRICE CATEGORIES

Price includes dinner and a half-bottle of house wine.
€€€€ = more than €60
€€€ = €40–60
€€ = €25–40
€ = under €25

Restaurants

Ristorante Abruzzi
1 Via del Vaccaro
06- 679 3897
L & D daily, closed Sat, Aug.
€€€ [p324, D1]
A family-run trattoria, specializing in dishes from the Abruzzo region. It offers high-quality food, including *bucatini amatriciana*, gnocchi (Thu), delicious roast lamb or suckling pig, and a good selection of antipasti.
Le Tamerici
79 Vicolo Scavolino

06-6920 0700
www.letamerici.com
D Mon–Sat.
€€€ [p324, D1]
Innovative, seasonal cuisine from an all-female team, with a minimalist decor providing dramatic contrast to the Baroque extravagance outside.
Vineria Il Chianti
81–82 Via del Lavatore
06-678 7550
www.vineriailchianti.com
L & D Mon–Sat.
€€ [p324, D1]
A buzzing, rustic locale with young staff and a Tuscan slant. Dishes are likely to include hearty soups, quiche and wild boar fillet.

Bars and Cafés

Dagnino
75 Via V. E. Orlando
06-481 8660

www.pasticceriadagnino.com
[p318, B3]
This olde-worlde Sicilian pasticceria is located in an anonymous gallery off the street. Try the delicious pastries.
Il Gelato di San Crispino
42 Via della Panetteria
www.ilgelatodisancrispino.it
Closed Tue
[p324, D1]
Ice cream like no other in a wide variety of flavours, served in paper cups as cones affect the taste according to its creators.
The News Café
72 Via della Stamperia
06-6992 3473
www.newscafe.it
[p324, D1]
Named after the racks of newspapers available for customers to read. A good all-day option for salads, soups and pastas.

The Spanish Steps, Rome's most popular meeting place.

PIAZZA DI SPAGNA AND TRIDENTE

The Spanish Steps provide a great spot for watching the world go by: buskers play guitars, romantics pay homage to Keats and Shelley, backpackers sunbathe on the steps and fashion-lovers crowd elegant shops in the streets below.

The Tridente is a mecca for anyone interested in fashion, shopping or art; some tourists never stray from here. The area takes its name from the trio of streets built in the 16th century to relieve congestion in Rome's cramped medieval centre. Via del Corso, Via di Ripetta and Via del Babuino emanate like the prongs of a fork from the Piazza del Popolo, for centuries the main entrance to Rome for travellers coming from the north.

PIAZZA DEL POPOLO

Piazza del Popolo ❶ is one of the most impressive squares in Rome. The paving was allegedly paid for by taxes levied on prostitutes, and the piazza was used for executions one time. In the 19th century, the square was remodelled by Valadier, who created the oval form.

The most striking feature of this elegant square is the **obelisk**. Stolen from Egypt by Emperor Augustus, it once decorated the Circus Maximus, where it was used as a turning point during chariot races.

Standing at the ends of Via del Babuino and Via del Corso are two churches designed by Carlo Rainaldi in the 1660s. Though they appear identical, one is octagonal and the other is dodecagonal. Stand between them for a good view down the Via del Corso to Piazza Venezia and the facade of the Vittoriano monument.

Santa Maria del Popolo ❷

Address: 12 Piazza del Popolo
Telephone: 06-361 0836
Opening Hours: Sun–Thu 7.30am–12.30pm and 4–7pm, Fri–Sat 7.30am–7pm
Entrance Fee: free
Transport: Flaminio

Main Attractions
Piazza del Popolo
Santa Maria del Popolo
The Corso
Casa di Goethe
San Lorenzo in Lucina
Spanish Steps
Keats-Shelley House
Via dei Condotti
Ara Pacis
Mausoleo di Augusto

Maps and Listings
Map, page 122
Shopping, page 130
Restaurants, page 132

Alfresco dinner in the Piazza del Popolo.

TIP

Two spas in the vicinity will boost your flagging spirits after too much sightseeing or shopping. Try the couple massage and rejuvenation treatments at the **Dermastir Spa** (6 Piazza di Spagna; tel: 06-6938 0852; www.dermastir.com), or join the international jet set indulging themselves at the spa of the stylish **Hotel de Russie** (9 Via del Babuino; tel: 06-328 881; www.lhw.com).

Caravaggio's Conversion of St Paul.

Across the piazza, by Porta Flaminia, is the church of Santa Maria del Popolo, built in 1472 over a pre-existing 11th-century chapel. According to legend, Emperor Nero was buried on the site by his spiteful lover, and 1,000 years later Pope Paschal II had the chapel constructed to rid the site of evil spirits.

The church was rebuilt in the late 15th century, and is packed with Renaissance masterpieces. The biggest attractions are the two paintings by Caravaggio, *The Conversion of St Paul* and *The Crucifixion of St Peter*, but also worth seeking out are the beautifully detailed frescoes by Pinturicchio, and Guillaume de Marcillat's exquisite stained glass inside the Bramante-designed apse.

The small Chigi Chapel was designed by Raphael for influential banker Agostino Chigi, who commissioned numerous works of art and architecture, including

the Villa Farnesina. Mosaics in the dome depict God creating the solar system and Chigi's astrological chart. The chapel was completed by Bernini, who added two of his characteristic statues, one of Daniel and one of Habakkuk.

THE CORSO

The most important of the trio of streets that fan out from the Piazza del Popolo is **Via del Corso**, a long thoroughfare that links the square with the Piazza Venezia, another of Rome's central squares and one of its most terrifying traffic roundabouts. The name "Corso" dates from the 15th century, when Pope Paul II introduced horse racing (*corse*) along its length. Pope Alexander VII straightened the road in the 16th century. The races were imitations of the ancient games (with all their atrocities), and it wasn't only horses that ran: there were races for prostitutes, for children, for Jews

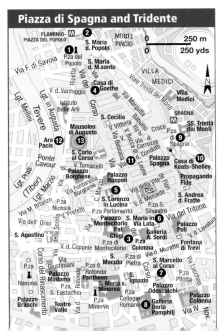

Piazza di Spagna and Tridente

and for the crippled. The German poet Goethe, who lived at No. 18 (see page 124), described the races in his *Italian Journey*. They were finally banned at the end of the 19th century.

Piazza Colonna ❸

These days, the only people racing along the Corso are politicians being whisked at high speed to **Palazzo Chigi** (guided tours only, email: visite@palazzochigi.it) the prime minister's official residence, and the neighbouring **Palazzo di Montecitorio**, the Chamber of Deputies (www.camera.it), both on **Piazza Colonna**. This square marks the halfway point of the Via del Corso.

The southern half of the Corso between Piazza Colonna and Piazza Venezia is lined with stately palaces, most of which are banks, while the northern half, between Piazza Colonna and Piazza del Popolo, is a much more pedestrian-friendly shopping area. In the early evening and on Saturdays, Romans swarm into town to stroll up and down and window-shop on this stretch of the Corso and the surrounding streets.

Dominating the Piazza Colonna is the street's only classical relic, the 30-metre (90ft) **Colonna di Marco Aurelio** (Column of Marcus Aurelius). It dates from AD 180, and the bas-relief around the shaft depicts the campaigns of Marcus Aurelius against the Germanic tribes and the Sarmatians. Stairs lead to the top, where the original statue of the emperor was replaced with one of the Apostle Paul in 1589.

Casa di Goethe ❹

Address: 18 Via del Corso; www.casadigoethe.it
Telephone: 06-3265 0412
Opening Hours: Tue–Sun 10am–6pm

One of the four lion fountains by Valadier (1823) that grace the Piazza del Popolo. In the background are Rainaldi's twin Baroque churches.

Piazza del Popolo.

FACT

Casa Rome has been called the city of obelisks – it has at least 13. Most were brought back by triumphant armies and erected in public places to show the power of the Empire, but some – such as the one at the top of the Spanish Steps – are Roman imitations of Egyptian originals.

Via del Corso.

Entrance Fee: charge
Transport: Flaminio

Not far from the Piazza del Popolo is the apartment where German poet Goethe lived for two years in the late 18th century. He shared the house with painter Hans Tischbein, whose depictions of the poet are on display.

You can peruse the writer's journals and a room dedicated to all his works, either written in, or inspired by, the Eternal City. Among them are *Iphigenia*, *The Roman Elegies*, *Faust*, *The Roman Carnival* and *Italian Journey*.

San Lorenzo, Santa Maria in Via Lata and San Marcello

Further down the Via del Corso, in a small square to the west, is the 12th-century church of **San Lorenzo in Lucina ❺** (16A Via in Lucina; tel: 06-687 1494; daily 8am–8pm; www.sanlorenzoinlucina.it).

It contains some busts by Bernini, and a grill, rumoured to be the very spot where the martyr St Lawrence was burnt to death for his refusal to hand over Church riches to the Roman city government. When questioned as to the whereabouts of the wealth, he is said to have presented the poor, crippled and homeless, declaring that they were the true treasures of the Church.

On the other side of the Corso from Piazza Colonna is **Santa Maria in Via Lata ❻**, which has an impressive facade by da Cortona. In a side street next to the church is one of Rome's "talking" fountains, the *facchino* (or water-bearer). In the days before freedom of speech, the *facchino* and other "talking statues" were hung with satirical and subversive messages and fulfilled much the same function as a newspaper (see page 163).

Another noteworthy church is **San Marcello al Corso ❼** (daily 7.30am–11pm, festive days from 9.30am; www.sanmarcelloalcorso.eu), further along the Corso towards Piazza Venezia, which has a Van Dyck crucifix in the sacristy (you need to ask to see it).

The palace on the right at the end of the Corso houses the **Galleria Doria Pamphilj ❽** (see page 155). There are several splendid buildings in the city called Doria Pamphilj (also spelt Pamphili), after one of the oldest aristocratic Roman families. One of their members, Giovanni Battista Pamphilj, became Pope Innocent X (1644–55). The current generation of the family still live in this *palazzo* and their private apartments are sometimes open for guided tours.

THE SPANISH STEPS

The sweeping Spanish Steps combine with the twin towers of the church of Trinità dei Monti on top and the harmonious square with its

bizarrely shaped fountain below to form one of the most distinctive of Roman scenes. **Piazza di Spagna** ❾ is so called because there has been

a Spanish Embassy to the Holy See here since the 17th century. The French, meanwhile, owned the land around the convent of **Trinità dei Monti** (church open Thu–Sun 6.30am–8pm, guided tours of the convent in Italian Sat 11am or French Tue 11am and Sun 9.15am) at the top of the steps, and so they claimed the right to pass through the square and named part of it French Square.

This petty rivalry between the French and Spanish reached a climax with the building of the Spanish Steps. The original design was intended to sing the praises of the French monarchy, and there was to have been a huge equestrian statue of Louis XIV. However, the Pope was against this idea, so when the architect de Sanctis finally started building the steps in the 18th century, the only reference made to France was the little fleur-de-lis on the pedestals.

The cascade of the Spanish Steps is perennially crowded with visitors. In spring, the crowds share the steps with pots of blossoming azaleas. The centrepiece of the square at the

FACT

Critics of Richard Meier's Ara Pacis Museum have likened it variously to a petrol station, a pizzeria and a giant coffin. Vittorio Sgarbi, a celebrity art critic and former Deputy Culture Minister, publicly set fire to a model of the building, and declared it "an indecent cesspit by a useless architect".

Reliefs on the Column of Marcus Aurelius.

The church of San Marcello.

GRAND TOURISTS

The term "Grand Tour" first appeared in 1670 in Richard Lassels's Voyage through Italy, when the British priest and traveller declared that "young lords" must visit Italy and France to educate themselves in the culture of antiquity. In many cases, the Grand Tour provided the only opportunity to view specific works of art, and possibly the only chance to hear certain musical styles. In the following centuries Italy's great cities became the main stops on a secular pilgrimage of English aristocrats and aspiring gentlemen wishing to complete their education. For the Romans, this procession of "Sirs" and "Miladies" represented an opportunity to cash in. Houses were rented out in the fashionable districts of Rome on the Corso and Piazza di Spagna, and tea shops (such as Babington's), hotels and cafés sprung up. With the arrival of mass transport in the middle of the 1800s, travel became cheaper and safer; many writers, including Byron and Shelley, felt that the Grand Tour was de rigueur. The dalliances and foibles of these British in Italy became the subject for literary satire in the novels of E.M. Forster and Henry James, many of which have been dramatised for cinema.

Roman Fashion

Many glamorous and highly sought-after couturiers are based in Rome, the hotspot being Via dei Condotti. Shopping around this legendary road is part of the Roman experience.

While most of the Italian fashion business is centred on Milan, there are a handful of top designers who have made their base in Rome. The most famous of these is undoubtedly Valentino, who opened his Roman studio in 1959 and is still enjoying success even after his retirement in 2007. His high-profile clients have included Sophia Loren, Audrey Hepburn and Jackie Kennedy.

Laura Biagiotti and Fendi are also big names in the world of international fashion who started in Rome. The former, who has been dubbed the "queen of cashmere", creates luxurious knitwear, silk separates and loose-fitting, feminine dresses. The designer is said to test-drive her designs personally for comfort. Her headquarters and home are located just outside Rome in the 15th-century castle of Marco Simone, a former medieval fortress. The four towers of the castle form the famous Biagiotti logo.

Streets that make dreams come true

The second of the two, Fendi, is a company created by a married couple and their five daughters. They first set up their flagship shop on Via Borgognona on the site of a former cinema in the early 1950s. Over half a century on, the shop is one of the largest in the area and sells beautiful bags, shoes, luggage and ready-to-wear clothes.

Two other legendary names are Fontana and Capucci. The heyday of the three Sorelle Fontana (Fontana Sisters) is associated with the glamorous *Dolce Vita* of the 1950s and 1960s, when droves of aristocratic women and just about all the successful foreign actresses in Rome visited their atelier. You can see their classic, elegant clothes at Via della Fontanella di Borghese. Roberto Capucci also emerged during the 1950s and is best-known for the sculptural quality of his garments that look as good off as on the body. His work has been shown in important design museums in Italy, Vienna, Munich and Paris, and he has a boutique/atelier on Via Gregoriana.

More recently, the young Gai Mattiolo has been making his mark both at home and abroad. He has his own-name boutique in the ultra-swanky Via Borgognona.

Of course, just about all the other well-known Italian designers, among them Versace, Armani and Trussardi, have shops in Rome as well. However, visitors who cannot afford top designer names should not be put off; there are plenty of boutiques selling clothes with far less frightening price tags.

Fendi started in Rome.

bottom of the steps is the fountain by Pietro Bernini, who was aided in its construction by his more famous son, Gianlorenzo. The so-called **Barcaccia** is a half-sunken boat fed by water from the ancient aqueduct *Aqua Virgo*.

The English ghetto

The Grand Tourists of the 18th century, most of whom were English aristocrats, stayed in this area on their visits to Rome (it came to be known as the English ghetto). In the 19th century many illustrious artists, writers and musicians followed in their footsteps: Keats, Tennyson, Stendhal, Balzac, Wagner and Liszt among them.

Keats-Shelley House ⑩

Address: 26 Piazza di Spagna; www.keats-shelley-house.org
Telephone: 06-678 4235
Opening Hours: Mon–Sat 10am–1pm, 2–6pm

Entrance Fee: charge
Transport: Spagna

In 1820, Keats spent the last few months of his life in a small room overlooking the Spanish Steps; he died of consumption there in 1821, aged just 25. In 1906, the house was bought by an Anglo-American association and turned into a museum and library dedicated to Keats and his fellow Romantics who had made Rome their home. The Keats-Shelley House has an intriguing collection of personal objects and documents relating to the lives of Shelley and Byron, but the main focus is on Keats – his prints, paintings, books and death mask are on display.

SHOPPING STREETS

The former artistic enclave is now the haunt of big spenders and wishful window shoppers who come to flex their credit cards in its elegant and expensive shops. The area

The twin towers of Trinità dei Monti atop the Spanish Steps.

Piazza di Spagna at night.

FACT

Byron, who had claimed that Rome was the city of his soul, was disappointed to find it "pestilent with English". His fellow Romantic poet Shelley was equally disturbed by the Brits abroad: "The manners of the rich English are wholly insupportable, and they assume pretences which they would not venture upon in their own country."

Keats-Shelley House.

Il Margutta RistorArte.

between Piazza di Spagna and Via del Corso is for dedicated fashionistas. Elegant **Via dei Condotti**  is designer-label heaven.

This street, plus the parallel **Via Borgognona** and **Via Frattina**, which are linked by the equally sumptuous **Via Bocca di Leone**, are home to all the top fashion outlets. **Via del Babuino** is lined with interesting design and antique shops. Parallel to this is **Via Margutta**, a pretty, narrow street (once home to Federico Fellini), with artists' studios, galleries and workshops. Twice a year (May/June and September/ October; www.centopittoriviamargutta. it), the street holds a special art show dedicated to the works of local painters. Matching the expensive shops in this area are some of the best hotels in Rome.

Towards the end of Via dei Condotti is the world-famous tourist trap **Antico Caffè Greco**, said to have been opened by a Greek merchant in 1760. The great and the good down the centuries have frequented this café, including Baudelaire, Wagner, Taine, Liszt, Stendhal, Goethe, Byron, Keats and Shelley.

The third road in the trident of streets, **Via di Ripetta** (*ripa* means river bank: a reminder that there was once a harbour here, back when ships still plied the Tiber) connects Piazza del Popolo to the Vatican, via the Mausoleum of Augustus and the Ara Pacis, two ancient monuments dating from the time of Augustus.

Ara Pacis Museum ⑫

Address: Lungotevere in Augusta; www.arapacis.it
Telephone: 06-0608
Opening Hours: daily 9.30am–7.30pm
Entrance Fee: charge
Transport: Flaminio

The **Ara Pacis**, a finely carved sacrificial altar built in 13 BC to commemorate the era of peace (*pax romana*) that followed Augustus' victories in Gaul and Spain, was painstakingly pieced together by archaeologists from original and reconstructed fragments, and erected in its current location by Mussolini in 1938. The altar is enclosed by a white marble screen decorated with reliefs illustrating mythological and allegorical scenes.

After decades of neglect and a series of botched restorations, the altar is now the principal exhibit in a new museum complex, designed amid great controversy by American architect Richard Meier and inaugurated in 2006. His striking glass-and-travertine design is the only work of modern architecture in the historic centre of Rome, and as such has provoked strong reactions (see page 125).

Mausoleo di Augusto ⑬

Behind the museum is the **Mausoleo di Augusto** (Mausoleum of Augustus), built between 28 and 23 BC, long before it was intended for use. The first person buried here was Augustus' nephew Marcellus, then Augustus himself in AD 14. It's hard to believe now that this overgrown ruin was one of the most magnificent sights in Rome, covered as it was with marble pillars and statues.

EAT

For a taste of old-fashioned English style in the heart of the capital, try Babington's Tea Rooms (23 Piazza di Spagna; tel: 06-678 0846). The creaky wood floors, serious black-skirted staff and all-round austere feel are like a trip back in time. However, the teapots for €12 a person will bring you right back to the present day, and to one of the world's most pricey piazzas.

Shoppers mix with designer labels in Via dei Condotti.

SHOPPING

Those into serious shopping and couture names head to the Piazza di Spagna area and explore the high-fashion temples that are Via dei Condotti, Via Bocca di Leone and Via Borgognona. Nearby Via del Corso is far more budget-oriented.

Accessories

Artigianato del Cuoio
90 Via Belsiana
06-8360 3008
Make your dream bag at this magnificent leather laboratory. Bring your design or describe your idea, choose the leather and accessories and let them do the rest. It takes about a week.
Furla
22 Piazza di Spagna

Shopping on Via dei Condotti.

06-6920 0363
www.furla.com
Italy's mid-market answer to the bag dilemma, with a widely varied, constantly changing range of leather bags, wallets and accessories for ladies and gents. Good quality, and pleasingly (almost) modest prices.
Profumum
10 Via di Ripetta
06-320 0306
www.profumum.com
Exclusive lines of perfumes inspired by the Italian flora and by life in Italy. Scents include clean linen, basil, salt, ocean, and many more, and the packaging is luxurious and modern. Expensive.
Sermoneta
61 Piazza di Spagna
06-679 1960

www.sermonetagloves.com
This 100 percent Italian store only sells gloves, in a multitude of colours, materials and styles.

Antiques

FLAIR
55B Via Margutta
06-3265 2067
www.flairhomecollection.com
This antique furniture shop goes beyond the traditional antique experience mixing vintage pieces with modern designs.

Books

Anglo-American Book Co
102 Via della Vite
06-679 5222
www.angloamericanbook.it
A good range of travel, non-fiction and children's books in English.
Libreria Il Mare
239 Via di Ripetta
06-361 2155
www.ilmare.com
The number one shop for lovers of the ocean and navigation, specializing in novels, manuals, guidebook, and reference material about the sea and its inhabitants. There's also a showcase with navigation instruments such as compasses and telescopes.

Clothing

Max&Co
46 Via dei Condotti
06-678 7946
www.maxandco.com
Max Mara's casual (and affordable) little sister stocks pretty summer dresses and well-structured basics and colourful accessories all year-round.
Patrizia Pepe
44 Via Frattina
06-678 1851
www.patriziapepe.com

Self-described as "rock style with a glamorous soul", the Florentine designer's collections are modern and feminine and come at user-friendly prices.

Crafts

Fabriano
173 Via del Babuino
06-3260 0361
www.fabrianoboutique.com
Quality writing paper, photo albums, wallets and travel diaries, all made in the renowned Fabriano factory, plus a section with drawing products for children.

Food

Enoteca al Parlamento
15 Via dei Prefetti
06-687 3446
www.enotecalparlamento.com
Hundreds of bottles of wine and liquor in a mind-boggling selection. Also carries a small range of wine-related gifts.

Home

C.U.C.I.N.A.
65 Via Mario de' Fiori
06-679 1275
www.cucinastore.com
Pasta makers, nonstick saucepans, culinary gadgets l and more. This trendy store sells good-quality kitchenware with an appealing mix of prices.

Jewellery

Bulgari
10 Via dei Condotti
06-696 261
www.bulgari.com
The supreme jeweller to royalty and the stars.

Markets

Mercato delle Stampe (Print market)
Largo della Fontanella Borghese
Mon–Sat 9.30am–6pm
This little market sells old and new prints as well as second-hand or antiquarian books.

La Soffitta Sotto i Portici
Piazza Augusto Imperatore, under the porticoes first and third Sun of every month, except Aug, 9am–sunset
www.collezionando.org
There's something Parisian about this antiques and collectors' market. Browse the stalls for small antique objects, mid-century modern items, porcelain, jewellery and ancient books. The porticoes make this market the perfect place on a rainy Sunday.

Shoes

Fratelli Rossetti
5a Via Borgognona
06-678 2676
www.fratellirossetti.com
One of Italy's most sophisticated shoe lines for men and women, from Milan. The design is sleek and classic. Also at 59/A Via del Babuino.

Geox
443 Via del Corso
06-6889 2720
www.geox.com
Comfortable, wearable and sexy shoes with a "breathing apparatus", as well as casual and classy jackets and coats.

High fashion

Dolce & Gabbana,
51–52 Via Condotti (women) and 93 Piazza di Spagna (men)
Fendi
420 Largo Goldoni
Versace
12 Piazza di Spagna
Giorgio Armani
77 Via dei Condotti
Gucci
8 Via dei Condotti
Hogan
110 Via del Babuino
Laura Biagiotti
26 Via Mario de' Fiori
Max Mara
28 Via Frattina also 17 Via dei Condotti
Missoni
78 Piazza di Spagna
Prada
88 Via dei Condotti
Roberto Cavalli
25 Via Borgognona
Valentino
38 Piazza di Spagna

Take your pick from an array of well-made Italian leather products.

RESTAURANTS, BARS AND CAFÉS

PRICE CATEGORIES

Price includes dinner and a half-bottle of house wine.

€€€€ = more than €60
€€€ = €40–60
€€ = €25–40
€ = under €25.

Restaurants

Al 34
34 Via Mario dei Fiori
06-679 5091
www.ristorparteal34.it
L & D Tue–Sun, D only Mon.
€€ [p316, E3]
The service is fast, the prices honest, the atmosphere lively and the food classical Italian. Sample the *tonnarelli al granciporro* (pasta with crab), the fresh fish *misto* (a mix of different fish), the home-made Neapolitan *caprese* cake, *semifreddo al torronocino* (nougat ice cream dessert) or the pear and chocolate tart.

Babette
1 D Via Margutta
06-321 1559
www.babetteristorante.it
L & D Tue–Sun, D only Mon.
€€ [p316, D2]
The atmosphere is that of a French brasserie from the early 1900s, but the cuisine is decidedly Italian, with traditional flavours and many new inventions from the chef. Breakfast is especially pleasant, with hot croissants and bread with jam. There's a buffet at lunchtime and menu à la carte in the evening. The outdoor tables spill out on the lovely piazzetta, but they go fast, so book ahead.

Il Gabriello
51 Via Vittoria
06-6994 0810
www.ilgabriello.it
D only Mon–Sat.
€€ [p316, E2]
Though below street level (it's the former wine cellar of a 17th-century palazzo), the setting is truly beautiful, with vaulted ceilings and the perfect lighting – only the music is sometimes a bit too loud. The family-run service adds a touch of home, and the cuisine serves traditional dishes made with high-quality raw materials. One example: beef fillet cooked in Brunello di Montalcino, or the usual *pasta cacio e pepe* (pasta with pecorino and black pepper).

Fiaschetteria Beltramme
39 Via della Croce
06-6979 7200
www.fiaschetteriabeltramme.info
L & D only daily.
€€€ [p316, E2]
This traditional, and always busy, restaurant near the Spanish Steps hasn't changed much since it opened in 1886. The menu is also very traditional, with a selection of delicious pasta and good meat dishes. Try the mouth-watering *abbacchio scottaditto* (roast lamb with potatoes).

'Gusto
9 Piazza Augusto Imperatore
06-322 6273
www.gusto.it
L & D daily, Br Sat–Sun,
Restaurant €€–€€€, pizzeria €–€€ [p316, D2]
'Gusto is an empire: a pizzeria downstairs, an upmarket restaurant upstairs, a wine bar on the other side, and an *osteria* next to that. There's even a well-stocked cookery store attached. The service is fast and friendly, and the general standard is high. An added feature is the outdoor seating most of the year under impressively austere 1930s porticoes that line the square. Booking advisable. Open late.

Hostaria dell'Orso
25c Via dei Soldati
06-6830 1192
www.hdo.it
D only Mon–Sat.
€€€€ [p324, B1]
Milanese superstar chef Gualtiero Marchesi is at the helm of the exclusive Hostaria dell'Orso in a *palazzo* that has been an inn since medieval times. Now a posh but hip restaurant-cum-piano bar-cum-disco, it has an expensive take on Italian haute cuisine that can be ordered à la carte or from four different set-price menus *(menù degustazione)*.

Life
28 Via della Vite
06-6938 0948
www.ristorantelife.it
L & D Tue–Sun, D only Mon.
€€–€€€ [p324, D1]
This restaurant and pizzeria is modern and minimal inside, and comfortable and romantic outside. Colourful art fills the walls and the atmosphere is youthful and relaxed. The bread, pasta and desserts are home-made and the pizza is light and crunchy, plus the menu lists the staples of Roman cuisine as well as a few creative dishes, focusing on both meat and fish recipes prepared with the freshest ingredients.

Il Margutta RistorArte
118 Via Margutta
06-3265 0577
www.ilmarguttavegetariano.it
L & D daily, Br Sun.
€€–€€€ [p316, E2]
This is one of Rome's oldest vegetarian restaurants and offers refined contemporary Italian cuisine. Walls are filled with modern art, echoing its location in the artsy Via Margutta. At lunch there is a set-price buffet, and there's a good brunch on Sunday.

Matricianella
4 Via del Leone
06-683 2100
www.matricianella.it
L & D Mon–Sat.
€€ [p324, C1]

Traditional Roman food in a cheerful setting. To start, try their crispy *fritto vegetale* (fried vegetables) and then, if you are a carnivore, the fettuccine with chicken liver and minced beef is a good bet. Closed three weeks in Aug.

Nino
11 Via Borgognona
06-679 5676
www.ristorantenino.it
L & D Mon–Sat.
€€–€€€ [p316, E3]
A cordial setting where genuine Tuscan food has been consumed for over 70 years. Sample the leek soufflé, wild boar with polenta, and pappardelle with hare sauce. The wine list is well thought out and has a good selection of half-bottles. At the upper end of the price scale, and well worth it. Closed Aug.

L'Osteria
16 Via della Frezza
06-3211 1482
www.gusto.it
L & D daily.
€€ [p316, D2]
Informal but chic, and further proof that anything the 'Gusto team does turns to gold. Furniture and details have some 1930s touches, and the menu is a skilful combination of the traditional and the contemporary, with 400 cheeses, cured meats, deep-fried delicacies, omelettes, soups and good main courses. All served with hearty home-made bread and excellent wines by the glass or bottle from a selection of 1,700 labels.

Otello alla Concordia
81 Via della Croce
06-679 1178
www.ristoranteotelloallaconcordia.it
L & D Mon–Sat.
€ [p316, E2]
Authentically Roman food (*rigatoni all'amatriciana*, lamb and *tiramisù*) and fresh fish served in a room overlooking a pretty little courtyard, used in summer. Book ahead.

PizzaRé
14 Via di Ripetta
06-321 1468
www.pizzare.it
L & D daily.
€ [p316, D2]
For a simple pizza after a heavy day spent in the Spanish Steps' clothing mecca, try PizzaRé, maker of the thick and crusty Neapolitan variety. Set-price menus including pasta and grilled meats at lunchtime.

Taverna Ripetta
158 Via di Ripetta
06-6880 2979
L & D Mon–Sat.
€€ [p316, D2]
Romantic and atmospheric, this restaurant is perfect for lunch as well as dinner. The menu incorporates pasta, meat and fish. Try the gnocchi with basil and cherry tomatoes, and the outstanding *semifreddo* for dessert. Open late.

Bars and Cafés

Antico Caffè Greco
86 Via dei Condotti
www.anticocaffegreco.eu
[p316, E3]
With its marble tables and red-velvet chairs, this historic establishment is frequented mostly by tourists, but the bar out the front makes delicious coffee. Drink it standing at the bar, as it's much cheaper than when you are sitting at a table.

Babington's Tea Rooms
23 Piazza di Spagna
06-678 6027
www.babingtons.com
[p316, E2]
The English teahouse was founded in 1835 and is still run by the same family. Order English and continental breakfasts, a traditional brunch, cocktails and excellent tea. All cakes, breads and muffins are baked fresh daily. Elegant, and decidedly expensive.

Bar Caffè Ciampini
29 Piazza S. Lorenzo in Lucina
06-687 6606
www.ciampini.com
[p324, C1]
A pleasant café in one of Rome's cosiest piazzas. They make their own delicious ice cream.

Buccone
19 Via di Ripetta
06-361 2154
www.enotecabuccone.com
[p316, D2]
This enoteca existed long before wine bars became fashionable, and it is a joy just to take in the sheer authenticity of this high-ceilinged, old-fashioned emporium crammed with bottles of wine and regional specialities.

Ciampini al Café du Jardin
Piazza Trinità dei Monti
06-678 5678
www.caffeciampini.com
[p316, E2]
For the ultimate view of Rome, climb up the Spanish Steps and turn left to enter this enchanted garden, open only in summer, where you can have light meals and cocktails as the sun sets on the Eternal City.

Enoteca Antica di Via della Croce
76b Via della Croce
06-679 0896
www.anticaenoteca.com
[p316, E2]
One of the most appealing wine bars in the area. It's cosy in winter in its cellar-like interior, and delightful in summer if you can nab one of the few outdoor tables. You can just sit and drink wine, or you can eat here too.

Recafè
36 Piazza Augusto Imperatore
06-6813 4730
http://recafe.it
[p316, D2]
An ultra-modern pizzeria-restaurant-café-bar.

Rosati
5 Piazza del Popolo
06-322 5859
www.barrosati.com
[p316, D2]
Long-time rival of Canova (16 Piazza del Popolo) on the opposite side of the piazza, Rosati wins hands down for ambience. Furthermore, its cakes are mouthwatering, and the cocktails are a cut above the usual.

Striking a pose in St Peter's Square.

THE VATICAN AND PRATI

The Vatican City is a shrine to the power and
extravagance of the Catholic Church through the
ages, and to its extraordinary artistic taste.

The fabulous wealth and extravagance of the Catholic Church
through the ages is celebrated
without restraint in the Vatican State.
The immense basilica of St Peter's,
with its dome by Michelangelo and
an interior sumptuously bedecked
with Bernini's glistening creations,
is impressive enough. Then there
are the Vatican Museums, mile upon
mile of rooms and corridors containing historic treasures, and, of course,
the Sistine Chapel.

Covering a total area of little more
than 40 hectares (100 acres), Vatican
City is by far the world's smallest
independent sovereign entity with its
population of 842, only 30 of whom
are women. The Lateran Treaty of
1929, concluded between Pope Pius
XI and Mussolini, established its terri-
torial limits. The Vatican has its own
stamps, currency, media, railway and
police force – the Swiss Guards. The
city is roughly trapezoidal in shape,
bounded by medieval walls on all
sides, except on the corner where the
opening of St Peter's Square marks
the border with Rome.

PIAZZA SAN PIETRO

Piazza San Pietro (St Peter's Square)
❶ was laid out by Bernini in 1656–67

*View of the keyhole-shaped square from
the dome.*

for Pope Alexander VII. Its double-
colonnaded wings symbolise the
outstretched arms of Mother Church,
embracing and protecting the congregation. The piazza itself is keyhole-
shaped, echoing St Peter's role as
holder of the keys to heaven. In the
centre are fountains by Maderno and
della Fontana, and an Egyptian obelisk, brought to Rome by Emperor
Caligula in AD 37. Between the
obelisk and each fountain is a round
marble slab, from where the spec-
tator obtains a typically Baroque

FACT

St Peter's is the longest basilica in the world. The nave is the size of two football fields and the baldacchino is as high as a nine-storey building. The church has 21 altars, 14 chapels, 9 domes and capacity for 60,000 people.

illusion: that each colonnade has only a single row of columns, the other three having disappeared.

Basilica di San Pietro ❷

Address: Piazza San Pietro; www.vatican.va
Telephone: 06-6988 3731
Opening Hours: daily 7am–7pm, until 6.30pm in winter (no bare legs or shoulders)
Entrance Fee: free for the basilica; charge for dome and sacristy
Transport: Ottaviano-San Pietro

At the end of the square, above a triple flight of steps, stands the **Basilica di San Pietro** (St Peter's Basilica), an undeniably impressive structure, but an unfortunate mixture of conflicting architectural styles. Built on the site of St Peter's martyrdom in AD 67 during Nero's persecutions of the Christians, the original Constantinian church was of typical basilican form – a Latin cross with a nave, side aisles and a transept. It was lavishly

decorated with mosaics, paintings and statuary, but became so dilapidated that rebuilding became unavoidable.

In 1506, Julius II decided on a complete reconstruction and commissioned Bramante, whose plan for the new basilica was a Greek cross surmounted by a gigantic dome. On Bramante's death in 1514, the four central piers and the arches of the dome had been completed. Raphael (d. 1520) then took over, and was followed by Sangallo (d. 1546); both men bowed to the clergy's wish for greater capacity by designing a nave and altering the ground plan to that of a Latin cross.

In 1546, however, before this could be realised, the 72-year-old Michelangelo was summoned by Pope Paul III. He expressed his preference for the original Greek cross and central dome of Bramante; seeing the Pantheon's dome as unambitious, though, he developed his own version of Brunelleschi's Florentine

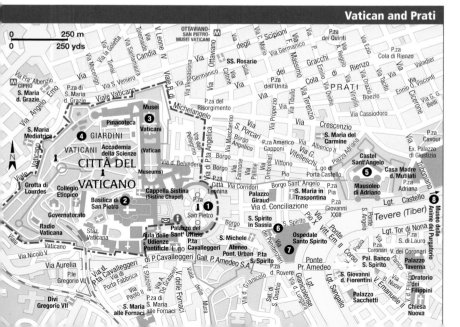

and dead Christ, which he sculpted in 1499 when only 25. Mary is seated on a rock (the rock of St Peter) holding Christ's lifeless body, her face filled with sorrow. It is an incredibly moving work and the only one Michelangelo ever signed.

Halfway down the nave the 13th-century statue of St Peter by Arnolfo di Cambio is so widely venerated that its foot, kissed by devout pilgrims for over seven centuries, is almost worn away.

In the centre of the basilica, directly under the dome is Bernini's **baldacchino** (1633), commissioned by the Barberini Pope Urban VIII. This huge bronze canopy (the largest free-standing bronze structure in the world) rises 26 metres (66ft) over the holiest part of the church, the legendary tomb of St Peter. The twisted columns are replicas of the ones that Christ apparently leant against in the Temple of Solomon. It was cast from metal stripped from the Pantheon's dome, leading locals

Inside St Peter's Basilica.

The Polizia in St Peter's Square.

cupola, and substituted Bramante's piers with new ones of tremendous strength. The entire plan was realised after Michelangelo died in 1564; construction work was continued until 1590, when Pope Paul V decided that the Latin cross was more appropriate, demanding a nave.

Maderno extended Michelangelo's building to give it its current form, adding the portico in 1614. The building was consecrated in 1626, 1,300 years after the construction of the original basilica. Seen from the square, Maderno's portico robs Michelangelo's dome of much of its power, though from a distance the cityscape is still dominated by the cupola.

St Peter's treasures

As you pass into the **portico**, the statue of Constantine on the left is by Bernini. Look up, opposite the 15th-century bronze central doors, to see a restored remnant of the original 13th-century mosaic, *La Navicella*, by Giotto. Inside the basilica, turn right for *La Pietà*, Michelangelo's remarkable statue of the Madonna

to quip, "What the barbarians didn't do, the Barberini did". Bernini added the vine leaves and the bees, symbols of the Barberini coat of arms.

To the right of the baldacchino, stairs lead down to the **grottoes** (daily 8am–6pm, until 5.30pm in winter; free) containing the tombs of several popes, including that of the late Pope John Paul II.

On the apse wall, framed by the baldacchino, is another Bernini creation, the **Cattedra di San Pietro** (1665), a gilded bronze throne said to have been the episcopal chair of St Peter. It is supported by statues of the four fathers of the Church, and above it angels and putti surround a halo of gilt stucco with a key to heaven and the dove of the Holy Spirit.

Don't miss the ghoulish **tomb of Alexander VII**, another of Bernini's patrons, to the left of the transept. Just above the door is Bernini's last work, representing a skeletal allegory of death clutching an hourglass, reminding us that death comes to us all. The draped skeleton is surrounded by four statues representing Justice, Truth, Prudence and Chastity.

Pope Francis during his weekly audience in St Peter's Square.

The dome

The entrance to the **dome** (daily 8am–6pm, till 5pm in winter; closed during ceremonies; charge) is on the right of the portico. The long climb to the top (there are 320 steps from where the lift stops) is rewarded by extensive views across the city.

The **Vatican Gardens** can be seen from the dome, but if you want a closer look you will have to book in advance (see page 139).

THE VATICAN MUSEUMS ❸

Address: 100 Viale Vaticano; www.museivaticani.va
Telephone: 06-6982/ 698 83145
Opening Hours: Mon–Sat 9am–6pm (last admission 4pm), 9am–2 (last admission 12.30pm) last Sun in the month; end Apr–Jul and Sept–Oct also Fri 7–11pm (last admission 9.30pm, booking required); no bare legs or shoulders
Entrance Fee: charge; last Sun in the month is free

AN AUDIENCE WITH THE POPE

For many, the highlight of a Rome visit is attending Mass in St Peter's, or a Wednesday morning audience with the Pope. Mass is celebrated several times daily in St Peter's in Latin or Italian. Confessions are heard in English and many other languages in all four main Roman basilicas.

Anyone can attend an audience with the Pope, but if you want a seat in a special sector close to the Pope, you need to write in advance to the Prefettura della Casa Pontificia, 00120 Città del Vaticano, or fax them on 06-6988 5863 (www.vatican.va/various/prefettura/en/biglietti_en.html). Specify the preferred date and give a local phone number and address (your hotel) for ticket delivery. Alternatively, get your tickets in person (through the bronze door watched over by Swiss Guards, to the right of Saint Peter's).

The general audiences are held either in St Peter's Square or in the Audience Room on Wednesday at 10am or, during the summer, at Castel Gandolfo, the Pope's summer residence. There is no charge for attending an audience.

If you are in Rome for Christmas or Easter and want to attend Midnight Mass or Holy Week celebrations, ask the tourist information service for times and other information, as you may need tickets for some events.

Transport: Ottaviano-San Pietro, Cipro-Musei Vaticani

The Vatican Museums are a good 15-minute walk from St Peter's Square; just follow the walls north until you reach the entrance. Expect a long queue, especially at weekends and on the last Sunday of the month, when the place gets mobbed as admission is free. To help visitors out, the museum authorities have devised four routes lasting from 1.5 to 5 hours. All, including the shortest, take in the Sistine Chapel.

There are several collections in all, plus the papal apartments, but the undisputed highlights are the Sistine Chapel and the Raphael Rooms. Because different visitors have different tastes and because of the vast amount of exhibits contained in the museums, no single route is described here, only the main highlights. You'll find plenty of detailed information at the entrance.

Sistine Chapel

No visit to the Vatican is complete without a look inside the **Sistine Chapel**. The walls, depicting scenes from the lives of Christ and Moses, were painted by some of the greatest masters of the Renaissance: Botticelli, Perugino, Ghirlandaio and Signorelli.

TIP

Tours of the Vatican Gardens must be booked in advance through the Vatican tourist office (tel: 06-6988 4676; every day except Wed and Sun; guided tour only). To visit St Peter's Necropolis, beneath the basilica, contact the Vatican's Ufficio Scavi (tel: 06-6988 5318; Mon–Sat 9am–3.30pm; no children under 15; guided tour only).

A curve of Bernini's colonnade in Piazza San Pietro.

The magnificent dome of St Peter's Basilica.

It is Michelangelo's sublime frescoes, however, which have made the chapel universally famous (see page 148).

The Raphael Rooms

The Stanze di Raffaello are four rooms decorated by Raphael in the 16th century at the request of Pope Nicholas V. The first room, the **Sala di Constantino**, was the last to be painted and, since Raphael was on his deathbed, is mainly the work of his pupils. The frescoes depict scenes from the life of Constantine.

The **Stanza di Eliodoro** was decorated in the years 1512–14. The subject matter alludes to events in Pope Julius II's life. *Expulsion of Heliodorus*, with angels chasing a thief out of the temple, refers to Julius's success in expelling the enemy from Italy.

The next room, **Stanza della Segnatura**, was where the Pope's council met to sign official decrees. The frescoes (1509–11) mix pagan and Christian themes. In the *School of Athens* fresco, representing the triumph of philosophical truth, Raphael portrays ancient characters with the features of contemporary heroes.

Michelangelo is said to have made his mark on the less spiritual side of the Vatican as well. Word has it that the master designed the blue-, yellow- and red-striped uniforms (the colours of the Medici popes) of the Vatican's famous Swiss Guards. The uniforms have not changed since the corps was instituted in the 16th century.

Giuseppe Momo's magnificent helicoidal staircase (1932).

The bearded figure of Plato in the centre is da Vinci; Bramante appears as Euclid in the foreground, and the thoughtful figure of Heraclites

on the steps is Michelangelo. The *Parnassus* fresco, representing poetic beauty, features Homer, Virgil, Ovid, Dante and Boccaccio.

The last room, the **Stanza dell' Incendio di Borgo**, takes its name from the fresco depicting a terrible fire in the Borgo in 847, miraculously extinguished by Leo IV making the sign of the cross. This room was painted after the first half of Michelangelo's Sistine ceiling was uncovered, and direct influences can be seen in the monumentality of the figures.

For information on the other Vatican collections, see Treasures of the Vatican, page 146.

Vatican Gardens ❹

Address: Viale Vaticano; www.museivaticani.va
Telephone: 06-6988 4676
Opening Hours: guided tours (walking or open bus) every day except Wed and Sun
Entrance Fee: charge; ticket also grants entry to the Vatican Museums
Transport: Ottaviano-San Pietro, Cipro-Musei Vaticani

A place of meditation for the popes since 1279, the gardens were commissioned by Nicholas III who wanted an orchard, a lawn and a vegetable garden. The most important improvements were carried out in the 16th and 17th centuries by artists, including Bramante and Pirro Logorio. Renaissance culture, philosophy and art had an influence on the gardens' landscape, demonstrated by small temples and grottoes dedicated to the Virgin, and the impressive fountains. The ship-shaped Fountain of the Galley shoots water from its cannons, and the Eagle Fountain celebrates the arrival of water from the Acqua Paola aqueduct at the Vatican. There's also a French Garden, rare tree species and a notable example of Italian-style gardening, with hedges, trees and bushes trimmed to perfection to convey a sense of symmetry.

Castel Sant'Angelo ❺

Address: 50 Lungotevere Castello; http://castelsantangelo.beniculturali.it
Telephone: 06-681 9111
Opening Hours: Tue–Sun 9am–7.30pm
Entrance Fee: charge, free first Sun of the month
Transport: Lepanto

Castel Sant'Angelo is approached from across the Tiber by means of the delightful **Ponte Sant'Angelo**, a pedestrian bridge adorned with

KIDS

If you're travelling with children, be sure to visit the Castel Sant'Angelo; with its ramparts, trapdoors, prison chambers, drawbridges and cannonballs galore, it will keep them amused for hours.

Frescoes in the Stanza della Segnatura in Apolistic Palace.

PAPAL INSIGNIA

Wherever you see a coat of arms with the crossed keys of St Peter topped with the triple crown, you will know that the building, sculpture or painting on which it appears was a papal commission. Each papal dynasty had its own insignia. Red balls signify the Medici popes, for example, while bees represent the Barberini, the greatest patrons of the Baroque. The Barberini bees can be spotted all over Rome, from Triton's Fountain to the baldacchino in St Peter's. Other interesting papal symbols to look out for are dragons, doves, fleurs-de-lis, cypress and olive trees, stars and hills.

FACT

The eye-rolling, ecstatic expressions of Bernini's ten angels on the Ponte Sant'Angelo, and the fact that they seem to be battling with the wind with garments fluttering, has earned them the nickname "the breezy maniacs".

statues of saints Peter and Paul and 10 angels sculpted by Bernini and his students in the 1660s. The three central arches were part of the bridge Hadrian built in AD 136 to link his mausoleum – now the Castel Sant'Angelo – to the centre of the city. Most of the present bridge dates from the 17th century, but it was altered in the late 19th century to accommodate the new Tiber embankment.

Construction of the castle began in AD 123, and 16 years later it became Hadrian's mausoleum. It has since been a fortress, a prison and the popes' hiding place in times of trouble, thanks to the *passetto*, the corridor that connects the Vatican Palace with the castle. The castle houses artefacts from all periods of Roman history, and many of the rooms, such as the Sala Paolina painted by del Vaga in 1544, are beautifully frescoed.

The papal chambers and other rooms are accessible via the spiral ramp inside, which is still in an excellent state of preservation. At the top of the ramp are the terraces and café, both with superb views of the Dome of St Peter's and the rest of Rome. (It was from this parapet that Puccini's heroine, Tosca, plunged to her death.) The gigantic bronze statue of the Archangel Michael that crowns the citadel was placed here in 1753.

THE BORGO AND VIA DELLA CONCILIAZIONE

If you've energy left after visiting St Peter's and the Vatican Museums, wander the warren of pedestrian streets just east of the Vatican. The first pilgrims to St Peter's were housed in hostels here, and the area is still a colony of international pilgrims today, making it the place to go for anyone wishing to buy religious items.

The relaxed charm of this atmospheric neighbourhood will soothe your tired feet as you meander along its medieval lanes and admire its ancient, ivy-clad *palazzi*. The quarter was formerly known as the Città Leonina after Leo IV, who built the fortified walls and connected the Vatican to Castel Sant'Angelo by an

SHOPPING

Pleasant Via Cola di Rienzo provides a relaxing mid-range shopping experience. Via della Conciliazione, linking the Vatican with Castel Sant'Angelo, offers a wide selection of religious artefacts including Vatican coins, statues, stamps, religious books and souvenirs.

Accessories

Coccinelle
255 Via Cola di Rienzo
06-324 1749
www.coccinelle.it
Luxuriously soft leather bags and pocketbooks in the colours of the season.
Mandarina Duck
206 Cola di Rienzo
06-687 4610
www.mandarinaduck.com

Bolognese designer of pretty and functional bags and luggage.
Sabon
241 Via Cola di Rienzo
06-320 8653
www.sabon.it
Soaps, lotions and bath products with exotic and old-fashioned scents for an "affordable luxury" experience.

Clothing

Carla G
134 Via Cola di Rienzo
06-324 3511
www.carlag.it
Classy, well cut and very sassy garments for charming women.
Gente
277 Via Cola di Rienzo
06-321 1516

www.genteroma.com
Women disappear for hours in this fabulous boutique carrying superb designer clothes, accessories and shoes, and lesser-known (but equally chic) brands.
Iron G
50 Via Cola di Rienzo
06-321 6798
www.iron-g.com
Get club-ready and a bit extravagant at this twenty-something magnet.

Food

Castroni
196 Via Cola di Rienzo
06-687 4383
www.castroni.it
The hands-down favourite for Italian speciality items, international treats and amazing gifts.

overhead passageway. Unfortunately a large part of the Borgo and its olde-worlde atmosphere were destroyed when Mussolini decided that St Peter's needed a more grandiose approach and tore the area in two with the Via della Conciliazione, which ruins the effect of Bernini's piazza, but allows for a full view of St Peter's.

An interesting sight on Via delle Conciliazione is the church of **Santa Maria in Traspontina** (Mon–Sat 6.30am–noon, 4–7.15pm, Sun 7.30am–1pm), which stands on the site of an ancient Roman pyramid, said to have been Romulus' Tomb. The church was built in 1527 and houses the columns to which Saints Peter and Paul are thought to have been chained before their martyrdom. Further down, the style of **Palazzo Torlonia Giraud** (30 Via delle Conciliazione; closed to public), closely resembles that of Palazzo della Cancelleria (the papal chancellery) and its facade is an example of Roman Renaissance. The Palazzo was built for a cardinal in 1496, but

has had many owners, including the nobleman Giovanni Torlonia, after whom it was named, some members of the Medici family and Queen Christina of Sweden.

South of the boulevard is **Borgo Santo Spirito**. The church of **Santo Spirito in Sassia ❻**, built for the Saxons in 689, was rebuilt in the 16th century. Next door, the **Ospedale Santo Spirito ❼** was set up by Pope Innocent III in the 13th century as an orphanage for unwanted babies. Within the hospital is the small **Museo Storico dell'Arte Sanitaria** (3 Lungotevere in Sassia; Mon, Wed, Fri 10am–noon, booking required on other days, guided tours, tel: 06-689 3051; www.museiscientificiroma.eu/arte-sanitaria), with an array of medical paraphernalia, and two frescoed wards.

PRATI

North of the Vatican lies the elegant residential area of Prati. Until the late 19th century, Prati was characterised by vast vineyards and gardens, hence the name, which means "meadows". The

FACT

The Museum of the Souls of Purgatory is housed within the Sacro Cuore del Suffragio (Sacred Heart of Suffrage), and was founded by Jouet, a missionary from Marseille.

Castel Sant' Angelo from the pedestrian Sant' Angelo bridge.

The Borghese Papal Insignia – the dragon and eagle.

SHOP

Another feature of Prati is its markets. The wholesale flower market at 45 Via Trionfale has blooms and plants at give-away prices. Essentially a trade market, it is open to the public on Tuesday mornings. Nearby Mercato Trionfale is one of the city's largest, and runs along Via Andrea Doria. Here you'll find fresh produce, as well as clothing and homeware. There's also a superb covered food market at Piazza dell'Unità.

The Vatican Gardens.

quarter was built in its present shape in response to an urgent need to expand the city after it was proclaimed capital of the newly unified nation in 1870.

Its strategic position just outside the Vatican walls makes this district convenient for sightseeing and shopping. Prati may lack the medieval charm of the Centro Storico, but if you want to get a deeper understanding of the real fabric and rhythm of everyday Roman life, then venturing into this neighbourhood is a great way to start.

Prati is easily reached on metro line A (get off at Lepanto, Ottaviano-San Pietro or Cipro-Musei Vaticani), or one of the many bus routes that terminate at Piazza del Risorgimento.

Most of the shops are concentrated around Via Cola di Rienzo and Via Ottaviano, around Piazza Mazzini, which is laid out in a large star-shaped plan, and Piazza Cavour, immediately recognisable by its towering palms. Facing Piazza Cavour, with its rear towards the west bank of the Tiber, is the colossal **Palazzo di Giustizia** (Palace of Justice), dubbed *il palazzaccio* (the big, ugly building).

Its river-front facade is crowned with a bronze chariot and fronted by statues of the great men of Italian law.

Museo delle Anime del Purgatorio ❽

Address: 12 Lungotevere Prati
Telephone: 06-6880 6517
Opening Hours: daily 7.30–11am, 4.30–7.30pm
Entrance Fee: free
Transport: Lepanto

A small neo-Gothic church on the Tiber's banks houses what is perhaps the strangest museum in Rome: the **Museo delle Anime del Purgatorio** (Museum of the Souls of Purgatory), which some say holds proof of the existence of an afterlife. Following a fire that destroyed part of the church in the late 1800s, Father Jouet recognised the face of a suffering man in one of the smoke stains on the wall and, interpreting it as a sign from the otherworld, he decided to collect items to testify to the existence of Purgatory. Handprints on Bibles, faces marked on missals and stained nightgowns are among the few items on display in the small showcase.

RESTAURANTS, BARS AND CAFÉS

PRICE CATEGORIES

Price includes dinner and a half-bottle of house wine.

€€€€ = more than €60
€€€ = €40–60
€€ = €25–40
€ = under €25.

Restaurants

Dante Taberna de' Gracchi
266/268 Via dei Gracchi
06-321 3126
www.tabernagracchi.com
L & D Mon–Sat.
€€–€€€ [p316, B2]
A relaxing pastel-coloured interior and classic cuisine based mostly on fresh fish, and a different soup every day. Choose a fine wine from an endless list.

Il Matriciano
55 Via dei Gracchi
06-321 3040
L & D Thu–Tue.
€€ [p316, B2]
Just around the corner from St Peter's this restaurant has served genuine local food for over 90 years. Its signature dish is an excellent spaghetti all' amatriciana (spaghetti with tomato, onion and cured pork sauce).

Napul'è
89–91 Viale Giulio Cesare
06-323 1005
www.napularte.it
L & D daily.
€ [p316, B2]
Neapolitans approve of the pizza at this southern restaurant. Choose from 40 different styles, all boasting the typical thick crust (as opposed to the thin Roman pizza). Also serves pasta and meat dishes from the Campania region.

Osteria dell'Angelo
24 Via G. Bettolo
06-372 9470
L Tue–Fri, D Mon–Sat.
€–€€ [p316, B2]
This neighbourhood trattoria with

a fixed-price evening menu, including house wine, is always packed to the gills. Try the fritti to begin with, then a flavourful version of the Roman standard tonnarelli cacio e pepe (pasta with pecorino and black pepper). Booking advisable. No credit cards.

La Pergola dei Cavalieri Hilton
101 Via A. Cadlolo, Monte Mario
06-3509 2211
www.romecavalieri.it
D Tue-Sat, Aug closed.
€€€€ [off map p316, A1]
German superstar chef Heinz Beck has made this a place worth making a detour for. Enviable views, attentive staff and ultra-refined food. Elegant dress code.

Settembrini
25 Via L. Settembrini
06-323 2617
http://viasettembrini.com
L & D Mon–Fri, D only Sat. Closed Aug.
€€€€ [p316, C1]
Serving both sushi and seafood pasta, Settembrini explores various cuisines and manages to combine them skilfully. The cheese and cold meat platters are the result of long ingredient research and the wine list is spectacular.

Siciliainbocca
26 Via Faà di Bruno
06-3735 8400
www.siciliainbocca.com
L & D Mon–Sat.
€€ [p316, B1]
Come here for a cheerful ambience and good Sicilian food seasoned with the island's flavours: lemons, olives, capers and plenty of sunshine. Their classic ricotta-filled cassata is excellent.

Taverna Angelica
6 Piazza Capponi
06-687 4514
www.tavernaangelica.com
L & D Sun, D only Mon–Sat.
€€ [p316, B3]

Massimo Pinardi's restaurant has only been around a few years, but it quickly earned a reputation for high-quality food. Try smoked goose breast with celery, apple and walnuts, pasta with fennel and anchovy, or grilled swordfish with pesto.

Zen
243 Via degli Scipioni
06-321 3420
http://zenworld.eu/roma/ristorante.html
L & D Tue–Fri & Sun, D only Sat.
€€–€€€ [p316, C2]
High-standard, fresh Japanese food is Zen's strong point. Pick your dishes as they roll past you on the city's first sushi and sashimi conveyor belt, or order the tempura and other heftier dishes à la carte.

Bars and Cafés

Antonini
19–29 Via G. Sabotino
06-372 5052
www.antoniniroma.it
[p316, B1]
This pasticceria makes the kind of cakes you bring to dinner parties when you want to impress – and is also a perfect place for an aperitif.

Gelateria dei Gracchi
272 Via dei Gracchi
06-321 6668
www.gelateriadeigracchi.it
[p316, C2]
Owner Alberto is an artist with a passion for ice-cream making, and the recipes he follows are more than 100 years old. His gelato flavours are all-natural, with real fruit and absolutely no additives.

Pellacchia
103 Via Cola di Rienzo
06-321 0807
[p316, C2]
This ice-cream parlour makes its own ice cream on the premises and is deservedly famous.

TREASURES OF THE VATICAN

Many visitors to the Sistine Chapel feel a sort of sensory overload, known as "Stendhal's Syndrome": a natural response to the Vatican's artistic riches.

The Vatican Museums house one of the biggest and most important art collections in the world. They merit a lifetime's study, but for those with little time, here are the must-sees.

The Sistine Chapel (see page 148) and the four Raphael Rooms are the star attractions. The Museo Pio-Clementino has some of the greatest sculptures of antiquity. The Pinacoteca houses an extensive collection of paintings from Byzantine times to the present, with works by Giotto, Bellini, Titian, da Vinci, Raphael, Caravaggio and many others.

The Vatican Library contains a priceless collection of illuminated manuscripts and early printed books. The Chapel of St Nicholas has some exquisite frescoes by Fra Angelico, and frescoes by Pinturicchio can be seen in the Borgia Apartment.

The Modern Religious Art Collection displays works by Paul Klee, Francis Bacon, Max Ernst and Henri Matisse, among others. The Etruscan Museum has many artefacts found in tombs of the mysterious pre-Roman civilisation (see page 279). The Gregoriano Profano Museum houses finds from the Baths of Caracalla, on the old Via Appia.

Galleria delle Carte Geographiche (Gallery of Maps): this superb barrel-vaulted gallery is frescoed with maps of Italy. Most were designed by a 16th-century monk.

The Essentials

Address: 100 Viale Vaticano; www.musei vaticani.va
Tel: 06-6988 3145
Opening Hours: Mon–Sat 9am–6pm, last entry at 4pm
Entrance Fee: charge
Transport: Ottaviano-San Pietro, Cipro-Musei Vaticani

Paul Klee's City with Gothic Cathedral in the Vatican's Modern Religious Art Collection.

The Pinacoteca contains superb paintings, including The Last Communion of St Jerome by Domenichino on the left.

Detail from Raphael's School of Athens (1510–11) showing Plato and Aristotle with students including Michelangelo (with his famous boots on), who considered Raphael an arch-rival. See it in the Raphael Rooms.

CLASSICAL MASTERPIECES

The Vatican Museums are packed with antiquities and artistic treasures.

The Museo Pio-Clementino houses some of the greatest sculptures of antiquity. In the Octagonal Courtyard of the Belvedere are three classical masterpieces: the Atleta Apoxyomenos, depicts an athlete washing himself after a race; the Apollo del Belvedere, depicting the Greek sun god; the Laocoön, a 1st-century BC copy of an older bronze sculpture, found near Nero's Golden House and depicting a Trojan priest of Apollo and his two sons struggling with two writhing sea serpents.

The Hall of the Greek Cross (Sala a Croce Greca) houses porphyry sarcophagi of Emperor Constantine's mother and daughter. The Circular Hall (Sala Rotonda) has a huge gilded bronze statue of Hercules and a colossal head of Jupiter of Otricoli. In the Hall of the Muses (Sala delle Muse) there are statues of Apollo and the Muses; in the centre, the Belvedere Torso (1st century BC) is a Greek work that was admired greatly by Raphael and Michelangelo.

The Animal Room (Sala degli Animali) is worth visiting for its remarkable animal statues. The Gallery of Statues (Galleria delle Statue) has more Roman copies of Greek originals. The Mask Room (Gabinetto delle Maschere) houses intricate 2nd-century AD mosaics of theatrical masks from Hadrian's Villa.

Laocoon is a 1st-century BC copy of a 3rd century BC bronze sculpture and was found near the Domus Aurea by the Colosseum.

SISTINE CHAPEL

The realistic dynamism of the human figures and the mastery of colour and light still astonish visitors to this day, as they did Michelangelo's contemporaries.

A detail of Botticelli's The Temptation of Christ before restoration.

The Sistine Chapel was built by Sixtus IV in 1473–81 as the official private chapel of the popes. It was also used for the conclaves by which a new pope is elected, a function the chapel preserves today. Michelangelo was engaged to paint the ceiling by Pope Julius II in 1508, but initially expressed his desire to decline: he was intimidated by the scale of the commission as he felt that he was more of a sculptor than a painter. Though untried at the art of fresco painting, Michelangelo finally accepted and worked single-handedly, lying on his back, for four years (1508–12). When the work was unveiled, it set the seal on his reputation as the greatest living artist. Goethe once wrote that "without having seen the Sistine Chapel one can form no appreciable idea of what one man is capable of achieving."

The ceiling depicts scenes from Genesis, starting with God dividing light from dark and ending with the drunkenness of Noah. The sides show the ancestors of Christ and, on marble thrones, the prophets and the classical sybils who prophesised Christ's coming. Above these are the ignudi, nude figures holding up festoons with papal symbols and medallions. In the four corners are scenes of salvation, including the dramatic hanging of Haman, and Judith swiping off Holofernes's head.

Critics cannot agree if the ceiling is a neo-Platonic statement or a theological programme devised with the help of religious experts, including, perhaps, Julius II.

Michelangelo's celebrated ceiling of frescoes in the Sistine Chapel.

The Fall of Man. One of the nine ceiling panels depicting stories of the Creation, the Fall and Noah. The panels (painted in reverse order) are as follows: 1) Separation of Light and Darkness 2) Creation of Sun, Moon and Planets 3) Separation of Land and Sea 4) Creation of Adam 5) Creation of Eve 6) the Fall, and Expulsion from Paradise 7) the Sacrifice of Noah 8) the Flood 9) the Drunkenness of Noah.

Towards the centre of the ceiling you will be able to make out the outstretched finger of the Creation of Adam, the Sistine Chapel's most iconic image.

THE LAST JUDGEMENT

Some critics say the overall theme of the Sistine Chapel is salvation, reaching its climax in the *Last Judgement* fresco on the end wall (painted by Michelangelo between 1535 and 1541). It depicts a harrowing image of the souls of the dead rising up to face the wrath of God. The good are promoted to heaven, while the damned are cast down into hell. The figure of St Bartholomew is depicted to the right of the beardless Christ, carrying his flayed skin in his left hand. The tragic face depicted on it is Michelangelo's self-portrait; his pained expression reflected the spiritual crisis he was going through and his contemporaries' lack of comprehension.

The fresco aroused violent controversy. The nudity of the figures was criticised as indecent, but Michel-

angelo's patron, Paul III, was overwhelmed by the work, truly appreciating its greatness. Some of his successors were not so enlightened. In 1564, Pope Paul IV, in a fit of prudery, ordered drapery to be painted over some of the nude figures.

The other paintings in the Sistine Chapel have been understandably overshadowed by Michelangelo's work. But the earlier frescoes on the lower walls illustrating scenes from the lives of Moses and Christ are worthy of more than a passing glance. They include works by Pinturicchio, Botticelli, Luca Signorelli and Perugino, who painted the fresco Giving of the Keys to Saint Peter (1481) pictured above.

The Last Judgement fresco.

The Pantheon, Piazza della Rotunda.

PIAZZA NAVONA AND THE PANTHEON

The Pantheon has stood in the heart of Rome for almost 2,000 years, while Piazza Navona is built on the foundations of a Roman stadium. Today this compact area is filled with Baroque buildings, churches and picturesque alfresco cafés.

The area loosely referred to as the Centro Storico (the Historic Centre) is contained between the great bend of the Tiber to the west and Via del Corso to the east. In ancient times, the area centred on the Campus Martius (Field of Mars), an army training ground dedicated to the Roman god of war that lay outside the Pomerium, the sacred boundary of the city. It was here, in front of the nearby Temple of Apollo (three pillars of which can still be seen next to the Teatro di Marcello), that generals returning from their military campaigns reported to the Senate.

As building space around the central Fora became scarce, the city gradually spread beyond the ancient walls and out towards the Tiber. By Imperial times the old Campus Martius had all but disappeared, and the area was filled with theatres, baths, porticoes and arenas, and dotted with verdant public parks. All that is left to remind us of the existence of the Field of Mars is an elegant little square and street called Piazza and Via di Campo Marzio.

Rome's population shrank in the Middle Ages due to devastating plagues and the relocation of the Empire's capital to Constantinople. Those who remained moved towards

the Tiber. The river was good for defence purposes, for water, to which there was no access further inland because so many of the ancient aqueducts had been destroyed, and because it provided a transport route safe from highway bandits. The river current also turned floating mills, which were tied up between the banks.

The ruins in the area provided building materials for new houses, churches and papal complexes. Some were used as forts or – as with the Pantheon – as churches. Almost all

Main Attractions

The Pantheon
Santa Maria sopra Minerva
Galleria Doria Pamphilj
Government buildings
San Luigi dei Francesi
Piazza Navona
Palazzo Altemps
Museo di Roma
Ponte Sant'Angelo
Via dei Coronari

Maps and Listings

Street musicians.

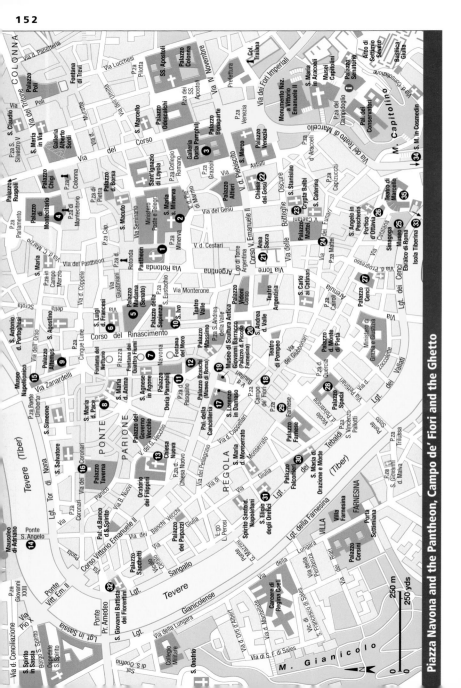

Piazza Navona and the Pantheon, Campo de' Fiori and the Ghetto

the major medieval, Renaissance and Baroque buildings in the Centro Storico are either expressions of an increasingly powerful Church, or reflect the intense competition for power and prestige among Rome's rich and aristocratic families.

But the Historic Centre has more to offer than churches and palaces. Its tangle of streets and alleys has been the home of the craft guilds since medieval times, when these quarters were full of *botteghe* (workshops). The types of trade may have changed, but trade is still the lifeblood of the district. There are antique shops and fairs in and around Via dei Coronari and Via dell'Orso, while Piazza della Fontanella Borghese is the site of a print market.

AROUND PIAZZA DELLA ROTONDA

The Piazza della Rotonda is one of the busiest squares in the city. It's worth trying to beat the crowds by getting here as early as you can.

The Pantheon ❶

Address: Piazza della Rotonda; www.pantheonroma.com

Telephone: 06-6830 0230
Opening Hours: Mon–Sat 9am–7.30pm, Sun 9am–6pm
Entrance Fee: free
Transport: Barberini, 30, 40, 62, 64, 81, 87, 492,

Street theatre artist.

One of the most memorable and impressive of Rome's many architectural marvels is the **Pantheon** (Basilica di Santa Maria ad Martyres), the best-preserved ancient building in Rome. Originally built as a temple to all the gods, its subsequent conversion into a church in 609 saved it from being torn down. Only 15 metres (45ft) above sea level, the Pantheon is now the lowest point in Rome. The ditch around it shows just how much the rubble has raised Rome over the centuries: in ancient times one looked up to the Pantheon, not down.

As the inscription over the portico informs us, the statesman Marcus Agrippa, son-in-law of Augustus, built the original Pantheon in 27 BC in honour of the victory over Antony and Cleopatra at Actium. Agrippa's building, however, was severely damaged by fire in AD 80 and was completely rebuilt by Hadrian (AD

The Pantheon at night.

SHOP

One of the most interesting streets is Via dei Cestari (connecting the Pantheon and Largo Argentina). It is lined with shops selling religious raiment and equipment for the Catholic priesthood. Many facades incorporate old guild signs or pieces of ancient marble.

117–38), who has been credited as the building's architect, not just its patron.

The portico is stately and imposing: 16 massive Corinthian columns support a roof with a triangular pediment (the notches cut into the portico columns are said to have supported stalls for a fish and poultry market in the Middle Ages). The walls are 6 metres (20ft) thick and the huge bronze doors 8 metres (24ft) high. But the most striking aspect of the building is, of course, the dome.

The Pantheon contains the tombs of kings and painters, Raphael (1483–1520) being one of them. The marble floor is an 1873 restoration.

Santa Maria sopra Minerva

Southeast of the Pantheon, **Santa Maria sopra Minerva** ❷ (www. santamariasopraminerva.it; Mon–Fri 7.30am–7pm, Sat 7.30am–12.30pm, 3.30–7pm, Sun 8am–12.30pm, 3.30–7pm) is the only truly Gothic church in Rome. Built in the 8th century on the site of a temple of Minerva, its present form dates from around 1280 when it was rebuilt by Dominicans. Its most striking feature is the beautiful, Giotto-blue vaulted ceiling.

The interior of the Pantheon's dome.

The church houses the tombs of several popes and cardinals, and the relics of St Catherine of Siena (the patron saint of Italy who died in the Dominican convent here in 1380). The last chapel on the right is decorated with a fresco of *The Assumption* by Filippino Lippi. In the bottom section the portraits of two young boys represent two Medici princes, future popes Leo X and Clement VII. To the left of the altar stands a Michelangelo sculpture of Christ the Redeemer, whose nudity shocked the Church at the time. It was carved as a nude figure in Florence and then sent to Rome, where it was ineptly finished by pupils.

Outside in Piazza Minerva, the jovial little **elephant statue** with an ancient Egyptian obelisk on its back was designed by Bernini in 1667.

On nearby Via del Pie' di Marmo (Street of the Marble Foot), set on a pedestal in a shadowy corner is the massive and very worn foot of an ancient Roman statue.

THE PANTHEON DOME

A perfect hemisphere, and a symbol of beauty and harmony, the Pantheon dome had a profound impact on the architects of the Renaissance, influencing Brunelleschi's cathedral in Florence and Michelangelo's design for the dome of St Peter's. The height of the dome is the same as its diameter: 43.3 metres (142ft). The hole (oculus) in its centre is still the only source of light. On sunny days a beam of light pours through the oculus and moves around the Pantheon's interior, illuminating the frescoes and tombs. Originally, the dome was covered in bronze, but the Byzantine emperor Constans II stripped the outer layer off and took it to Constantinople in 667. Almost 1,000 years later, in 1620, the Barberini Pope Urban VIII had the inner layer melted down to make cannons for Castel Sant'Angelo and Bernini's baldacchino in St Peter's. This act of papal vandalism inspired the quip that "What the barbarians didn't do, the Barberini did". Every year on Pentecost, a shower of rose petals falls through the Pantheon's open oculus thanks to a group of firemen who scale the exterior wall of the Pantheon and this sight is almost as interesting as the petal rain itself.

Beyond stands the church of **Sant'Ignazio di Loyola** (daily 7.30am–12.20pm, 3–7.20pm), built between 1627 and 1685 to honour St Ignatius, founder of the Jesuit order. The interior is the usual Baroque combination of gold embellishments, marble and statuary, but the highlight is Andrea Pozzi's fantastic trompe l'œil views of heaven.

Just south of here (off Via del Corso) is Piazza del Collegio Romano and the entrance to the Galleria Doria Pamphilj.

Galleria Doria Pamphilj ❸

Address: Via del Corso 305; www.doriapamphilj.it
Telephone: 06-679 7323
Opening Hours: daily 9am–7pm
Entrance Fee: charge
Transport: 8, 62, 64, 85, 175, 492, 630, 850

The Galleria Doria Pamphilj contains one of the best art collections in Rome, with over 400 paintings from the 15th to 18th centuries. The 17th-century palace was the residence of the once-powerful Doria Pamphilj dynasty (it is still the property of the Pamphilj family, who live in the opposite wing). Every inch of wall space in the ornate State Apartments is taken up with paintings, in keeping with the interior fashions of the time. The finest room here is the 18th-century Gallery of Mirrors – a Versailles in miniature. The light pouring in from the windows on both sides is reflected in the mirrors and gold frames to dazzling effect. The gallery is lined with sculptures, and ceiling frescoes depict the Labours of Hercules.

The collection was begun by Pamphilj Pope Innocent X, who was crowned in 1644, and expanded by subsequent generations. It includes the portrait of Innocent X by Velázquez (painted in 1649), with a penetrating gaze and a ruthlessness expression. Nearby is a bust of the Pope by Bernini, Titian's Salomé (one

theory suggests that John the Baptist's head is a self portrait of Titian and Salomé that of a lover who rejected him), a double portrait by Raphael, and two masterpieces by a young Caravaggio – Rest on the Flight to Egypt, much lighter than the rest of his oeuvre, and the Magdalene.

The Government buildings

Rome is still the centre of Italian government, and there are two important government offices in heavily guarded old palazzi in this area. Behind Piazza Colonna, **Palazzo di Montecitorio** ❹ (www.camera.it; free first Sun of the month, except Jul, Aug and first week of Sept) is where the Chamber of Deputies has met since 1871. Before that, it was the Papal Tribunal of Justice. Bernini drew up plans for the building in 1650, and Carlo Fontana saw the design and building through to completion in 1697. Virtually all that remains of the 17th-century design is the convex curve of the facade – designed to make the building look even bigger than it is – and the rusticated columns.

The Egyptian obelisk in front of the palazzo dates from the 6th

Bernini's marble elephant on Piazza Minerva supports a 6th-century obelisk.

Priestly parade.

EAT

Avoid the overpriced cafés on Piazza Navona. For a glass of wine and plate of cheese, cold cuts, pâté or any combination of snacks and salads, the Cul de Sac wine bar on Piazza Pasquino is a good place to know about.

century BC. It was used by Emperor Augustus for an enormous sundial he laid out in 10 BC. The sundial was discovered in the crypt of the nearby church of San Lorenzo in Lucina.

Another ancient relic that was adapted to modern usage lies in the nearby Piazza di Pietra, east of Piazza della Rotonda. The **Palazzo della Borsa** takes its name from its one-time role as Rome's stock exchange. Prior to that, the building, with its 11 ancient columns, was a customs house, and originally, in the 2nd century AD, it was the Temple of Hadrian, which is how it is mostly referred to now.

The Senate has occupied the elegant **Palazzo Madama** ❺ (www.senato.it; the first Sat of the month except Aug, 10am–6pm; free) between Piazza della Rotonda and Piazza Navona since 1870. It was built for the Medici family in the early 16th century, and several of its members lived here before becoming Pope.

The palace gets its name from the Habsburg Madama Margherita (1522–86), the illegitimate daughter

Titian's Salomé in the Galleria Doria Pamphilj.

of Emperor Charles V and the wife of Alessandro de' Medici.

Caravaggio chapel

Opposite is the Baroque church of **San Luigi dei Francesi** ❻ (10am–12.30pm, 3–7pm, closed Thu pm), the French national church in Rome, built in 1589. It contains works by Giacomo della Porta and Domenico Fontana, but it is the three Caravaggio masterpieces in the Capella Contarelli, showing scenes from the life of St Matthew (The Calling of St Matthew, The Martyrdom of St Matthew and St Matthew and the Angel – painted between 1599 and 1602) that make a visit very worthwhile. These wonderful and moving paintings demonstrate Caravaggio's astounding mastery of light and dramatic realism. Have a euro handy to light the chapel up.

AROUND PIAZZA NAVONA

Piazza Navona ❼ is one of the most animated squares in Rome, invariably full of Romans and foreign visitors wandering among stalls set up by hopeful artists, relaxing with a coffee in one of the many bars, or stopping for a chat by its gushing fountains.

Piazza Navona was built over the remains of the emperor Domitian's ancient athletics stadium: the stand forms part of the foundations of the flanking houses, and you can see one of the original entrances just behind the north end of the square.

The stadium originally measured 50 by 275 metres (150 by 825ft), with the seats rising to 35 metres (105ft). It was used for athletic contests and horse races, and was probably still in use when the Goths invaded in the 5th century. However, the plundering of its fabric began under Constantius II (third son of Constantine the Great), who carried off works of art and decorative features in 356 to adorn his new residence in

Constantinople, after the seat of the Empire had been moved there.

Three fountains

The piazza owes its Baroque appearance to the Pamphilj Pope, Innocent X (1644–55), who enlarged his family palace and commissioned the square's magnificent centrepiece, Bernini's **Fontana dei Quattro Fiumi** (Fountain of the Four Rivers). The rivers in question – the Danube, the Ganges, the Nile and the Plate – are represented by four huge allegorical figures that in turn represent the four continents Europe, Asia, Africa and America. The Nile is blindfolded because the source of the river was then still a mystery. Rising above the statues is an obelisk taken from the Circus of Maxentius. The obelisk is topped by the figure of a dove with an olive branch to show that this once pagan monument has been converted into a Christian one.

To the south of the square is the **Fontana del Moro** (Fountain of the Moor). Its central figure (which looks more like a Triton than a Moor)was designed by Bernini.

TIP

In summer, the courtyard of Sant'Ivo alla Sapienza hosts classical concerts. It is a great opportunity to view Borromini's marvellous Baroque church in a different light, especially because the site is only open on Sundays , and for just a couple of hours. For programme information call 06-0608 and press 2 for English.

Vaulting in Santa Maria sopra Minerva, the only true Gothic church in Rome.

The **Fontana del Nettuno** (Fountain of Neptune) at the northern end was originally just a large basin. The sculptures were added in the 19th century to create symmetry.

Gelato time in Piazza Navona.

The 6th-century BC Egyptian obelisk stands in front of the Palazzo di Montecitorio, home to the lower house of government.

Bernini's Fontana dei Quattro Fiumi.

Churches and palaces

Pope Innocent also commissioned the Borromini facade of **Sant'Agnese in Agone** (www.santagneseinagone.org). Here, it is said, the saint was pilloried and stood naked in the stocks until her hair miraculously grew to protect her modesty. Inside the church there are underground chambers where you can see the ruins of the stadium of Domitian, a Roman mosaic floor and medieval frescoes on the wall.

To the left of the church is **Palazzo Doria Pamphilj** (not to be confused with the Galleria Doria Pamphilj), designed by Rainaldi in the mid-17th century. It now houses the Brazilian Embassy.

Just off the square is the church of **Santa Maria della Pace ❽**, rebuilt in 1482 and then restored in 1656, when the convex, Baroque facade was added. The church contains Raphael's frescoes of The Four Sybils.

The nearby **Santa Maria dell' Anima** (daily 9am–12.45pm, 3–7pm; www.pisma.it) is the German-speaking church of Rome and was founded in 1500, although the present building was heavily restored in the 19th century. Apart from a Romano altarpiece, most of the works of art inside are by pupils and followers of Caravaggio, Michelangelo and Raphael.

Palazzo Altemps ❾

Address: 46 Piazza di Sant'Apollinare (nr Piazza Navona); http://archeoroma.beniculturali.it
Telephone: 06-3996 7700
Opening Hours: Tue–Sun 9am–7.45pm
Entrance Fee: charge (combination ticket valid for three days includes Palazzo Massimo alle Terme, the Baths of Diocletian and Crypta Balbi)
Transport: 70, 81, 87,116T, 186, 492, 628

Just north of Piazza Navona, Palazzo Altemps is one of the four sites of the Museo Nazionale Romano that holds the state collection of ancient treasures; the rest of the collection is split between Palazzo Massimo alle Terme, the Terme di Diocleziano, and the Crypta Balbi.

Full of tranquil rooms set around a central courtyard, this airy museum contains many treasures of classical

statuary and art, most of which come from the priceless collection amassed by Cardinal Ludovisi. The prize exhibit is the Ludovisi Throne, a decorative Greek sculpture, thought to date from the 5th century BC, which Mussolini sold to Hitler in 1938, and which is now believed to be one of a pair. Upstairs, the vaulting of the loggia is intricately painted with a vine-covered pergola full of winged putto, flowers, fruits and exotic birds, inspired by the flora and fauna imported by the explorers of the New World. It is lined with busts of the 12 Caesars.

Other masterpieces here include an incredibly well-preserved carved sarcophagus from the 3rd century and the moving *Galata Suicide*, said to have been commissioned by Julius Caesar, purchased by the cardinal at the same time as the Dying Gaul, now in the Capitoline Museum (see page 91).

The palazzo also contains many frescoes and bas-reliefs, a private

chapel and parts of the ancient Roman houses on which its foundations can be seen.

East of Piazza Navona, on the parallel Corso del Rinascimento, is the **Palazzo della Sapienza**, which housed the headquarters of Rome's oldest university, La Sapienza, until it moved to the Stazione Termini area in 1935. It is now home of the State Archives (www.archiviodistatoroma.beniculturali.it). In the square is Borromini's **Sant'Ivo ⑩** (Sun 9am–noon, closed Jul–Aug), a Roman Baroque church with a striking, white, spiralling bell tower and unusual facade. On the main altar is a 1661 canvas by da Cortona showing St Ivo and other saints surrounded by angels.

Piazza di Pasquino

Off the southern end of Piazza Navona is **Piazza di Pasquino ⑪**. The mutilated marble torso leaning against the wall is thought to date from the 3rd century BC. It was found in Piazza Navona and brought here in the 15th century when it became one of Rome's "talking statues".

TIP

For nearly a century, La Mostra dell'Antiquariato, a twice-yearly antiques market, has been held on Via dei Coronari. Every May and October dealers literally roll out the red carpet along the street and stay open for late-night shopping, while torches and candles light the way.

The Galleria Doria Pamphilj.

St Matthew and the Angel by Caravaggio.

SHOPPING

Old bottegas, small boutiques and vintage shops define the shopping character of this area. Via del Governo Vecchio and Via dei Coronari are Rome's best destinations for antique lovers. Via del Governo Vecchio is also known for its vintage shops. The tangle of roads around the Pantheon is packed with small shops selling luxurious souvenirs, such as high-quality stationery and all-Italian perfumes, as well as clothes by lesser-known designers.

Accessories

Borsalino
72a Via di Campo Marzio
06-678 3945
www.borsalino.com
For a classic Italian hat, there is no competition. This time-honoured hat maker is the only place to go.

Clothing

Davide Cenci
1/7 Via Campo Marzio

Silk ties for sale.

06-699 0681
www.davidecenci.com
Designer suits, shoes, and any type of accessories by the most elegant Italian and international labels, for both women and men.

Jewellery

Massimo Maria Melis
57 Via dell'Orso
06-686 9188
www.massimomariamelis.com
Custom-made jewellery, inspired by Roman and Etruscan artefacts.

Shoes

Petrocchi
2 Vicolo Sugarelli 06-687 6289
www.calzoleriapetrocchi.it
Elegance, good taste and class are the secret of this shoemaker's success.
The shoes are hand-crafted from the finest leathers and designed in a variety of made-to-measure, ready-to-wear styles.

Tod's
53a Via del Codotti
06-699 1089
www.tods.it
Diego Della Valle's shoes, bags and leather accessories, sold here, have become cult luxury items in Italy and abroad.

Souvenirs

Cartoleria Pantheon
15 Via della Rotonda
06-687 5313
www.pantheon-roma.it
A well-stocked card store featuring hand-bound leather notebooks that make perfect gifts or souvenirs.

Ai Monasteri
72 Corso Rinascimento
06-6880 2783
http://aimonasteri.it
Sells teas, honeys, liqueurs, ointments and potions made by monks from all over Italy.

Il Papiro
5 Via del Pantheon
06-679 5597
www.ilpapirofirenze.it
A stationery store featuring Florentine stationery with the typical marbleized pattern, quill pens, and beautiful notebooks and albums.

Toys

Città del Sole
65 Via della Scrofa
06-6880 3805
www.cittadelsole.it
A store for progressive parents and their progeny, crammed with the best educational toys, games and books from the world over.

Al Sogno
53 Piazza Navona
06-686 4198
www.alsogno.com
Historic toy store specialising in all kinds of toys, from wooden trains to giant teddy bears, that are sure to drive any toddler crazy.

The statue leans against a wall of the **Palazzo Braschi**, one of the last papal palaces built in Rome, in the 18th century. The palazzo is home to the Museo di Roma.

Museo di Roma ⑫

Address: 10 Piazza San Pantaleo; www.museodiroma.it
Telephone: 06-0608
Opening Hours: Tue–Sun 10am–7pm
Entrance Fee: charge
Transport: as for Palazzo Altemps

The Palazzo Braschi was built by Cosimo Morelli in the closing years of the 18th century as a papal residence for Pius VI (the chapel and staircase are by Valadier). It houses a sizeable collection of art and artefacts that document the daily life of Roman nobility from medieval times to the beginning of the 20th century.

Part of the collection is housed in the Museo di Roma in Trastevere,

and the rest is shown in rotation. Most interesting among the paintings, which are of more historic than artistic value, is the series illustrating Roman festivities and processions.

Palazzo Massimo alle Colonne, next door to the Braschi, was designed in 1536 by Baldassare Peruzzi for the Massimo family, who occupy it to this day (open 16 Mar 7am–1pm). The building is screened by a fine curved portico of Doric columns visible from the Via del Paradiso. Behind the palace, in Piazza de' Massimi, is an ancient column that may have come from the remains of Domitian's stadium.

AROUND CORSO VITTORIO EMANUELE II

Towards the Tiber end of the Corso Vittorio Emanuele II stands the 16th-century **Chiesa Nuova** ⑬ (www.vallicella.org), built for San Filippo Neri, founder of a great spiritual order. St Philip had wished the interior to be plain, but in the centuries after his death his disciples commissioned da Cortona to paint the magnificent frescoes that

KIDS

Housed inside Bramante's gorgeous cloister of Santa Maria della Pace, the bistrot of the Chiostro del Bramante exhibition space (5 Arco della Pace) is a pleasant getaway for an afternoon tea, and serves delicious cakes. It is also one of the very few openly child-friendly spots in Rome, with a changing table – a rare find in the city.

Inside Santa Maria della Pace.

The traffic-free Ponte Sant'Angelo is Rome's loveliest bridge.

TIP

From December until early January, Piazza Navona hosts a colourful Christmas fair at which all sorts of decorations, toys, sweets and Baroque-style Nativity scenes are sold. It lasts until the Epiphany (6 January), when friendly old ladies on broomsticks *(befane)* hand candy to well-behaved children.

The much-quieter backstreets.

Street artist entertaining the crowd in Piazza Navone.

decorate the vault, apse and dome. Among the church's other treasures are three altarpieces by Rubens.

Next to the church is the **Oratorio dei Filippini**, built by Borromini between 1637 and 1662 as a place of worship for St Philip Neri's fraternity. St Philip was a strong believer in the spiritual benefit of music and instituted the musical gatherings that later became known as oratorios. The building now houses the Capitoline Historical Archives (www.archivio capitolino.it) and the Vallicelliana Library (www.vallicelliana.it). Its facade was inspired by "the human body with open arms so as to embrace everyone who enters".

In **Piazza della Chiesa Nuova** is a 17th-century fountain that came from the Campo de' Fiori. On the rim of its basin is the inscription: *Ama Dio e non fallire – Fa del bene e lascia dire* (Love God and don't fail – Do good and make sure people talk about it).

The nearby **Palazzo del Governo Vecchio** was the residence of the governor of Rome from 1624 until the mid-18th century.

The embankment

A little further west along Corso Vittorio Emanuele II is the Palazzo del Banco di Santo Spirito. Its facade (1520s) is by Antonio da Sangallo the Younger. From here, Via Banco di Santo Spirito leads to the lovely **Ponte Sant'Angelo** ⑭.

At the southern end of the next bridge upriver, Ponte Umberto I, is the **Museo Napoleonico** ⑮ (www. museonapoleonico.it; Tue–Sun 10am–6pm; free). Among the Bonaparte family memorabilia is a cast of the right breast of Napoleon's sister, Pauline, made by Canova in 1805, when he started work on *Venus Victrix*, now in the Galleria Borghese.

The nearby **Via dell'Orso** used to be lined with inns and was a favourite haunt of courtesans. Today, the area is better-known for its antique shops, interspersed with classy boutiques selling modern designer furniture. The **Via dei Coronari** ⑯ is packed with some of the best antiques and fine-arts shops in Rome.

Talking Statues

Rome's "talking statues" were the mouthpieces of discontent in the city during the Renaissance, serving as an outlet for a form of anonymous political expression.

Rome's "talking statues" are a tradition born in the 1500s, when the citizens were governed directly by the Papacy. To avoid punishment they would secretly hang their caustic criticism on a statue. This political dissidence often took place at night, the Romani enjoying a good laugh in the morning before the insults were removed by the authorities. The statues soon earned nicknames, the best-known being the Pasquino. This torso of a male figure, possibly from the 3rd century BC, is in such poor condition that it is hard to know who, or what, it represents. The roots of his nickname are recounted in a Roman legend saying he was "discovered" near a barber's shop or inn run by a Signor Pasquino.

The Pope vs. Pasquino

The best-known "pasquinata" barb is a pun against Pope Urban VIII. This Pope from the Barberini family commanded Bernini to strip the ancient Roman bronze parts of the Pantheon to make the great baldacchino canopy for St Peter's altar. *"Quod non fecerunt barbari, fecerunt Barberini"* ("What the barbarians didn't do, the Barberini did") quipped Pasquino. This statuesque satire became so fervent that Pope Adrianus VI (1522–23) wanted Pasquino cast into the Tiber. The risk of ridicule for punishing a lump of stone saved the statue from the river bed – but severe laws were issued to stop the practice, and Pasquino was put under surveillance.

Marforio is known as Pasquino's friend. He and Pasquino were a bantering double act: one posing questions about politics and popes, the other retorting ironically. Marforio's statue – a reclining river god – is now in the Capitoline Museum.

The Facchino (Porter) is a small fountain on Via Lata (just off the Via del Corso). Dressed in a typical porter's costume, nobody knows who made the statue – though it was once, wrongly, attributed to Michelangelo.

Madama Lucrezia sits on the corner of Piazza San Marco (next to Piazza Venezia). This marble is probably associated with the goddess Isis. Her nickname derives from a 15th-century Lucrezia who fell in love with the married king of Naples. Lucrezia came to Rome to ask the Pope to let the king divorce, but permission was denied.

The statue of the Babuino (Baboon) gives the Via del Babuino its name. His wicked grin and his grubby brown torso make him one of the best-known of the talking statues – which became known collectively as *il Congresso degli Arguti* (the Shrewd Congress).

The marble torse on Piazza Pasquino is still festooned with comments on the events of the day.

RESTAURANTS, BARS AND CAFÉS

PRICE CATEGORIES

Price includes dinner and a half-
bottle of house wine.
€€€€ = more than €60
€€€ = €40–60
€€ = €25–40
€ = under €25.

Restaurants

Da Baffetto
18 Piazza del Teatro di Pompeo
06-6821 0807
www.pizzeriabaffetto.it
D Sun–Mon, L Sat–Sun
€ [p324, B2]
One of the city's legendary pizzerias.
Not the best pizza in town, but
almost, its typically thin base always
on the right side of crusty. Be prepared to queue or book early. No
frills, no tablecloths, no credit cards.

Casa Bleve
48 Via del Teatro Valle
06-686 5970
www.casableve.comL & D Mon–Sat
€€ [p324, B2]
Set against the stunning backdrop
of the restored Palazzo Medici

Osteria dell'Ingegno.

Lante della Rovere. An enormous
semicircular counter is laden with
all kinds of cold meats, salads and
cheeses. With an exceptional wine
list, this is a high-level *enoteca*
worth seeking out. Closed three
weeks Aug.

Clemente alla Maddalena
4 Piazza della Maddalena
06-683 3633
www.clementeallamaddalena.it
L & D daily
€€€ [p324, C2]
The owner prides himself on the
freshness of the ingredients, and
the menu changes according to
the season, with fresh fish,
selected meat cuts, and porcini
mushrooms in autumn. The setting
is charming and elegant, and
there's a pleasant terrace for the
summer. Closed two weeks in Aug
and three weeks in Jan.

Il Convivio Troiani
28 Vicolo dei Soldati
06-686 9432
www.ilconviviotroiani.com
D only Mon–Sat, L by request for groups of
8 and over
€€€€ [p324, B1]
Run by three brothers, Il Convivio is
one of the city's foremost gastronomic temples. Equal emphasis is
placed on vegetable, fish and meat
options, but they are always combined with something unexpected.
Three elegant rooms and well-
trained staff make for a truly
rounded gourmet experience.

Cul de Sac
73 Piazza di Pasquino
06-6880 1094
www.enotecaculdesac.com
L & D daily
€€ [p324, B2]
One of the best-stocked wine bars
in Rome. Space may be tight, but
the atmosphere, prices and array of
cheeses, cold meats, Middle East-
ern-influenced snacks, hearty
soups and salads all hit the right
spot. It gets packed, so be prepared
to queue as bookings aren't taken.

Al Duello
11a Via della Vaccarella
06-687 3348
L & D Mon–Sat
€€ [p324, B1/2]
Named after the famous duel, in
which Caravaggio killed his friend
Ranuccio, this welcoming trattoria
commemorates the painter's
wrongdoings. Try typical Roman
dishes, including the artichokes
that caused Caravaggio's fight with
a waiter. Service is attentive and
friendly, the food is good and the
wine selection sophisticated.

Enoteca al Parlamento Achilli
15 Via dei Prefetti
06-687 3446
www.enotecaparlamento.com
L & D daily
€€€ [p324, C1]
Located right in front of the Italian
Parliament building, this small restaurant is a favourite among politicians and journalists. The menu is
varied and seasonal and follows
the main rules of Roman cuisine –
with some imaginative detours.
Fabulous wines.

Il Fico
49 Via di Monte Giordano
06-687 5568
www.ilfico.com
L & D daily
€€ [p324, A2]
This friendly eatery is very reasonably priced for its location, a stone's
throw from Piazza Navona. All
dishes are made with fresh seasonal ingredients. Try the pasta
with mussels, pecorino cheese
and cherry tomatoes.

Fortunato al Pantheon
55 Via del Pantheon
06-679 2788
www.ristorantefortunato.it
L & D daily
€€–€€€ [p324, C2]
A place for those who don't want to
take risks but want to eat well and
be served quickly and efficiently.
Simple classical dishes, such as
spinach and ricotta ravioli cooked

with butter and sage, grilled squid or veal served with rocket.

Maccheroni
44 Piazza delle Coppelle
06-6830 7895
www.ristorantemaccheroni.com
L & D daily
€€ [p324, B1/2]
A lively trattoria with several rooms and some outdoor tables. It attracts a youngish clientele drawn by fair prices and typical, competent cuisine.

O' Pazzariello
19 Via Banco di Santo Spirito
06-6819 2641
L & D Tue–Sun
€ [p324, A2]
With an exhibitionist pizza chef and *simpatico* waiters, this is a sure bet for a fun and affordable evening. The pizzas are thick-crusted and range from small to gigantic.

Osteria dell'Ingegno
45 Piazza di Pietra
06-678 0662
http://osteriaingegno.it
L & D Tue–Sun
€€ [p324, C2]
Much frequented by politicians due to its location near parliament, this modern *osteria* specialises in light, inventive dishes. The sweets are home-made and the wines well chosen.

L'Osteria di Memmo
22-23 Via dei Soldati
06-6813 5277
www.osteriademenmo.it
L & D Mon–Sat
€€–€€€ [p324, B1]
In an old *palazzo*, three elegant rooms have been made over in modern minimalist style. The menu is creative, though first courses are a bit hit and miss. However, the main courses, desserts and wines compensate for any shortcomings.

La Rosetta
8 Via della Rosetta
06-686 1002
www.larosetta.com
L & D Mon–Sat, D only Sun
€€€€ [p324, C2]
One of the best seafood restaurants in Rome, where the produce

is guaranteed to have been caught that morning and prepared by an experienced chef. Unless you go for the "working lunch" or a set-price *degustazione* (tasting) menu, your bill is likely to tip the €100-a-head mark for a full meal. A cheaper option is its Oyster Bar.

Terra di Siena
77–78 Piazza Pasquino
06-6830 7704
www.ristoranteterradisiena.com
L & D Mon–Sat
€€ [p324, B2]
Carnivores flock to this family-run restaurant, with dishes including succulent beef tagliata and the famed Fiorentina steak. The menu is 100 percent Tuscan, and portions are generous. A wide variety of Chianti wines.

Tre Archi da Loreto
233 Via dei Coronari
06-687 5890
L & D Mon–Sat
€ [p324, A2]
Situated right in the heart of Rome's nightlife hub, this popular trattoria gets pretty busy on weekends. The two rooms are small and loud, and the food is traditional Roman, with lots of primi and meat dishes. The portions are generous, and the prices more than fair considering the area. Book ahead.

Vecchia Locanda
2 Vicolo Sinibaldi
06-6880 2831
www.vecchialocanda.eu
D only Mon–Sat
€€ [p324, C3]
In a pedestrianised alleyway, this rustic restaurant offers decent if a little unadventurous food. A nice touch is that you can choose which home-made pasta to go with which home-made sauce.

Bars and Cafés

Caffè Novecento
12 Via del Governo Vecchio
06-686 5242
www.caffenovecento.it
[p324, B2]
For a genteel snack lunch or tea with home-made cake, head to this delightful café, not far from

Piazza Navona.

Caffè Sant'Eustachio
82 Piazza Sant'Eustachio
06-6880 2048
www.santeustachioilcaffe.it
[p324, C2]
The recipe for success at this celebrated espresso bar seems to lie in the water, coming from a 2,000-year-old aqueduct, and in the wood-roasted Sant'Eustachio coffee blend.

La Caffettiera
65 Piazza di Pietra
[p324, C2]
A smart café where you can enjoy Neapolitan goodies or relax with a cappuccino after a busy day's sightseeing.

Giolitti
40 Via Uffici del Vicario
06-699 1243
[p324, C2]
www.giolitti.it
This famous ice-cream place has been scooping dozens of flavours since 1900, and has an olde-worlde dining room inside.

Grom
30a Via della Maddalena
www.grom.it
[p324, C1]
Artisanal organic *gelato* made with top-quality local ingredients but produced in industrial quantities. The cups and spoons are environment-friendly, and the ice cream so special that people usually line up a second time after their first cone.

Chiostro del Bramante Cafe Bistrot
5 Via Arco della Pace
06-06 6880 9035
http://chiostrodelbramante.it
[p324, B2]
Cheerful place in a tranquil setting of the Bramante's Cloister with surprisingly modern decor. Teas, coffees, cakes and light lunches. Good value.

Tazza D'Oro
84 Via degli Orfani
[p324, C2]
06-6789792
www.tazzadorocoffeeshop.com
This small bar serves some of the tastiest coffee in town. Standing room only.

Nuns at Campo de' Fiori produce market.

CAMPO DE' FIORI AND THE GHETTO

People have lived and worked in this picturesque part of Rome since the Middle Ages. The tangle of cobbled streets and alleys lead to the vibrant Campo de' Fiori market square and beyond into Europe's longest-surviving Jewish community.

The southern part of Rome's Centro Storico is a triangle of tightly packed streets between the Corso Vittorio Emanuele II, Via Arenula and the river, with the lively little market square of Campo de' Fiori at its hub. In ancient times this area was part of the Field of Mars (Campus Martius), a main training ground for the Roman army, until Julius Caesar's reign when the moneyed citizens of Imperial Rome moved in and built great complexes and theatres. By the Middle Ages, the area was a warren of small, dark, narrow streets, with the eastern side occupied by the Ghetto, lively now but a poignant reminder of the Jewish community's suffering.

In 1880, the rulers of a newly unified Italy set about putting their mark on the city and built the Corso Vittorio over the ancient tract of Via Trionfale and the winding, medieval Via Papale, destroying beautifully proportioned Renaissance squares and buildings in the process.

The resulting avenue had none of the grandeur that was intended, and today it's a traffic-choked thoroughfare that disrupts the beauty and harmony of the medieval streets around it.

Jewish quarter.

AROUND CORSO VITTORIO EMANUELE II

Set off down the Corso from the Ponte Vittorio Emanuele and then turn right into **Via dei Banchi Vecchi**. At No. 22 is the fanciful facade of **Palazzo dei Pupazzi**, built in 1504 and decorated with elaborate stucco designs by Mazzoni. This street leads to Via del Pellegrino, which winds past artisans' workshops, bookshops and antique dealers to **Palazzo della Cancelleria** ⑰, a splendid Renaissance palace built

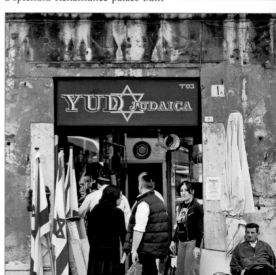

WHERE

The small crumbling archway you will find on your right when walking down Via del Pellegrino to Campo de'Fiori leads to the Arco degli Acetari, a charming medieval piazzetta, hardly known to tourists and even some Romans. The postcard-perfect buildings and the piazzetta's warm colours have the feel of some quiet, sleepy Italian village.

Fresh produce at Campo de' Fiori.

Novelty t-shirts can all be bought at Campo de' Fiori.

between 1485 and 1527. The architect is unknown but the beautiful courtyard is attributed to Bramante, who also modified the adjoining 4th-century basilica of **San Lorenzo in Damaso**. Bramante had a reputation for destroying medieval monuments (the ancient St Peter's basilica is a prime example), which earned him the nickname *Maestro Ruinante* (Master Ruiner).

The palace was built for Cardinal Raffaele Riario, who is said to have financed it from the proceeds of one night's gambling, before being confiscated by the Pope and used as the Apostolic Chancery. The Sala Riaria and the Salone dei Cento Giorni (the only two rooms of the palace that can be seen, Tue pm and Sat am), along with the Salviati chapel (Mon and Thu pm), can be visited by appointment only a month in advance (tel: 06-6989 3405).

Campo de' Fiori ⓲

South of the Cancelleria is the lively **Campo de' Fiori** (Field of Flowers), so named because it used to be a meadow that sloped down towards the Tiber. It has been the site of a produce market for centuries and was one of the liveliest areas of medieval and Renaissance Rome, when

cardinals and pilgrims would rub shoulders with fishmongers, vegetable-sellers and prostitutes.

The Campo de' Fiori is the most secular of Roman squares, for although it is as old as Rome itself, it has never been dedicated to any cult and to this day is free of churches. Its present aspect dates from the end of the 15th century, when the whole area was reshaped. It was surrounded by inns for pilgrims and travellers (there are still plenty of hotels in the area if you don't mind the noise). During the Renaissance, some of these hotels were the homes of successful courtesans, Vannozza Catanei, mistress of the Borgia Pope Alexander VI, among them. On the corner of the square and Via del Pellegrino you can see her shield, which she had decorated with her own coat of arms and those of her husband and lover.

Today, the Campo flourishes, thanks to a perfectly balanced infrastructure. It has everything from a butcher's and a baker's shop to clothes boutiques, a cinema and a bustling morning food market.

At night, the Campo plays host to hundreds of Romans and visitors who frequent the bars and restaurants or simply hang out under the statue of Bruno, sipping beers until late into the night. Then the Campo has only a few hours to breathe before the market traders arrive to set up their stalls at the crack of dawn.

The streets around Campo de' Fiori still retain the names of trades originally practised in them. Via dei Baullari, the luggage-makers, leads to Piazza Farnese; Via dei Giubbonari, named after the sellers and makers of *gipponi* or bodices, is still lined with clothes shops, which are among some of the cheapest in town.

Museo di Scultura Antica Giovanni Barracco ⑲

Address: 166 Corso Vittorio Emanuele; www.museobarracco.it
Telephone: 06-0608
Opening Hours: June–Sept Tue–Sun 1–7pm, Oct–May 10am–4pm
Entrance Fee: free
Transport: 40, 46, 62, 64, 70, 81, 87, 116, 190, 492, 628, 916

FACT

With its reputation for being a carnal, pagan place, the Campo de' Fiori was a natural spot to hold executions. Of all the unfortunate victims, Giordano Bruno was the most important figure to be burnt at the stake here, in 1600. A priest and philosopher, he was found guilty of freethinking, claiming that the earth was not the centre of the universe but revolved round the sun, a belief which cost him his life.

Visit Roscioli Alimentari for gourmet food.

TIP

Via dei Cappellari just off Campo de'Fiori, was where the hat-makers once congregated, but is now full of furniture restorers, gilders and carpenters practising their trade on the street.

Turning back up Via dei Baullari to Corso Vittorio, you reach **Palazzo Piccola Farnesina** in Piazza San Pantaleo. Built for a French prelate, Thomas Leroy, in 1523 and decorated with fleurs-de-lis, this elegant Renaissance palace is now home to the Museo Barracco, a prestigious collection of antique sculpture. Artworks include Assyrian bas-reliefs, Attic vases, rare examples of Cypriot art and exceptional Phoenician, Etruscan and Roman pieces. It's easy to see why Giovanni Barracco, who spent his life collecting these masterpieces, called ancient sculpture "the mother of all the arts".

Further along Corso Vittorio, the magnificent church of **Sant'Andrea della Valle** ⓴ (daily 7.30am–12.30pm, 4.30–7.30pm) has the second-largest dome in Rome after St Peter's. Its design is largely by Maderno, with frescoes by Lanfranco and Domenichino. The church is the setting for Act I of Puccini's much-loved opera, *Tosca*.

The church stands over some of the remains of the **Teatro di Pompeo**, a huge complex that spread from Campo de' Fiori to the temples at Largo Argentina. It was built in 55 BC as part of a plan to introduce some culture to Rome, but the Romans preferred the blood-and-guts entertainment of gladiators, fake battles and animal fights. You can ask one of the priests to take you downstairs for a look.

Next to the theatre was the **Curia Pompeia** where Julius Caesar was stabbed to death on the Ides of March (15 March), 44 BC. Remains of the theatre have been discovered in the cellars of the surrounding houses, and are visible at the Da Pancrazio (92 Piazza del Biscione; www.dapancrazio.it) and Costanza Hostaria (65 Piazza del Paradiso; www.hostariacostanza.it) restaurants, and in the breakfast room of Hotel Teatro di Pompeo (www.hotelteatrodipompeo.it), for those in the mood to eat or sleep amid famous ruins.

Largo di Torre Argentina

Next stop on Corso Vittorio is Largo di Torre Argentina, one of the busiest crossroads in the city and a major bus interchange. Its architecture

The evocative Crypta Balbi.

– *palazzi*, banks and insurance companies – isn't very exciting. Only Teatro Argentina, a state-funded theatre and official home of the Teatro di Roma (www.teatrodiroma.net), radiates any atmosphere.

The real attractions lie in the middle of the square, several metres underground. During attempts to improve the road system in the 1920s, archaeologists excavated four temples (street levels in ancient times were some 10 metres/30ft below today's level). The **Area Sacra** ㉑ (www.sovraintendenzaroma.it; closed for restoration) dates from Republican times, around the 3rd and 4th centuries BC. It is not known to which gods the temples were consecrated, so they are known simply as temples A, B, C and D. Some of the remains, inhabited by Rome's many stray cats, can be seen from above.

East of the square is the church of the **Gesù** ㉒ (www.chiesadelgesu.org; daily 7am–12.30pm, 4–7.45pm), more properly called Santissimo Nome di Gesù. Built between 1568 and 1584 with funds provided by the powerful Cardinal Alessandro Farnese, it was Rome's first Jesuit church. The flamboyance of its design and decoration look forward to the Baroque churches of the next

Flowers for sale at Campo de' Fiori.

Two of Rome's many stray cats.

ROME'S CAT WOMEN

Rome's stray cat population numbers in the hundreds of thousands. Originally said to have boarded Rome-bound ships from Egypt, the felines found their home amid the ancient monuments. Since the 1929 excavation of the **Area Sacra** of Torre Argentina, stray cats have been taking refuge in the protected archaeological area. As their numbers grew, volunteer cat caretakers, referred to as gattare (cat women), fed and cared for the cats until an official sanctuary was established in 1993. The organisation receives donations and support from all over the world, and has even established a cat adoption agency. Largo di Torre Argentina;www.romancats.com; tel: 06-6880 5611.

The Area Sacra is beloved by stray cats.

century. The founder of the Jesuit order, St Ignatius Loyola, is buried in the opulent Cappella di Sant'Ignazio di Loyola, built by Andrea del Pozzo in 1696. Above the chapel's altar is a statue of the saint, framed by gilded lapis lazuli columns. Loyola's living quarters, in the Casa Professa del Gesù, can be visited Mon–Sat 4–6pm and Sun 10am–noon.

Crypta Balbi ㉓

Address: 31 Via delle Botteghe Oscure; http://archeoroma.beniculturali.it
Telephone: 06-678 0167
Opening Hours: Tue–Sun 9am–7.45pm
Entrance Fee: charge
Transport: 30, 40, 44, 46, 62, 63, 64, 70, 80, 87, 190, 492, 628, 780, 781, 810, 916, H, C3

Not far from the Gesù church is the Crypta Balbi, one of the four homes of the Museo Nazionale Romano collection (see page 158). This huge courtyard, originally annexed to a theatre built for Augustus at the end of the 1st century AD, was excavated in 1981 and forms the basis for the fascinating Crypta Balbi Museum.

Snapshot of the Jewish Ghetto.

It combines state-of-the-art technology with the preservation and interpretation of archaeological finds on the site itself, tracing the development of Roman society from antiquity to modern times. The ruins beneath the structure can be visited once an hour (on the hour) for short periods, and reveal the expansive lobby of the theatre, built by Cornelius Balbus, a friend of Augustus.

Piazza Mattei ㉔

Just south of here is the cosy little **Piazza Mattei**, with a funky bar, a couple of trendy boutiques and one of Rome's most delightful fountains as its centrepiece. The Fontana delle Tartarughe (Tortoise Fountain) was sculpted by Taddeo Landini in 1585 and depicts four youths gently pushing four tortoises towards the water above. The tiny bronze turtles were added later, possibly by Bernini.

JEWISH GHETTO

The Ghetto lies in the area between Largo Argentina, the river, Via Arenula and Teatro di Marcello. The first wave of Jewish settlers came

in the 2nd century BC, and thrived peacefully here until Titus' victory over Jerusalem in AD 70, after which their status changed from free men to slaves (the Colosseum workforce was largely made up of Jewish slaves).

In the centuries that followed, their fortunes and status fluctuated. In the Middle Ages the Jewish population enjoyed relative freedom, and were generally appreciated for their financial and medical skills. But then in 1555, Pope Paul IV's zero-tolerance policy culminated in a papal bull ordering the confinement of the Jewish population into an enclosed area around the Portico d'Ottavia, which became known from then on as the Ghetto. The area was surrounded by high walls with doors that were locked from the outside at night.

The walls of the Ghetto were destroyed in the revolutionary year of 1848. When Rome fell to King Emmanuel II's troops in 1870, ending papal dominion over the city, the Jews were finally given the same rights as other Italian citizens. But persecution resumed with the outbreak of World War II, when the Fascist regime deported 1,024 Jews to Nazi concentration camps.

Today, the area retains its Jewish heritage, and the streets are dotted with kosher shops and restaurants.

The Synagogue ㉕

Address: Tempio Maggiore, Lungotevere Cenci; museum: www.museoebraico.roma.it
Telephone: 06-6840 0661
Opening Hours: June–Sept Sun–Thu 10am–5.15pm, Fri 10am–3.15pm, earlier closing rest of year; guided tours in English every hour
Entrance Fee: charge (includes guided tour)
Transport: 23, 30, 44, 51, 63, 81, 83, 85, 87, 118, 130, 160, 170, 280, 628, 715, 716, 780, 781, 810, H, C3,
The Synagogue, consecrated in 1904, was built to a great height to send a message to the Vatican across the Tiber. On 13 April 1986, Pope John Paul II and Rabbi Elio Toaff held a historic meeting here marking the first time that a bishop of Rome had prayed in a Jewish house of worship. Pope Benedict XVI repeated the event on 17 January 2010.

Sculpture in Museo Barracco.

In front of Portico d'Ottavia.

Borromini's statue in Palazzo Spada is a clever optical illusion.

Genteel Via Giulia.

Attached to the Synagogue (make sure you carry some form of ID, as security is strict) is the **Museum of Jewish Culture**. The museum recounts the story of Rome's Jewish population through art, relics and a documentary film. Six exhibition spaces contain treasures from the community, including Renaissance-era embroidery, stunning ritual items and original marble blocks from some of the *Cinque Scole*, Rome's five ancient synagogues.

Portico d'Ottavia ㉖

The church of **Sant'Angelo in Pescheria** (Wed and Sat 4–8.30pm, first Mon 3–6pm), where Jews were once forced to attend penitential services, was built on the ruins of the Portico d'Ottavia, originally the entrance to a colonnaded walkway erected in 147 BC by Augustus to display statues captured from Greece. It was dedicated to his sister, Octavia, the abandoned wife of Mark Antony. In the Middle Ages, the ruin was used as a covered fish market – above the arch of the portico, there is a Latin inscription demanding that all the fish exceeding the length marked have to be decapitated and their heads given to Conservatori (this was the preferred part for making fish soup).

Via del Portico d'Ottavia still has several medieval houses. At the end (No. 1) is **Casa di Lorenzo Manili** (not open to the public). Lorenzo Manili had this house built in 1468 and adorned it with a classical plaque. The Latin inscription dating the building employs the ancient Roman calendar that used the founding of Rome as its starting point. According to this, the year 1468 was 2221. Original Roman reliefs are embedded in the facades, as well as a fragment of an ancient sarcophagus.

TOWARDS PIAZZA FARNESE

A short distance west of here is the **Palazzo Cenci** ㉗, the family palace of the infamous Beatrice Cenci, who attracted sympathy for killing her brutal father, but was nevertheless condemned to death for witchcraft and murder, and beheaded on Ponte Sant'Angelo in 1599. Only parts of the original medieval building remain. The present facade and details are Baroque. Note the architectural quirk of an indented balcony on the front facing Via Arenula.

Crossing back over Via Arenula, Via degli Specchi leads to **Palazzo Monte di Pietà**, which was set up as a pawnshop in the 16th century. From here, turn left and then right into Via Capo di Ferro.

Palazzo Spada ㉘

Address: 13 Piazza Capo di Ferro; http://galleriaspada.beniculturali.it
Telephone: 06-2258 2493
Opening Hours: Sun–Mon 8.30am–7.30pm
Entrance Fee: charge
Transport: 8, 23, 63, 116, 280, 780, 810, H
The large building on your left, with the facade covered in stucco reliefs by

Mazzoni, is Palazzo Spada. The Spada family bought the palace in 1632 and Borromini restored it, adding the ingenious corridor to the courtyard. Borromini raised the floor and shortened the columns to create a false sense of perspective, making the corridor appear much longer than it actually is. At the end, a statue was placed against a painted garden backdrop. The statue is less than 1 metre (3ft) tall but from afar it seems to be life-size.

The *palazzo* is also home to the **Galleria Spada**, which has a fine collection of paintings, including work by masters Rubens, Domenichino, Guercino, Tintoretto, Reni and Artemisia, amongst others.

Piazza Farnese 29

The end of the street opens into Piazza Farnese, linked by a short street back to Campo de' Fiori. Its twin fountains incorporate two huge basins from the Baths of Caracalla. You'll want to linger in this picturesque square, and there's an inviting (if overpriced) bar where you can stop for refreshment.

The **Palazzo Farnese**, a masterpiece of High Renaissance architecture, was commissioned by Cardinal Alessandro Farnese in 1517. The palace cost so much that for a while even the Farnese finances were strained. The original designs were by da Sangallo, but Michelangelo took over the work. When he died, Vignola and della Porta finished it off. Annibale Carracci frescoed the main salon. In 1874 Palazzo Farnese became the French Embassy, and it is now open to the public (one hour visits at 3, 4 and 5pm Mon, Wed and Fri. Book at least a week in advance (www.inventer rome.com, ID required).

Via Giulia

Near the palace is Via Giulia, named after Pope Julius II who commissioned it as a monument to the Apostolic Church. When Bramante began work on it in 1508, the intention was to make it Rome's most important thoroughfare, connecting the Vatican with Ponte Sisto and the Ripa Grande harbour, and thus the centre of papal Rome. The centrepiece of the street was to be the Palazzo dei

EAT

The Ghetto is a great place to find that unique hybrid, Roman-Jewish food, and other non-Italian delicacies. If it's bagels, muffins and chocolate chip cookies you're after, head for La DolceRoma bakery, an Austrian-owned spot at 20b Via del Portico d'Ottavia (www.ladolce roma.com).

A guided tour on wheels in Piazza Farnese.

Tribunali, but the building failed to get beyond the foundations stage.

The street became a prestigious address, and many high-profile people lived in its sumptuous palaces, including Antonio da Sangallo, Raphael and Benvenuto Cellini. The parties in Via Giulia were among the best in Rome, and on one occasion wine gushed from the Mascherone Fountain for three full days.

All this is hard to believe now, as the street is quiet and lined with expensive antique shops and art galleries. The elegant arch crossing the street was designed by Michelangelo and was intended to connect Palazzo Farnese with the Villa Farnesina across the Tiber, but the bridge was never built.

Next to the arch stands the church of **Santa Maria dell'Orazione e Morte** (closed for renovation), which was redesigned by Ferdinand Fuga (1733). Fuga was a member of the Compagnia della Buona Morte, an association whose purpose was to give a decent burial to the poor. Grotesque and macabre arabesques of human bones – children's skulls,

Restaurant in the Jewish Ghetto.

Tiber Island on a sunny day in Rome.

collarbones, ribs – decorate the walls of the crypt (daily 4–6pm). The walls and the ceiling are covered with reliefs and mosaics.

Adjacent to the church is **Palazzo Falconieri** ㉚, which was modernised by Borromini for the Falcone family and is framed by two falcons' heads on female torsos. It is now the Hungarian Academy (www.roma.balassiintezet.hu), and occasionally opens for exhibitions and concerts.

Off Via Giulia, in Via Sant'Eligio, is the beautiful little 16th-century church of **Sant'Eligio degli Orefici** ㉛ (Mon–Fri 9.30am–1pm, call no 7), designed by Raphael, with a dome by Peruzzi.

Further along the street, past the derelict church of **San Filippo**, is the fortified building of the **Carceri Nuove** (New Prison), built in 1655 to replace the gruesome prisons of Tor di Nona and the nearby torture chambers of the Savella family, who until then were the papal gaolers.

Continuing past the Palazzo dei Tribunali, you come to several important Renaissance *palazzi*, including da Sangallo the Younger's palace at No. 66 and one of Raphael's houses at No. 85. The street ends with the church of **San Giovanni Battista dei Fiorentini** ㉜ (www.sangiovannideifiorentini.net; daily 7.25am–noon, 5–7pm; museum Mon–Sat 9.30am–noon; free), built in various stages by Sansovino, da Sangallo the Younger, della Porta and Maderno. The facade was added in the 18th century. Inside, there is a delightful sculpture of St John by the Sicilian Mino del Reame over the sacristy door, and an impressive apse altar by Borromini with a marble group, the *Baptism of Christ*, by Antonio Raggi. Both Borromini and Maderno are buried in the church.

TIBER ISLAND ㉝

The Isola Tiberina is a pretty island in the middle of the Tiber. It has long been associated with healing. Legend has it that in 293 BC the Romans asked the Greeks, and their god Aesculapius in particular, for help overcoming a plague. They were sent a ship full of snakes, whose venom was used to cure ailments. The plague was defeated and a temple to Aesculapius duly erected. The church of San Bartolomeo was built on the ruins of this temple in the 10th century. The island is also the site of the Fatebenefratelli (the "do-good-brothers") hospital founded in 1548.

The two bridges linking Isola Tiberina to the shore are among the oldest structures still in use in Rome. The **Ponte Fabricio** (leading to the north bank) was built in

The shop on the corner of Via del Portico d'Ottavia is a famous Jewish bakery specialising in a ricotta and black cherry torte. Ask for a slice of torta di ricotta e visciole. The tiny Forno del Ghetto is technically open Mon–Thu 8am–8pm, but the goodies are often gone by noon.

A riverboat plies its way down the Tiber.

RIVER BOAT TRIPS

Rome launched a tourist riverboat service on the Tiber in 2003. A fleet of steamboats, led by the flagship *Rea Silvia* started sailing between the Duca D'Aosta Bridge and Ponte Marconi in Trastevere. Today, the services available include hop-on hop-off trips with commentary (€18, daily every hour, 10am from Molo Sant'Angelo and 10.35am from Molo Tiberina), romantic evening cruises with dinner (€60, weekends) and aperitivo cruises (€40, weekends). For information and bookings, www.battellidiroma.it.

TIP

The best way to get a glimpse of the magnificent frescoed ceilings of Palazzo Farnese is to walk by just after sundown, while people are still inside, and lights are on. If you're en route to dinner in the area it's worth a look.

62 BC by the civil engineer Lucius Fabricius, and there's an inscription to prove it. The **Ponte Cestio** was built in 42 BC by Lucius Cestius and restored in AD 370. The central arch is all that remains from that date; the rest is a late 19th-century reconstruction. This bridge leads into the heart of Trastevere.

Off the eastern end of the island are the remains of Rome's first stone bridge (142 BC), known as the **Ponte Rotto** (Broken Bridge). Most of what remains is from a 1575 reconstruction by Gregory XIII, the rest of which was washed away in 1598. The modern bridge behind it, **Ponte Palatino**, is sometimes called the English Bridge, because it is one of the very few stretches of road in Rome where cars are driven on the left.

Michelangelo's arch, part of an uncompleted bridge on Via Giulia.

Santa Maria in Cosmedin

Address: 18 Piazza Bocca della Verità

SHOPPING

Via dei Giubbonari and the surrounding streets are lined with small shops for the young and youthful, while the Ghetto is the place to go for kitchenware and, of course, Judaica objects.

Books

Libreria del Viaggiatore
78 Via del Pellegrino
06-6880 1048
This miniature shop is packed to the brim with guidebooks, travel literature and maps.

Clothing

Ethic
11 Piazza B. Cairoli (end of Via dei Giubbonari)
06-6880 6035
www.ethic.com
A women's casual wear chain that mixes styles, genres and fabrics with a penchant for the ethnic or

unusual. Great looking, well priced pieces.
Momento
9 Piazza Cairoli (end of Via dei Giubbonari)
06-6880 8157
www.momento-shop.it
Choose from flowing boho dresses and enough shoes and bags to fill a million closets.

Crafts

Cartoleria Sec
85 Via Arenula
06-6880 1457
Pens and notebooks, art supplies and cards, as well as selected gifts, have been filling the shelves of this two-level stationery shop for over a century.

Home

Spazio Sette
7 Via dei Barbieri
06-686 9747

www.spaziosette.comChoose from gorgeous Venini glass objects, sleek Flos lamps, Kartell chairs and a wealth of kitchen utensils at one of Rome's premier furniture and home furnishings stores, specializing in Italian design.
Tè e Teiere
37 via dei Banchi Nuovi
06-686 8824
www.teeteiere.com
A tea-lover's haven in a coffee-oriented city, with expert staff to boot.

Shoes

Nuyorica
36–37 Piazza Pollarola
06-6889 1243
This boutique is also a shoe-lover's dream, and includes selections by Marni, Balenciaga, Rodolphe Menudier and Sigerson Morrison. Very hip, but pretty pricey.

Telephone: 06-678 7759
Opening Hours: daily 9.30am–5pm
(6pm in summer)
Entrance Fee: free
Transport: 23, 30, 44, 51, 81, 83, 85,
87, 118, 160, 170, 280, 628, 715,
716, 781, 810, C3

Back on the mainland, east of the
bridge, is the **Piazza della Bocca
della Verità**, once the site of the
Forum Boarium, the cattle market of Ancient Rome. The square
is named after the Bocca della
Verità, which is in the portico
of the church of Santa Maria in
Cosmedin. First built in the 6th century, with additions made throughout the centuries, the church is a
lovely mixture of early Christian,
medieval and Romanesque design.
The floors were replaced with stunning Cosmati pavements, and a bell
tower was erected in the 12th century. You'll find a Roman bathtub
on the altar, used for baptisms, and
an 8th-century mosaic in the sacristy. The name Cosmedin is Greek
(it means "splendid decoration"),
and Rome's oldest Greek Christian
community has been worshipping
here since the 700s.

Temples of Hercules and Portunus

In the piazza are two well-preserved
Republican-era temples. The round
one was restored and determined
by archaeologists to be the oldest
marble structure in the city, built in
the 1st century BC to Hercules. The
nearby square temple is dedicated to
Portunus, the god of harbours, which
makes good sense considering the
vicinity of the Tiber.

Theatre of Marcellus ㉟

What looks like a smaller version
of the Colosseum attached to a
Renaissance *palazzo* is in fact the
remains of the Teatro di Marcello.
The once-glorious performance
space was completed under the reign
of Emperor Augustus, who named it
after his nephew Marcellus. In its heyday, the 20,000-seat theatre flaunted
three tiers, each supported with a different style of column, from the basic
Doric to the extravagant Corinthian,
and the top level, which has collapsed, was adorned with decorative
theatre masks. In summer, the Teatro
Marcello area becomes the stage for
a number of classical music concerts.

TIP

If you're not too
squeamish, pay a visit to
the Criminology Museum
(29 Via del Gonfalone;
tel: 06-6889 9442; Tue–
Sat 9am–1pm, Tue and
Thu also 2.30–6.30pm;
www.museocriminologico.it).
It displays articles
relating to some of Italy's
most sensational crimes,
the clues and evidence
used to incriminate the
culprits, and the
gruesome instruments
used to extract
confessions and punish
the guilty.

*Santa Maria in
Cosmedin.*

RESTAURANTS, BARS AND CAFÉS

PRICE CATEGORIES

Price includes dinner and a half-bottle of house wine.

€€€€ = more than €60
€€€ = €40–60
€€ = €25–40
€ = under €25.

Restaurants

Antica Trattoria Polese
40 Piazza Sforza Cesarini
06-686 1709
www.trattoriapolese.com
L & D Wed–Mon
€€ [p324, A2]
Less packed than its rowdier neighbour Da Luigi, Polese has the better outdoor seating in a small piazza off Corso Vittorio, and a more refined Roman menu based on what is available at the market that morning. In the evening, pizza is also on the menu.

Ba'Ghetto
57 Via del Portico d'Ottavia
06-6889 2868
www.kosherinrome.it
L & D Mon–Thu, L only Fri, D only Sat
€€€€ [[p324, C4]
The Jewish, Libyan and Roman specialities are all strictly kosher. Try the fried *carciofi alla giudia* artichokes and ask the staff to decipher the complicated Arabic dish names on the menu.

La Casa Bleve
48 Via del Teatro Valle
06-686 5970
www.casableve.com
L & D Mon–Sat
€€ [p324, C3/4]
A quintessentially Roman *enoteca* (wine bar) whose buffet is loaded with dozens of delicacies such as smoked swordfish, salmon rolls, *sformati* (flans) and cod carpaccio. Locals come here for the good food, well-chosen wine list and the *simpatia* of its husband-and-wife owners, Tina and Anacleto. .

Ditirambo
74 Piazza della Cancelleria

06-687 1626
www.ristoranteditirambo.it
L & D Tue–Sun, D only Mon
€€ [p324, B3]
The atmosphere is busy but convivial. The varied menu includes numerous and unusually creative vegetarian options, such as ricotta flan with raw artichokes and a pomegranate vinaigrette, and wholemeal pasta with red onions and pecorino cheese. There are many good cuts of meat and plentiful fish dishes. The desserts are home-made, fresh and heavenly; the wine list is extensive and the waiters happy to tell you all about it.

Ar Galletto
104 Piazza Farnese
06-686 1714
www.ristoranteargallettoroma.com
L & D daily
€–€€ [p324, B3]
A simple trattoria with Roman classics such as *spaghetti alla carbonara*, *abbacchio* (lamb) and *involtini* (meat rolls). The view of Michelangelo's Palazzo Farnese and Bernini's two fountains is unforgettable.

Da Giggetto al Portico d'Ottavia
21/22 Via del Portico D'Ottavia
06-686 1105
www.giggetto.it
L & D Tue–Sun
€€ [p324, C4]
It may be very popular with tourists, but don't let that put you off. The standards are reliably high as they take their Roman-Jewish cooking very seriously here, and the service is equally efficient and pleasantly old-fashioned. Try one of five menus, all of which usually include *carciofi alla giudia* (deep-fried whole artichokes), stuffed courgette flowers or salted cod filets.

Da Luigi
23–24 Piazza Sforza Cesarini
06-686 5946
www.trattoriadaluigi.com
L & D Tue–Sun

€€ [p324, A2]
Traditional Roman fare at this always-packed venue on a small square off Corso Vittorio Emanuele. There's a pleasant breeze and a convivial atmosphere amongst the outdoor seating on the square.

Nonna Betta
16 Via Portico d'Ottavia
Tel 06-6880 6263
www.nonnabetta.it
L & D Sun–Thu, L only Fri, D only Sat
€–€€ [p324, C4]
The name means "Grandma Betta", as the recipes at this restaurant have been handed down through the generations. The cuisine is traditional Roman and certified kosher, and specialities include ravioli in orange sauce, pasta with chickpeas and many fish dishes.

Il Pagliaccio
129a Via dei Banchi Vecchi
06-6880 9595
www.ristoranteilpagliaccio.com
L & D Wed–Sat, D only Tue
€€€ [p324, A2]
This smart restaurant has a limited but creative menu with an emphasis on beautiful presentation and quality ingredients. It's expensive but well worth it.

Dar Pallaro
15 Largo del Pallaro
06-6880 1488
www.trattoriaderpallaro.com
L & D Tue–Sun
€ [p324, B3]
This quintessentially Roman trattoria is owned by the jovial Fazi couple and is a reliable favourite for those with big appetites and smaller budgets. There is no menu, but for about €20 (house wine and water included) you are served several courses that will leave you more than satisfied. No fish. Open past midnight. No credit cards.

Piperno
9 Via Monte de'Cenci

06-6880 6629
www.ristorantepiperno.it
L & D Tue–Sat, L only Sun
€€€€ [p324, C4]
In a small quiet piazza in the ghetto, Piperno serves Jewish-style (but not at all kosher) dishes, such as their special *cacio e pepe* (pecorino and black pepper) recipe, which includes lard, and very-well fried and crunchy Jewish artichokes. The elegant setting and fine dishes justify the bill, and reservations are required.

Dal Pompiere
38 Via S. Maria dei Calderari
06-686 8377
www.alpompiereroma.com
L & D Mon–Sat
€€–€€€ [p324, B/C4]
Waistcoated waiters dance attendance on customers in the wood-panelled and frescoed rooms of this fine restaurant occupying the first floor of the Palazzo Cenci. The food is Roman-Jewish and consistently good – which means the tables are consistently full.

Renato e Luisa
25 Via dei Barbieri
06-686 9660
www.renatoeluisa.it
D only Tue–Sun
€–€€ [p324, B3]
A reliable and affordable trattoria in a rustic, simple setting, serving classic dishes accompanied by good house wines. You could start with fettuccine with pachino tomatoes and buffalo ricotta, followed by turkey cooked with rosemary and honey, rounded off with a perfect crème brûlée.

Roscioli
21 Via dei Giubbonari
06-687 5287
www.salumeriaroscioli.com
L & D Mon–Sat
€€ [p324, B3]
This family-run deli-cum-restaurant receives rave reviews for its authentic produce and inventive food combinations, such as their signature dish, *tonnarelli* with grouper fish, pistachios and fennel seeds.

Sora Margherita
30 Piazza delle Cinque Scole
06-687 4216
L & D Mon–Sat
€ [p324, C4]
A small, basic trattoria in the heart of the former Jewish Ghetto, serving simple and hearty fare (much of it vegetarian) accompanied by bread from renowned Trastevere bakery La Renella. The sweets are home-made, and the highly palatable local wine is from Velletri outside Rome. No credit cards.

Taverna degli Amici
37 Piazza Margana
06-6992 0637
www.latavernadegliamici.netL & D Tue–Sun
€€–€€€ [p324, C3]
A refined alfresco restaurant in an ivy-draped square in the Ghetto district. It serves subtly different versions of Roman classics as well as plenty of interesting vegetarian dishes.

Trattoria Moderna
16 Vicolo dei Chiodaroli
06-6880 3423
L & D Tue–Sun, D only Mon
€€ [p324, B3]
A lively restaurant with appealing decor. The owners are experienced Roman restaurateurs, and the menu is classical Mediterranean with some modern touches.

Bars and Cafés

Alberto Pica
12 Via della Seggiola
[p324, B4]
This award-winning ice-cream maker has been making *gelato* all his life and is rather better at it than most. People travel from all over Rome to enjoy his superlative ice creams.

Barnum
87 Via del Pellegrino
06-647 0483
www.barnumcafe.com
[p324, A3]
Inspired by the world of circus, this cafè combines food, drinks, art and performances. The circus-themed furnishings are listed on the menu and are for sale.

Enoteca Bartaruga
26 Via dei Funari 06-6476 0525
[p324, C4]
Bohemian-styled interiors and occasional live concerts are the main elements of chic bar, a favourite among local celebrities and models.

Centrale Ristotheatre
6 Via Celsa
06-678 0501
http://teatrocentrale.it
[p324, C3]
A former theatre that attracts a thirty-something Roman crowd looking for a quirky night out. It has a bar with a lounge area and restaurant with live music, theatre or cabaret. From 7.30pm–midnight on Sundays there's an all-you-can-eat buffet, plus one drink for a set price.

Filettaro a Santa Barbara
88 Largo dei Librari
06-686 4018
[p324, B3]
For over 100 years this little shop has been serving fried cod fillets for a quick snack on the go. Juicy and delicious, definitely a must-try.

Il Goccetto
14 Via dei Banchi Vecchi
06-686 4268
[p324, A2]
This enoteca has been serving good wines and even better cheeses for over two decades in this medieval bishop's palace. Some 800 labels are available, of which about 40 can be tasted by the glass.

Kosher Bistrot
68/69 Via Santa Maria del Pianto
06-686 4398
www.kosherbistrotcaffe.com
[p324, C4]
Tables spill onto the pedestrianised streets of the Jewish ghetto for a pleasant snack, lunch, or drink in the sun.

Sciam
56 Via del Pellegrino
06-6830 8957
[p324, B3]
A laid-back Middle Eastern tearoom with a tempting selection of sweet and savoury dishes. You may even be tempted to take a puff of the aromatic hookah pipes. Open until 2am.

Harry's Bar on Via Veneto.

VIA VENETO AND VILLA BORGHESE

The country estates of wealthy Romans were carved up after Unification and transformed into elegant boulevards. Only the Villa Borghese was saved and turned into a vast public park containing some of the city's finest museums.

Leading north from the city centre, the once-glamorous Via Veneto takes us to the green heart of Rome, the Villa Borghese gardens, which also house three important art galleries, an Etruscan museum and Rome's zoo.

VIA VENETO

The southern end of **Via Veneto** begins in **Piazza Barberini ❶**, a busy square with a cinema and fast-food joints. In its centre sits, rather forlornly, Bernini's **Fontana del Tritone** (Triton Fountain). Via Veneto itself, lined with plane trees and pavement cafés, was once the symbol of Roman fashion and style. However, the glorious days of *La Dolce Vita*, immortalised on screen by Fellini, are long gone and the intellectuals have drifted to Piazza del Popolo and the area around Piazza Navona. The long, twisting avenue is now filled for the most part with luxury hotels, embassies and offices, as well as numerous anonymous restaurants with glass-enclosed outdoor seating, hungry for the tourist dollar. Only a few historic cafés – Harry's Bar (www.harrysbar.it) at No. 150 and the Art Deco Doney (www.restaurantdoney.

com) at No. 125 – still bear witness to the street's heyday as the place to be seen in Rome.

Santa Maria della Concezione ❷

Address: 27 Via Vittorio Veneto; www.cappuccinilazio.com
Telephone: 06-8880 3695
Opening Hours: daily, church: 7am–1pm, 3–6pm, museum and crypt: daily 9am–7pm
Entrance Fee: charge
Transport: Barberini

Via Veneto ends at the Porta Pinciana, part of the old Roman Aurelian walls.

At the southern end of the Via Veneto, this Baroque church also goes by the name of I Cappuccini (The Capuchins). The Capuchin friars broke away from the Franciscans in 1525, but still emulate the humble lifestyle of their patron saint, dressing in a simple brown robe with a cord belt, and sandals without socks. This church has been the home of the Capuchin order in Rome since 1631.

It has two noteworthy paintings: *The Archangel Michael Slaying the Devil* by Guido Reni and *St Paul's Sight Being Restored*, by Pietro da Cortona. But the main draw is Caravaggio's masterpiece, *Saint Francis in Mediation*, and the crypt, which contains the bones and skulls of 4,000 Capuchin friars, ornately displayed.

Horti Sallustiani

The **Horti Sallustiani** (Gardens of Sallust; www.hortisallustiani.it; group visits only, by request Sat 9am–1pm, Mon 9.30–11.30am) are located between Via Veneto and the Villa Borghese Gardens. Gaius Sallustius, a historian and profiteer who made enormous fortunes out of the campaigns of 40–30 BC, embellished his home with magnificent gardens. Soon hailed as one of the wonders of the world, they were quickly appropriated by the Empire. Vespasian and Titus preferred this part of Rome to the Palatine.

Fountains, pools and mosaic floors once drew awed visitors. Now the gardens lie 15 metres (45ft) below street level, buried by the rubble from collapsed houses and the building activity of the 19th century. Archaeological finds from the gardens include the obelisk at the top of the Spanish Steps and those on show as part of the collection of the Museo Nazionale Romano (see page 158).

In the Middle Ages, the family of Ludovisi Boncompagni injected new life into the by then unkempt gardens by planting 30 hectares (74 acres) of vineyards. They lasted until the property boom of the 1880s, which spelt their demolition. The Società Generale Immobiliare, backed mainly by German and French capital, made an irresistible

Gran Caffè Roma on Via Veneto.

offer to the Ludovisi princes, and the villa was split up. All that remains is the 16th-century **Casino dell'Aurora** in the gardens of the Swiss Cultural Institute.

Palazzo Margherita ❸

The other part of the gardens spared by developers is **Palazzo Margherita**, which was completed in 1890 and now houses the American Embassy. One of the Ludovisi princes had this gigantic building constructed as a substitute for his lost garden, but his money ran out and he had to sell it to the Savoy royal family, who moved the queen mother in. It bears her name to this day.

SANTA MARIA DELLA VITTORIA ❹

Address: 17 Via XX Settembre; www.chiesasantamariavittoriaroma.it
Opening Hours: daily 8.30am–noon, 3.30–6pm
Entrance Fee: free
Transport: Repubblica

To the south of the *palazzo*, on the corner of Piazza San Bernardo and Via XX Settembre, stands the church of **Santa Maria della Vittoria**, begun by Carlo Maderno in 1605. It contains Bernini's famous Baroque Cornaro side chapel, which uses natural lighting effects to highlight the *Ecstasy of St Teresa*, a sculpture of Teresa of Avila, one of the great saints of the Counter-Reformation, portrayed with open mouth and half-closed eyes at the climax of her vision of Christ. She described how an angel pierced her heart with a flaming golden arrow. It has prompted many writers and critics over the centuries to suggest that the love she is experiencing may not be entirely divine.

VILLA BORGHESE

At the northern end of Via Veneto, outside the Porta Pinciana, is the **Villa Borghese**, which was founded at the beginning of the 17th century by Cardinal Scipione Borghese Caffarelli, a nephew of Pope Paul V. The family later extended their property by buying some nearby land, so that 100 years ago the park encompassed 75 hectares (190 acres), which the Borghese family frequently

FACT

That most popular of Italian drinks, cappuccino, is named after the garb worn by Capuchin monks. The colour of the milky coffee is reminiscent of their brown robes and the pointed hoods of the peaks of milky foam. The word cappuccino literally means "little hood" or "monk's cowl".

Entrance to the National Gallery of Modern Art, housing a collection of 19th- and 20th-century art, including a group of paintings by the Macchiaioli, Italy's answer to France's Impressionists.

BONE IDOLS

Beneath the church of Santa Maria della Concezione is an extraordinary crypt that contains the bones of 4,000 monks. Many churches have charnel houses, but this arrangement of skeletal remains into intricate designs is unique. The crypt is full of unusual tableaux: brown-cowled skeletons bow to visitors under arches of hip bones and pelvises; an infant skeleton attached to the ceiling brandishes a scythe, surrounded by rosettes made from vertebrae; a large clock comprises finger and foot bones. And in case this is not enough to remind you of mortality, a sign ominously informs us that: "What you are now, we once were. What we are now, you shall someday be". When the Marquis de Sade visited the crypt in 1775, he wrote, "I have never seen anything more striking", and he probably meant it in a positive way.

The origins of this death cult are unclear. The church says that when French Capuchin friars came to Rome they found a shortage of burial space and created this monument. There is also the legend of "a half-mad monk with time on his hands and a certain passion for tidiness". Whatever the motives, this is Rome's most artistic cemetery.

opened to the public. Property developers cast a greedy eye on the villa in the late 19th century, and their plans provoked the first battle to save the Romans' traditional society promenade.

Eventually, in 1901, the state bought the villa and, two years later, gave it to the people. The Villa Borghese, along with the Pincio Gardens and the Villa Giulia, is now home to a handful of museums, a cinematic cultural centre and the city zoo.

The **Villa Borghese Gardens** are laid out over rolling hills with winding paths, little lakes, statues and pretty flower beds. On Sunday, the people of Rome take over the park. Every corner is full of picnicking families, strolling lovers, cyclists and joggers, and squealing children at play.

There are several entrances to the park, but the main one is at the top of Via Veneto, at Porta Pinciana.

Carlo Bilotti Museum ⑤

Address: Viale Fiorello La Guardia, Villa Borghese; www.museocarlobilotti.it
Telephone: 06-0608
Opening Hours: June–Sept Tue–Fri 1am–7pm, Sat–Sun 10am–7pm, winter Tue–Fri 10am–4pm, Sat–Sun 10am–7pm
Entrance Fee: free
Transport: Flaminio

A wide *viale* leads downhill from the Porta Pinciana, passing the **Galoppatoio** (horse track) on the left and a statue of Goethe on the right. A little further ahead, the old orangery (Aranciera) has been restored and transformed into a museum containing a collection of works by Carlo Bilotti, an Italo-American collector who favoured modern art. The core of the collection is made up of 22 paintings and sculptures by Giorgio de Chirico. There is also a portrait of the larger-than-life arts patron Larry Rivers, and one of Bilotti's wife and

In the Santa Maria della Concezione crypt.

Via Veneto and Villa Borghese

Cardinal by Giacomo Manzù. The complex regularly houses important modern and contemporary art exhibitions.

Pincio Gardens **6**

From Piazzale Canestre walk down Viale delle Magnolie and head over the bridge, crossing busy Viale del Muro Torto below, into the **Pincio Gardens** at the southwest corner of the park. These formal gardens were designed by Valadier in the 19th century. Look out for the fanciful water clock and the **Casina Valadier**, once an elegant café visited by the intellectuals of the Roman *belle époque*. Nowadays, it is an expensive restaurant with a fabulous view from its terrace (tel: 06-6992 2090; www.casinavaladier.com; Tue–Sun 12.30–3pm, 7.30–11pm).

Outside the restaurant is a stand full of bicycles and pedal carts for hire – not a bad idea, especially if you plan on visiting the museums across the park. The romantic terrace of the Pincio overlooks Piazza del Popolo and offers a splendid vantage point to view the city. It's

daughter, the *Portrait of Tina and Lisa Bilotti* (1981) by Andy Warhol. Other key works include *Summer* by Gino Severini and the large bronze

In its Dolce Vita heyday, the five-star Excelsior on Via Veneto played host to some of the most glamorous stars of the day. Many a tempestuous scene between hot-headed lovers Frank Sinatra and Ava Gardner was played out within its walls.

Retreat to the park if the heat gets too intense.

TIP

Just inside the Villa Borghese park, on the other side of the Porta Pinciana, stands the Casa del Cinema (www.casadelcinema.it). The lovely converted villa boasts several screening rooms (showing the occasional film in English), a book and DVD shop, and a cinema library containing scripts and movie stills. The CineCaffè (www.cinecaffe.it; daily 9am–7pm), which serves drinks and light meals in an airy atmosphere, is an appealing place.

The Pincio Gardens.

a particularly delightful spot for an evening stroll.

Villa Medici ❼

Further down the Pincio hillside is the majestic **Villa Medici** (www.villamedici.it). Rebuilt in the 16th century for the Crescenzi family, it was then passed to the Medicis, before being confiscated by Napoleon in 1803 and made the home of the French Academy. It is open for occasional exhibitions and concerts. There are also guided tours of the gardens and villa (Tue–Sun 9.30am–5.30pm, English at noon; tel: 06-6761 311; café daily 8am–7pm).

Giardino del Lago ❽

Backtrack and cross the bridge to where a wide *viale* leads up to **Piazza di Siena** on the right. This oval track is the site of the International Horse Show in May – an important social and sporting event.

To the left is the pretty **Giardino del Lago**, with a tiny lake in the middle of which stands a reproduction of a Greek temple of Aesculapius. Rowing boats can be hired for a brief paddle. Nearby, you will find the **Fountain of Fauns**, created in 1929 by Giovanni Nicolini.

Galleria Nazionale d'Arte Moderna e Contemporanea ❾

Address: 131 Viale delle Belle Arti; www.gnam.beniculturali.it
Telephone: 06-3229 8221
Opening Hours: Tue–Sat 8.30am–7.15pm, Sun 2–7.30pm
Entrance Fee: charge; free first Sun of the month
Transport: 3, 19, 88, 95, 490, 495, M
Two sloping ramps lead to Viale delle Belle Arti and the neoclassical facade of the **Galleria Nazionale d'Arte Moderna** (GNAM). It has a permanent collection of 19th- and 20th-century pieces (dating until the 1960s) by Italian and foreign artists including de Chirico, Van Gogh, Modigliani, Degas, Cézanne, Courbet, Kandinsky, Mondrian, Klimt, Henry Moore and others. The gallery also frequently hosts travelling exhibitions of international importance. There is a café and a bookshop.

andersen.beniculturali.it; Tue–Fri 9am–7.30pm; free) is a branch of the GNAM, and offers a look at the Norwegian-American artist, whose bold, bronze statues of men in all their glory were not always so well received.

Next door, in the Piazza Winston Churchill, is the **Accademia Britannica (British School at Rome)**, designed by Lutyens and home to visiting scholars (www.bsr.ac.uk).

Museo Nazionale Etrusco di Villa Giulia ⑩

Address: 9 Piazzale di Villa Giulia; www.villagiulia.beniculturali.it
Telephone: 06-322 6571
Opening Hours: Tue–Sun 8.30am–7.30pm
Entrance Fee: charge; free first Sun of the month
Transport: Flaminio

Nearby **Museo Henrik Christian Andersen** (20 Via Pasquale Stanislao Mancini, Piazzale Flaminio; tel: 06-321 9089; www.museo

To the west of the modern art gallery is Rome's Museum of Etruscan Art. It is housed in the Villa Giulia, a splendid late-Renaissance palace built as a summer villa for Julius III between 1551 and 1553. The museum gives a unique insight into

View from the Pincio hills.

A typical Sunday in the park.

Every summer, on the night of Saint Lawrence (10 August), many Romans head to the Pincio Hill's gardens and point their noses towards the sky to wait for the shower of Perseid meteors. Lie down on the grass while you count the falling stars, and make a wish each time you see one. If you haven't caught any, not to worry! Scientists say the shower usually goes on for a few days, so come back tomorrow.

Fonte Gaia in the Villa Borghese gardens.

the life and art of the enigmatic pre-Roman civilisation of the Etruscans. Among the many outstanding exhibits are the sweet 6th-century BC sarcophagus of a married couple – *degli Sposi* – from the excavations in Cerveteri, and a 6th-century bronze statue of Apollo of Veio. These and other pieces form one of the finest collections of Etruscan art in the world, rivalled only by that of the Vatican.

Some of the collection is on show in the restored 16th-century Villa Poniatowski (Tue–Sat 9am–1.30pm, Sun only guided tour by request) nearby. Once part of the Villa Giulia complex, it was renovated in the early 19th century by the Polish Prince Stanislao Poniatowski.

The zoo (Bioparco) ⓫

Address: Piazzale del Giardino Zoologico; www.bioparco.it
Telephone: 06-360 8211
Opening Hours: Apr–Oct Mon–Fri 9.30am–6pm, Sat–Sun till 7pm (except Oct), Nov–Mar 9.30am–5pm
Entrance Fee: charge

Transport: Flaminio
The road leading uphill to the left ends at the entrance to the zoo, or Bioparco, its official eco-friendly name. In the past the zoo had a reputation for being neglected, but in recent years there have been some worthy and fairly successful attempts to phase out the caging of exotic animals and keep other specimens in more humane, purpose-built environments that more closely resemble their natural habitats.

Galleria Borghese ⓬

Address: 5 Piazzale del Museo Borghese; www.galleriaborghese.it
Telephone: 06-32810
Opening Hours: Tue–Sun 9am–7pm, controlled entry every two hours on the hour until 5pm, by reservation only
Entrance Fee: charge; free first Sun of the month
Transport: 53, 61, 9, 83, 91, 116, 120F, 150F, 160, 223, 360, 490, 495, 590, 910, C3, MA1, MA2
In the eastern corner of the park, one of the world's great private art collections is housed in the Casino Borghese, built as a summer home for the worldly, pleasure-loving Cardinal Scipione Borghese between 1613 and 1615. The cardinal was a great patron of the arts and laid the basis for the remarkable collection of paintings and sculptures on view today (see page 198).

NORTHEAST OF THE CITY

To the northeast, **Via Salaria** crosses the suburbs and leads out to the Sabine Hills, and onward to the Adriatic coast. This old Roman road is named after the salt *(sale)* that was transported into Rome from the sea and through the hills. Just before the Salaria Bridge (1874), is the hill of Monte Antenne where the Sabine settlement of the Antemnae is said to have stood. It is here that the Romans, under Romulus, supposedly kidnapped the Sabine

women to populate their growing empire. Via Salaria was an important street and, in the early years of Christianity, many churches and catacombs were built here.

Catacombe di Priscilla ⑬

Address: 430 Via Salaria; www.catacombepriscilla.com
Telephone: 06-8620 6272
Opening Hours: Tue–Sun 8.30am–noon, 2.30–5pm, closed Aug or Jul
Entrance Fee: charge
Transport: 63, 83, 92, 310

Entered through the cloister of a Benedictine monastery, the 13km (8-mile) network of catacombs evolved between the 1st and 4th centuries. Seven early popes and numerous martyrs were buried here, hence the high-quality frescoes and stucco decorations. The catacombs extend under the park of Villa Ada, now the Egyptian Embassy but formerly Victor Emmanuel II's hunting lodge. It is surrounded by a beautiful park that is open to the public.

Quartiere Coppedè ⑭

To the east of Via Salaria, just off Piazza Buenos Aires, is the fashionable Quartiere Coppedè, a residential area named after a Florentine architect who designed many buildings here between 1921 and 1926, using Art Nouveau-inspired motifs. Of particular interest is Piazza Mincio, a square with an unusual fountain of frogs that Gabriele d'Annunzio described as "a genuine disgrace to Rome". Coppedè, whose buildings were the last notable architecture of pre-Fascist Rome, intended this square to show a harmony between the individual details of each house and the great tradition of Florentine craftsmanship.

MACRO ⑮

Address: 138 Via Nizza; www.museomacro.org
Telephone: 06-0608

Opening Hours: Tue–Sun 10.30am–7.30pm, Testaccio Tue–Sun 4–10pm
Entrance Fee: charge; free first Sun of the month
Transport: 38, 60, 60L, 62, 80, 82, 89, 90,

At the beginning of Via Nomentana, set in a former Peroni brewery, is the Museo d'Arte Contemporanea di Roma (MACRO). One of two sites (the other is in Testaccio, see page 218), it houses artworks by the key figures in Italian contemporary art. There is also a café and museum shop on site.

Villa Torlonia ⑯

Address: 70 Via Nomentana; www.museivillatorlonia.it
Telephone: 06-0608
Opening Hours: museum: Tue–Sun 9am–7pm, park: 9am–one hour before sunset.
Entrance Fee: charge
Transport: 3, 19, 36, 60, 62, 84, 90

Further east, on Via Nomentana, the Villa Torlonia was the last great villa built in Rome. In the

WHERE

Northeast of the city on the other side of Villa Ada is the chic residential area of Parioli, housing Rome's first mosque. Built in 1992, it serves a Muslim population of 100,000 and is the largest mosque in Europe to date. Noted for its modern feel and contextual design, the mosque sits on over 3 hectares (7.5 acres) of verdant park space and its interior follows a forest motif. To reach the mosque, take the local Viterbo-bound train to Acqua Acetosa (Campi Sportivi).

Giardino del Lago.

North and Central Rome

VILLA ADA

VILLA BORGHESE

VILLA GLORI

VILLA FLAMINIA

FLAMINIA

PARIOLI

PINCIANO

SALARIO

TRIESTE

VILLA TORLONIA

Catacombe di Priscilla

Moschea di Roma (Rome Mosque)

Villa Ada

Stazione Campi Sportivi

Stazione Acqua Acetosa

Stazione Euclide

Villa Glori

SS. Cuore Immacolato di Maria

Auditorium Parco della Musica

Palazzetto dello Sport

Stadio Flaminio

MAXXI

Ponte Milvio

Stadio d. Marmi

Stadio Olimpico

Foro Italico

Rai Auditorium

Ministero degli Affari Esteri

S. Roberto Bellarmino

S. Filippo Neri

Museo Africano

Museo Zoologia

Bioparco

Museo Canonica

Galleria Borghese

Galleria Naz. d'Arte Moderna

Accademia Britannica

Accademia di Belle Arti

Accademia di Romania

Museo Etrusco di Villa Giulia

Explora il Museo dei Bambini

Villa Ruffo

Staz. Flaminio

PIAZZALE FLAMINIO

S. Maria

Piazza d. Popolo

Casa di Goethe

Museo Henrik Christian Andersen

Tempio d. Esculapio

Tempio d. Diana

Muro Torto

Villa Medici

Chiesa Luterana

Galleria Borghese

Porta Pinciana

Ple Brasile

Porta Pindiana

Mausoleo d. Lucilio Petro

Museo di Arte Contemporanea di Roma (MACRO)

Quartiere Coppedè

Villa Albani

SS. Martiri Canadesi

Mausoleo di S. Costanza

S. Agnese fuori le Mura

Villa Mirafiori

Istituto Poligrafico dello Stato

Istituto Storico e di Cultura dell'Arma del Genio

Ministero della Difesa

Ministero dei Lavori Pubblici

Ministero dei Trasporti

CONI

Casa Internazionale dello Studente

Piscina

Ple della Farnesina

Stadio d. Farnesina

500 m

500 yds

N

early 19th century, the aristocratic Torlonia family contracted French architect Valadier to design the villa, which had a small lake, guesthouse, sports field and Temple of Saturn. The splendid three-storey residence, the Casino Nobile, was Mussolini's home from 1924 until 1943 (his rent was 1 lira a month). It was then occupied by Allied Forces, but after the war it was left to disintegrate.

Following 50 years of neglect the palace has been restored to something of its former glory, and was opened to visitors in 2006. The rooms are lavishly decorated – the chandeliered ballroom is the grandest – though furnishings are sparse, as so much was looted or destroyed. You can also visit the network of bunkers Mussolini had built in case of air raids or gas attacks (www.bunkerdiroma.it; guided tours only).

While you're in the Villa Torlonia grounds, the **Casina delle Civette** (Owl House) is also worth a visit. The Swiss chalet-style residence was built in 1840 and restored in the 1920s in the Art Nouveau style, with stained-glass windows featuring idyllic scenes of flora and fauna.

Nearby, a small medieval building houses **Technotown** (www.technotown.it; Tue–Sun 9.30am–7pm, in summer Tue–Fri 5–11pm,

Hunting and war scenes on a gilded silver bowl, Museo Etrusco di Villa Giulia.

Ponte Milvio when love locks were still allowed.

BRIDGE LOVE-LOCKS

For years, the ancient Ponte Milvio bridge was a pilgrimage site for thousands of lovers who sealed their *amore* by fixing a padlock to the bridge's historic lamp-posts and throwing the key into the river. This tradition started in 1992, after Federico Moccia published his novel *Tre Metri Sopra Il Cielo* (Three Metres Above The Sky). In 2006, politicians began wondering whether it was acceptable that the 19th-century lamp-posts by Valadier should bear the weight of so many padlocks and measures to ease the load were sought. However, in September 2012, all of the locks were removed, after rust from them was deemed to be harming the fabric of the bridge.

KIDS

If you've children in tow when exploring the Villa Borghese area, two good places to know about are the zoo and the nearby Explora Museum (80/86 Via Flaminia; tel: 06-361 3776; www.mdbr.it), a science museum full of interactive displays to keep them amused.

Balloons for sale outside the zoo.

Museo Nazionale delle Arti del XXI Secolo.

Sat–Sun 1–11pm), a hands-on science and technology museum designed for 11–15-year-olds. See website for events and special activities.

Sant'Agnese fuori le Mura ⑰

Address: 349 Via Nomentana; www.santagnese.com
Telephone: 06-8620 5456
Opening Hours: church: daily 7.30am–noon, 4–7.30pm, catacombs and mausoleum: Mon–Sat 9am–noon, daily 3–5pm
Entrance Fee: charge for catacombs
Transport: 60, 60L, 82, 90, 309

Continuing down Via Nomentana, you come to Sant'Agnese fuori le Mura, an important early Christian church built over the site of the tomb of St Agnes in the mid-4th century by Princess Costantina, daughter of the Emperor Constantine. It was rebuilt by Pope Honorius I in the 7th century. The relics of St Agnes are housed in the high altar. Every 21 January, the saint's day, two lambs are blessed and shorn to make woollen robes for the Pope.

The adjoining catacombs are remarkably well preserved. The nearby church of St Costanza, built as Constantina's own mausoleum, contains some interesting

4th-century mosaics depicting scenes of the *vendemmia* (grape harvest).

FLAMINIA

Northern Rome is connected to the city by the Via Flaminia, which begins at Piazza del Popolo and continues in a straight line all the way to the historic Ponte Milvio (see page 196), a Roman footbridge that offers wonderful views of the Tiber. From here it's a short walk to the Foro Italico sports centre, one of the most intact examples of Fascist-era architecture in the city.

Foro Italico ⑱

The Foro Italico sports complex was designed for Mussolini in the late 1920s by prominent architect Enrico del Debbio. This district was formerly dominated by the **Stadio dei Marmi**, built in the style of a Greek stadium and surrounded by 60 marble figures of athletes in heroic poses. Today, it is dwarfed by the **Stadio Olimpico**, (www.coni.it) the huge football and athletics stadium immediately behind it, with

capacity for 80,000 spectators. This is where the opening ceremony of the 1960 Olympics took place, and, when the World Cup was held here in 1990, the stadium was extended into the Monte Mario behind it.

The stadium now hosts football matches most Sundays during the season, and is the venue for much passion and excitement – and also, unfortunately, disruption when the two home teams, AS Roma and SS Lazio, come together in a match.

The Auditorium ⑲

Address: 30 Viale Pietro de Coubertin; www.auditorium.com
Telephone: 06-8024 1281
Transport: Flaminio, then tram 2

Back on the south side of the Tiber, just north of the Parioli district and east of Flaminio, is the largest arts complex of its kind in Europe. The state-of-the-art Auditorium Parco della Musica designed by Genoese architect Renzo Piano opened in 2002. The huge venue is set in open parkland, with a 7,600-seat capacity spread over three concert halls. It has a large outdoor amphitheatre

TIP

Add some romance to your jaunt in the Villa Borghese park. Pick up a gourmet picnic-to-go from nearby Piazza di Spagna-area restaurant GiNa (7a Via San Sebastianello; tel: 06-678 5201; www.gina roma.com). Luxury packs come complete with chequered cloth, plates, flatware, wineglasses, a bottle of your wine of choice, a thermos of espresso and fresh sandwiches.

Villa Medici.

FACT

Ponte Milvio is one of Rome's oldest bridges. Dating back to 2 BC, it is one of only three bridges that stood in the ancient city. It was the site of the great battle between rivals for the Imperial crown: Constantine and Maxentius. On the eve of the battle in AD 312 Constantine had a vision of Christ, and converted to Christianity. He went on to win the battle and turn the Roman Empire to Christianity.

A modern Olympian at the Foro Italico.

and even incorporates a ruined Roman villa, unearthed during construction. There also several free museums on the site, including archaeological and of musical instruments. The "city of music" offers an excellent programme of international music and dance. See the website for up-to-date details.

MAXXI ⑳

Address: 4A Via G. Reni;
www.fondazionemaxxi.it
Telephone: 06-320 19540
Opening Hours: Tue–Fri and Sun 11am–7pm, Sat 11am–10pm
Entrance Fee: charge
Transport: Flaminio, then tram 2

Designed by award-winning Anglo-Iraqi Zaha Hadid and inaugurated in May 2010, the National Museum of 21st-century Art (MAXXI) is a three-level curved concrete box with its uppermost level reaching skywards. The minimalist interior is a sensual maze of metal and cement waves pulsing through the galleries resembling,

as the architect said, "curves unwinding like a ribbon in space".

The MAXXI's collection represents acclaimed Italian and international artists, with works from the 1960s onwards, and is Italy's first national museum dedicated to innovation in architecture as well as art. Part national museum, part private foundation, each year the MAXXI awards the Italian Prize for Contemporary Art, in a competition open to artists under 45 years of age and resident in Italy. Along with a cash prize, the winning artist's work becomes part of the permanent collection.

A visit to the MAXXI can satisfy a quick contemporary art fix or be an all-day affair. The complex has an auditorium, library and media library, bookshop, cafeteria, bar/restaurant and galleries for temporary exhibitions, performances and educational activities. The large open square in front of the museum hosts artworks and live events, and the exterior walls are utilised for street art.

RESTAURANTS, BARS AND CAFÉS

PRICE CATEGORIES

Price includes dinner and a half-bottle of house wine.

€€€€ = more than €60
€€€ = €40–60
€€ = €25–40
€ = under €25.

Restaurants

Cantina Cantarini
12 Piazza Sallustio
06-474 3341
www.ristorantecantinacantarini.it
L & D Mon–Sat
€€ [p318, B2]
A high-quality family-run trattoria where the price is still right. Dishes are meat-based the first part of the week, fish-based Thu–Sat.

Casina Valadier
Pincio Gardens, Villa Borghese
06-6992 2090
www.casinavaladier.it
L & D daily
€€€ [p316, E2]
The service can be indifferent and the quality of the food is not necessarily reflected in the price, but you might be prepared to risk it just to enjoy the location.

Girarrosto Fiorentino
46 Via Sicilia
06-4288 0660
www.girarrostofiorentino.it
L & D daily
€€€ [p318, A2]
An island of reliability in a sea of tacky venues. The service is faultless, and wall-hangings give it a pleasantly dated look. All the classic Roman dishes are on offer, along with some Florentine specialities, including wonderful T-bone steaks.

Moma
42/43 Via San Basilio
06-4201 1798
www.ristorantemoma.it
L & D Mon–Sat
€€€ [p318, A3]
Excellent food beautifully presented. You can choose between a light lunch and more formal dining on the upper level. The menu is a mix of traditional Italian cuisine and more adventurous dishes. Booking essential.

Papà Baccus
30 Via Toscana
06-4274 2808
www.papabaccus.com
L & D Mon–Fri, D only Sat
€€€ [p318, A2]
Renowned for its attentive service and Tuscan cuisine. Meat features heavily, but there are fish and vegetarian options too.

La Terrazza dell'Eden
49 Via Ludovisi (Hotel Eden)
06-4781 2752
www.dorchestercollection.com
L & D daily
€€€€ [p318, A2]
One of the capital's top restaurants, with a panoramic terrace that's as much of a draw as the food; try the risotto with melted taleggio and aubergine.

Bars and Cafés

Caffè delle Arti
73 Via Gramsci
06-3265 1236
www.caffedelleartiroma.com
[p316, E1]
In Villa Borghese's National Gallery of Modern Art, this is considered one of the finest museum cafés in Italy with a beautiful terrace and interior.

Doney
145 Via Veneto
06-4708 2783
www.restaurantdoney.com
[p318, A2]
This luxurious café harks back to dolce vita glamour. A good bet for everything from breakfast to dinner, cocktails and aperitifs.

Enjoy an alfresco meal at Casina Valadier.

GALLERIA BORGHESE

This is one of the finest collections of paintings and statuary in Rome, as well as a magnificent palace.

The Galleria Borghese is housed in an early 17th-century *palazzina* built for Cardinal Scipione Borghese. The cardinal was a great patron of the arts and laid the basis for the remarkable collection of paintings and sculptures on view today. In his lifetime, he collected hundreds of classical statues and antiquities, including a marvellous mosaic of gladiators on display on the ground floor. Between 1801 and 1809 the sculpture collection was severely depleted, when over 500 pieces were sold to Napoleon. These now make up the Borghese Collection of the Louvre in Paris, but the Roman collection still fills 20 rooms across two floors. The cardinal was an early patron of Bernini, and his collection includes his best work, including his dramatic statue of *David*, *Apollo and Daphne* and *Pluto and Persephone*. Scipione was also one of the few cardinals to appreciate Caravaggio, and his works sit alongside other great Italian masterpieces by Raphael, Correggio, Titian, Perugino, Lotto, Domenichino, Giorgione, Dossi and Bassano, as well as by works Rubens and Cranach.

Raphael's celebrated Deposition, 1507.

The Essentials

Address: 5 Piazzale del Museo Borghese; http://galleriaborghese. beniculturali.it
Tel: 06-32810
Opening Hours: Tue–Sun 9am–7pm; entrance every two hours on the hour until 5pm
Entrance Fee: charge
Transport: 5, 19, 52, 53, 861, 98, 83, 91, 116, 120F, 150F, 160, 204, 217, 223, 360, 490, 495, 590, 910, 926, C3, MA1, MA2

David and Goliath, by Caravaggio, 1606. The head of Goliath is a self-portrait, said to be a sign of contrition by the artist for the murder he had recently committed.

Titian's Sacred and Profane Love, c1515, made for an aristocratic wedding, is loaded with symbolism.

One of the highlights of the collection is the sensual statue of Pauline Bonaparte by Canova. The 19th-century femme fatale, whose conquests in the bedroom matched her brother's on the battlefield, was appropriately sculpted as Venus Victrix. When asked how she could possibly have posed so scantily dressed, she replied, "The studio was heated."

The gleaming Galleria Borghese is made of creamy white travertine which reflects the light.

THE PATRON'S PALACE

The Casino Borghese was built in the 17th-century outskirts of the city as a summer house for the pleasure-loving cardinal Scipione Borghese, and was completed in 1615. As a close associate of the Pope, he entertained many high-profile guests in his *palazzina*. The ancient statuary and the building itself, modelled on the classical villa, recalled the glories of Imperial Rome, and with the precious art collections on display, were a forceful demonstration of the cardinal's power. The villa is richly decorated with stuccos, ancient marble, paintings and frescoes, including an impressive trompe l'oeil by Mariano Rossi in the first Salone. The Sicilian artist made such good use of foreshortening that his painting appears almost three-dimensional.

In his will, Cardinal Borghese stated that the villa and grounds should never be separated. In 1902, the entire Villa Borghese estate was bought by Umberto I of Italy and presented by him to the city.

Venus and Cupid with a Honeycomb, by German painter Lucas Cranach the Elder (1531).

A typical Roman street in Trastevere.

TRASTEVERE AND THE GIANICOLO

Now the gentrified turf of bourgeois Romans and expats, Trastevere retains a special charm from its days as Rome's working-class district "across the Tiber". Rising behind it, the Gianicolo hill offers some of the best views of the city.

Across the river (*trans Tiberim*) from the Centro Storico lies Trastevere, which has always stood apart from the rest of the city. The area has a long history as the residence of outsiders: in Roman times it was settled by sailors, foreign merchants and a large Jewish community which later moved across the river. Over time, Trastevere's separation from the rest of the city resulted in the development of its own customs, traditions and dialect.

For centuries, the *Trasteverini* considered themselves to be *i romani de Roma*: Rome's Romans – a cohort of proud working men and women who faced life with a quick-witted sardonic joy. The energy of life on the streets of *er core de Roma* – the heart of Rome – nurtured some of the city's great artistic talent. The actor Alberto Sordi turned Trastevere's backstreets dialect into his comedy trademark. Inventor of the Spaghetti Western, Sergio Leone, grew up in Viale Glorioso, and his neighbourhood school was also the Alma Mater to film music maestro Ennio Morricone.

But the old *Trasteverini* are a dying breed. After the war, the area's down-at-heel charm attracted gentrifying expats and middle-class

Trastevere is quiet by day.

Romans. Inhabitants with roots going back generations departed for housing on Rome's periphery. The new *Trasteverini* are more likely to be artists, actors and film stars in residence.

Fortunately, Trastevere has kept some of its idiosyncrasies, even if many of the old *trattorie* and *osterie* have given way to pizzerias, pubs and trendy wine bars. During the day, it is left to its sleepy self: residents exercise dogs and do their daily shopping, while children play

Main Attractions

Santa Maria in Trastevere
Museo di Roma in
  Trastevere
San Francesco a Ripa
Santa Cecilia in Trastevere
Villa Farnesina
Palazzo Corsini
Orto Botanico
Bramante's Tempietto

Maps and Listings

and the elderly sit outside their houses or on the benches in the piazzas. In the evening, the streets and squares are packed with locals and tourists, who flock here to eat, drink or stroll among stalls selling ethnic jewellery, and fortune tellers shuffling their cards.

One major blot on this appealing landscape is the amount of graffiti scrawled across walls and doors, as well as late-night drunk and disorderly behaviour, quite common in and around the main square. Locals are campaigning hard for the mayor to address these social problems and for stronger policing in the area.

PIAZZA SANTA MARIA IN TRASTEVERE

This cobbled square is the throbbing heart of the neighbourhood and is one of the most charming piazzas in Rome. There's a steady ebb and flow of tourists and locals

Marble statue of St Cecilia in her eponymous church.

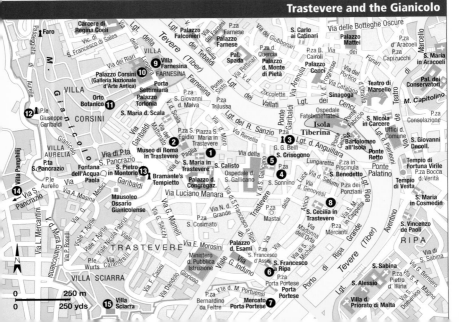

Trastevere and the Gianicolo

their details. *The Life of the Virgin* series is by Cavallini (1291). Also worthy of note are the 21 granite columns that divide the nave from the aisles. These were taken from classical buildings including the Baths of Caracalla.

Museo di Roma in Trastevere ②

Address: 1B Piazza Sant'Egidio; www.museodiromaintrastevere.it
Telephone: 06-0608
Opening Hours: Tue–Sun 10am–8pm
Entrance Fee: charge
Transport: bus: 8, 125, 780, tram: H

Northwest of the square, this small museum, housed in a beautifully restored Carmelite convent, is dedicated to Roman folklore. The exhibition on the upper floor begins with a collection of watercolours by Ettore Roesler Franz (1845–1907), known as "Lost Rome". They present a rose-tinted Rome as it was before the urban restructuring of the 1870s, through romantic scenes of daily life in and around the Tiber.

Piazza Santa Maria in Trastevere.

The facade of Santa Maria in Trastevere.

whiling away their time in the cafés or sitting on the steps of the **fountain** (1692) around which musicians perform in summer.

Santa Maria in Trastevere ①

Address: Piazza Santa Maria in Trastevere
Opening Hours: daily 7.30am–9pm, Aug 8am–noon, 4–9pm
Entrance Fee: free
Transport: bus: 8, 23, 125, 280, 780, tram: H

The piazza is named after the basilica on its eastern side, one of the oldest churches in Rome and one of the first to be dedicated to the Virgin. It was founded in the 3rd century, and rebuilt in the 12th century, although the portico was added in 1702. The 12th- and 13th-century mosaics, both inside and outside the church, are spectacular, and it is worth taking a pair of binoculars to enjoy

EAT

Brush up on your bad language and visit one of Trastevere's most popular restaurants, La Parolaccia, (3 Vicolo del Cinque; www.cenciolaparolaccia.it; D Mon–Sat), where food is served accompanied by bawdy language (the restaurant's name means swear word) and a brusque, but entertaining, Roman manner.

At the far end of the floor is a series of life-size reconstructions of Roman life in the 18th century, and a room chock-full of objects from the studio of popular Trastevere poet Carlo Alberto Salustri (1871–1950), known as Trilussa (he is also remembered in a statue that graces the Piazza Trilussa).

The staircase features casts of the so-called "Talking Statues" (see page 163). The ground floor of the museum is used for temporary exhibitions, often focusing on photography and new media.

The atmosphere is more brisk and businesslike in **Piazza San Cosimato** to the south, where the daily food market is surrounded by grocers, bars, restaurants, a hospital and a playground.

VIALE DI TRASTEVERE

Palm trees in the botanical gardens.

Trastevere is now home to trendy boutiques and restaurants.

Like every old quarter of Rome, Trastevere had to make sacrifices when the capital started expanding after 1870. Many historic buildings and streets were destroyed in order to make way for the **Viale di Trastevere**, a broad boulevard that cuts through the patchwork of

Trastevere's little streets. At its northern end, on the banks of the Tiber, is **Piazza G.G. Belli** ❸, named after the much-loved 19th-century Roman

BRAMANTE'S TEMPIETTO

When the centre of the Renaissance shifted from northern Italy to Rome at the end of the 15th century, the atmosphere of the Eternal City gave the architects of the day fresh impetus to rediscover the styles and motifs of antiquity. Donato Bramante had learnt his trade in the north and moved to Rome in 1499. He transformed the classical manner of the 15th century into a more monumental style, and because of this he is remembered as one of the fathers of modern architecture. His Tempietto di San Pietro in Montorio (1502) is the first monument of the High Renaissance style. It possesses a gravity all of its own – not surprising, considering its location: it marks the spot that was believed to be the site of St Peter's crucifixion. On closer inspection, you will notice there is very little surface decoration, and the colonnade is also unadorned. Too small to fit a congregation (5 metres/15ft in diameter), the circular temple supports a classical entablature, which lends further weight and severity. These features, combined with the perfect classical proportions, make the Tempietto a brilliant homage to antiquity and an example for many later architects such as Palladio.

dialect poet, Giuseppe Gioacchino Belli (1791– 1863) whose statue stands here.

Behind Piazza Belli is **Piazza Sidney Sonnino ④**. The Torre degli Anguillara, the last of many towers that once guarded Trastevere, is marked with a plaque commemorating Dante's stay here in 1300. The nearby church of **San Crisogono ⑤** (daily 7–11.30am, 4–7.30pm) was built over one of the oldest sites of Christian worship in Rome, dating from the 3rd century. The facade is a 17th-century copy of the medieval original. Inside are remains of a 5th-century basilica.

San Francesco a Ripa ⑥

Address: 88 Piazza di San Francesco d'Assisi; www.sanfrancescoaripa.com
Opening Hours: daily 8am–1pm, 2–7.30pm
Entrance Fee: free
Transport: bus: 8, 780, tram: H

On the south side of the Viale di Trastevere is the church of San Francesco a Ripa. Dedicated to St Francis, who stayed in a convent near here, it contains a powerful late work by Bernini, the statue of The Blessed Ludovica Albertoni. From a wealthy family, she spent her fortune and ruined her health caring for the poor.

Renowned for her religious ecstasies, she became known as a miracleworker and, it was said, had the gift of levitation. Her ecstatic expression is reminiscent of Bernini's more famous statue of St Teresa in Santa Maria della Vittoria.

Porta Portese

The church is not far from **Porta Portese**, a gateway built by Urban VIII on the site of the ancient Porta Portuensis. Rome's cheap and cheerful **flea market ⑦** is held here on Sunday mornings.

Santa Cecilia in Trastevere ⑧

Address: 22 Piazza di Santa Cecilia
Opening Hours: church and crypt daily 10am–1pm, 4–7pm, frescoes daily 10am–12.30pm
Entrance Fee: charge for frescoes
Transport: bus: 8, 780, tram: H

FACT

Trastevere was the site of Rome's notorious old prison, the Carcere Regina Coeli. In the 18th century, women would pay "prison singers" to sing their messages from the piazza, which their incarcerated loved ones could hear from inside.

The superb mosaics inside Santa Maria in Trastevere.

KIDS

The Piazza Garibaldi in Trastevere is home to a puppet theatre (Sat–Sun 10.30am–1pm, 4–7pm), which has entertained children for decades. Please give generously, as it survives on donations from the public.

Nestling in a quiet and secluded part of Trastevere, this church is dedicated to the martyr St Cecilia, traditionally regarded as the inventor of the organ and the patron saint of music. Condemned to death for her faith in 230, she was to have been executed by means of suffocation, but when this failed, an executioner was despatched to behead her. She survived three strokes of the axe, living for a further three days and converting 400 pagans before she finally died. In 1599, her tomb was opened and her body, in a semi-foetal position, was found in a miraculous state of preservation. The artist, Maderno, made a beautiful statue of the saint, which can be seen beneath the high altar. The 13th-century frescoes by Pietro Cavallini in the adjacent convent are worth a look.

VIA DELLA LUNGARA

Tempietto di San Pietro.

Via della Scala leads from Piazza Sant'Egidio to the **Porta Settimiana**, a gate erected by Emperor Septimius Severus and replaced by Pope Alexander VI in 1498. From here Via Garibaldi climbs to the Gianicolo. This route was used in the Middle

Bernini's statue of The Blessed Ludovica Albertoni.

Ages by pilgrims en route to the Vatican, before the building of the *"retifili"* – the long, straight roads built by the Renaissance popes. The longest of these is Via della Lungara, laid out in the early 16th century to connect Trastevere with the Borgo. It's a short walk from the Porta Settimiana along Via della Lungara to the Villa Farnesina, a Trastevere gem.

Villa Farnesina

Address: 230 Via della Lungara; www.villafarnesina.it
Telephone: 06-6802 7268
Opening Hours: Mon–Sat 9am–2pm, second Sun of the month 9am–5pm; guided tours in English at 10am
Entrance Fee: charge
Transport: 125

This sumptuous villa was built between 1508 and 1511 for the fabulously wealthy papal banker, Agostino Chigi. Renowned for his lavish banquets, Chigi was also a noted patron of the arts and had his villa decorated with a series of

beautiful frescoes by some of the best artists of the time. The highlights of the downstairs rooms are Raphael's sensual *Triumph of Galatea* and *Three Graces*. Upstairs is a fine *trompe l'œil* depicting contemporary views of Rome by Peruzzi, and Sodoma's magnificent *Wedding of Roxanne and Alexander*.

Palazzo Corsini ⑩

Address: 10 Via della Lungara;
http://galleriacorsini.beniculturali.it
Telephone: 06-6880 2323
Opening Times: Wed–Mon
8.30am–7.30pm
Entrance Fee: charge; free first Sun of the month
Transport: 125

Built in the 15th century for a wealthy cardinal, this *palazzo* opposite the Villa Farnesina now houses part of the **Galleria Nazionale d'Arte Antica** collection, which includes works by Fra Angelico, Rubens, Van Dyck, Caravaggio and Luca Giordano (whose *Christ among the Doctors* is one of the collection's key works). The rest of the collection is in Palazzo Barberini (see page 117).

Orto Botanico ⑪

Address: 24 Largo Cristina di Svezia;
https://web.uniroma1.it/ortobotanico
Telephone: 06-4991 7108
Opening Hours: Mon–Sat
9am–6.30pm in summer, until 5.30pm in winter
Entrance Fee: charge
Transport: 8, 23, 280

Originally part of the Corsini palace grounds, the botanical gardens are now open to the public. There are about 7,000 plants on display, including a scented garden for the blind and a collection of medicinal herbs. On the slopes up to the Gianicolo is a series of tiered fountains.

THE GIANICOLO

The **Gianicolo** (Janiculum hill) is climbed from Trastevere via the long and winding Via Garibaldi. The hill was the site of one of Italy's decisive battles for independence, when in 1849 Garibaldi and his army defeated French troops sent to restore papal rule. At noon, a cannon blast sounds to commemorate the struggle for liberation.

Opposite the church of San Pietro in Montorio, a striking white monument is Mussolini's tribute to the heroes of the Risorgimento (1848–70). On it is written the slogan "Roma o morte" (Rome or death), Garibaldi's famous war-cry uttered on this spot.

In the Porta Portese flea market.

SHOP

Rome's most famous flea market is Porta Portese, held on Sunday 6am–2pm on Via Portuense and adjacent streets between Via Ettore Rolli and Porta Portese. Go early if you want to get the bargains and avoid the crowds.

Piazzale Garibaldi

You can either walk or hop on a bus (115 or 870) up the hill to Piazzale Garibaldi. The broad square is dominated by an **equestrian monument** to the freedom fighter, while further north is another for his wife, the intrepid Anita, represented as an Amazon. Views from the terrace are magnificent.

Via Garibaldi

If you're catching the bus up to the Piazzale it's worth jumping off on the way up at the church of **San Pietro in Montorio**, with works by Vasari, del Piombo and Bernini, but most importantly **Bramante's Tempietto** (Tue–Sun 9.30am–12.30pm, 2–4.30pm; free), one of the gems of the Renaissance. During the bloody fighting that took place in 1849, the wounded were brought into the church, which was right next to the battlefield. A commemorative plaque

Villa Farnesina.

SHOPPING

Trastevere is known for its small artisan's bottegas and little shops that are a delight to explore.

Accessories

Artigianino
49 Vicolo del Cinque
06-6067 6064
www.artigianino.com
Bags, wallets, belts and all things leather in all colours of the rainbow and with prices ranging from €5 to €300.

Books

Almost Corner Bookshop
45 Via del Moro
06-583 6942
This Australian-run bookshop stocks well-chosen and reasonably priced titles.

Open Door Bookshop
23 Via della Lungaretta
06-583 6942
Second-hand books in English, many of which are about Rome, feature here.

Department stores

Oviesse
62 Viale Trastevere
www.ovs.it
Basic department store for household goods, clothes and cosmetics. For affordable Italian fashion, check out the girls' line, especially designed for Oviesse by Fiorucci.

Gifts

Dolceidea
27 Via San Francesco a Ripa
06-5833 4043
www.dolceidea.com

Luxurious chocolates in all shapes and sizes, sugared almonds, praline boxes, and ice cream, all made in Naples by maitre chocolatier Gennaro Bottone.

Polvere di Tempo
59 Via del Moro
06-588 0704
www.polvereditempo.com
This unusual shop sells beautiful handmade copies of ancient time-measuring instruments, including sundials and sand clocks, as well as ancient globes.

Markets

Porta Portese
Trastevere
Sun 6am–2pm
This is the best flea market in Rome. Skill is required to get a real bargain, but it's great fun. Hang onto your bags and look out for pickpockets.

Paul V to grace the end of an ancient aqueduct built by Trajan.

FURTHER AFIELD

Southwest of Trastevere lies the green and well-heeled **Monteverde Vecchio** residential zone, built in the late 19th and early 20th centuries. Here also is the vast **Villa Pamphilij park** ⓮ (entrance on Via di San Pancrazio; dawn–dusk; bus 115, 710, 870 to Piazzale Aurelio), the largest green space in Rome, with undulating terrain, fields, picturesque walkways, pine forests, fountains, lakes and gardens, a theatre museum, a bistro and pony hire.

The basilica of **San Pancrazio** (Piazza San Pancrazio; www.sanpancrazio. org; Mon–Sat 9am–noon, 5–7pm, Sun 8am–1pm, 5–8pm; bus 75) was founded in the 6th century on the burial site of a young Roman martyr, who was beheaded for his faith in 304. Underneath the church are the **catacombs of San Pancrazio** (Wed 9.30am–noon, 4.30–7pm, Thu 9.30am–noon).

Not far to the east is another, far smaller but beautifully designed park and house, the **Villa Sciarra** ⓯. The park boasts botanical plants and statues of mythological figures.

on the outside of the church, with a French cannonball stuck to it, marks the event.

A little further uphill stands the **Fontana dell'Acqua Paola**, a fountain commissioned in 1612 by Pope

Via Garibaldi locals.

Catching some rays on the Gianicolo.

RESTAURANTS, BARS AND CAFÉS

PRICE CATEGORIES

Price includes dinner and a half-bottle of house wine.

€€€€ = more than €60
€€€ = €40–60
€€ = €25–40
€ = under €25.

Restaurants

Antica Pesa
18 Via Garibaldi
06-580 9236
www.anticapesa.it
D only Mon–Sat
€€€ 324, A4]
This historic restaurant serves up all the usual Roman classics, along with some surprises: try the ravioli with white truffles, or steak with strawberries and balsamic vinegar. Booking advised.

Antico Arco
7 Piazzale Aurelio
06-581 5274
www.anticoarco.it
L & D daily
€€€ [p320, B2]
Excellent restaurant on the Gianicolo hill, with a mix of traditional and innovative dishes. The speciality is risotto with a Piedmontese cheese.

Da Enzo Al 29
29 Via dei Vascellari
06-5812 260
www.daenzoal29.com
L & D Mon–Sat
€€ [p320,
Small and lively place with friendly and efficient staff. Roman staples done exceedingly well, plus some mouthwatering desserts.

Bir & Fud
23 Via Benedetta
06-4547 3223
http://birefud.blogspot.com
L & D daily
€–€€ [p324, A4]
A high-end pizzeria with a passion for quality ingredients. Choose from a large selection of fried antipasti and more than 100 labels of local and international beers, mainly from small, family-run breweries.

Checco er Carettiere
10 Via Benedetta
06-580 0985
www.checcoercarettiere.it
L & D daily
€€–€€€ [p324, A4]
A pleasant outdoors section and a steadfast Roman menu of fish and meat make this a sure bet. Sweets and ice cream are homemade.

Il Ciak
21 Vicolo del Cinque
06-589 4774
http://ristoranteilciak.com
D only Mon–Sat, L & D Sun
€€ [p324, A4]
Game hanging in the windows testifies that this is a meat-eating venue. Dishes based on hearty Tuscan recipes and served with the house Chianti.

La Cornucopia
18 Piazza in Piscinula
06-580 0380
www.ristorantecornucopia.com
L & D daily
€€ [p320, D2]
Specialising in fish dishes, this restaurant's other selling point is its lovely garden, which is a pleasant place for dinner in the summer months.

Enoteca Ferrara
1a Via del Moro
06-5833 3920
www.enotecaferrara.it
D only daily
€€€–€€€ [p324, B4]
Minimalist decor and creative menu with organic ingredients. Comprehensive wine selection (850 labels). Light snacks or full meals. Reservations essential at weekends.

La Fraschetta
134 Via S. Francesco a Ripa
06-581 6012
www.lafraschetta.com
L & D daily
€€ [p320, C2]
Simple pizzeria and trattoria menu served with house wine in a jovial atmosphere.

Alle Fratte di Trastevere
49–50 Via delle Fratte di Trastevere
06-583 5775
http://allefratteditrastevere.com
L & D Thu–Tue
€€ [p320, C2]
A family-run, authentic Trastevere trattoria serving up Roman dishes with Neapolitan touches – try the oven-roast sea bream. In summer, request one of the few outside tables.

La Gensola
15 Piazza della Gensola
06-581 6312
www.osterialagensola.it
L & D daily
€€€ [p320, D2]
A homey atmosphere, a spontaneous and friendly service and art on the walls are the main elements here. Great cuisine specializing in rare and precious ingredients such as sea anemone, Sicilian tuna and king crab.

Glass Hostaria
58 Vicolo del Cinque
06-5833 5903
www.glass-restaurant.it
D only Tue–Sun
€€€ [p324, A4]
Ultra-modern Glass offers creative Italian cuisine and attentive service. Though the cutting-edge design won't be to everyone's taste, it does make a change from Trastevere's predominantly red-checkered-tablecloth trattoria decor.

Jaipur
56 Via di San Francesco a Ripa
06-580 3992
www.ristorantejaipur.com
L & D Tue–Sun, D only Mon
€€ [p320, C2]
If you just can't face another pizza, Jaipur is one of the city's

best Indian restaurants, with friendly service and a great selection of tandoori dishes. Particularly strong on vegetarian options.

Le Mani in Pasta
37 Via de' Genovesi
06-581 6017
www.lemaniinpasta.net
L & D Tue–Sun
€€ [p320, D2]
Inviting and friendly restaurant serving meat and fish carpaccios; home-made pastas are cooked in a myriad of different ways. No menu, but the prices are reasonable. Booking advised. Closed three weeks Aug.

Ai Marni
53 Viale Trastevere
06-580 0919
D only Thu–Tue
€ [p320, D2]
Not the most inspiring of interiors, but a Rome classic for its thin crusty pizzas, large antipasti buffet, low prices and its quicker-than-lightning, brusque Roman service.

Paris
7a Piazza San Calisto
06-581 5378
www.ristoranteparis.it
L & D Tue–Sat, L only Sun
€€€ [p320, C2]
Reliably excellent traditional Roman-Jewish cuisine, such as golden deep-fried vegetables and coda alla vaccinara (braised oxtail with tomatoes, celery and white wine), characterises this eaterie. Small outdoor eating area. Closed for three weeks in Aug.

Dar Poeta
45–46 Vicolo del Bologna
06-588 0516
www.darpoeta.com
D only daily
€ [p324, A4]
Pizzas made with a blend of yeast-free flours, which creates an incomparably fluffy base, and tasty toppings. No reservations.

Spirito Divino
31a/b Via de' Genovesi
06-589 6689
www.spiritodivino.com

D only Mon–Sat
€€ [p320, D2]
History permeates this restaurant that stands atop the remains of a synagogue and an ancient Roman house. Classic dishes are served, many based on recipes used in Ancient Rome. The wine list is international and has won plaudits.

Trattoria degli Amici
5 Piazza Sant'Egidio
06-580 6033
www.trattoriadegliamici.org
L & D Mon–Sat, L only Sun
€€ [p324, A4]
This restaurant gives work experience to mentally and physically handicapped people. There's a friendly atmosphere, hearty Roman cooking and great value for money. Popular so book ahead. Closed throughout Aug.

Da Vittorio
14a Via di San Cosimato
06-580 0353
www.davittorioatrastevere.it
D only daily
€€ [p320, C2]
One of Trastevere's most popular pizzerias, Da Vittorio serves up delicious Neapolitan-style pizza: try the house special Vittorio, with a classic topping of mozzarella, tomato and basil. Great atmosphere and good value.

Bars and Cafés

Akbar
51 Piazza in Piscinula
06-8975 61519
www.ak-bar.com
[p320, D2]
Tables in all styles and colours surrounded by vintage chairs give this corner bar an artsy feel. Open morning to night, Akbar serves a lunch and dinner buffet for €8–10. Live music in the evening.

Baretto
27F Via Garibaldi
06-589 6055
[p324, A4]
A retro feel, a fabulous position between Trastevere and Giani-

colo, and plenty of outdoor space have turned this bar into a popular pre- and post-dinner stopover. Live music and film screenings in summer.

Bar San Calisto
3–4 Piazza San Calisto
[p320, C2]
This neighbourhood bar is small and plain but nevertheless pulls in an incredibly mixed crowd. Its chocolate ice cream and hot chocolate in winter are deservedly famous.

Caffè del Gianicolo
5 Piazzale Aurelio
[p320, B2]
On the scenic Gianicolo hill, this is a simple bar where light snacks and fruit-shakes can be consumed indoors and out.

Caffè di Marzio
15 Piazza Santa Maria in Trastevere
[p320, C2]
The best-priced café in lovely Piazza Santa Maria in Trastevere, which offers excellent opportunities for people-watching.

Freni e Frizioni
4–6 Via del Politeama
06-4549 7499
www.freniefrizioni.com
[p324, B4]
A buzzy bar open for breakfast, lunch and dinner, but most popular for aperitifs in the early evening, when the crowds spill out onto the piazza outside.

Friends Art Café
34 Piazza Trilussa
06-581 6111
www.cafefriends.it
[p324, B4]
The ever-popular café is open all day long until late at night, and is a good place for a quick bite or an expertly mixed cocktail.

Ombre Rosse
12 Piazza Sant'Egidio
06-588 4155
[p324, A4]
This is the perfect place for a cocktail or beer. Set in a picturesque piazza, it boasts a lively atmosphere and is open all day every day (except Sunday morning).

The entrance to Parco Savello.

AVENTINO AND TESTACCIO

The most southerly of Rome's hills, the Aventine has always been a tranquil and sought-after residential area. Testaccio, once a busy working river port, is still one of the city's most down-to-earth and genuinely Roman districts.

The Aventine hill is now one of the most desirable places in which to live in Rome, a peaceful oasis conveniently close to the city centre. Considered the "Sacred Mount" in ancient times, it is the site of pagan temples and of some of Rome's earliest Christian churches.

For centuries, the Aventine lay outside the city walls. It remained virtually uninhabited until 494 BC when the plebeians retreated here to organise the first general strikes against patrician rule. During the latter years of the Republic, it was the residence of foreign merchants and nouveau riche plebeians.

By the Imperial era, the hill had moved right up the social scale. The aristocracy moved in and built magnificent temples and luxury villas on it. In subsequent centuries, several churches were built on the ancient sacred sites. Today, the Aventine remains a well-to-do neighbourhood.

THE AVENTINE HILL

High on the hill is the **Parco Savello**, the gardens once surrounding the 12th-century residence of the noble Savello family. Today the park is a serene destination for walks or picnics, lined with orange trees and overlooking St Peter's dome which, thanks to an optical illusion, appears farther away as you move towards it from the park's entrance.

Santa Sabina and Sant'Alessio ❶

Address: 1 Piazza Pietro d'Illiria
Opening Hours: daily 8.15am–12.30pm, 3.30–6pm
Entrance Fee: free
Transport: 51, 81, 85, 87, 118, 160, 628, 715, 810, C3

Main Attractions
Santa Sabina
Piazza dei Cavalieri di Malta
Piramide di Caio Cestio
Cimitero Acattolico
Testaccio
Mattatoio
Centrale Montemartini
Garbatella
San Paolo fuori le Mura
EUR

Maps and Listings
Map, page 214
Shopping, page 216
Restaurants, page 222

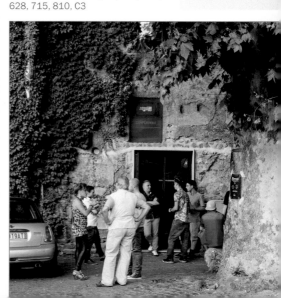

The pace is a lot slower up here.

A Maltese cross in Piranesi's Piazza dei Cavalieri di Malta.

The gardens flank the early Christian basilica of Santa Sabina, skilfully restored to its near-original state in 1936. It was built in the 5th century by a priest from Dalmatia, Peter of Illyria, on the site of the house of a martyred Roman matron called Sabina. The broad nave is lined with elegant Corinthian columns, relics of a temple which once stood here. The west door, made of cypress wood, is as old as the church; its carved panels depict biblical scenes, including the earliest known representation of the Crucifixion.

Next door, the church of **Sant' Alessio** has a fine Romanesque *campanile* (bell tower). A pretty courtyard leads into a Baroque interior with a gilt-covered relic of a staircase, beneath which St Alexis is said to have lived and died.

The Knights of Malta

From here, Via Santa Sabina leads into **Piazza dei Cavalieri di Malta** ➋. The square is named after the ancient chivalric order founded in 1080 as the Hospitallers of St John to run a hospital for pilgrims in Jerusalem. The Hospitallers became

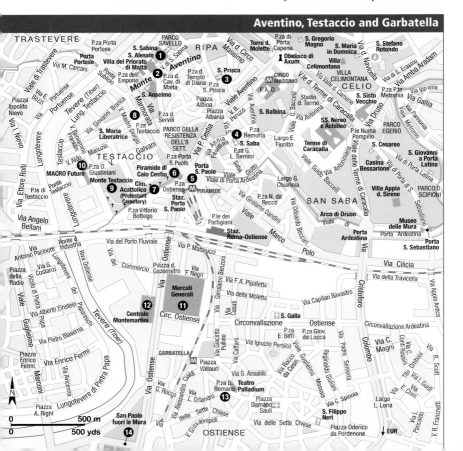

a powerful military order, based in Malta until they were expelled by Napoleon in 1798. The Knights of Malta have been based in Rome ever since.

The square was designed by the 18th-century engraver Piranesi and has heraldic symbols containing allusions to the military prowess of the knights. Piranesi was also responsible for the monumental gate to the **Priorato di Malta**, the residence of the Grand Master of the order.

Santa Prisca and San Saba

Down the hill and to the northeast is the church of **Santa Prisca** ❸ (11 Via di Santa Prisca; daily 7.30am–noon, 5–6.30pm), said to occupy the site of a 3rd-century house belonging to Prisca and Aquila, who invited St Peter to dine here. Beneath the church are the remains of a *mithraeum*, a grotto to the ancient god Mithras (www.coopculture.it; guided

tours only, second and third Sat of the month).

Further down the hill you come to the Viale Aventino, which divides the main Aventine Hill from the smaller one known as *Il Piccolo Aventino*. On the right are remnants of the city walls dating from the 4th century BC.

Across Piazza Albani, Via San Saba leads to the pretty 10th-century church of **San Saba** ❹ (20 Piazza G. Bernini; www.sansaba.it; daily 8am–noon, 4–7.10pm), founded in the 7th century by exiled Palestinian monks. Ancient sculptural fragments are displayed in its portico, and the interior has some Cosmatesque work and remains of a 13th-century fresco of St Nicolas.

PIRAMIDE

Originally called the Porta Ostiense, because it marked the beginning of the road to Ostia, **Porta San Paolo** ❺ is one of the best-preserved of the ancient city gates. It was renamed after St Paul who entered Rome through it. It houses a small Museo della Via Ostiense (Tue–Sun 9am–1pm) which documents the

FACT

The ashes of Romantic poet Shelley are in the Protestant Cemetery. He drowned off the coast of Viareggio and was cremated in the presence of Lord Byron. His heart, however, was snatched from the pyre and was buried alongside Mary Shelley in an English churchyard.

The moving inscription on Keats' tomb.

Ceiling detail, Sant'Alessio.

This door leads to the gardens of the Priorato di Malta. Peek through the keyhole for an unusual view of the dome of St Peter's framed by a tree-lined avenue.

Piazza Testaccio architecture.

long history of the road that links Rome with the seaside town of Ostia. Among exhibits are ancient monuments that once stood by the road, prints and photographs. Impressive though the gateway is, it is overshadowed by the **Piramide di Caio Cestio ⑥**, (www.coopculture. it; guided tours only) the tomb of a vainglorious Roman officer, Gaius Cestius, buried here in 12 BC.

Cimitero Acattolico ⑦

Address: 6 Via Caio Cestio; www. cemeteryrome.it
Telephone: 06-574 1900
Opening Times: Mon–Sat 9am–5pm, Sun 9am–1pm
Entrance Fee: free
Transport: Piramide

Adjoining the pyramid is Rome's **Cimitero Acattolico**, known in English as the Protestant Cemetery. Romantic poets Shelley and Keats (the latter dying in a house overlooking the Spanish Steps), and the son of the German writer Goethe are buried here. The cemetery is perhaps more properly regarded as the burial place of non-Catholics rather than just foreigners, and it also contains the graves of a number of prominent Italians, including Antonio Gramsci, founder of the Italian Communist Party.

TESTACCIO

Testaccio, the area west of Porta San Paolo, doesn't feature on most tourist itineraries, but it's worth a visit if you want to experience a genuine Roman working-class district, before it goes the way of Trastevere and gentrification changes its character for good.

By the Middle Ages Testaccio had largely been abandoned, and wasn't developed into a residential area until the end of the 19th century when rows of low-cost tenement blocks with internal courtyards were built to house the workers. Many of these so-called *case popolari* are still rent-controlled working class residences, though the influx of a new generation of more moneyed residents drawn to the fashionable district is driving property prices up.

Testaccio is now one of the most culturally active areas in Rome, with theatres, a cinema, a music school and some of the liveliest nightlife in town. Many of the old wine cellars have been transformed into clubs and late-night bars.

Piazza Testaccio ⑧

Despite its ongoing gentrification, Testaccio still retains something

SHOPPING

Shopping in this working-class neighbourhood gravitates around the market on Piazza Giustiniani. The few shops in Testaccio mainly sell household items and food, with the occasional exception.

Rome. Stock up on goodies to bring home, or buy your takeaway lunch for a luxurious picnic.

Food

Volpetti
47 Via Marmorata
06-574 2352
www.volpetti.com
Probably the best deli in

Shoes

Boccanera
36 Via Luca della Robbia
06-575 0847
www.boccanera.it
Find all the big Italian (and some foreign) brands under one roof. including Hogan, Tod's, Prada and those Italian icons, Dolce & Gabbana.

location in Piazza Testaccio to Piazza Giustiniani in 2012, is a testimony to this.

To the south lies **Via Galvani**, home to some trendy minimalist restaurants serving fusion cuisine. Via Galvani leads to Monte Testaccio, which is bounded by **Via di Monte Testaccio**, an uninhabited, quasi-rural lane that is best visited at night when its clubs, bars and restaurants, housed in unlikely looking warehouses and low buildings, really get going.

Monte Testaccio ❾

The heart of the district is the 35-metre (105ft) -high Monte Testaccio, or "Hill of Shards", which gets its name from the broken bits of amphorae that can be found here. Testaccio was basically an ancient landfill site. The amphorae used to transport oil and wine was neatly dumped here once their contents had been unloaded in the warehouses of the Republican port that lined the Tiber between Ponte Testaccio and Ponte Aventino. Today the mound is closed to

of an authentic working-class appeal. The daily produce market, transferred from its historic

TIP

Several of the clubs and restaurants built into Monte Testaccio offer a view of the amphorae shards at their lower levels. One of the finest displays can be seen in the back room of Ketumbar (24 Via Galvani; www.ketumbar.it; tel: 06-5730 5338). The oriental-inspired fusion restaurant and bar attracts a hip crowd, and the food is a break from everyday Italian.

Detail from the terraces of stacked amphora.

Fresh produce at the indoor market.

the public, but you can arrange guided visits (tel: 06-0608). Views of the Tiber valley from the top are splendid.

MATTATOIO

Between Monte Testaccio and the river lies the Mattatoio, the city's former slaughterhouse dating from 1891, when the cattle market was moved here from Piazza del Popolo. For decades, the Mattatoio was the main source of revenue for Testaccio, but in 1975 it was pensioned off when a modern "meat centre" was built outside the city. Today, the buildings house a contemporary art gallery, a cultural center, the university's architecture department and a farmers' market on Sundays.

MACRO Future

Address: 4 Piazza Orazio Giustiniani; www.museomacro.org
Telephone: 06-0608
Opening Hours: open for exhibitions only Tue–Sun 4–10pm

Porta San Paolo and the Piramide di Caio Cestio.

Entrance Fee: charge
Transport: Piramide

This is one of two sites occupied by the Museo d'Arte Contemporanea di Roma (see page 191. This gallery hosts impressive art shows and installations, often in collaboration with the big guns on the contemporary art scene, including MoMa and PS1.

SOUTH OF THE CENTRE

First impressions of **Ostiense**, a former industrial district south of Testaccio, are not favourable. But for those interested in discovering the face of modern Rome, it's worth delving beneath the grubby surface of this up-and-coming young area. Bars, restaurants and clubs are mushrooming in the streets around **Via Ostiense**.

Rome's former wholesale food market, the vast **Mercati Generali** ⓫, is undergoing a Covent Garden-style makeover led by Dutch architect Rem Koolhaas, who is transforming the area into a state-of-the-art shopping and leisure district.

Centrale Montemartini ⑫

Address: 106 Via Ostiense; www.
centralemontemartini.org
Telephone: 06-0608
Opening Hours: Tue–Sun 9am–7pm
Entrance Fee: charge
Transport: Garbatella

Just a 10-minute walk from the Piramide di Caio Cestio is Ostiense's main attraction. What began as a temporary solution to the overcrowding of the Capitoline Museums has become a delightful landmark museum. Four hundred pieces of Roman sculpture are on permanent display in a converted electricity power plant. The juxtaposition of statues with machinery, tubes and furnaces makes this a highly unusual venue. The occasional live jazz performance adds a classy soundtrack.

Garbatella

On the other side of Via Ostiense is the vibrant working-class neighbourhood of Garbatella (Metro B Garbatella, exit left side), worth visiting both for its old-Rome authenticity and for the

architecture. The area was conceived and constructed in the 1920s during the post-WWI building boom. First intended for city workers and immigrants, the quarter was modelled on the English "garden city", which laid out two- or three-storey buildings in plots with plentiful gardens and gathering space, in the hopes that newcomers to the city would thrive among their Roman neighbours in communal harmony. The architects in charge of the project, Sabbatini and Giovannoni, added character to what might otherwise have been run-of-the-mill housing projects, with balconies, chimneys, floral embellishments and arches.

Piazza Bartolomeo Romano ⑬, one of the neighbourhood's most characteristic squares, is home to the **Teatro Palladium** (http://palladium.uniroma3.it; tel: 06-5733 2768). Today the arts centre stages international music and dance performances and participates in the prestigious multimedia Romaeuropa Festival (www.romaeuropa.net).

Street art in Ostiense.

Centrale Montemartini.

EUR

The stark district was Mussolini's attempt to build a city fit for Fascists. Today it is a sought-after residential neighbourhood.

The rather clumsy acronym EUR stands for the Esposizione Universale di Roma (Universal Exhibition of Rome), which was to have been held in 1942 to mark the 20th anniversary of Mussolini's accession, but because of the war it never took place. The slightly hilly site, south of San Paolo, was intended to form an impressive entrance to a new town extending all the way to Ostia. But by the time the Fascist regime was over, only two palaces on either side of Via Cristoforo Colombo had been built.

Metaphysical landscapes

A start had been made on **Palazzo della**

Palazzo della Civiltà del Lavoro, the symbol of EUR.

Civiltà del Lavoro (Palace of the Civilisation of Labour; www.eurspa.it), popularly known as the "square Colosseum". Piacentini's plans for the new town combined monumental grandeur and a repetitive motif: square pillars, square ground plans and square roofs. The buildings radiate a cold beauty that is all the more striking because, in the city's centre, nothing is rarer than a straight line. After the war, Mussolini-style architecture gave way first to glass facades and reinforced concrete, and then to post-modernism. The result is a largely unplanned mishmash of styles.

But it is not all modern. There is a reminder of Ancient Rome in the form of the **Abbazia delle Tre Fontane** (www.abbaziatrefontane.it), the 8th-century abbey on the northeast slope of the EUR hill. This is where St Paul was reputedly beheaded.

Museums are EUR's main attraction. The **Museo Nazionale Preistorico-Etnografico Luigi Pigorini** (www.pigorini.beni culturali.it; Mon–Sat 9am–6pm, Sun 9am–1.30pm; charge) on Piazza Marconi has a large collection of prehistoric artefacts. Next to it, the **Museo Nazionale delle Arti e Tradizioni Popolari** (www.idea. mat.beniculturali.it; Tue–Sun 8.30am–7.30pm; charge) presents a lively portrayal of Rome's social history (though everything is labelled in Italian). But the most interesting of all is the **Museo della Civiltà Romana** (10 Piazza G. Agnelli; www. museociviltaromana.it), which chronicles every aspect of Ancient Roman life, but unfortunately it's closed for renovation.

In recent years, the EUR has experienced an architectural revival in the city's attempt to turn the neighbourhood into yet another tourist attraction. Rome's new Aquarium will host hundreds of Mediterranean species inside an innovative seethrough structure embedded under the EUR lake (www.acquariodiroma.com), while renowned architect Fuksas will inaugurate his so-called "cloud", a suspended glass structure hanging from the ceiling of his new congress building.

The quickest way to reach EUR is by metro on the B line, but there are many bus services from the city centre.

San Paolo fuori le Mura ⑭

Address: 190 Via Ostiense; www.
basilicasanpaolo.org
Telephone: 06-6988 0800

Opening Hours: daily 7am–6.30pm;
paid sites from 8am
Entrance Fee: charge for cloister,
Pinacoteca and archaeological site
Transport: San Paolo

In an unappealing site between Via Guglielmo Marconi and the Tiber stands San Paolo fuori le Mura, one of Rome's four patriarchal basilicas.

Built on the site of St Paul's tomb, it was once the most glorious church in Rome, but it was sacked by Saracens, then in 1823 almost completely destroyed by a fire. It may have lost much of its ancient splendour, but it's impressive nonetheless. Remnants of the original basilica include a set of doors dating back to the 11th century, engraved with stories from the Bible, and a Gothic tabernacle by Arnolfo di Cambio, rising over the high altar.

The 13th-century mosaic in the apse depicting Christ and Saints Peter, Paul, Andrew and Luke, was the work of Venetian craftsmen sent to Rome by the Doge. The cloisters are among the most beautiful in Rome.

FACT

St Paul was martyred in AD 67 at Aquae Salviae, about 3km (2 miles) from San Paolo fuori le Mura. Legend relates that when he was beheaded, after having converted one of Nero's favourite concubines, milk instead of blood flowed from his veins.

Try before you buy at the Volpetti delicatessen in Testaccio.

Teatro Palladium.

RESTAURANTS, BARS AND CAFÉS

PRICE CATEGORIES

Price includes dinner and a half-bottle of house wine.
€€€€ = more than €60
€€€ = €40–60
€€ = €25–40
€ = under €25.

Restaurants

Agustarello
100 Via G. Branca
06-574 6585
L & D Mon–Sat
€€ [p320, D4]
This restaurant specialises in cooking with the "poor" ingredients that this area – one of the city's most authentic – is famous for: *coda alla vaccinara* (oxtail in a tomato-based stew), tripe and the like.

Angelina
24a Via Galvani
06-5728 3840
www.ristoranteangelina.com

Estrobar at the Abitart hotel.

D only daily, B Sun
€€ [p320, D4]
White-washed vintage cupboards, butcher counters and country-style tables make up this contemporary osteria housed in an old meat warehouse. The menu includes the typical Testaccio dishes, with many offal recipes. The roof opens up for dining under the stars. Sunday brunch.

Le Bistrot
160 Via delle Sette Chiese
06-512 8991
www.ristorantelebistrot.com
L & D Mon–Fri, L only Sat
€€–€€€ [off map, p320, E4]
A little way from Testaccio in villagey Garbatella, this cosy restaurant offers a variety of vegetarian dishes; the menu is split between pasta and dishes with a French slant.

Bucatino
84 Via della Robbia

06-574 6886
www.bucatino.com
L & D daily
€ [p320, D4]
Bucatini alla amatriciana is the dish that gave the name to this trattoria specializing in authentic Roman cuisine. The interiors remain unchanged since the 1960s, with wood-panelled walls and wooden tables. Service is fast (sometimes even too fast) and the evenings are loud and definitely informal – and people keep coming back.

Cantina Castrociclo
35 Viale degli Astri
06-520 4979
www.cantinacastrociclo.it
D & L Tue–Sat, early D Mon
€€ [off map, p320, D4]
More than just a wine bar, the menu at this *enoteca* in EUR includes a wide range of dishes for a complete dinner. Apart from the usual (but delicious) cold platters, Castrociclo serves ravioli with parmesan, and meat stews. Wine lovers have a wealth of labels to choose from.

Checchino dal 1887
30 Via di Monte Testaccio
06-574 6318
www.checchino-dal-1887.com
L & D Tue–Sat, L Sun
€€€ [p320, D4]
Typical Roman cuisine excellently prepared. Known throughout the city so booking is advisable. Closed Aug.

Stazione di Posta
Largo Dino Frisullo (Città dell'Altra Economia)
33-3418 7870
www.stazionediposta.eu
D only Mon, L & D Tue–Sat
€–€€ [p320, C4]
Situated in the eco-space of the former slaughterhouse, this trattoria serves simple dishes made with organic ingredients from local producers. Try the small selection of natural wines and beers.

Estrobar
20 Via P. Matteucci (Abitart Hotel)
06-5728 9141
www.estrobar.com
D only Mon–Sat
€€€ [p320, D4]
This classy restaurant within the designer Abitart hotel has an arty theme. Exhibitions of young artists' work provide a suitable backdrop for the sophisticated menu. There's also a tasting menu.

Da Felice
29 Via Mastro Giorgio
06-574 6800
www.feliceatestaccio.it
L & D Mon–Sat daily
€€ [p320, D4]
A Testaccio institution, this bustling restaurant serves up classics of Roman cuisine such as roast lamb with rosemary potatoes. Closed three weeks Aug.

Junsei
69 Via Galvani
06-575 4012
www.junsei.it
L & D daily
€€–€€€ [p320, C/D4]
A great Japanese restaurant serving sushi in unusual varieties, and many fusion dishes like black cod from Alaska marinated in miso, or blue fin tuna with yosuponzu sauce.

Ketumbar
24 Via Galvani
06-5730 5338
www.ketumbar.it
L & D daily
€€–€€€ [p320, D4]
Sleek, minimalist interior. Food might include sushi, nasi goreng and braised tuna fillets with parmesan wafers. Music gets louder as the evening wears on.

Manali
108 Via Avignone
06-8992 7741
www.ristorantemanali.it
L & D Mon–Fri, D only Sat
€€ [off map, p320, D4]
This pleasant, airy restaurant near the lake in EUR offers creative Mediterranean cooking, using seasonal ingredients. Home-made desserts include a

delicious white chocolate mousse *cannolo*.

Remo
44 Piazza S. Maria Liberatrice
06-574 6270
D only Mon–Sat
€ [p320, D4]
This is one of the best pizzerias in the area, with good starters on the menu. No booking.

Tuttifrutti
3a Via Luca della Robbia
06-575 7902
D only Mon–Sat
€ [p320, D4]
Hidden down a side street is this friendly, charming restaurant. The menu changes on a daily basis but always contains Italian classics such as *cacio e pepe* (pasta and baked lamb). Closed two weeks Aug.

Bars and Cafés

Andreotti
54/56 Via Ostiense
06-575 0773
www.andreottiroma.it
[off map, p320, D4]
A historic *pasticceria*, where they'll

Popular Checchino.

not only serve you a perfect cappuccino, but also beautifully wrap up any pastries you want to take with you.

Doppio Zero
68 Via Ostiense
06-5730 1961
www.doppiozeroo.com
[off map, p320, D4]
This chic, New York-style café with its own bakery offers great bread and pastries at breakfast time, light meals and snacks, as well as a selection of delicious cakes in the afternoon.

Oasi della Birra
38 Piazza Testaccio
06-574 6122
[p320, D4]
This is a popular meeting spot for young Romans, with a choice of more than 500 beers from all over the world.

Il Seme e la Foglia
18 Via Galvani
06-574 3008
[p320, D4]
A trendy spot to enjoy an espresso or cappuccino, or linger a bit longer over a light lunch.

CELIO AND SAN GIOVANNI

The Lateran, on the eastern extremity of the Caelian hill slightly off the beaten track, was once the centre of the Catholic Church, hence this area is packed with striking ancient monuments and churches steeped in history.

hen the Lateran Palace was the seat and residence of the popes (from the 4th century until the papacy's temporary move to Avignon in 1309), the Lateran was the centre of the Catholic Church. On the return of the papacy to Rome in 1377, the Pope's official residence was moved to the Vatican, but the Lateran remained an important centre for the Church – popes were still crowned here until 1870.

PIAZZA DI SAN GIOVANNI

At the heart of the Lateran district is **Piazza di San Giovanni**, flanked by the **Palazzo Lateranense** (Lateran Palace; www.museivaticani.va; visits by appointment only). The original papal residence, founded in the 4th century, was damaged by fire and fell into ruin. In 1586, Pope Sixtus V commissioned Domenico Fontana to build a new palace as a papal summer residence, though it was never used as such. Fontana's Baroque palace now houses the offices of the diocese of Rome (of which the Pope is bishop). It was the site of the historic meeting that led to the 1929 Lateran Treaty, which established the current boundaries of the Vatican and stabilised its relationship with the Italian state.

San Giovanni in Laterano ❶

Address: 4 Piazza San Giovanni in Laterano
Telephone: 06-6988 6433
Opening Hours: daily 7am–6.30pm, museum 10am–7.30pm
Entrance Fee: free
Transport: San Giovanni

Next to the palace stands the mighty **San Giovanni in Laterano**, the "mother of all churches" and the first Christian basilica in Rome, founded by Constantine the Great. The church has stood here since

Baths of Caracalla.

The cloisters (daily 9am–6pm) of San Giovanni in Laterano are a high spot of any tour of the basilica. Completed around 1230, they are the work of father-and-son team Jacopo and Pietro Vassalletto, supreme masters of the Cosmatesque school of mosaic work. Note how the columns are inlaid with chips of coloured glass and marble, which were plundered from ancient remains.

313, but it has burnt down twice and been rebuilt several times. As a result, it is a mixture of styles from the exquisite 4th-century baptistery to the majestic Baroque interior.

The east facade, through which you enter, is the work of Alessandro Galilei (1732–5), but it was Fontana who designed the north facade, when he was rebuilding the Lateran Palace.

The central doorway has the original bronze doors taken from the Roman Curia of the Forum. The facade is crowned by 15 huge statues of Christ and the Apostles, visible for miles around. Most of the marble-clad interior is the result of remodelling by Borromini (1646), but some of the works of art and church furnishings are far older. They include a fragment of fresco attributed to Giotto (1300) and a 14th-century Gothic baldacchino from which only the Pope is allowed to celebrate Mass. The

nave's gilded wooden ceiling was completed in 1567. Other features of note include the Baroque frescoes and reliefs of the transept, and the peaceful 13th-century cloisters.

The baptistery

The **Battistero Lateranense** (Baptistery; www.battisterolateranense.it; daily 9am–12.30pm, 4–6.30pm; free) was part of the original complex, built by Constantine around 320; it was rebuilt in its present octagonal shape in the 5th century. In the earliest days of Christianity, all Christians were baptised here. The chapels of San Giovanni Evangelista (St John the Evanglist) and Santi Rufina e Secunda (the original entrance) contain a series of exquisite 5th-century mosaics.

Standing 30 metres (100ft) high, the **obelisk** on the square is the tallest and oldest in Rome; it honours the Pharaoh Tutmes III and once stood in the Circus Maximus.

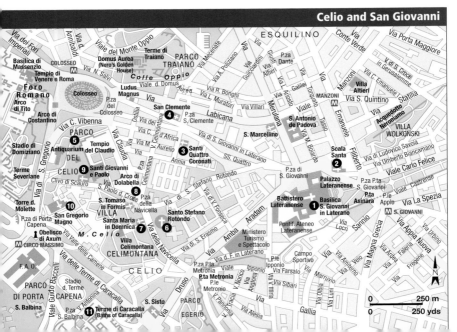

Celio and San Giovanni

Entrance Fee: free
Transport: San Giovanni

Across the street from the Lateran Palace is the entrance to the Scala Santa, said to be the stairs that Christ ascended when he was tried by Pontius Pilate. Brought to Rome from Jerusalem by Constantine's mother, Helena, they are protected under a layer of wood, but you still have to mount them on your knees, and the devout (who arrive in bus loads) do so slowly, stopping on each of the 28 steps to pray.

You can cheat and walk up one of the side staircases to the **Sancta Sanctorum** (Holy of Holies; tel: 06-772 6641; Mon–Sat 9am–12.40am, 3–5.10pm, closed Sun; charge), where there is a painting of Christ – said to be the work of St Luke and an angel.

Scala Santa ❷

Address: Piazza San Giovanni in Laterano; www.scala-santa.it
Opening Hours: daily 6am–1.30pm,

Santi Quattro Coronati ❸

Address: 20 Via dei SS Quattro; www.aulagoticasantiquattrocoronati.it
Opening Hours: limited access on special dates (see website for details),

The ancient bronze doors of San Giovanni in Laterano.

Scala Santa draws penitent pilgrims.

WHERE

Close to Piazza San Giovanni in Laterano, a small museum (145 Via Tasso; www.viatasso.eu; Tue–Sun 9.30am–12.30pm, Tue, Thu and Fri also 3.30–7.30pm; free), housed in the building that once hosted the Nazi headquarters in occupied Rome, commemorates Italy's liberation from Nazism and Fascism through the photographs and biographies of the heroes of the Resistance. The cells where prisoners were brought for interrogation are still in their original state, with goodbye messages to their loved ones scrawled on the walls.

The entrance to the 5th-century Santo Stefano Rotondo.

book in advance.

Entrance Fee: charge

Transport: 3, 8, 51, 85, 87, 117, 810

Originally part of the fortress that protected the Lateran Palace, the "Four Crowned Saints" belongs to a community of silent Augustine nuns. The present church, built over the remains of a much larger 4th-century edifice, dates from the 11th century.

Inside the complex, you can admire the beautiful 12th-century cloisters, with slender columns and a fountain, and also the **Chapel of San Silvestro**. This 13th-century chapel contains an endearing fresco illustrating the conversion of Constantine to Christianity by Pope St Sylvester (who was Pope at the time). You can see the emperor suffering from what looks like the advanced stages of a skin disease, then travelling to Rome to be cured by the Pope. A mosaic depicts St Helena's discovery of the True Cross, which she found at the same time as the Scala Santa.

San Clemente ❹

Address: 95 Via Labicana;

http://basilicasanclemente.com

Telephone: 06-774 0021

Opening Hours: Mon–Sat 9am–12.30pm, 3–6pm, Sun noon–6pm

Entrance Fee: free; charge for excavations

Transport: Colosseo

The basilica of **San Clemente** is one of Rome's most fascinating churches, with some of the finest mosaics and frescoes in the city. Run by an order of Irish Dominicans, it is in fact two churches, one built on top of the other, beneath which lie still earlier remains. The present church dating from the 12th century is built in basilica form with three naves divided by ancient columns. In the apse is a beautifully detailed mosaic depicting the cross as the Tree of Life nourishing all living things. Against a background of brilliant gold, the crucified Christ is depicted in jewel-like blues, reds and greens.

In the **Chapel of St Catherine** are some lovely early Renaissance frescoes of the life of St Catherine of Alexandria by Masolino (1383–1447) and Masaccio (1401–28). You can see Catherine praying while the

---

MITHRAS

Mithraism was a mystery religion that came from the Eastern Mediterranean in the 2nd century BC and was practised throughout the Roman Empire from the 1st century BC to the 5th century AD. It is difficult to unravel the exact workings and beliefs of Mithraism as the rituals were the secret of its exclusively male members. It was particularly popular with the army, with followers of the cult enduring severe ordeals, involving heat, cold and hunger. One ritual involved being locked in a coffin for several hours. Worship took place in a temple or *mithraeum* – a cave constructed to resemble Mithras' birthplace, which always contained a space for ritual banquets, a blue ceiling with the stars and planets, and a tauroctony, a depiction of Mithras as he slays the cosmic bull and gives birth to the universe.

One extraordinary aspect of Mithras is the similarity with the life of Christ. Mithras' birth was over the winter solstice, he became a travelling teacher who performed miracles, had 12 disciples, was called the Good Shepherd and the Messiah, had a last supper, was buried in a tomb, rose three days later on Sunday, and was celebrated once a year in the spring.

wheel to which she was strapped and tortured to death is prepared.

To the right a staircase leads down to a 4th-century church, with fine 11th-century frescoes of miracles being performed by St Clement, the fourth pope.

Temple of Mithras

An ancient stairway leads deeper underground to a Roman alley and a maze of damp corridors and eerie chambers. Down here is the earliest religious structure on the site, a 2nd-century **Temple of Mithras**, dedicated to the Persian god whose cult spread to Rome.

THE CELIO

The Celio (Caelian hill), incorporated into the city in 7 BC when the defeated citizens of the rebellious city of Alba lived there, is one of the seven classical hills of Rome. Today it is home to Villa Celimontana, surrounded by a pleasant park.

Parco del Celio ❺

Sprinkled with ancient ruins and some fine early medieval churches, Villa Celimontana was once a vineyard, and was bought by the

Enjoying the shade by San Clemente.

Santi Quattro Coronati fresco.

The ceiling of San Clemente.

Shopping for bargains.

Mattei family in the 16th century, who turned it into gardens and an art gallery. The villa is now a public park – a calm sanctuary of greenery and birdsong in a chaotic city. There are two entrances; the main gateway is on Piazza della Navicella.

A short driveway leads to the villa building, which is now the home of the Italian Geographical Society. To the left of the building are some winding pathways, a pristine lawn, and views over southern Rome and the Baths of Caracalla. To the right of the main building is a charming sloping area planted with trees and offering plenty of picnic spots. The park is often home to art exhibitions and special events; in the summer a series of evening jazz concerts is held here.

On the southeastern edge of the park is the 5th-century church of **Santo Stefano Rotondo** ❻ (tel: 06-421 199; Tue–Sat 9.30am–12.30pm, 2–5pm, Sun 9.30am–12.30pm; bus 673, 81), one of the few remaining circular churches in the city. The soft natural light that filters through its windows reveals gruesome 16th-century frescoes of martyred saints by Pomarancio.

SHOPPING

With its 2km (1.5 miles) of shops, Via Appia Nuova is one of Rome's more popular shopping streets. The portion of this street running from Porta San Giovanni to Piazza Re di Roma is lined with more expensive shops. After the Re di Roma roundabout, browse the bargain shops and less pricey department stores.

Department store

Coin
7 Piazzale Appio
06-702 7392

www.coin.it
Four floors of brand-name clothing and shoes, luxurious cosmetics and some well-made and imaginative linen and household items.

Market

Mercato di Via Sannio
Via Sannio, Piazza San Giovanni in Laterano
Mon–Fri 8am–2pm, Sat 8am–5pm
This outdoor market sells new and second-hand clothes; the occasional vintage gem can be found here for a bargain price.

Santa Maria in Domnica ❼

Address: 10 Via della Navicella
Telephone: 06-7720 2685
Opening Hours: daily 9am–noon, 3.30–6pm
Transport: 81, 673

On the other side of Via della Navicella is the 9th-century church of Santa Maria in Domnica. In the apse is a magnificent mosaic of the Virgin and Child surrounded by saints and angels in a garden of paradise – the man on his knees at the Virgin's feet is Pope Paschal I, who commissioned the mosaic.

Turn left outside the church to reach Via di San Paolo della Croce, which is straddled by the dramatic 1st-century **Arco di Dolabella** ❽, part of Nero's great aqueduct. Next to the arch, the gateway of **San Tommaso in Formis** (Sat–Sun 9.15am–12.30pm) is

decorated with a 13th-century mosaic showing Christ with two freed slaves, one black and one white.

Santi Giovanni e Paolo ❾

Address: 13 Piazza Santi Giovanni e Paolo
Telephone: 06-700 5745
Opening Hours: daily 8.30am–noon, 3.30–6pm
Entance Fee: free
Transport: Circo Massimo

The Via di San Paolo della Croce leads to the church of Santi Giovanni e Paolo. The first church here was built in the 4th century, but the present one is mainly 12th-century, with an early 18th-century interior. The 13th-century bell tower was built into the remains of a temple of Claudius. The church also gives access to the remains of houses dating back to the 1st century AD (13 Via Clivio di Scauro; www.case romane.it; Thu–Mon 10am–1pm, 3–6pm; charge).

San Gregorio Magno ❿

Address: 1 Piazza di San Gregorio
Telephone: 06-700 8227
Opening Hours: daily 9am–1pm, 3.30–7pm
Entrance Fee: free
Transport: Circo Massimo

TIP

The remains of the *caldarium* (hot room) in the Terme di Caracalla is used to stage the Teatro dell'Opera's annual outdoor opera and ballet festival in July and August (www.operaroma.it).

The Persian god Mithras.

Tranquil Parco del Celio.

Another noteworthy church in this area is the 17th-century **San Gregorio Magno**. Founded by St Gregory in the 6th century, the church is run by Benedictine monks. Inside, the medieval chapels of Santa Barbara and Sant'Andrea are of particular interest, the latter with frescoes by Guido Reni and Domenichino. The chapel of St Sylvia dates from the 17th century.

The Baths of Caracalla ⑪

Address: 52 Viale delle Terme di Caracalla; www.coopculture.it
Telephone: 06-3996 7700
Opening Hours: Tue–Sun 9am–one hour before dusk, Mon 9am–2pm
Entrance Fee: charge; free first Sun of the month
Transport: Circo Massimo

In AD 212 these were the most luxurious baths in Rome and the city's largest until the completion of the Baths of Diocletian a century later.

Pony rides are available in the Parco del Celio, which also has a children's playground.

The imposing Baths of Caracalla.

In their heyday, these baths could accommodate 1,600 people. Visitors could enjoy the use of libraries and

lecture rooms, a gymnasium and a stadium, quite apart from the complex of saunas and pools.

The interior was sumptuously decorated with marble, gilding and mosaics. The unearthed statues are now scattered among various collections, but the buildings are still impressive, their vaults rising 30 metres (100ft).

Fragments of mosaic are scattered around the Baths of Caracalla.

RESTAURANTS, BARS AND CAFÉS

PRICE CATEGORIES

Price includes dinner and a half-bottle of house wine.
€€€€ = more than €60
€€€ = €40–60
€€ = €25–40
€ = under €25.

Restaurants

I Clementini
106 Via San Giovanni in Laterano
06-4542 6395
www.iclementini.it
L & D daily
€ [p322, B2]
Service is friendly and the food is traditional at this old neighbourhood trattoria. Try the *pasta ai clementini* (garlic, hot pepper and cherry tomatoes), or good old classics like carbonara and *amatriciana*.

Crab
2 Via Capo d'Africa
06-7720 3636
www.ristorantecrab.it
L & D Tue–Sat, D only Mon
€€€ [p, B2]
A reputable but expensive seafood restaurant with the best oysters in town, as well as every kind of crustacean and mollusc imaginable.

Isidoro
59a Via San Giovanni in Laterano
06-700 8266
www.hostariaisidoro.com
L & D daily
€–€€ [p322, B2]
Fifty pasta first courses, most of which are suitable for vegetarians, although on Fridays many are fish-oriented.

Ai Tre Scalini
30 Via dei SS Quattro
06-709 6309
www.ai3scalini.com
L & D Tue–Sun
€€ [p322, B2]
Modern, inviting decor and convenient for the Colosseum. Equally strong on meat, fish and pasta. If it's too hot outside, try one of the naturally cool rooms on the lower level.

Bars and Cafés

Palazzo Manfredi
125 Via Labicana
06-7759 1380
www.palazzomanfredi.com
[p322, B2]
The rooftop bar of this hotel gives you an unparalleled view of the Colosseum. A charming place for an atmospheric *aperitivo*.

Shamrock
26d Via Capo d'Africa
06-700 2583
www.shamrockroma.it
[p322, B2]
A lively bar offering Guinness on tap, reasonable pub food and board games.

The cobbled streets of Monti.

MONTI AND ESQUILINO

This sprawling area centres on the Esquiline and Viminal hills that lie between the Colosseum and Stazione Termini. Wander the streets of bohemian Monti and multicultural Esquilino, take in the their fine churches and visit Roman antiquities.

I n ancient times Monte Esqui-lino, the largest of Rome's seven hills, was the site of communal burials for slaves and executed prisoners. Emperor Augustus transformed the area into an aristocratic residential zone with palatial villas and idyllic gardens. Maecenas, a rich bon vivant and Augustus' life-long friend, built himself a luxury villa on the hill, and Virgil and Horace also had homes here. Nero built his magnificent Domus Aurea on the Oppian Hill (Colle Oppio), which was later incorporated into the foundations of Trajan's Baths. Pope Sixtus V's magnificent villa stood on the site of what is now Termini Station. While the wealthy lived in luxury on the breezy summit, the foot of the hill was occupied by the slums of the densely populated Suburra district.

Many of the ancient palaces and villas of the area were cleared or built over to make way for the boulevards flanked by stately *palazzi* built after Unification in 1870.

MONTI

These days traffic thunders along Via Nazionale and Via Cavour, two characterless thoroughfares intersecting

the area, but between the lower end of them is a cluster of pretty, narrow, cobbled streets lined with bars, restaurants and boutiques, which make up the heart of the trendy bohemian Monti district. To the east, centred on the faded splendour of Piazza Vittorio, lies the Esquilino quarter, now the capital's prime multicultural district, with many shops and restaurants owned and run by North Africans, Indians and Chinese.

The western side of the Esquiline hill, known as Rione Monti or simply

Trendy locals.

Steep steps link San Pietro in Vincoli with Via Cavour.

called Monti, is now a lively district popular with artists, artisans and boutique-owners, and has a number of notable churches.

Santa Maria Maggiore ❶

Address: Piazza Santa Maria Maggiore; www.vatican.va
Telephone: 06-6988 6800
Opening Hours: daily 7am–6.45pm
Entrance Fee: free
Transport: Termini

According to legend, in August of AD 352, following a vision of the Virgin Mary, Pope Liberius witnessed a snowfall on the summit of the Esquiline hill. To commemorate the miracle he built the basilica of Santa Maria Maggiore.

The church is the only one of the four patriarchal basilicas in Rome to have retained its paleo-Christian structures. The 18th-century Baroque facade gives no indication of the building's true antiquity, but step inside and its venerable origins become apparent. The striking gilded coffered ceiling and elaborate chapels are 16th- and 17th-century additions, but the mosaics that decorate the triumphal arch and the panels high up on the nave walls are the original 5th-century ones. To the right of the main altar is the burial place of Bernini, Rome's Baroque genius.

Santa Prassede ❷

Address: 9 Via Santa Prassede
Telephone: 06-488 2456
Opening Hours: daily 7.30am–noon, 4–6.30pm (from 8am Sun)
Entrance Fee: free
Transport: Termini

South of Santa Maria Maggiore is **Santa Prassede**, built by Pope Paschal I in the 9th century. He commissioned mosaic-workers from Byzantium to decorate the apse, the triumphal arch and the chapel of San Zeno, reintroducing an art that had not been practised in Rome for three centuries – with stunning results.

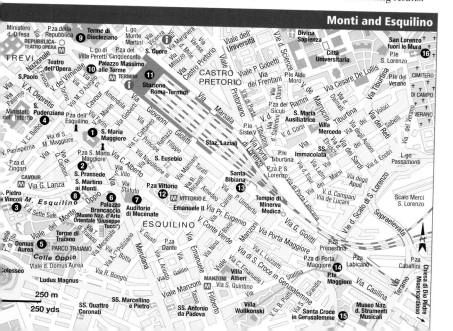

Monti and Esquilino

San Pietro in Vincoli ❸

Address: 4 Piazza di San Pietro in Vincoli
Telephone: 06-9784 4950
Opening Hours: daily 8am–12.30pm, 3–7pm (6pm in winter)
Entrance Fee: free
Transport: Cavour

From Piazza dell'Esquilino, in front of Santa Maria Maggiore, the busy Via Cavour descends the hill towards the Forum. Halfway down, a steep flight of steps leads to Via delle Sette Sale and San Pietro in Vincoli.

The church of St Peter in Chains was founded in the 5th century as a shrine for the chains said to have bound St Peter during his imprisonment in Jerusalem. They are preserved beneath the high altar in a bronze-and-crystal reliquary. Over the centuries the church was rebuilt and restored many times, but the ancient Doric columns lining the nave remained. The church is also home to Michelangelo's monumental *Moses*, part of the unfinished tomb that the artist was preparing for Pope Julius II.

Offbeat Monti

The cobblestone streets between Via Cavour and Via Panisperna are lined with artisans' shops, funky clothes shops, cool bars and ethnic restaurants. This area retains traces of its medieval past, as well as an intimate village atmosphere. Here you'll find some of the most interesting boutiques and workshops in town.

Just off Via Panisperna is the beautifully restored Piazza degli Zingari, where gypsy *(zingari)* caravans once congregated. From the square, Via Urbana leads to the church of **Santa Pudenziana** ❹ (8.30am–noon, 3–6pm), built over a house where St Peter allegedly stayed. Dating from the 4th century, its apse is decorated with one of the earliest known Christian mosaics.

OPPIO

The **Oppian hill**, site of Nero's legendary Golden House – the **Domus Aurea** ❺ (see page 110), is now an unkempt park strewn with rubbish and home to lots of stray cats, but there are some lovely views of the Colosseum from up here, and it's pleasant to get away from the bustle of the city. Cutting through this area is the busy Via Merulana.

Museo Nazionale d'Arte Orientale ❻

Address: 249 Via Merulana
Telephone: 06-4697 4832
Opening Hours: Tue, Wed and Fri 9am–2pm, Thu, Sat and Sun 9am–7.30pm
Entrance Fee: charge
Transport: Vittorio E

The 19th-century Palazzo Brancaccio houses the Museum of Oriental Art, a small but impressive collection ranging from 6,000-year-old Middle Eastern pottery to 18th-century Tibetan fans and ancient artefacts from the Swat culture in Pakistan. The museum also includes sections on Nepal, India, China, Japan, Korea

TIP

If you are in the area on 5 August, head for Santa Maria Maggiore, where the Festa della Madonna delle Neve is celebrated. Thousands of white flower petals cascade down from the roof of the church, commemorating the legendary summer snowfall on the Esquiline hill.

The stunning coffered ceiling inside Santa Maria Maggiore.

TIP

The Museo Nazionale Romano's collection of classical Roman art and statuary is contained in four different sites: the Terme di Diocleziano and Palazzo Massimo alle Terme near the station, Palazzo Altemps by Piazza Navona and Crypta Balbi near the Jewish Ghetto. A €7 museum card, valid for three days, covers all four sites.

Urban expression in San Lorenzo.

Terme di Diocleziano.

and Southeast Asia. In the gardens are remains of Nero's water cistern, the Sette Sale, built for his private house and used to feed Trajan's Baths.

Further along Via Merulana is the **Auditorio di Mecenate** ❼ (visits must be booked in advance, tel: 06-0608), dating from 30 BC and believed to be the *nymphaeum* of Maecenas' villa. Inside are the remains of frescoes depicting garden scenes, birds and small figures.

Follow Viale del Monte Oppio downhill to the 8th-century **San Martino ai Monti** ❽ (7.30am–noon, 4–7pm), a damp, dark church dotted with mosaic remnants and classical statuary.

ESQUILINO

In many cities the area around the main train station is scruffy and insalubrious, and Rome is no exception to this, with Termini Station surrounded by shabby apartments and run-down hotels. In the last two decades, the Esquiline has undergone a series of changes and renovations, from the creation of the new ES Hotel to the restoration of the Art

Nouveau Ambra Jovinelli. The old Esquilino market on Piazza Vittorio was moved to the covered structure on Via Principe Amedeo, and more improvements are still in progress.

Terme di Diocleziano ❾

Address: 79 Via Enrico de Nicola; www.coopculture.it
Telephone: 06-3996 7700
Opening Hours: Tue–Sun 9am–7.30pm
Entrance Fee: charge
Transport: Termini

At the northern end of Piazza della Repubblica are the remains of the Baths of Diocletian, one of the four sites of the Museo Nazionale Romano. Early in the 4th century, these baths – then the largest and most beautiful of the city's 900 bath-houses – were a buzzing centre of social activity. They fell into ruin after the aqueduct that fed them was destroyed by invading Goths.

In the 16th century, the church of **Santa Maria degli Angeli** (tel:

06-488 0812; www.santamariadegli-angeliroma.it) was built inside the *tepidarium* (warm bath) to a design by Michelangelo. The interior exploits the massive vaulting of the ancient building to dramatic effect. Highlights include a painting by Domenichino of the *Martyrdom of St Sebastian* and an elaborate timepiece on the nave floor.

The splendid **Aula Ottagona** (Octagonal Hall, open for special exhibitions only; tel: 06-0608) round the corner is an integral part of the immense structure of the baths, in which sculptures from the museum collection are displayed.

Palazzo Massimo alle Terme ⑩

Address: 1 Largo di Villa Peretti
Telephone: 06-3996 7700
Opening Hours: Tue–Sun 9am–7.45pm
Entrance Fee: charge
Transport: Termini

On Piazza dei Cinquecento is the imposing Palazzo Massimo alle Terme, the main site of the Museo Nazionale Romano's museum quartet, where you'll find the most important part of its vast collection of Roman antiquities. There's a stunning array of statuary on the ground floor from the Republican Age (2nd–1st century BC) to the late Imperial Age (4th century AD), but best of all are the splendid floor mosaics and wall paintings from the houses of wealthy Romans, seen at their best in the delicate frescoes from the Villa di Livia, the house of Augustus' wife that once stood on the Via Flaminia. The frescoes decorated the dining room and depict a garden paradise.

Stazione Roma Termini ⑪

On the other side of the piazza is one of the few successful pieces of post-war architecture, the graceful ticket hall of **Stazione Termini**,

designed by Angiolo Mazzoni. Its undulating roof echoes the remains of the Servian Walls, which are visible through long glass windows. Uncovered during the building of the first station in 1867, they are believed to date from the reign of Servius Tullius (6th century BC). The revamped station now offers a vast selection of services including a shopping centre, an excellent art gallery (by platform 24), a gym, restaurants, a post office, a church and a medical centre.

The covered Nuovo Mercato Esquilino.

Towards Porta Maggiore

Directly south of the station is **Piazza Vittorio Emanuele II** ⑫. Built in the late 19th century to accommodate government ministries, it features one of the longest colonnades in Europe. A food market runs off the piazza on Via Ricasoli (Mon–Thu 9am–3pm, till 5pm Fri–Sat).

Several blocks east is the church of **Santa Bibiana** ⑬ (154 Via Giolitti; 7.30–10am, 4.30–7.30pm; www.santabibiana.com). Small enough to seem like a private chapel, it is one of Bernini's first architectural projects.

Admiring the statuary in the Palazzo Massimo.

FACT

The strange-looking block of marble sitting in front of Porta Maggiore recalls a car engine, but is instead the ancient tomb of a rich baker who asked to be buried in an oven-shaped structure. If you look closely, you will see that it is decorated with bas-reliefs depicting the art of bread-making.

Heading south on Via Giolitti, you pass the romantic remains of the 4th-century **Tempio di Minerva Medica**, a landmark if you arrive by train. To the southeast is **Porta Maggiore ⓴**, a wonderfully preserved 1st-century gate that also served as an aqueduct. You can still see the channels that carried the water. In 1917, a 1st-century underground basilica was discovered here, but it is not open to the public.

Santa Croce in Gerusalemme ⓯

Address: 12 Piazza Santa Croce in Gerusalemme
Telephone: 06-7061 3053

Opening Hours: daily 7am–12.45pm, 3.30–7.30pm
Entrance Fee: charge
Transport: bus: 81, 85, 810, tram: 3, 8

South of Porta Maggiore, along Via Eleniana, is the splendid white facade of Santa Croce in Gerusalemme, which was established in AD 320 by St Helena, Emperor Constantine's mother, to house fragments of the True Cross and other relics that she acquired on a visit to the Holy Land.

Next door, the **Museo Nazionale degli Strumenti Musicali** (www.museostrumentimusicali.it; charge; Tue–Sun 9am–7pm) has some 3,000

SHOPPING

Home to Rome's Chinatown, the Esquiline is the place to go for exotic foods, spices, teas and bargain stores. The quiet alleys of Monti are lined with the boutiques of up-and-coming designers, and with many artisan workshops. In between, Termini Station hosts an underground mall with many of the big chains, including Mango, Promod and Imaginarium.

Books

Borri Books
Termini Station
06-48 28 422
www.borribooks.com
A whole floor of English books inside the main train station, plus two more floors of Italian titles, maps, travel narrative, toys and children's books.

Department stores

MAS
11 Via dello Statuto
www.magazzinimas.it
Four floors of ceiling-high piles of clothes, bed linen, shoes, household objects and much more, some costing as little as €1. It's a stressful experience but skilled diggers always leave with bags full

of goods, including some brand-name items.

Upim
Piazza Santa Maria Maggiore
www.upim.it
Italy's most popular department store, selling youthful clothes, household goods with some designer items, economical cosmetics and an UPIM line of children's clothes.

Market

Nuovo Mercato Esquilino
Via Ricasoli
Mon–Thu 9am–3pm, till 5pm Fri–Sat
Rome's most multicultural produce market, with exotic herbs and spices, yams, sweet potatoes and okra, and lots of other goods including meat, seafood, fruit and vegetables at attractive prices. Bargaining with stallholders is part of the fun.

Shoes

Calzature Fausto Santini
106 Cavour
www.faustosantini.it
His main store is on Via Frattina, but this is where you get Santini's gems from past collections at half-price.

Mencucci
102 Via Cavour
06-4782 4405
This trendy shop dresses women from head to toe in select shoes and garments – but it's on the expensive side. For more affordable but equally stylish shoes, pay a visit to its nearby outlet store, on 92 Via Cavour.

Food and drink

Panella
54 Via Merulana
06-487 2651
www.panellaroma.com
This well established bread and pastry shop will tempt you with foodstuffs straight out of your dreams – until the prices wake you up, that is. It sells gluten-free and organic products and there is an excellent café serving fresh pizzas, panini, desserts and other treats, plus a garden where you can enjoy all these delicacies al fresco.

Trimani
20 Via Goito
06-446 9661
www.trimani.com
A good selection of top quality wines and tempting delicacies from one of Rome's oldest wine vendors.

pieces documenting musical history from antiquity to the 19th century.

Surrounding the church and the museum are the remains of the 3rd-century **Anfiteatro Castrense**. The section along Via Castrense is particularly well preserved.

SAN LORENZO

East of the railway tracks, beyond the ancient Porta Tiburtina, is the densely populated area of **San Lorenzo**, known as the student area of Rome. Built to house workers in the 1880s, but with few amenities or public services, the area has a reputation for being a focus for left-wing unrest. Today it is one of the city's liveliest districts, its streets – named after Italic and Etruscan tribes – filled with restaurants, artisans' workshops and cultural diversity.

Nearby is the Città Universitaria, one of Europe's biggest universities, which was constructed in the 1930s in typical Fascist style: big, white and imposing.

San Lorenzo fuori le Mura ⓰

Address: 3 Piazzale del Verano
Telephone: 06-491 511,

www.basilicasanlorenzo.it
Opening Hours: daily 7.30am–12.30pm, 3.30–7pm in summer, 7.30am–12.30pm, 4–8pm in winter
Entrance Fee: free
Transport: bus: 71, 19, 492, C3, C2, tram: 3

The area takes its name from the ancient basilica of San Lorenzo fuori le Mura (St Lawrence outside the Walls), which stands at the entrance to the vast Verano cemetery. One of Rome's first Christian places of worship, the basilica is made up of two churches joined together.

The raised apse is the nave of the Constantinian church erected in 330 (rebuilt in the 6th century with beautiful Corinthian columns); the 5th-century basilica next door forms the present nave. The two were joined together in the 8th century. The interior is decorated with early mosaics and some beautiful Cosmatesque work. To the right is the entrance to the pretty 12th-century cloister and underneath lies a labyrinth of catacombs. The church was badly bombed in World War II, but was soon restored to its former glory.

WHERE

The gardens of Piazza Vittorio Emanuele are filled with ancient ruins, including the so-called "Alchemy Gate", a monument built in the second half of the 1600s as a portal for the villa of marquis Palombara. The gate is decorated with enigmatic alchemical symbols, witnessing the marquis' passion for magical practices. Today, the gardens are a meeting place for the Esquiline's multiethnic population and the regular venue for the Chinese New Year celebrations.

The Chiesa di Dio Padre Misericordioso.

THE CHURCH OF SAILS

Rome's isolated eastern suburb of Tor Tre Teste has a church designed by Richard Meier that was inaugurated in 2003. The **Chiesa di Dio Padre Misericordioso** (www.diopadremisericordioso.it; 7.30am–12.30pm, 4–7.30pm) on Via Francesco Tovaglieri stands somewhat incongruously but majestically in the centre of a triangular site, with a public park on one side and several 10-storey apartment blocks on the others. Its three striking white shells of graduated height curve up like sails over the main body of the church. The stark white of the walls, a Meier trademark, creates a sensation of space and light, enhanced by the dizzying array of skylights and the walls of glass.

RESTAURANTS, BARS AND CAFÉS

PRICE CATEGORIES

Price includes dinner and a half-bottle of house wine.
€€€€ = more than €60
€€€ = €40–60
€€ = €25–40
€ = under €25.

Restaurants

Africa
26 Via Gaeta
06-494 1077
L & D Tue–Sun
€ [p318, B3]
Stewed dishes from Ethiopia and Eritrea, which you scoop up with flat bread. Some vegetarian options.

Agata e Romeo
45 Via Carlo Alberto
06-446 6115
www.agataeromeo.it
L (Tue–Fri) & D Mon–Sat
€€€€ [p322, B1]
Despite their weekend closing and the fact that the kitchen shuts down at 10.30pm, this is still one of the city's best dining experiences. Highly creative dishes (for example, Irish cod served in four different ways and trench-seasoned cheese soufflé with pear sauce). Huge wine selection from its renowned cellar. Booking essential. Closed two weeks Jan.

Gli Angeletti
3 Via dell Angeletto
06-474 3374
L & D daily
€€ [p324, E3]
Enjoying a great location, overlooking a picture-postcard piazza, Gli Angeletti serves up tasty dishes such as tagliolini with red onion, pancetta and balsamic vinegar, and duck breast in a marsala sauce.

Aromaticus
134 Via Urbana
06-488 1355
www.aromaticus.it
L & D Tue–Sun, 11am–9.30pm
€€ [p318, B4]
A mini-restaurant seating only 10 people created inside a plant nursery for herbs, with accordingly inspired recipes. The dishes served are all cold and raw and include salads and sandwiches, made with fresh leaves and edible flowers. When you are done eating, shop for delightful urban farming equipment.

Alle Carrette
14 Vicolo delle Carrette
06-679 2770
D only daily
€ [p324, E3]
Here, tucked away in a little side street close to the Forum, is what many consider the best pizzeria in the area. There's a beer tavern feel to it and some outdoor seating.

Cavour 313
313 Via Cavour
06-678 5496
www.cavour313.it
L & D daily
€–€€ [p324, E3]
This attractive *enoteca* has an impressive 1,000 bottles on its wine list. Friendly staff are happy to advise on which of their platters of cheeses and cold meats pairs best with your chosen vintage. Closed Sun in summer.

Formula Uno
13 Via degli Equi, San Lorenzo
06-445 3866
D only Mon–Sat
€ [p318, D4]
Genuine buffalo mozzarella on the pizzas makes this a cut above most pizzerias, and the fried *baccalà* (salt cod) is excellent.

Da Franco ar Vicoletto
1–2 Via dei Falisci, San Lorenzo
06-4470 4958
L & D Mon–Sat
€ [p318, D4]
A real neighbourhood trattoria with no frills, just lots of good and fishy food. Pick the set-price menu and the waiters will bring out dish after

dish of seafood served with pasta or salad, or simply grilled, roasted or fried.

Il Guru
4 Via Cimarra
06-474 4110
www.ilguru.it
D only daily
€€ [p324, E3]
To satisfy your need for something not pizza or pasta-based go to Guru, one of the most welcoming Indian restaurants in town. Choose various dishes from the classic tandoori or curry options or one of three fixed menus – vegetarian, fish or meat.

Hang Zhou
82 Via Principe Eugenio
06-487 2732
L & D daily
€ [p322, C1]
One of the better of the many Chinese restaurants in Rome, Hang Zhou offers a fixed menu or à la carte. Particularly good are the steam-cooked vegetable ravioli and the chicken with ginseng. The fried ice cream is delicious.

La Piazzetta
23a Vicolo del Buon Consiglio
06-699 1640
L & D Mon–Sat, L only Sun
€€ [p324, E4]
A popular restaurant that, due to its small size, can get packed out. Fish and large portions of perfectly cooked pasta are polished off with enthusiasm, and the in-house puddings are excellent. Some seating in the medieval lane outside in summer.

Rouge
6 Piazza dei Siculi
06-4436 2682
www.osteriarougeroma.it
L & D Mon–Sat
€ [p318, E4]
Non-matching, colourful tableware and chairs are their artful way to say "we are informal". This little restaurant boasts a hearty menu with Slavic influences (the chef is

Serbian), and the menu changes every night, so consult the blackboard.

Said
Via Tiburtina 135
06-446 9204
www.said.it
L & D Mon–Sat
€€ [p318, D4]
An old chocolate factory turned into a café and restaurant. While chocolate is the main reason people flock here (you can watch the *maîtres chocolatiers* at work), this is also a great venue for a salad lunch, soup or a full Italian dinner.

Tram Tram
44/46 Via dei Reti, San Lorenzo
06-490 416
http://tramtram.it
L & D Tue–Sun
€€ [p318, D4]
This small, cosy trattoria serves up Pugliese specialities such as linguine with squid and porcini.

Trattoria Monti
13a Via San Vito
06-446 6573
L & D Tue–Sat, L only Sun
€€ [p318, B4]
The owners are from the Marche region and the menu reflects this: home-made vegetable lasagne, chicken or rabbit in *potacchio* (with tomato, onion, garlic and rosemary), roast turkey with balsamic vinegar. There is fish on Friday, and the menu changes almost daily in this long and narrow, elegant trattoria.

Bars and Cafés

The Fiddler's Elbow
43 Via dell'Olmata
www.thefiddlerselbow.com
[p318, B4]
There's a pool table, a piano and a TV screen for sporting events at this small Irish pub near Santa Maria Maggiore.

Il Palazzo del Freddo di Giovanni Fassi
65–7 Via Principe Eugenio
www.palazzodelfreddo.it
[p322, C1]
This historic ice cream parlour has been here since 1880. Its huge, kitsch interior is filled with locals day and night (it's open until midnight) queuing to get their hands on some of the tastiest ice cream in the city. Their speciality is *gelato al riso* (rice ice cream).

Zest
171 Via Filippo Turati
www.radissonblu.com
[p318, C4]
For a contemporary experience worlds away from the multicultural area in which it stands, try the rooftop chill-out of the luxury Radisson Es. Blu Hotel. Sip a cocktail as you lounge on sofas and look out over the streamlined spectacle of Termini Station.

Upmarket bakery Panella.

Claudio aqueduct.

THE APPIAN WAY

Just outside the city walls the "Queen of Roads",
begun in 312 BC, was an important part of
Christian Rome. The old Appian Way is home to
ancient monuments, catacombs and dramatic ruins.

ome's first great military
road, the Via Appia Antica,
initially led to Capua 200km
(124 miles) away; by 191 BC it
extended to Brindisi, the main port
for Greece and the Eastern Empire,
and was known as the *regina viar-
ium*, "Queen of Roads". As Roman
law prohibited burial within the
city walls, the Appian Way became
lined with tombs, vaults and mausoleums. Later it became the site of
the first catacombs built by the early
Christians.

Although the Appian Way has
suffered greatly throughout the
centuries, with many of the monuments reduced to rubble, there is
still lots to see, and it is a wonderful area to spend a day. You can hire
bikes from the visitors' centre (see
page 247).

TO PORTA SAN SEBASTIANO

Once part of the Appian Way, the
Via di Porta San Sebastiano passes
through the **Parco degli Scipioni**
❶. At No. 9 is the **Sepolcro degli
Scipioni** (visits by appointment
only, tel: 06-0608), the mausoleum
of the powerful Scipio family. The
first family member entombed here
was L. Cornelius Scipio, a consul in

The Appian Way is closed to cars on Sunday.

298 BC. By the middle of the 2nd
century BC, the square tomb was
full and an annexe was dug adjacent to it.

Nearby is the 1st-century AD
Columbarium of **Pomponio Hylas**
(visits by appointment only, tel:
06-0608), which stored the cremated
remains of those too poor to build
their own tombs. Rich Romans often
had *columbaria* built for their freed-
men, but this was probably a commercial venture in which people
bought a slot.

Main Attractions
Museo delle Mura
Via Appia Antica
Domine Quo Vadis
Fosse Ardeatine
Catacombs
Circo di Massenzio
Tomb of Cecilia Metella

Maps and Listings
Map, page 246
Restaurants, page 249

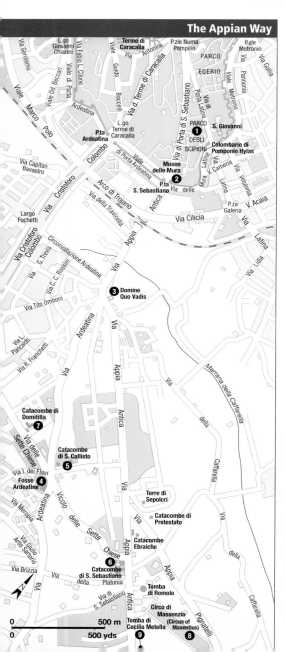

The Appian Way

Museo delle Mura ❷

Telephone: 06-0608
Opening Times: Tue–Sun 9am–2pm
Entrance Fee: free
Transport: 118

Porta San Sebastiano is the largest and best-preserved of the gateways in the Aurelian Wall, and inside, the Museo delle Mura gives a detailed account of the building of the walls, once almost 20km (12 miles) long with 381 towers. In AD 403, their height was doubled – to 12 metres (40ft). They were then 3.5 metres (12ft) thick and had 18 gates. Older buildings were incorporated into the walls.

A walk along the top gives some idea of the view the Imperial legionaries had as they watched for barbarian armies. Today, however, there are concrete blocks in every direction, except towards Via Appia, where the Campagna is almost in its original state.

When the Via Appia was extended outside the city walls to Capua, it followed an existing route to the Alban Hills and was the major campaign path for the conquest of southern Italy. In 190 BC it was extended via Benevento to Brindisi, connecting Rome with the eastern Mediterranean. When the Empire fell, the road decayed and was not used again until the time of Pius VI.

VIA APPIA ANTICA

Beyond the gate is Via Appia Antica. The first part, with the main monuments and sights, is not an entirely pleasant walk due to unrelenting traffic. About 1km (0.5 mile) down, on the left, is the church of **Domine Quo Vadis** ❸ ("Lord, where are you going?"), where the Apostle Peter, after escaping from a Roman prison, is said to have met Jesus. Jesus replied to Peter's question: "To let myself be crucified a second time."

Jesus is said to have left his footprints on the road and you can see a copy of the footprints on a marble slab inside the church (the original slab is preserved in the nearby basilica of San Sebastiano).

To the left of the church is the little Via della Caffarella, which leads into the Caffarella Valley, a lovely stretch of Roman countryside, scattered with ruins, sheep and farmhouses. If you take the right fork at Domine Quo Vadis and head along Via Ardeatina, you come to **Fosse Ardeatine ④** (174 Via Ardeatina; tel: 06-513 6742; Mon–Fri 8.15am–3.15pm, Sat–Sun till 4.30pm), a moving memorial to the 335 Italians who were murdered on 24 March 1944, in revenge for an ambush by Resistance fighters in which 32 Nazi soldiers were killed. The victims had nothing to do with the attack, but were rounded up, shot and buried in a mass grave. After the war, their bodies were retrieved and reburied in sarcophagi in the mausoleum.

Catacombs

On the way back to Via Appia are the **Catacombe di San Callisto ⑤** (Thu–Tue 9am–noon, 2–5pm). In the **Cripta dei Papi** (Crypt of the Popes), inscriptions of at least 10 bishops of Rome from the 3rd and 4th centuries have been discovered. Among them

is the first documented use of the title "Pope" for the bishop of Rome (from AD 298).

Also open to the public are the **Catacombe di San Sebastiano ⑥** (Mon–Sat 9am–5pm), the first of the underground burial sites to be so-called due to its proximity to a cave (from the Greek *kata*, near, and *kymbas*, cave), and the **Catacombe di Domitilla ⑦** (Wed–Mon 9am–noon, 2–5pm), one of the largest catacombs in Rome. Contrary to popular belief, the catacombs were not used for worship, nor for hiding in during times of Christian persecution; the excavated rooms were used for simple funeral ceremonies. See also Relics of the Catacombs, page 251.

Among the rows of shelves for the dead are a lot of small "tombs", used for the tragically high number of infant deaths, and some particularly large or imposing ones, usually belonging to martyrs who were reburied in Roman churches in the Middle Ages. Further along Via Appia, at No. 119a, are the Jewish catacombs of Vigna Randanini. These can only be visited on the occasion of particular events (call 06-0608 for information).

KIDS

The Caffarella Valley is a slice of Italian countryside in the city and a great place for the kids to explore. There is an old farmhouse, whose inhabitants still make cheese and bread, a "resident" white horse and hordes of sheep and cattle. There is also an educational vegetable garden, where kids can run freely as they try out the rudimentary irrigation system, and a prehistoric village to play in.

Cycling along the Appian Way.

VIA APPIA ON A BIKE

A ride along Via Appia is one of the best ways to get to know this ancient 'queen of roads'. Bikes can be hired from several infopoints, including the main one at 58/60 Via Appia Antica (tel: 06-513 5316; Mon–Sat 9.30am–1pm and 2–5 pm, Sun 9.30am–5.30pm, till 6.30pm in summer; book ahead if in a group). For information on other infopoints visit www.parcoappiaantica.it, where you can also find details and maps of cycling routes along the Appian Way, ranging from an easy 6km (4-mile) loop suitable for all to a 32km (20-mile) trail for more experienced cyclists. The best time to visit is on a Sunday or public holiday, when traffic is restricted.

Circo di Massenzio ❽

Address: 153 Via Appia Antica;
http://en.villadimassenzio.it
Telephone: 06-0608
Opening Hours: Tue–Sun
10am–4pm
Entrance Fee: free
Transport: 660

Worth seeing also are the **Circo di Massenzio** (Circus of Maxentius), built by the Emperor Maxentius, and the **Mausoleo di Romolo**, both from around AD 310. The Circus was used for chariot races and could seat 10,000 spectators. Maxentius' Imperial palace, **Villa di Massenzio**, is nearby (opening times as above).

The tomb of Cecilia Metella ❾

Address: 161 Appia Antica;
http://archeoroma.beniculturali.it
Telephone: 06-3996 7700
Opening Hours: Tue–Sun 9am–5pm
(closing time varies according to season)
Entrance Fee: charge
Transport: 660

The tomb of Cecilia Metella was built around 50 BC for the daughter of Quintus Metellus Creticus, conqueror of Crete. She was later the wife of Crassus, son of the famous member of the Triumvirate of Caesar's time. During the 14th century the tomb was incorporated into

Circo di Massenzio.

The San Sebastiano catacombs are one of the most popular to visit.

a fortress and crenallations added by the Caetani family, relatives of the Pope, who used to boost the family coffers by extracting tolls from passers-by.

After this, the Via Appia is far more rural, sparse and quiet, with overgrown ruins, fabulous gated modern villas and shady trees. The remains of tombs built by the great families of Rome dot the roadside. To the east, you can see the dramatic arches of the Claudio aqueduct, one of 11 that supplied Rome with water at the height of its power.

Beyond the crossing with Via Erode Attico, the remains in the farmland to the left are those of the 2nd-century AD **Villa dei Quintili** (1092 Via Appia Nuova; http://archeo roma.beniculturali.it; Tue–Sun 9am– 6.30pm in summer, closes earlier the rest of the year). If you look closely, you can see a *nymphaeum* and aqueduct arches. Finally, where Via Appia joins the road that leads back to Via Appia Nuova is **Casale Rotondo**, a late 1st-century BC tomb, with a farmhouse sitting on top.

TIP

Signs and symbols in the catacombs: **Dove holding a twig** – reconciliation between God and Man. **Anchor** – sign of hope. **Fish** – symbol of Christ (the initial letters of the Greek word for fish make the phrase "Jesus Christ, God's Son, Saviour"). **Dolphin** – coming to save the shipwrecked, Jesus the Saviour. **Jonah and the Whale** – the Resurrection.

Porta San Sebastiano.

RESTAURANTS, BARS AND CAFÉS

PRICE CATEGORIES

Price includes dinner and a half-bottle of house wine.
€€€€ = more than €60
€€€ = €40–60
€€ = €25–40
€ = under €25.

Ar Montarozzo
4 Via Appia Antica
06-7720 8434
www.ristorantearmontarozzo.com
L & D Tue–Sun
€€€
A lovely restaurant with garden for alfresco eating and a predominantly fishy menu – try the risotto with asparagus tips and prawns. All the usual Roman classics are here, too, and there's an extensive wine list, with 300 bottles.
L'Archeologia

139 Via Appia Antica
06-788 0494
www.larcheologia.it
L & D daily
€€–€€€
Set in a 16th-century house with a beautiful outdoor area and ancient ruins on view. Fresh fish daily. Excellent wine cellar in an old catacomb.
Hostaria Antica Roma
87 Via Appia Antica
06-513 2888
www.anticaroma.it
L & D Tue–Sun
€€€
This charming restaurant's garden features ancient Roman ruins. Specialities include gnocchi with clams and a succulent beef fillet with truffles.
Da Priscilla
68 Via Appia Antica
06-513 6379

www.trattoriapriscilla.com
L & D Mon–Sat, L only Sun
€
A rustic, authentic trattoria attached to an ancient Roman tomb. Pasta with wild boar ragù, lemon-scented meatballs and spaghetti with cheese and pepper are their most famous specialities, and the owners are friendly and fun.

Bars and Cafés

Appia Antica Caffè
173 Via Appia
www.appiaanticacaffe.it
On the corner of Via Cecilia Metella, this is a good place for a restorative coffee and a snack, before or after a brisk walk along the Appian Way's famous but sometimes wearying cobblestones. Closed Mon.

RELICS OF THE CATACOMBS

"A desert of decay, sombre and desolate; and with a history in every stone that strews the ground". Charles Dickens visited the catacombs in 1846.

An intricate carving.

For health reasons and habit, the Romans buried their dead outside the city walls, and the Appian Way is lined with monumental tombs. Burial land, however, was expensive and the less wealthy could only afford a place in one of the catacombs, whose labyrinthine galleries contain niches (loculi) built into the tufa rock. The largest catacombs are those of St Callistus, whose network of tunnels is 19km (12 miles) long and more than 20 metres (66ft) deep.

The catacombs were used by both Christians and non-Christians. While the pagan Romans preferred to be cremated, and therefore buried their ashes in urns, the Christian and the Jews buried their loved ones' bodies, which were embalmed or shrouded in linen and placed on ledges in the walls, sealed beneath marble slabs on the floor or interred in family vaults (cubicula). The Jews had their own separate catacombs.

The Christianisation of Rome led to the cult of the early martyrs, with pilgrimages and renewed interest in the catacombs. The frescoed interiors are adorned with Christian symbols or graffiti, from a dove, fish or anchor to acanthus leaves and vines. The catacombs of St Callistus contain the crypt of nine 3rd-century popes – the actual bones were removed when barbarian invaders attacked the tombs in the 8th century – as well as early Christian frescoes and paintings. While some are mossy and mouldering, the weather-worn tombs make an impressive proclamation of faith. Today, the Via Appia is an inspired or desolate scene, depending on one's mood.

Skulls and fragments of engravings in the catacombs of St Callistus.

The Last Supper fresco in the catacombs of St Callistus. Founded around the middle of the 2nd century AD, they are part of a huge complex of galleries, 19km (12 miles) long and more than 20 metres (66ft) deep. Callistus was the deacon in charge of the cemetery; he was born a slave and became Pope before dying as a Christian martyr in 222. These catacombs were only discovered in 1850.

This chamber, called the Hypogeum, is part of an underground tomb or ipogeo. These were often frescoed, depicting pagan scenes such as funerary feasts or blood sacrifice. Henrik Ibsen enjoyed lying among the tombs.

Many Jews converted to Christianity, but those who kept their faith were buried separately in the Jewish Catacombs.

SUBTERRANEAN SCENE

Three of the largest Roman underground burial sites are to be found in the vicinity of the Appian Way:

Catacombe di San Callisto (110/126 Via Appia Antica; tel: 06-513 0151; Thu–Tue 9am–noon, 2–5pm; bus 218, 118, 714). Rome's first official Christian cemetery encloses the crypts of many early popes and saints.

Catacombe di San Sebastiano (136 Via Appia Antica; tel: 06-785 0350; Mon–Sat 9am–5pm; bus 118, 218, 660). Three exquisitely preserved mausoleums and subterranean galleries over four levels.

Catacombe di Domitilla (282 Via delle Sette Chiese; tel: 06-511 0342; Wed–Mon 9am–noon, 2–5pm; bus 218, 714, 716, 160, 30). One of the earliest images of Christ as the Good Shepherd features among its sublime frescoes.

The following are in the northeast of Rome:

Catacombe di Priscilla (430 Via Salaria; tel: 06-8620 6272; Tues–Sun 8.30am–noon, 2.30–5pm; bus 63, 83, 92).

Catacombe di Sant'Agnese (349 Via Nomentana; tel: 06-8620 5456; Mon–Sat 9am–noon, 4–6pm, Sun and religious holidays 3–5pm; bus 36, 60, 90).

This fresco, a particularly delicate tomb decoration, is in the catacombs dedicated to the Roman soldier who became a Christian martyr (San Sebastiano).

Underground Rome has more to offer than catacombs. This 1st-century Temple of Mithras, dedicated to a polytheistic Persian cult, lies below San Clemente. In a relief, Mithras is depicted slaying a bull, the symbol of fertility.

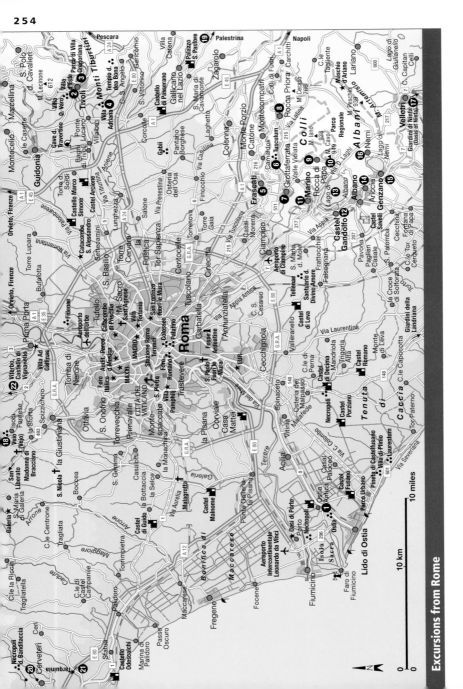

254

Excursions from Rome

EXCURSIONS FROM ROME

All roads may lead to Rome, but it's worth considering going in the opposite direction to explore the fertile, hilly areas, Etruscan and Roman sites, and Renaissance villas and gardens, all within easy reach of the capital.

Given that more than 20 million tourists pour into Rome each year, it's surprising that so few find their way into the Roman hinterland. The region of Lazio remains relatively unexplored, but has plenty to offer. As with any major metropolis, the area immediately around the capital doesn't instantly give way to a pastoral idyll. The shift from suburban sprawl and industrial development to rolling countryside is gradual. However, there are some delightfully picturesque pockets and landmarks to discover, all within easy reach of the city.

The Pope is not alone in choosing the gentle, wine-producing hills of the Castelli Romani south of Rome for his rural retreat. During the sweltering summers and at weekends Romans leave the capital in droves to indulge in the region's excellent food and wine – a favourite Italian

An evening view of Sperlonga, a port town south of Rome.

pastime – lounge around its lakes and enjoy the scenery. Sun-seekers head for convenient Lido di Ostia, but the resort of Fregene, north of the Tiber, has more cachet. Seawater quality, however, is poor in Fregene, and bathing is often prohibited for health reasons, so be prepared to bathe in one of the many beach-side pools available. The most scenic stretches of coast, however, are a lengthier drive away at the southern end of the Lazio coast, starting at the Circeo Promontory.

Villa d'Este fountain.

Ostia Antica, Hadrian's Villa and the Etruscan graves of Cerveteri draw romantics to their ruins. Lake Bracciano appeals to escapists, walkers, golfers and riders. Villa d'Este, with its pleasure palace and water gardens dominating the town of Tivoli, is a favourite spot for picnickers.

The most popular destinations make for perfect day trips, though some places may tempt you into an overnight stay. Most of these destinations are accessible by bus or train, but a hire car will give you much more flexibility and enable you to explore Lazio's countryside and coast at your leisure.

The Capitolium Curia, Ostia Antica.

OSTIA ANTICA

The evocative ruins of Ostia, surrounded by pines and flat coastal plains, make a good excursion from the hustle and bustle of Rome. For a sun, sea and sand break, head for Fregene or explore Lazio's more scenic southern beaches.

Main Attractions
Ostia Antica
Lido di Ostia
Fregene
Medieval Ostia

Maps and Listings
Maps, pages 254, 258
Restaurants, page 261

Accrording to legend, King Ancus Marcius founded a port town in the 7th century BC and named it **Ostia ❶** after the *ostium* or mouth of the Tiber. However, the archaeological evidence dates only to the second half of the 4th century BC, when fortifications were built around the town. Rome was very dependent on this one connection with the sea, because all its essential commodities – especially grain – were transported from Ostia along the **Via Ostiense**. It also became the main base of the Roman fleet in around 300 BC, and by the Imperial era had become a major city, with a population of about 80,000.

Rome's dependence on Ostia was good news for the port's inhabitants. The trade of imported goods from the West and East brought the local population wealth and luxury. The town even had special status, with the male inhabitants being freed from military service. There was also money to be made from holidaymakers. On hot summer days, when the stone streets of Rome practically blazed, Romans fled to the seaside resort.

However, when Emperor Augustus transferred the Roman naval base to Misenium, Ostia felt the loss of the free-spending sailors and all the associated trade. For a while, it remained the unloading point for the grain ships and, in AD 41–54, Claudius had new docks built, but the beginning of the end of Ostia was already evident – the harbour was silting up. Not even a new harbour basin – now the airport of Fiumicino – that was dug on the orders of Trajan (AD 98–117) could stop this process. The coastline gradually moved west, and today Ostia is several kilometres from the sea.

The beach at Ostia.

Mass exodus

Ostia's prosperity peaked in the early 2nd century, but its decline was steady and relentless. Emperor Constantine's decision to move the capital of the Empire to Constantinople in the 4th century, continual pirate attacks and, in the early Middle Ages, the threat of Saracen invasions, meant that Ostia's population was forced to leave their homes. Soon, the only inhabitants left were malarial mosquitoes.

At that time, the coastline was about 4km (2 miles) further inland than it is today. Luckily for archaeologists, the city was never repopulated, and it has been very well preserved under a bed of sand. Although the ruins were quarried for building materials in the Middle Ages, about two-thirds of the Roman town can now be seen, thanks to extensive archaeological excavation.

Since the 19th century, when excavations began under Popes Pius VII and Pius IX, this archaeological treasure house has been systematically laid bare. The better finds are on display in Rome's museums.

On the Decumanus Maximus.

Part of the well-preserved mosaic in the Baths of Neptune.

OSTIA ANTICA

Telephone: 06-5635 0215,
http://archeoroma.beniculturali.it
Opening Hours: Tue–Sun Apr–Sept 8.30am–7pm, till 6.30pm in Oct, Nov–Mar 8.30am–4.30pm

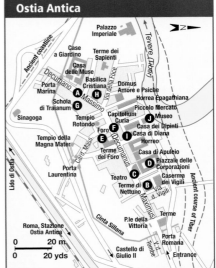

Ostia Antica

Entrance Fee: charge, free first Sun of the month

Transport: Ostia Antica/Scavi

Among the umbrella pines and wild flowers of the ancient site are the remarkably well-preserved remains of warehouses, shops, baths and barracks, temples and theatres. They give as good an insight into the everyday urban life of ancient Rome as the Forum, or even Pompeii. From the entrance, visitors follow the **Decumanus Massimo** Ⓐ, the same main road used by the Ancient Romans, which leads through the city centre. Worth noting en route are the **Terme di Nettuno** Ⓑ (Baths of Neptune), named after their glorious mosaic floor, and the **Teatro** Ⓒ (Theatre), which warrants a visit for the splendid views offered by its upper tiers. Underneath these tiers there would have been taverns and shops. Beside the theatre, three large masks have been mounted on tufa columns – they were originally part of the Theatre's decoration. In summer months, the Theatre is used to stage plays and concerts.

Also well worth looking at are the stalls in the **Piazzale delle Corporazioni** Ⓓ (Square of the Guilds), where lovely floor mosaics preserve the insignias of the various guilds, most of which were associated with the fitting and supplying of ships.

The Forum

The Decumanus Maximus leads to the **Foro** Ⓔ (Forum), where citizens congregated and justice was dispensed by city officials, and the **Capitolium Curia** Ⓕ, Ostia's largest temple, which was dedicated to Jupiter, Juno and Minerva. Beyond is the **Schola di Traianum** Ⓖ (School of Trajan), formerly the headquarters of a guild of merchants, and the **Basilica Cristiana** Ⓗ (Christian Basilica).

The workers of Ostia lived in *insulae*, Roman apartment blocks that were three or four storeys high. The **Casa di Diana** Ⓘ (House of Diana), near the Forum, is one of the smarter ones and is well preserved. It had a balcony on the second floor, its own private bathhouse and a central courtyard where there was a cistern to collect water.

TIP

In summer, all of Rome's trendiest nightclubs move to their respective beach locations in Ostia and Fregene. Be ready for long queues, and be sure to be wearing your best clothes, as the dress code is usually strict.

The Ostia Antica Teatro, still used to stage occasional summer performances.

Lazio Beaches

Sunseekers should avoid Ostia and head instead for the less busy beaches a little further afield, where the water is cleaner and the landscape more natural.

Lido di Ostia, just half an hour by train from Piramide, and the surrounding beaches are the most popular, and flocks of locals descend on them at weekends from late May. This cannot be attributed to the cleanliness of the water, but to its convenience as the nearest seaside resort to Rome and the fact that it is packed with amenities and a rather chaotic nightlife.

Most Italian beaches are organised around *stabilimenti balneari*, bathing establishments, which offer more than clean toilets, deckchairs, sunloungers and umbrellas for hire (for a daily fee).

Find long sandy beaches at Sperlonga.

Since many holiday-makers spend their whole day there, the complexes hire out sporting equipment, host children's activities, and have cafés that may include full-blown restaurants.

A more upmarket alternative to Lido di Ostia is **Fregene**, north of the Tiber, about 40km (25 miles) west of Rome. Once the glamorous retreat of the *dolce vita* set, this appealing resort is fashionable again. It's an hour's journey by bus from Lepanto metro station or by train from Termini to Maccarese, then bus to nearby Fregene.

The natural beauty of the dunes

Another alternative some 10km (6 miles) south of Ostia is the sand dunes of **Capocotta**. A once-infamous nudist beach (a respectable and predominantly gay section, known as Il Buco, remains, just beyond the gates, going towards Torvaianica), it has cleaned up its act and is now run by a Rome City Council-backed consortium that offers free *stabilimenti*. Located behind several gates, which close at about 7.30pm, this stretch of coastline is well kept and of some natural beauty, since it is located within the protected Parco del Litorale Romano. Take the Roma–Lido di Ostia train from Piramide but get off at Cristoforo Colombo, the last stop. Here you can hire a bike and pedal down the coast, or wait for the "Mare 2" bus.

Further south, **Anzio** and **Nettuno** are two nostalgic port towns with hotels, restaurants, seafront cafés and boutiques. For a heady mix of antiquity and sunbathing, head to the beach at Villa di Nerone, to which you can walk or cycle from the centre of Anzio. Here you can sunbathe in full view of the remains of Nero's palace. Trains to Anzio and Nettuno leave regularly from Roma Termini.

For the first really clean water and large sandy beaches south of Rome you will have to go a bit further, to **Sabaudia** (direct buses leave from the EUR Fermi metro stop), or the ancient Roman port of **Sperlonga** (about halfway between Naples and Rome).

An interesting insight into the sort of housing used by ancient Romans, it also incorporates a tavern on the ground floor, complete with a marble counter on which customers were served their sausages and hot wine (sweetened with honey), as well as ovens, storage facilities and an outdoor beer garden.

The Museum

North of the Casa di Diana, a Renaissance building houses the **Museo ❶**. Originally built for storing salt from the nearby salt pans, today the excavation museum contains a collection of sculptures, tools, mosaics, sarcophagi and a variety of other finds from the site, which help to build a picture of daily life in Ostia.

MEDIEVAL OSTIA

Before heading either back to Rome or on to the beaches of Ostia, while here don't miss the opportunity to visit the medieval town of Ostia.

Developed around the ruins of Gregoriopolis, a fortified citadel built on the orders of Pope Gregory IV between 827 and 844, Ostia was a medieval village within defensive walls; its inhabitants worked in the nearby saltpans.

After it had been destroyed by invading forces in 1408, Martin V built a defensive tower against the barbarians and Saracens. This tower became the centre of a castle built by Pontelli later in the same century for the future Pope Julius II, then a cardinal. However, the attacks continued and, together with the silting-up of the river and a huge flood in the 16th century, drove the inhabitants away.

Castello di Giulio II (16 Piazzale della Rocca; tel: 06-5635 8044; free), as the castle is now known, has some interesting features, such as scarped curtain walls, which were innovative at the time, but became commonplace in the 16th century. Unfortunately, it closed down for renovation at the end of 2014 and now can't be visited. Check http://archeoroma.beniculturali.it for the most up-to-date information.

You can also see the fortress's museum, its church, Santa Aurea, and the Palazzo Episcopale, official residence of the bishop of Ostia. The latter houses some notable frescoes by Peruzzi.

TIP

The Pontine archipelago is a group of volcanic islands just off the coast of Lazio. Ponza is the largest and best equipped with hotels and restaurants, and is a popular weekend getaway with Romans. A trip to this picture-postcard island is a relaxing way to round off a Roman holiday. There's a regular ferry service from Anzio, the nearest port to Rome, and the journey time is about 70 minutes. For more information visit www.ponza.com.

Fisherman in Anzio.

RESTAURANTS

PRICE CATEGORIES

Price includes dinner and a half-bottle of house wine.
€€€€ = more than €60
€€€ = €40–60
€€ = €25–40
€ = under €25

Allo Sbarco di Enea
675 Via dei Romagnoli
06-565 0034
Daily 12.30–2.30pm and 7.30–11.30pm
€€€
Right next to the entrance to the ruins, this reliable fish restaurant is perennially popular.

Il Monumento
8 Piazza Umberto I
06-565 0021
www.ristorantemonumento.it
L & D Tue–Sun 12.30–3.30pm and 8–11pm
€€–€€€
Close to one of the entrances to the medieval town of Ostia, this restaurant offers a great selection of fish dishes – the house special is spaghetti with shellfish and squid. Carnivores are well provided for with classic Italian dishes such as chicken with white wine, rosemary and garlic.

A fresco in the Villa d'Este.

TIVOLI

Pressed against a hillside with commanding views of the plains below, this small workaday town was once home to Roman emperors and Renaissance aristocrats. The historic villas are testament to its glory days as a retreat for the rich.

Tivoli is one of many towns set in the hills outside Rome that has long served as a getaway for Romans during the hot summer months. The town itself would be unremarkable, but for its famous villas and gardens that make it a popular attraction and a worthwhile day trip. The Renaissance Villa d'Este, of Tivoli fountains fame, and the Villa Gregoriana park are within the town. While the impressive remains of Hadrian's Villa are a couple of kilometres south of it. Tivoli is about 31km (19 miles) east of Rome.

If you're driving, take the A24 Roma–L'Aquila motorway and exit at Tivoli e Castel Madama. Alternatively, trains for Tivoli depart from Stazione Tiburtina, or you can take a bus (journey time approximately 45 minutes) from Ponte Mammolo station on metro line B.

VILLA D'ESTE ❷

Address: 1 Piazza Trento, Tivoli; www.villadestetivoli.info
Telephone: 077-433 2920
Opening Hours: Tue–Sun 8.30am–6.30pm in summer, till 4pm in winter
Entrance Fee: charge
Transport: Tivoli

The Villa d'Este – a Unesco world heritage site – is a big tourist draw. The villa itself is worth a visit, with its beautiful frescoes, but the main reason people come here is to see the wonderful fountains and waterworks.

Originally a Benedictine convent, the building was converted into the Governor's Palace in the 13th century. In 1550, Cardinal Ippolito d'Este, son of Lucrezia Borgia and grandson of Pope Alexander VI, was elected governor. He immediately set about renovating the villa and its

Main Attractions
Villa d'Este
Villa Gregoriana
Villa Adriana

Maps and Listings
Map, page 254
Restaurants, page 267

Oval fountain in the villa gardens.

TIP

On some summer weekends, the Villa d'Este extends its opening times until midnight for visitors to enjoy the spectacle of the fountains beautifully floodlit. Visit the website for current dates.

gardens, to turn it into something befitting his aspirations to the papacy. Ippolito commissioned Pirro Ligorio to design the grounds. Ligorio, who had studied the nearby Hadrian's Villa, excavated the hillside, laid it out in terraces and built an aqueduct and underground canal, fed by the River Aniene, to supply the extensive waterworks. The gardens took seven years to complete, and their beauty and ingenuity created the desired impact.

Ippolito d'Este never did make pope, but he did leave a memorial to himself in the fountains, which have delighted visitors for centuries and served to inspire waterworks all over Europe. After the decline of the Este family, the Habsburgs inherited the villa, but they were poor caretakers. After World War I, the Italian State took it over and began the long task of its restoration.

The gardens

A walk through the terraced gardens, geometrically laid out with more than 500 fountains, is a delight. The first glimpse you get of the gardens is from the upper terrace, which offers

a wonderful vista of the lawns, fountains and walkways that fan out from the central axis that runs down the hill. The café here is a good spot to

Avenue of a Hundred Fountains.

View of the "Rometta" fountain and the plains below Tivoli.

relax and take in the view of the gardens and the valley below.

As you wend your way from top to bottom, the main fountains to look out for include the **Viale delle Cento Fontane** (Avenue of a Hundred Fountains), a row of close-set pipes that spray water into the air, which terminates at one end with the **Fontana dell'Ovato** (Oval Fountain) decorated with nymphs, and at the other with the **Rometta** (Little Rome), a miniature representation of Roman landmarks. Halfway along is the **Fontana dei Draghi** (Fountain of Dragons), made in honour of Pope Gregory XIII, who was once a guest here, and whose papal insignia included a dragon.

One of the most inventive of these playful creations was the **Fontana dell'Organo Idraulico** (Fountain of the Hydraulic Organ), designed with an elaborate water-operated organ. Recently restored, it can be seen in operation every two hours from 10.30am. Notice the two upper reliefs portray Apollo and Orpheus playing the lyre and the violin. The **Fontana della Civetta e degli Uccelli** (Fountain of the Owl and the Birds) was another ingenious invention, designed to reproduce the screech of an owl and birdsong through water power.

One word of warning: avoid the temptation to drink or touch the water – it comes from the polluted River Aniene.

PARCO DI VILLA GREGORIANA ❸

Address: Largo Sant'Angelo; www.villagregoriana.it
Telephone: 06-3996 7701
Opening Hours: Tue–Sun 10am–6.30pm in summer, till 4pm in winter (Dec–Feb by appointment only).
Entrance Fee: charge
Transport: Tivoli

Tivoli's watery attractions don't all flow in the Villa d'Este. The town is full of ancient remains of temples and other buildings – some (such as the Temple of Vesta) are extremely well preserved, while others have been incorporated into medieval churches.

Not far from the Temple of Vesta is the entrance to Villa Gregoriana, a dramatic and steep wooded park set in a rocky gorge. It was created in 1835 at the request of Pope Gregory XVI, whose aim was to avert frequent flooding of the town by diverting the flow of the River Aniene here.

Steep paths lead down to the villa's galleries, terraces and belvederes, from which visitors can admire the great waterfall and the nearby grottoes, both natural and artificial.

VILLA ADRIANA ❹

Address: Via Tiburtina, 6km (4 miles) southwest of Tivoli
Telephone: 0774-382 733. Reservations: 06-3996 7900
www.villaadriana.beniculturali.it
Opening Hours: Oct–Jan 9am–5pm, Mar and Oct till 6.30pm, Apr–Sept 9am–7pm
Entrance Fee: charge
Transport: Tivoli and bus CAT no. 4

A detail along the avenue of a Hundred Fountains.

The Tempio di Vesta overlooks the Parco di Villa Gregoriana in the gorge below.

TIP

There is a café just outside the site of Hadrian's Villa, but you might want to consider packing a picnic. There are plenty of benches and shady spots amid the olive trees to sit and enjoy lunch surrounded by the ruins.

Archway in the thick boundary walls.

The Canopus, Villa Adriana.

Even more impressive than the Villa d'Este are the ruins of Hadrian's Villa, the most magnificent country residence of Imperial times.

When Rome was flourishing, Tivoli (ancient Tibur), in the foothills of the Sabine Hills, was a favoured retreat for wealthy citizens. Among the frequent guests at their splendid villas were Horace, Catullus, Maecenas, Sallust and Emperor Trajan.

In AD 117, Hadrian started to build a luxurious refuge for himself at the foot of the hill on which Tivoli stands. The emperor was a skilled architect (he was the creator of the Pantheon), and his plan was to reconstruct the monuments that had most impressed him on his travels through the Empire, particularly in Greece and Egypt. Another innovation was his idea of scattering the individual buildings over the 60 hectares (148 acres) of the park, rather than grouping them in a central complex. All the buildings were connected by covered walkways and underground passages (*cryptoportici*), to protect against the weather.

Just before entering the ruins, take a look at the model reconstruction of the villa, which gives a good impression of the sheer scale and splendour of Hadrian's grand design.

Beautiful imitations

One of the most noteworthy structures is the colonnaded garden court,

known as the **Pecile**, a reproduction of the Stoa Poikile Hadrian had seen in Athens. The surrounding wall, 230 metres (760ft) long, has survived on the north side, as has a basin in the centre. On the inner side once stood a covered, pillared entrance.

One of the most outstanding buildings to survive is the **Teatro Marittimo** (Maritime Theatre), a circular building with a columned porch, inside which a circular moat surrounded an island that was reached by two wooden swing bridges. On the island stood a miniature villa where the emperor could relax in safety and privacy.

Between the Pecile and Maritime Theatre, the remains of a great dome that once covered the **Terme** (Baths) demonstrate the very high architectural standards that were employed.

The most ambitious of Hadrian's replicas was the **Canopus**, a copy of the famous Temple of Serapis near Alexandria in Egypt. A 15km (10-mile) canal, lined with luxury residences and statues, led from the River Nile to the Temple. Hadrian tried to imitate the scenario by creating a 119 metre (390-ft) -long canal, by the side of which stood marble architraves and copies of Egyptian statues.

Reclining statue near the Canopus.

The southern bank was originally occupied by a copy of the Serapis shrine, but all that remains is a large niche in the rock and a big chunk of rock lying in the water basin.

Excavations of the villa, first carried out to obtain marble, have turned up more than 300 statues, as well as friezes, frescoes and mosaics. The museum near the Canopus displays various minor finds, but the majority of statues and other finds are now on display in museums throughout the world.

Hadrian didn't enjoy his Imperial palace for long – he died only four years after it was completed.

RESTAURANTS, BARS AND CAFÉS

PRICE CATEGORIES

Price includes dinner and a half-bottle of house wine.

€€€€ = more than €60
€€€ = €40–60
€€ = €25–40
€ = under €25

Restaurants

Osteria La Briciola
106 Via Tiburtina Valeria 36km
0774-418 421
www.osterialabriciola.it
D Tue–Fri, L Sat–Sun

€€–€€€
Small and cozy bistro with a large terrace overlooking green hills. Excellent food based on seasonal produce, with good value tasting menus plus a long list of wines from nearly every region, served by the glass or bottle.

Sibilla
50 Via della Sibilla
0774-335 281
www.ristorantesibilla.com
L & D Tue–Sun €€€
A few minutes from Piazza Garibaldi, Tivoli's central square, this historic restaurant has hosted popes, kings

and emperors – but the charming staff welcome all, and the menu of classic Italian dishes won't disappoint. The shady terrace, with views of nearby Villa Gregoriana, is a lovely spot in warm weather.

Bars and Cafés

Pippo
2 Via San Valerio
This small place in the heart of town makes exceptional (and filling) sandwiches with your favourite ingredients. Don't miss the preparation show!

GREEN RETREATS

Lazio has many hidden gardens, both formal and wild. Best enjoyed in the warmer months, these retreats offer respite from the city's hustle and bustle.

A trip out of the city in search of the region's little-explored gardens is a welcome antidote to the weight of all that history. Options range from densely flowered oases such as the Giardini della Landriana and wild, medieval Ninfa, to wildlife sanctuaries such as the peaceful Oasi di Porto and fairytale gardens like the fountain-filled Villa d'Este and the Castello di Vignanello. Gardens generally open to the public from April to October, to coincide with the flowering season. Some gardens put on special events to showcase the plants in bloom; the most popular are the springtime flower shows at the Giardini della Landriana.

All the gardens illustrated here are within easy reach of Rome, and make good day-trip destinations for those willing to hire a car; if you're reliant on public transport, Villa d'Este and the Oasi di Ninfa are just a short train ride away.

If you've got kids to entertain, visit the Park of Monsters in Bomarzo (www.sacrobosco.it; 8am–7pm, till sunset in winter; tel: 07-6192 4029). Created in

San Liberato overlooks Lake Bracciano. It is full of exotic specimens such as Japanese cherries and tulip trees, and has a delicate, manicured rose garden.

1552 for Pier Francesco Orsini as a memorial for his late wife, the garden contains giant sculptures such as the huge boulder carvings of an ogre whose mouth you walk in, whales, dragons and Sleeping Beauty.

The Castello di Vignanello is a beautiful villa that has been owned by the aristocratic Ruspoli family for centuries. Ottavia Orsini, an ancestor of the Ruspolis, can be credited with the garden's creation, widely regarded as one of the most beautiful Italian parterres. The perfectly rectangular space is subdivided by mixed hedges of bay, laurel and box; the boxes-within-boxes form patterns, tracing the initials of their creator in the central beds.

Giardini della Landriana's grounds are divided into 30 "rooms" separated by hedges and paths. Don't miss the Valley of the Roses: hundreds of varieties bloom in romantic disarray across the hillside overlooking the lake, in beds bordered by thyme, lavender and clove pinks, interspersed with slim cypresses.

Oasi di Ninfa has retained its otherworldly appeal: plants and trees grow unchecked amid the moss-covered parapets and crumbling towers.

Oasi di Porto (www.oasidiporto.it) is surprisingly peaceful considering it's just over 1km (0.5 mile) from Fiumicino Airport. A vast lake makes an ideal habitat for migratory birds, and the surrounding parkland is dominated by imposing Roman pine trees, oaks and poplars. Guided tours by horse-drawn cart can be organised.

A DAY IN THE GARDEN

The grounds of the magnificent Villa d'Este in Tivoli (www. villadestetivoli.info) are dotted with water features, from dramatic, gushing waterfalls to musical fountains, nymphaeums and grottoes. See it illuminated at night if you get the chance. For more information see page 263.

Oasi di Ninfa was a prosperous city in medieval times, but destroyed in a bloody civil war in 1382. Its ruins were restored and botanical species planted in the 1920s. Open Apr–Oct on most weekends; www. fondazionecaetani.org. Take a regional train to Latina railway station (35 minutes), then a taxi.

Giardini della Landriana (www.aldobrandini.it) are distinctive for their orderly, geometric design. Opening times vary, call in advance tel: 6081 532. By car, take the Via Pontina out of Rome until the Campo di Carne exit. Follow Via Campo di Carne until you reach the gardens at No. 51.

San Liberato (www.sanliberato.com) overlooks Lake Bracciano and is full of exotic specimens such as Japanese cherries. Open by appointment only, tel: 06-998 05460. By car, take the Cassia Veientana towards Viterbo. Take the Trevignano-Mazzano exit, and at Trevignano take the Settevene-Palo road to Bracciano up to No. 33.

Oasi di Porto is an ideal habitat for migratory birds. This nature reserve boasts many Mediterranean plants, too. For details tel: 06-588 0880. Open mid-Oct to mid-June, Thur and Sun 10am–4pm. Take the Roma–Fiumicino motorway, pass the airport exit and follow the viaduct towards Ostia. Take the first right to Fiumicino, then immediately left onto Via Portuense; the entrance to the Oasi is 3km (2 miles) along the road.

A carved eagle detail at Villa d'Este.

Castel Gandolfo and Lago di Albano.

CASTELLI ROMANI

For a leisurely country drive through towns and villages famous for their food and wine, hire a car and tour this group of small towns southeast of Rome – a popular weekend retreat for the city's inhabitants.

Rome

Southeast of Rome lie the Colli Albani, a group of volcanic hills that form a vast horseshoe-shaped crater 60km (37 miles) in circumference. Within this giant horseshoe are a number of smaller craters, two of which contain the beautiful lakes of Nemi and Albano.

Thirteen towns in the Alban Hills are known collectively as the "Castelli Romani" (Roman Castles). The name stems from the fact that they evolved around the feudal castles of Roman patrician families who sought refuge here when anarchy ruled in Rome. The Castelli are best explored by car, though they can be reached by Cotral buses, which depart from the car park at Anagnina station at the end of metro line A. Frascati is reached by car on Via Tuscolana; Castel Gandolfo, Albano and Ariccia by Via Appia Nuova. Lake Albano, Marino, Genzano and Nemi are reached by Via dei Laghi, which leaves Via Appia Nuova just south of Ciampino Airport.

FRASCATI ⑤

Frascati, which takes its name from the thatch (*frasche*) used to roof its huts, turned from a small settlement into a town in 1197, when the ancient city of Tusculum was destroyed and its population settled here. During World War II, it was seat of the German High Command and suffered heavy damage from Allied bombing, which left much of the town destroyed. Many of its historic buildings, including several churches, were rebuilt after the war.

Frascati is the nearest of the Castelli Romani, only 21km (13 miles) away from Rome. One of the best times to visit is in October, when the grape harvest begins; a *frasca di lauro*, a laurel twig, is displayed; the

Main Attractions
Frascati
Tusculum
Grottaferrata
Rocca di Papa
Monte Cavo
Marino
Genzano
Nemi
Oasi di Ninfa

Maps and Listings
Map, page 254
Restaurants, page 277

In the Oasi di Ninfa.

TIP

In June, hydrangea producers come to Frascati from all over Italy to compete in the lovely hydrangea festival. July and August are also eventful with food and wine festivals, theatre performances and concerts, and a celebratory gathering of vineyard-owners and farm labourers.

smoke of the first wood fires mixes with the sweet scents from the vineyards, and a fat, fresh *porchetta* (whole roast pig stuffed with aromatic herbs, for which the region is known) lies on the counter of every *alimentari* (local grocery).

Wine and porchetta

The town's trademark is its wine – a light, quaffable wine with a faint, refreshing prickle – which is a product of the rich volcanic soil. In Italy, Frascati is drunk mostly by the *Frascatani* themselves. Much of the stuff on sale in supermarkets bears little relation to the drink served in the *cantine* (wine shops or bars), which ranges from pale to dark yellow.

Most of the exported wine comes from neighbouring towns and villages rather than Frascati itself, but the reason it is so poor is that most is based on the rather bland Trebbiano grape: only the better producers – Fontana Candida and Colli di Catone (especially Colle Gaio) – use Malvasia. For more information on wine producers and wine tours and

tastings in Frascati, visit the tourist office on Piazza Marconi.

Begin with a walk around town, starting at **Piazza San Pietro**. From here, go through the little *galleria* (walkway) next to the cinema to **Piazza del Mercato**, where there is a closed produce market and plenty of stalls where you can get a good sandwich bursting with *porchetta*. Go left past the market and you will find several wine shops and bars in **Via Regina Margherita** and further on in **Piazza del Olmo**, that allow customers to bring *cibo proprio* (their own food).

Frascati villas

Frascati is not only famous for its wine, but also for its palaces and gardens. Next to the bus station is the park of **Villa Torlonia**, originally part of a 16th-century estate that was bombed in World War II. Now only the gardens, and the striking Teatro delle Acque (Theatre of the Waters) fountain designed by Carlo Maderno, remain.

Standing majestically above the town, with commanding views of the surrounding countryside and, on a clear day, Rome, is the **Villa Aldobrandini**. Built in 1602 for Pietro Aldobrandini, a nephew of Pope Clement VIII, the villa is still occupied by the Aldobrandini family and closed to the public, but you can visit the grounds (entrance off 11 Via Mazzarino; www.sovraintendenzaroma.it free; daily dawn till dusk).

Back down on the main square, the former stables of the villa have been sensitively restored and converted by Massimiliano Fuksas into a fabulous space for high-profile art exhibitions. **Le Scuderie Aldobrandini** (6 Piazza Marconi; tel: 06-941 7195; http:// beni-culturali.provincia.roma.it; Tue–Fri 10am–6pm, till 7pm Sat–Sun) is also the new home for the Tuscolano Museum, displaying finds from the nearby ancient city of Tusculum.

Piazza del Mercato, Frascati.

del Popolo; www.abbaziagreca.it; tel: 06-945 9309; daily 6am–12.30pm, 3.30pm–sunset; free) was founded in 1004 by Nilus, a monk from Calabria fleeing north to find a site safe from attack by Saracens. Under Byzantine rule, southern Italy had a large Greek minority, whose descendants survive today in a few remote areas.

The monastery was built on the remains of a sepulchre dating from the Republican era. The abbey church, **Santa Maria di Grottaferrata**, is decorated with some fine mosaics and has beautiful frescoes by Domenichino in the Cappella dei Santi Fondatori. On Sunday morning, Mass is celebrated according to the Greek Orthodox rite.

From here, you can see the cross atop the hill at **Rocca Priora ❽**, the highest town in the Castelli at 768 metres (2,520ft), which is often covered in snow in winter.

A shrine to the Virgin on Monte Cavo.

Enjoying Frascati wine in a backstreet cantina.

Remains of the amphitheatre at Tusculum.

TUSCULUM ❻

About 5km (3 miles) from the Villa Aldobrandini is the site of the ancient hill town of Tusculum. The city of the Latins (founded, according to legend, by Telegonus, son of Circe and Ulysses) was a monarchy before it fell within Rome's sphere of influence in the 6th century BC.

Later, in 340 BC, the city participated in the revolt against the Romans. From the 10th to the 12th centuries, the counts of Tusculum ruled over it – as well as Rome. In 1191, the Romans destroyed the town as an act of revenge for its subjugation, and its inhabitants fled to Frascati. Few ruins remain, but the views from up here are splendid, and it's a nice spot for a picnic.

GROTTAFERRATA ❼

It's only a few kilometres from Frascati to **Grottaferrata**, known for its Greek Orthodox abbey. The **Abbazia di San Nilo** (128 Corso

ROCCA DI PAPA ❾

The town of **Rocca di Papa** ("The Pope's Rock") lies a few miles away, on the northern flank of the **Monte**

EAT

The wine shops in Frascati will let you bring your own food, providing plates and cutlery for only a couple of euros, plus the price of the wine you are kindly asked to order. Buy your lunch from a nearby *alimentari*, and enjoy a lovely indoors picnic.

Detail of a fresco by Domenichino, in the chapel dedicated to Saints Nilo and Bartholemew.

Santa Maria di Grottaferrata.

Cavo, the highest peak of the Alban Hills (949 metres/3,114ft). This attractive medieval town has a *quartiere bavarese*, named after the Bavarian mercenaries who were stationed here by Emperor Ludwig III in the 1320s. Rome is only a few miles away and yet the city, whose lights twinkle like glow worms below, couldn't seem more distant.

The wine of Monte Cavo is excellent, and a particularly delicious local speciality, the *sfogatello* mushroom, is worth seeking out.

MONTE CAVO

From Rocca di Papa, you may want to climb to the peak of **Monte Cavo**, following Via Sacra through the oak woods. The summit is a little disappointing because it is covered in hundreds of TV antennae. These stand over the remains of the ancient shrine of Jupiter, worshipped by the 47 federated Latin cities, and a more recent monastery. Despite the antennae, the view is fantastic.

MARINO

Marino, another of the Castelli Romani noted for its wine, holds a

celebrated wine festival each October. The town's fountains flow with wine, and there's plenty of wine tasting, eating and parading through the streets. The main square, **Piazza Matteotti** (named after the Socialist leader murdered by Mussolini) is dominated by the Fountain of the Moors, built in honour of the *condottiere* (mercenary admiral) of the papal fleet, Marcantonio Colonna, victor of the sea battle of Lepanto in 1571.

The **Madonna del Rosario** church is well worth a visit. Built in 1713, it is the most beautiful rococo church in Lazio.

CASTEL GANDOLFO

The pope's summer residence at Castel Gandolfo is beautifully situated 400 metres (1,300ft) above the crater rim of Lago di Albano. This was the site of Alba Longa, the city founded by Aeneas. After a long struggle between Alba Longa and

Rome, the latter won. Alba Longa was destroyed as a punishment for treachery, but the temples were spared. They are said to have occupied the exact spot of the papal villa.

The Holy See acquired Castel Gandolfo at the end of the 16th century, and in 1628 Pope Urban VIII commissioned Maderno to design a villa here. Completed by Bernini, the **Papal Palace** is linked by bridges and loggias to the other two pontifical villas, Villa Barberini and Villa Cybo. The gardens are closed to the public for security reasons. In summer, the Pope holds the angelus prayer at midday on Sunday on the **Loggia della Benedizione**.

Stendhal, Goethe and Gregorovius all had a high opinion of Castel Gandolfo, and modern Romans love it, too, particularly because it is so close to **Lago di Albano** ⑬. The clean water of this volcanic lake invites boating and swimming, but in the middle, where it is 170 metres (558ft) deep, there are dangerous currents. There is a delightful footpath, 10km (6 miles) long, around the lake. On Sunday, it is as crowded as the seaside.

To the southwest of the lake, the supposed tombs of the Horatian and Curatian families can be seen in **Albano Laziale** on the right-hand side of Via Appia Nuova, if you are travelling in the direction of Ariccia. The local park has remains of the **Villa of Pompey**.

Ariccia ⑭ itself contains a number of works by Bernini. He restored the **Palazzo Chigi** (tel: 06-933 0053; www.palazzochigiariccia.it; Tue–Sun 11am–6pm, till 5pm in winter) and designed the church of Santa Maria dell'Assunzione and the pilgrim sanctuary of Santa Maria di Galloro. Like Frascati, the town is famous for its *porchetta*.

GENZANO ⑮

Further along Via Appia Nuova, on the southeastern edge of the little crater-lake of Nemi, is the medieval town of Genzano, famous for its Flower Festival and its bread. The *Infiorata* takes place on the "Corpus Domini" Sunday, usually in June, when the main street leading up to the church of **Santa Maria della Cima** is carpeted with holy pictures made from 5 tonnes of flower petals gathered by the townsfolk.

Villa Aldobrandini's own organic Frascati is for sale on the premises.

Castel Gandolfo overlooking Lago di Albano.

KIDS

The Genzano Flower Festival (Infiorata) takes place every year on Corpus Domini Sunday, with thousands of flowers creating 250 meters (820ft) of artistic images and designs on Genzano's main road. On the following day around sunset, children are allowed to run through the petals, and to destroy the gorgeous compositions.

Villa Aldobrandini.

Etruscan figurine in the Sanctuary of Diana, Nemi.

NEMI ⑯

Set on a spur of rock above the lake of the same name is Nemi, known for its *fragole di bosco* (wild strawberries) and the Strawberry Festival on the first Sunday of June, when free fruit is distributed. This unspoilt little village, surrounded by woods, was once home to a sacred shrine to the goddess Diana, in whose honour Caligula built two huge, ornate barges. These were sunk by the emperor's enemies and were only raised in the 1920s, then destroyed when the building they were kept in caught fire during an Allied air raid in 1944.

The **Museo delle Navi Romane** (15 Via Diana; tel: 06-6501 0089; http://archeoroma.beniculturali.it; closed for restoration) displays one-fifth scale models of the Imperial boats, plus some of the decorative elements that survived and objects from Diana's sanctuary, the site of which can be visited on request.

OASIS OF NINFA ⑰

Southeast of the Castelli Romani, about 60km (38 miles) from Rome,

the Oasi di Ninfa is one of the most evocative places in Lazio. If you are in a hire car and in the vicinity, a visit to these medieval ruins overgrown with exotic plants is worth considering. For more information, see page 269.

THE NEMI SHIPS

Since ancient times, rumours about two large ships lying on the bottom of Lake Nemi stimulated the imagination of the local population. The extravagant vessels, allegedly decorated with splendorous mosaics and ivory friezes, had been built by Caligula as a tribute to Diana, the goddess of hunt. Legend had it that the Emperor used them for pleasure trips and entertainment, often simulating ship battles, until he himself sank them, say the locals, amid a drunken orgy. This legend was kept alive by the many fishermen who, throughout the ages, often found Roman objects in their nets.

People tried to recover the two boats for centuries, but the first one who actually proved their existence was Mussolini in the late 1920s. After draining the lake, his workers managed to dig the vessels out of the mud and proudly presented their finding to the excited Italian population. In 1932, the boats were placed in the new Museo delle Navi Romane in Nemi. The legendary descriptions matched reality, but the ships' "new life" didn't last very long: in 1944, a fire (probably started by the German soldiers stationed in the area) destroyed them and most of the objects they contained. The few remaining pieces and artefacts are now housed in the museum.

RESTAURANTS

PRICE CATEGORIES

Price includes dinner and a half-bottle of house wine.

€€€€ = more than €60
€€€ = €40–60
€€ = €25–40
€ = under €25.

Castel Gandolfo

Ristorante Bucci
31 Via de Zecchini
06-932 3334
www.ristorantebucci.it
L & D Thu–Tue, D only Fri
€€–€€€
With great views of Lake Albano from its terrace, this family-run restaurant is strong on pasta dishes and meaty *secondi*.

Frascati

Genzano Da Pelliccione
13 Piazza Mazzini
06-936 4480
http://osteriapelliccione.it
L & D Mon–Sat
€€
Choose from more than 20 first courses and 18 second courses, including offal options like tripe with mint and pajata. The owner's wife goes out of her way to please children, proposing recipes to suit their palates. Pleasant (and breezy) open-air patio in summer.

Osteria Pietrino e Renata
70 Via Generale Roberto Lordi
06-9724 9478
www.pietrinoerenata.com
L & D Tue–Sun
€€
One of the best restaurants in the region, serving dishes made with seasonal ingredients. Specialities include zucchini flowers stuffed with mozzarella, fettuccine with chicken livers, papardelle with porcini mushrooms, and bean, barley and black cabbage soup. Good wine list.

Da Una Cantina
7/9 Viale Regina Margherita
06-941 7379
www.ristorantedaunacantina.it
D only Tue–Sat, L only Sun
€–€€
Situated in the heart of Frascati's Centro Storico. Chefs Mariella and Giacomo change the menu on a monthly basis according to what's in season; dishes are prepared using the freshest of ingredients. Has an excellent wine list. Booking is advised.

Grottaferrata

La Briciola
12 Via D'Annunzio
06-945 9338
L & D Tue–Sat, L only Sun
€€€
A competent exponent of the hearty fare that the Castelli Romani hill towns are known for: lamb stew and chickpea, barley and chestnut soup are typical dishes. Leave room for dessert, though – the pear and chocolate *millefoglie* is divine.

Marino

Al Cantuccio
6 Piaza Risorgimento
06-938 8906
www.alcantuccio.it
L & D Tue–Sun
€–€€
This friendly, family-run trattoria serves up excellent cooking at very reasonable prices. Try the outstanding beef tagliata with rosemary. Tables are set up on the pretty terrace in summer.

Trattoria la Credenza
4 Via Cola di Rienzo
06-938 5105
www.lacredenzadicesare.it
D only Tue–Sat, L only Sun
€€€
Authentic Castelli cuisine such as *zuppa di baccalà e ceci* (salt-cod and chickpea stew), *coratella d'abbacchio* (lamb offal with artichokes) and *fagioli con le cotiche* (pork and beans).

Nemi

Il Castagnone
Diana Park Hotel, 44 Via Nemorense
06-936 4041
www.hoteldiana.com
L & D Tue–Sat, L only Sun
€€
This family-run hotel restaurant offers classic Italian cuisine and great lake views from the summer dining terrace.

Rocca di Papa

La Longarina
1 Via dei Colli
06-949 5135
www.lalongarina.it
L & D Tue–Sun
€€
Surrounded by woodland, this restaurant is a tranquil place to sample the regional cuisine. Pasta dishes include the tasty fettuccine with porcini mushrooms and bacon. Meat is cooked on the grill in front of diners, with cuts generous enough to suit the hungriest of carnivores. The crispy pizza, cooked in a wood-fired oven, is also tempting.

Lamb chops are on the menu at Il Castagnone's.

Il Palazzo Papale, the jewel of Viterbo.

ETRUSCAN TOWNS

The Etruscans built a series of cities, founded leagues and painted frescoed tombs in northern Lazio more than 2,700 years ago. The remains of these cities make for a fascinating archaeological excursion.

here are many Etruscan settlements within Central Italy and some of the most important are in Lazio. Touring Etruria by car is probably the best way to take in the sites, though they can all can be reached by train from either Trastevere, Ostiense or Termini stations in Rome, or on a COTRAL bus from certain metro stations (ask at the tourist office for details).

Anyone whose curiosity is aroused by this mysterious and once powerful ancient race will find the well-preserved ruins of these archaeological sites fascinating. Some historical background will enhance the experience and help decode the ruins as well as the collections of Etruscan artefacts displayed in many city museums.

Etruscan origins

In about 800 BC, Etruscans settled on the west coast where Tuscany and Lazio are today. The origins of the Etruscans still puzzle scholars, but wherever they came from, they were a highly civilised people who had a hearty appetite for life. Hundreds of Etruscan tombs have survived, many with wall paintings depicting dancing, dinner parties and music-making. Other paintings show battle and hunting scenes. The Etruscans

A fine Etruscan fresco.

were also extremely skilled craftsmen, whose speciality was metalworking. Italy was rich in minerals, and trade in metal goods soon became the basis of an active urban society. Cities sprang up where previously there had only been simple villages.

Each Etruscan city supported itself by trade. Eager to obtain luxury goods from the Greek colonists, the Etruscans developed overland routes to reach the Greek cities. These cut straight through Latium, the plain south of the Tiber occupied by

Main Attractions
Veio
Palestrina
Cerveteri
Tarquinia
Viterbo

Maps and Listings
Map, page 254
Restaurants, page 285

Italian natives called Latins. One of their trading posts on the route south was a Latin village called Rome, originally only a cluster of mud huts. Under the influence of the Etruscans the settlement flourished. They drained the swamp that became the Roman Forum and built grand palaces and roads.

For 300 years, Etruscan kings ruled Rome, but by the 5th century BC their power was fading. The last king, Tarquin the Proud, was driven out when the Romans opted for a Republic. After this the Etruscans stayed north of the Tiber and their influence declined.

The Apollo of Veio, a masterpiece of Etruscan art, whose knowing, mysterious smile bears some resemblance to that of Leonardo's Mona Lisa.

VEIO ⑱

The Etruscan city closest to Rome is Veio, once the largest in southern Etruria. Unlike other sites, where only tombs remain, the **Archaeological Area of Veio** (Località Isola Farnese, Via Riserva Campetti; tel: 06-3089 0116; Tue–Sat 9am–7pm in summer, Tue, Wed, Fri, Sun 8am–2pm, till 4pm Thu, Sat in winter), which lies

The 2,000-year-old Nile Mosaic in the Palazzo Barberini, Palestrina.

within the protected Parco di Veio (www.parcodiveio.it), includes parts of a swimming pool and the lower section of a temple. The striking Portonaccio sanctuary was located outside the city walls. Originally, it had a terracotta roof and was decorated with a series of larger-than-life statues of various gods. A block of tufa stone and an underground gallery are the only ruins left from this construction. The famous **statue of Apollo**, dating from the 6th century BC, was found in the temple dedicated to Minerva.

PALESTRINA ⓽

Ancient **Praeneste** (modern Palestrina) is one of the oldest towns of Latium (Lazio). According to myth, it was founded by Telegonus, son of Ulysses and Circe. The town was flourishing in the 8th century BC, but it wasn't until the 4th century that it became part of Rome. During the civil war between Marius and Sulla, Marius fled to Praeneste, which was besieged by Sulla's troops and eventually destroyed.

Sulla wanted to make amends and so ordered the reconstruction of the **sanctuary of Fortuna Primigenia**, the mother of all gods. In the Middle Ages a new town rose on its ruins.

In 1944 bombs destroyed part of the town, bringing the temple to light and prompting excavations.

The temple was one of the grandest of antiquity. It comprised a series of terraces on the slopes of Mount Ginestro connected by ramps. Adorned with statues and blazing with torches, the complex must have been an impressive sight, which could be seen from afar. The goddess Fortuna was worshipped in the upper part of the shrine. In the 16th century, a palace was built into this upper circle of the temple, occupied first by the patrician Colonna family and then by the Roman Barberinis, who expanded it in the 1640s.

Museo Nazionale Archeologico di Palestrina

Address: 1 Piazza della Cortina
Telephone: 06-953 8100
Opening Hours: daily 9am–8pm
Entrance Fee: charge
The Colonna-Barberini Palace now houses the Palestrina Museum, where countless busts and other local finds

The majestic entrance to the Palazzo Barberini which sits atop the site of Praeneste.

In the 17th century Praeneste changed its name to honour its most famous native son, Pierluigi di Palestrina, born here in 1525. His distinguished career as a composer included many years as an organist and choirmaster at St Peter's in Rome.

Palestrina's 12th-century belltower.

are on display, including the badly damaged remains of the statue of Fortuna. The Nile Mosaic on the top floor is the museum's prize exhibit. Dating from the 1st century BC, it shows, in detail, the Nile valley after the annual flood, a scene teeming with peasants, fishermen, priests, soldiers and animals.

Access to the excavated site (with a ticket bought from the museum) is opposite the palace. The lower part of the shrine is buried beneath the old town of Palestrina, which is enclosed within the temple's extensive walls. In the central **Piazza Regina Margherita** the Seminario incorporates the remains of the *area sacra*. Most archaeologists agree that this was the entrance to the **Oracle** – one of the most important of ancient times.

CERVETERI ⓴

Ancient remains, even older than those at Ostia, can be found near Cerveteri, where an Etruscan settlement called Kysry was established

about 45km (28 miles) northwest of Rome and only 6km (4 miles) from the sea. In the 7th and 6th centuries BC, Kysry became one of the most powerful cities in Etruria, with a population of around 25,000. Revenue came mostly from rich ore deposits in the nearby Tolfa Hills, but there were also strong commercial ties with Hellenic lands, the influence of whose merchants made it the centre of a lively and sophisticated cultural life.

Kysry maintained good relations with its Roman neighbours. But eventually the barbaric strength of rising Rome wiped away what had been a refined and joyous civilisation. Under Roman rule the town became known as Caere. It grew steadily poorer, but was not abandoned until the Middle Ages, when the population then moved east to Ceri, renaming their abandoned town Caere Vetus, which evolved into Cerveteri.

Necropoli della Banditaccia (di Cerveteri)

Address: Via della Necropoli della Banditaccia, 2km (1.25 miles) from Cerveteri centre; www.tarquinia-cerveteri.it
Telephone: 06-994 0651
Opening Hours: Tue–Sun 8.30am–till one hour before dusk
Entrance Fee: charge

Nothing remains of the ancient town bar a few walls, but it is worth going to look at the excavation of Caere's necropolis on a hill, an atmospheric site with countless tombs carved into the soft tufa rock.

The oldest tombs (8th century BC) have a small circular well where the urns containing the ashes of the dead were placed. The first chamber tombs, also cut into the stone and covered with rocky blocks and mounds *(tumuli)*, appeared as early as the 7th century BC. The noble Etruscans were either enclosed in great sarcophagi with their effigies on top, or laid out on stone beds in their chamber tombs. In the 6th

TIP

The best way to reach Cerveteri from Rome by public transport is to take the *regionale* (ie not an Inter-City or Eurostar) train to Pisa, which stops at the town. Alternatively, a COTRAL bus leaves from Lepanto station on metro line A.

Telephone: 06-8852 2517
Opening Hours: Tue–Sun 8.30am–7.30pm
Entrance Fee: charge

Excavations of the tombs not already plundered revealed goods of gold, silver, ivory, bronze and ceramic. The vases show strong Greek influence as well as the excellent quality of Etruscan craftsmanship. Some of the objects found in the graves, including domestic implements, vases and terracotta lamps, are housed here in the 16th-century Palazzo Ruspoli. However, finds from Cerveteri are scattered as far afield as the British Museum, the Louvre in Paris, the Vatican's Museo Gregoriano and the Villa Giulia in Rome, which includes the famous sarcophagus of the married couple, the Sarcofago degli Sposi.

TARQUINIA ㉑

The Etruscan town of Tarquinia stood on a hill northwest of the picturesque medieval town bearing the same name. The town existed as early as the 9th century BC, but by the 8th and 7th centuries BC it was a rich and powerful city and became an

and 5th centuries BC, the so-called cubic graves became common. These rectangular tombs were laid out in regular rows of streets, reflecting the social changes that had taken place in the city. By then, prosperity had spread to the lower classes and a social levelling had taken place. From the 4th to the 1st century BC, the dead were buried in underground tombs called *hypogaea*, fairly plain by comparison to the earlier tombs.

The largest tomb in Cerveteri is the Tomba dei Rilievi. Other important tombs to look out for include the Tomba della Capanna, Tomba dei Dolii, Tomba dei Letti e dei Sarcofagi, Tomba dei Vasi Greci, Tomba della Cornice and Tomba degli Scudi e delle Sedie. Virtual reconstructions show how the tombs might have looked like more than 2,000 years ago.

Museo Nazionale Cerite

Address: Palazzo Ruspoli, Piazza Santa Maria; www.tarquinia-cerveteri.it

The 7th-century Tomba della Cornice, Cerveteri.

Visiting the Cerveteri necropolis.

TIP

If you are exploring the area north of Rome by car, consider a trip to Lago di Bracciano, famous for fishing and water sports. In Bracciano, Castello Orsini-Odescalchi is worth visiting, but more idyllic is the medieval village of Anguillara on the lake's southern shores.

The 6th-century BC sarcophagus of a married couple, discovered in Cerveteri, can be seen in the Villa Giulia Etruscan Museum in Rome.

active commercial and industrial centre. Its political supremacy extended over a vast area inland as far as the Cimini Mountains and Bolsena Lake.

Necropoli dei Monterozzi (di Tarquinia)

Address: Strada provinciale Monterozzi Marina–Tarquinia (Viterbo)
Telephone: 0766-840 000
Opening Hours: Tue–Sun 8.30am–7.30pm in summer, till one hour before sunset in winter
Entrance Fee: charge

The Necropoli di Tarquinia, together with that of Cerveteri, is the most important Etruscan burial site. It stands on a hill south of the original town, occupying an area 5km (3 miles) long by 1km (0.62 mile) wide. Some tombs are painted with frescoes that are a precious document of Etruscan life, depicting banquets, dancing and musicians, athletics or gladiatorial fights, funeral processions, and even erotic scenes.

At any given time no more than 15 of the 6,000 tombs are accessible, as they are opened in rotation in an effort to preserve the delicate paintings. The Tomba della Caccia e della Pesca (530–20 BC), which shows some

lively fishing and hunting scenes, and the Tomba del Cacciatore (the Tomb of the Hunter, 530–10 BC) are among the oldest. The Tomba delle Leonesse (Tomb of the Lionesses) shows a pronounced Greek influence. One of the best known is La Tomba dell'Orco (4th century BC), which depicts a banquet attended by the prominent Surinna family.

Museo Nazionale Tarquinense

Address: Palazzo Vitelleschi, Piazza Cavour; www.tarquinia-cerveteri.it
Telephone: 0766-850 080
Opening Hours: Tue–Sun 8.30am–7.30pm
Entrance Fee: charge

This museum in the atmospheric medieval town of Tarquinia houses one of the most important collections of Etruscan artefacts in Italy, most of which were discovered in the necropolis. It also boasts a great collection of Greek pottery.

VITERBO ㉒

Viterbo's roots can be traced right back to the Etruscans. Crammed with medieval alleyways, porticoes, noble fountains and fine squares, alongside

CITIES FOR THE DEAD

Every Etruscan town or village had another "city for the dead" built outside its walls. For the Etruscans, life in the next world was just as important as life on earth – perhaps even more so, judging by the fact that dead were buried in larger spaces than the living inhabited. The Necropoli della Banditaccia, for example, is organised in a city-like plan, with actual roads and neighbourhoods. The Etruscans believed not only in the everlasting soul but in the survival, in some shape or form, of the human body after death, so the tombs had to be suitably equipped for the deceased to carry on living in the next world in the way he or she had become accustomed to living on earth. Accordingly, the dead were supplied with food and jewellery and surrounded with all the things that they had loved most when alive – even household furniture, such as beds and chairs, were carved out of the rock, giving a detailed impression of Etruscan everyday life. The Etruscan cemeteries of Cerveteri and Tarquinia reflect the different types of burial practices and through the images depicted they give us an idea of the daily life and achievements of the Etruscan culture.

is the 13th-century **Palazzo Papale**, a favourite residence of the popes. On the same square the Romanesque **cathedral of San Lorenzo** was built on top of an Etruscan citadel. The shop-lined **Corso Italia** leads to the **Piazza del Plebiscito**, dominated by the town hall and governor's palace. To the east the medieval **San Pellegrino quarter**, a labyrinth of narrow alleyways, arches and hidden corners, is the most atmospheric part of town.

Just outside the city wall, east of the centre, the **Museo Civico** (2 Piazza Crispi; tel: 0761-348 275; www.visit.viterbo.it; Tue–Sun 9am–6pm) contains a collection of Etruscan finds such as sarcophagi with bas-reliefs, pottery urns and vases, and some bronze idols. There is also a small collection of paintings. Adjacent to the museum is the convent church of **Santa Maria della Verità**, worth visiting for its beautiful 13th-century cloister and the Mazzatosta chapel, frescoed by Lorenzo da Viterbo, a pupil of Piero della Francesca.

TIP

Many of the most valuable finds from the Etruscan towns have been transferred to Rome. The most important Etruscan collections can be seen at the Villa Giulia (see page 189) and the Etruscan Museum in the Vatican (see page 146).

A pork butcher in Viterbo.

bustling streets lined with shops, cafés and restaurants, this characterful town, just 98km (60 miles) from Rome, is ideal for a day trip. The most notable of its many historic buildings

RESTAURANTS, BARS AND CAFÉS

PRICE CATEGORIES

Price includes dinner and a half-bottle of house wine.
€€€€ = more than €60
€€€ = €40–60
€€ = €25–40
€ = under €25.

Cerveteri

Agroturismo I 4 Ricci
Via del Casalone snc Borgo S. Martino
06-9920 7118
www.agriturismo4ricci.it
L & D Fri–Wed
€€€
Located in the beautiful countryside, with magnificent views over nearby hills, this welcoming place serves traditional Latium dishes made of fresh, locally

sourced produce, including hare and rabbit.

Palestrina

L'Oracolo
16 Piazza Garibaldi
06-953 7705
L & D Tue–Sun
€–€€
This small trattoria serves both restaurant fare and pizza, but the latter, prepared in the view of diners and cooked in a wood-fired oven, are the main draw.

Tarquinia

Arcadia
6 Via Mazzini
0766-855 501
www.arcadia-ristorante.it
L & D Tue–Sun

€€–€€€
This restaurant, right in the centre of historic Tarquinia, has a fish-based menu, an extensive wine list and charming staff.

Viterbo

Buongusto
107 Corso Italia
393 661 9127
www.buongustopiadineria.it
L & D Tue–Sun
€
This small but cosy restaurant is famous for its excellent *piadine*, a typical flour flatbread prepared in the Romagna region. There are 40 different types on offer with fillings ranging from the classic *crudo e mozzarella* to sweet *crema de nociolle*.

INSIGHT GUIDES TRAVEL TIPS
ROME

TRANSPORT

GETTING THERE AND GETTING AROUND

GETTING THERE

By Air

Scheduled flights from around the world land at the main airport, **Aeroporto Leonardo da Vinci** in Fiumicino (tel: 06-65951; www.adr.it), about 35km (22 miles) southwest of Rome. The airport is served by most major national carriers, including Alitalia and British Airways. Along with several American carriers, Alitalia operates daily flights from New York and other US cities.

Low-cost airlines, including RyanAir and easyJet, fly in to **Ciampino Airport** (tel: 06-65951; www.adr.it), the city's second airport, about 12km (7 miles) southeast of the city (for information on getting into the city from the airport, see pages 289).

By Rail

Rome is well served by rail connections to the majority of major European cities, and the national railway, **Ferrovie dello Stato**, is efficient and relatively inexpensive. There are several categories: reservations are required for the Frecciarossa (Eurostar) and T-Biz, the fastest and most luxurious trains, and optional (but highly recommended) for the InterCity. You pay a supplement to use these lines, but they save time. Regional trains (called regionale or interregionale) are slower as they stop at many stations.

To buy a ticket or book a seat, go to a travel agent *(agenzia di viaggio)* in the city, or in Stazione Termini, where there are plenty of easy-to-understand ticket machines. You can also book by credit card online (www.trenitalia.com) or by phone (tel: 892 021, no prefix; from landline phones only; 24-hours daily, press 2 for information; from abroad call: +39 06-6847 5475). You can then pick up your tickets at machines at Termini Station or from the conductor on the train (ask for the "ticketless" option when booking). Both the website and phone service offer in-depth timetable information. If you're planning a lot of rail travel, it pays to look into various rail-pass offers at home and in Italy.

The regionale and InterCity train tickets are valid for two months after the date of issue, and must be stamped on the day you travel at one of the machines at the head of each platform, otherwise you will be fined. Eurostar tickets always have a booking time printed on them.

Stazione Termini is the main railway terminal, the meeting point of the two metro lines and the main stop for many city buses.

AIRLINES

Alitalia
Tel: 06-2222 (Rome)
Tel: 0333 566 5544 (UK)
Tel: 800-223 5730 (USA)
www.alitalia.com
British Airways
Tel: 02-6963 3602 (Italy)
Tel: 0844-493 0787 (UK)
Tel: 1-800-airways (USA)
www.britishairways.com
Delta
Tel: 892-006 or 02-3859 1451 (Italy)
Tel: 020 7660 0767 (UK)
Tel: 800-241 4141 (USA)

www.delta.com
easyJet
Tel: 199-201 840 (Italy)
Tel: 0843-104 5000 (UK)
www.easyjet.com
Ryanair
Tel: 895-589 5509 (Italy)
Tel: 0871-246 0000 (UK)
www.ryanair.com
United Airlines
Tel: 06-6605 3030 (Italy)
Tel: 0845-6076 760 (UK)
Tel: 1-800-united-1 (international destinations from USA)
www.united.com

There is a tourist office opposite platform 24, and a hotel reservation booth opposite platform 20, as well as a luggage deposit, cafés, restaurants and fast-food outlets, a bookstore, a shopping gallery, a telephone office and even an art gallery.

The official taxi rank is in front of the station. Do not be tempted by offers from unofficial cab drivers in the station interior.

By Coach/Bus

Most coaches arrive at the main terminus on Via Marsala next to Stazione Termini. If you are travelling on a COTRAL bus, the network which serves the Lazio region, you will arrive and depart from a metro stop: Lepanto and Ponte Mammolo for the north, Anagnina and EUR Fermi for the south, and Tiburtina for the east.

By Road

European (EU) driving licences are valid in Italy. Travellers from other countries normally require an international driving licence. Carry your licence, plus the vehicle registration and insurance (Green Card) documents with you when driving. If driving your own car, you may wish to take out extra insurance to cover home recovery in case of a breakdown.

Tolls are payable on motorways, including the A1. Pay in cash, with credit cards, or with the special motorway magnetic cards available at service stations.

Motorists arriving in Rome from all directions will first hit the Grande Raccordo Anulare (GRA), the ring road. It is busy and can be alarming, but is usually the quickest way to reach one of the entry roads into the centre. During rush hour, however, traffic jams are frequent.

The A1 Autostrada del Sole leads into the GRA from both north and south, as does the A24 from the east. If you arrive on the Via del Mare from the coast (Ostia), you can either switch to

Taxis outside Termini station.

the GRA or continue straight on into the centre.

When leaving the GRA, follow white signs for the road you want (blue ones usually lead away from the centre). The city centre sign is a white point in a black circle on a white background.

GETTING AROUND

From the Airport

From Fiumicino, there are frequent train services to the city – every 15–30 minutes to Trastevere Station and every 30 minutes (every 15 minutes in peak time) to Stazione Termini. Trains to Stazione Termini (the Leonardo Express) run from 6.23am to 11.23pm; the journey takes around 30 minutes and the ticket costs €14. If you're travelling to one of the suburban rail stations such as Trastevere, Ostiense and Tiburtina, take one of the regional trains bound for Orte, which run from 5.57am to 11.27pm; tickets cost €8. At night there's a COTRAL bus that leaves from the international arrivals terminus every 75 minutes bound for the Termini and Tiburtina railway stations. Taxi rates are

capped by law; a taxi from Fiumicino to the centre for four people should cost no more than €48. If you suspect you are being fleeced, ostentatiously make a note of the driver's licence number and report any problems; tel: 066-7107 0721 or 06-0606.

From Ciampino, the best way to reach the centre is to take the Terravision, Schiaffini or SIT-busShuttle coaches, which depart from outside the arrivals building and drop you off at Via Marsala, by Stazione Termini. The journey takes 40 minutes and tickets cost €4–6 one way and can be bought

Two wheels are better than four.

All tracks lead to Rome.

on board. Book online at www.ter-ravision.eu, www.schiaffini.it, www.cotralspa.it or www.sitbusshuttle.it (at least 24 hours before departure) to be sure of a seat. There is at least one coach for every scheduled Ryanair and easyJet flight arriving or departing. Alternatively, the fixed price for a taxi from Ciampino to the city centre is €30. Report any problems to 06-0606.

Orientation

It sometimes seems that all Roman roads lead to Piazza Venezia. This can produce traffic chaos, but from a visitor's point of view the square is a useful orien-

tation point at the centre of ancient, medieval and modern Rome.

To the south of Piazza Venezia, the three roads, Via dei Fori Imperiali, Via di San Gregorio and Via delle Terme, thread between the greatest monuments of Ancient Rome to the Terme di Caracalla. Northwards, Via del Corso runs through the commercial heart of modern Rome to Piazza del Popolo. To the west, Corso Vittorio Emanuele II leads through the heart of medieval Rome and across the Tiber (Tevere) to St Peter's and the Vatican. Eastwards Via Nazionale, Piazza della Repubblica and Piazza dei Cinquecento lead to Stazione Termini.

An easy and pleasant way to get an overview of the city is to walk or catch a bus up the Gianicolo (Janiculum hill) behind Trastevere. Alternatively, take the elevator (€7) to reach the top of the Vittoriano monument (Piazza Venezia).

Public Transport

Public transport is quite efficient and inexpensive, but over-crowded at peak hours. Tickets are available from bars, tobacconists and newspaper kiosks that display the ATAC (city bus com-

pany) emblem, and from vending machines in metro stations and bus terminals. Once validated in the metro turnstile or machine at the back of the bus, single-use tickets (BIT), valid for 100 minutes and costing €1.50, offer unlimited bus or tram journeys and one metro ride. One-day tickets (BIG) cost €7, two-day tickets €12,50, and three-day tickets €18. Weekly tickets *(carta settimanale)*, which cost €24, are also available. A €36 Roma Pass (www.romapass.it), valid for 48 hours or 3 days, entitles the user to free public transport, free entry to two museums, and discounts at other museums visited thereafter and certain shops and theatres.

Passengers caught without a ticket will be fined €51 on the spot. The amount doubles if you cannot pay immediately.

Buses and Trams

Bus and tram services run from 5.30am to midnight, with an all-night service on 22 bus lines, denoted by the letter "N" after the number. Bus and tram stops are clearly marked, and most list route numbers, the main destinations along each route and lines with night service.

Board buses at either the front or rear doors and stamp your ticket immediately. Ring the bell to request the next stop and exit through the centre doors.

The 40 Express is the quickest way to get from the station to the city centre and then St Peter's. Along with the 64 (a slower version of the 40 Express with more stops), it is one of the city's most popular bus routes, so watch out for pickpockets.

Five electric minibuses serve the narrow streets of the Centro Storico: the most useful are the 116, which passes through or alongside Campo de'Fiori, Piazza Farnese, Piazza Navona, the Pantheon and Piazza Barberini; the 119, which serves the area around Piazza del Popolo and

BUS TOURS

Several companies run hop-on/hop-off bus tours, including Opera Romana Pellegrinaggi (ORP; www.operaromanapellegrinaggi.org). Its 11-stop Roma Cristiana Open Bus tour starts at San Pietro in Vaticano (first departure 9.30am) and ends in Campo de Fiori in Trastevere (last departure 6pm). It offers on board commentary in 8 languages and costs €15 (one trip), €20 (one day) or €23 (48 hours). Rome Open Tour (www.romeopentour.com) also runs daily bus tours from Termini to St. Peter's. Several 3–9 hour bus tours in various combina-

tions, including meal options with prices ranging from €37 – 130, are provided by Enjoy Rome (www.enjoyrome.com). Due to environmental concerns and the narrow streets in the historic centre, tour buses are only allowed to stop in a few places (rarely the best from the tourists' point of view) so it can be just as fruitful to use public transport; three electric minibuses (nos 116, 117 and 119) are particularly useful as they crisscross the historic centre, passing by its main attractions. For timetables and routes, see www.atac.roma.it.

An ATAC bus.

Boats

The riverboat company Battelli di Roma (www.battellidiroma.it) organises hop-on hop-off tourist cruises with commentary and romantic tours on weekends (see page 177). Boats depart from Ponte Sant'Angelo and the Tiber Island (Isola Tiberina). Pleasure trips run daily every 30 minutes from 10am to 8.30pm, while dinner cruises only run Thursday–Saturday. Ask at the tourist information points for more details or contact Battelli di Roma; tel: 06-9774 5498.

Taxis

Licensed taxis are white and always have a meter. If you are approached inside railway stations or at the airport by someone muttering 'Taxi, taxi,' always refuse as they are likely to charge you far more than the official rate.

There are ranks outside Termini Station, outside both airports, and in many parts of the Centro Storico, such as Largo di Torre Argentina and Piazza Venezia. Otherwise you can always hail a taxi on the street as long as it has a light on, indicating it is free, or call 06-0609.

Prices for licensed taxis are fixed and start with a minimum fee of €3. Surcharges are made for each large piece of luggage

Piazza di Spagna, and the 117, which goes from Piazza del Popolo to Basilica San Giovanni in Laterano.

Bus 81 runs from the Colosseum to Piazza del Risorgimento near the Vatican Museums. If you are visiting the catacombs, take bus 118 from the Piramide metro stop to the Via Appia. The No. 8 tramline links Largo Argentina in the centre to Trastevere and Monteverde in the west. From Piazza di Spagna to Stazione Termini, take metro line A. For the Colosseum, do the same and change at Termini to line B.

For information on trams, buses or the metro call the 24-hour infoline 06-57003, or go to www.atac.roma.it, which has a useful route planner.

COTRAL runs regional buses that connect Rome to the airports, the rest of the province and the Lazio region (www.cotralspa.it).

Metro

The metro operates from 5.30am–11.30pm and until 12.30am on Saturday night. The city is served by two metro lines (A and B), which intersect at

Stazione Termini. There are only two lines because of the problems of circumnavigating the numerous unexcavated ruins underground. A third metro line © is slowly being constructed, but it is likely to be years before it is fully operational. A section connecting Monte Compatri/ Pantano to the Parco di Sentocelle (to be extended eventually to Fori Imperiali) opened in 2014, but it does not connect with the other two lines so is of limited use.

One of Rome's few remaining tram lines.

A Roman's ideal city runaround.

and for journeys after 10pm and on public holidays. By law every taxi should have a card listing the various rates and charges.

Driving

Generally, a car is of little use within the city. Parking is hard to find, one-way systems are complex and much of the city centre is closed. Non-resident drivers are not allowed inside the city center's ZTL (Limited Traffic Zone) during the day and on some nights (mainly on weekends). Cameras at the entrance of the restricted area film licence plates, and cars

Traffic cops have their work cut out in Rome.

without a permit will receive a fine each time they pass under the camera. The cameras are easily seen as they always come with an electronic sign that says whether the cameras are on *(varco attivo)*, meaning that access is restricted, or off *(varco non attivo)*, indicating that access is open to everyone.

If you need to reach a hotel in a traffic-restricted area you must make arrangements with reception before arriving. Local drivers have a very personal set of rules and codes that allow for much flashing of lights, tooting of horns and rampant acceleration at what looks like vastly inopportune moments to anyone non-Roman. If you are not deterred by such problems or if you wish to make extensive trips out of town, you might want to hire your own vehicle (see page 293). Note that all cars are required by law to keep their low-beam lights on at all times on motorways and dual carriageways.

There is a large car park under Villa Borghese (entrance at the top of Via Veneto) and one on the Gianicolo hill near the Vatican called Terminal Gianicolo (entrance from Piazza della Rovere). Several of the four- and five-

star hotels in the centre have their own garage or protected parking: ask when booking. Few two- or three-star hotels are able to help with parking.

Given the lack of parking spaces, it is not surprising that a lot of cars are towed away in Rome – over 10,000 a year – so if your car is no longer where you left it, this, rather than theft, may be the reason. The Ufficio Rimozione of the traffic police *(Vigili Urbani)* will be able to tell you if this is the case. The fines you will have to pay to get your car back are high. Contact Vigili Urbani; tel: 06-67691 or 06-0606.

A lot of cars are clamped. If this happens to you, a note on the windscreen will give you the number to call.

If you think that your car has been stolen, you can report it at the nearest police station.

Breakdown Service

The Italian Automobile Association (ACI) provides an emergency breakdown service. If you need repairs, look in the Yellow Pages *(Pagine Gialle;* www.paginegialle.it) for the nearest mechanic *(autofficina)*, or ask the ACI. ACI breakdown and information service, freephone: 803-116.

Bicycles and Mopeds

Romans tend to cycle, if at all, on weekends away in Tuscany with their mountain bikes. However, on car-free Sundays you will see them darting along the Via dei Fori Imperiali. Riding in one of the parks is a pleasant alternative to the city streets.

The transport company have launched a public bike scheme called BikeSharing, allowing you to borrow the city's bikes from various stands across the city. The procedure, however, is quite complicated and is mainly designed for locals: you must first enrol at one of 10 authorised ticket offices, located inside the main Metro stations (check www.bike-sharing.roma.it for details), and pay €10 to charge an electronic "smartcard" that gives you access to the bikes. Using the bikes costs €0.50 every 30 minutes.

Sundays are a good time to cycle along the Appian Way as traffic is restricted. You can rent a bike from the visitors' centre (see page 247).

Bicycle and moped rental companies in the city include:

Bici & Baci
5 Via del Viminale
Tel: 06-482 8443 (mopeds also)
www.bicibaci.com

Collalti
82 Via del Pellegrino
Tel: 06-6880 1084
www.collaltibici.com

Touring Rome by moped or Vespa is not advisable for beginners or the nervous. You will need to show your licence when hiring a moped, and leave a deposit. Motorcycle rental companies include:

Scooters for Rent
84 Via della Purificazione
Tel: 06-488 5485
www.rentscooter.it

On Foot

In much of the city centre the best way to get around is on foot. Most of the main sights are within easy walking distance of each other, although there are

Pleasure boat on the Tiber.

some for which you may want to use public transport.

Some parts of the centre are for pedestrians only, such as the second half of Via del Corso, roughly from the Piazza San Silvestro to Piazza del Popolo and Piazza Navona. This pedestrianised area includes the section that goes from Largo Argentina past the Pantheon to the Parliament.

Moped riders in particular, but also some car drivers, often decide that they are exempt

from this rule and drive along pedestrian zones.

Cross the road with confidence, staring down nearby drivers. If you wait timidly at a pedestrian crossing for the traffic to stop, you will spend the whole day there.

Most of the centre of Rome is reasonably safe, even at night, though the areas around Stazione Termini can be deserted and, despite recent improvements, are still rather seedy and should be avoided.

CAR HIRE

Prices per day at all the major international firms start at approximately €60 for the smallest cars. Expect to pay a generous surcharge if you want unlimited mileage, and check exactly what is included in the insurance you are offered. All the major firms have offices at the airports and railway station; they all have online booking services with sections where you can work out how much the rental will cost. Avis, Europcar and Hertz probably provide the best cover, but Italy Rent, which also has an office at the airport, offers

very good deals. The main rental companies are:

Avis
Tel: 06-481 4373
www.avisautonoleggio.it
Europcar
Tel: 06-488 2854
www.europcar.it
Hertz
Tel: 06-474 0389
www.hertz.it
Italy Rent
Freephone: 800-930 032
www.italyrent.it
Maggiore
Tel: 06-488 0049
www.maggiore.it

Several airlines also have an online car-hire booking service, though this is usually more expensive:

easyJet
Tel: +44-(0)871-384 9829; lines open 24 hours a day and 365 days a year for bookings.
www.europcar4easyjet.com
KLM Royal Dutch Airlines
Internet bookings only: www.klm.com
Opodo (a company jointly owned by a number of European airlines)
Tel: +44-0871-277 0090
www.opodo.com

ACTIVITIES

THE ARTS, NIGHTLIFE, ANNUAL EVENTS, SPORT AND FESTIVALS

THE ARTS

Theatre

As plays are nearly always performed in Italian, an evening at the theatre is only recommended for fluent Italian-speakers. A notable exception is theatrical events related to the Romaeuropa Festival (see Festivals, page 296) or some of the original-language performances put on at the ever-reliable **Teatro Argentina** (52 Largo Argentina; tel: 06-684 0003 11/14; www.teatrodiroma.net). However, in some cases it is worth attending a classical drama or play in translation, if the venue itself

The Teatro Argentina.

provides the drama – particularly summer events held outdoors, whether in amphitheatres, such as the one at **Ostia Antica** (Scavi di Ostia Antica, 717 Viale dei Romagnoli; tel: 380 584 4086), or at other classical sites. Roman theatre embraces mainstream and contemporary, but the emphasis is on the tried and trusted Italian dramatists (such as Carlo Goldoni and Luigi Pirandello), musicals, or lighter, frothier stuff, often translated. However, the university theatres and smaller venues do stage experimental or fringe productions (known as "Teatro off"). One of the most interesting of these is the revamped **Teatro Palladium** (8 Piazza Bartolomeo Romano; tel: 06-5733 2768; www.teatro-palladium.it), which is attached to the University Roma 3 and puts on an interesting range of readings, films, dance and theatre events. The theatre season runs from October to early June, but there are numerous summer events linked to specific Roman festivals. Rome also has a last-minute theatre box office where unsold tickets can be bought on the day for up to 50 percent off. The counter is located at 20 Via Bari (Piazza Salerno; tel: 06-4411 7799; Tue–Sat 1–7pm, Sun 10am–1pm,

closed July and August; Policlinico metro stop line B).

The English Theatre of Rome (tel: 06-687 9419; www.rometheatre.com) has an interesting and varied programme of small-scale productions, with five English-language productions per season, usually put on at the intimate Teatro L'Arciliuto in the Centro Storico.

Opera and Ballet

The opera and ballet season runs from October to June at the Teatro dell'Opera, 1 Piazza Beniamino Gigli; tel: 06-481 601; www.operaroma.it. The ticket office is open Mon–Sat 10am–6pm, Sun 9am–1.30pm, but tickets can also be bought on its website and picked up at the opera house on the night of the performance. Ticket prices run from reasonable to exorbitant. The outdoor summer opera series (same number as above) has been held in a variety of venues in past years, the current one being the Baths of Caracalla.

The best bet for international and contemporary dance is the **Teatro Olimpico** (17 Piazza Gentile da Fabriano; tel: 06-326 5991; www.teatroolimpico.it). Ticket office is open daily 10am–6pm (Mon–Fri in summer).

Classical Music

There is a wide range of venues for classical music. The season runs from October to June, but with special summer concerts there's something going on just about all year-round.

The renowned, high-profile Accademia di Santa Cecilia (www.santacecilia.it), and its symphonic and chamber orchestras, hosts all its principal concerts from October to May at the **Auditorium Parco della Musica** (30 Viale Pietro de Coubertin; tel: 06-8024 1281; www.auditorium.com). Designed by Genoese architect Renzo Piano, it features three concert halls with excellent acoustics. A 10-minute tram ride from Piazzale Flaminio (just above Piazza del Popolo), the complex also features a large inner courtyard, which is used for outdoor concerts and events, such as the ice rink around Christmas.

There are many other venues for classical music, including churches and outdoor venues all over Rome in summer, many

GETTING TICKETS

Venues have ticket offices, phone booking lines and online booking possibilities. Failing that, the best agencies for tickets to all kinds of events are:

Feltrinelli
11 Largo Torre Argentina
Tel: 199 151 173
www.lafeltrinelli.it
Viva Ticket
Freephone: 892 234
www.vivaticket.it (tickets can also be bought online and picked up at the venue beforehand)
Orbis Servizi
37 Piazza Esquilino (behind Santa Maria Maggiore)
Tel: 06-4827 403
Ricordi Mediastores
506 Via del Corso
Tel: 06-361 2370

of them part of the Estate Romana series of events. Some of the most atmospheric venues are the Terme di Caracalla, the Teatro di Marcello, the Fori Imperiali and the Terrazza del Pincio. Ask at a tourist information point for the monthly guide to cultural events, called *L'Evento*, or check the local press for more information on classical music events.

Museums and Galleries

The Roma Pass is an integrated ticket that costs €36, lasts three days and gives you free entrance to the first two museums or archaeological sites you visit (most major sites are included in the scheme; call 06-0608 or see www.romapass.it for details). The card also entitles you to reduced admission on any further sites you visit. Full access to the public transport system is included in the price. The pass is sold at all of the sites involved, at tourist information kiosks and at Fiumicino Airport's tourist information office in Terminal C.

A €6,5 Biglietto 4 Musei (four museums combined ticket), valid for three days, is available and covers Palazzo Altemps, Palazzo Massimo, Terme di Diocleziano, and Cripta Balbi. A €27,5 ticket (Roma Archeologia Card), valid for seven days, covers the sites of the Museo Nazionale Romano and the Colosseum, the Palatine, the Roman Forum, the Baths of Caracalla, the Tomb of Cecilia Metella and the Villa of the Quintili. They can be bought from any participating site.

Museums are usually closed on Monday, though there are some exceptions. Important art exhibitions are usually open daily.

Music Venues

Alexanderplatz
9 Via Ostia (Prati)
Tel: 06-3972 1867

Sculpture of Constantine's hand at the Museo Capitolino.

http://alexanderplatzjazzclub.com. When the big names come to town, they often come to this jazz club and restaurant, which runs the summer jazz series at the Villa Celimontana.
Beba do Samba
8 Via dei Messapi (San Lorenzo)
Tel: 328-575 0390
www.bebadosamba.it
Located in the student district of San Lorenzo, this is a buzzy venue with live music (generally jazz or world) most nights.
Big Mama
18 Via San Francesco a Ripa (Trastevere)
Tel: 06-581 2551
www.bigmama.it
The blues club in Rome, but also hosts jazz and rock musicians.
Brancaleone
11 Via Levanna (Nomentana)
Tel: 339-507 4012
www.brancaleone.it
One of the liveliest of Rome's *centri sociali*, attracting high-quality DJs and live acts.
Casa del Jazz
55 Viale di Porta Ardeatina (Aventine)
Tel: 06-704 731
www.casajazz.it
A classy villa and park hosting high-level jazz concerts nightly.
Contestaccio
65b Via di Monte Testaccio
Tel: 06-5728 9712

Rome's marathon begins and ends in Via dei Fori Imperiali.

www.contestaccio.com
Well-known bands as well as emerging talents perform here every night.

Cinema

Virtually all films on general release are dubbed into Italian. For English-speaking cinema, try the following (films are marked VO – *versione originale*):
Alcazar, 14 Via Cardinale Merry del Val; tel: 06-588 0099. The current film playing is shown in its original version on Monday.
Nuovo Olimpia, 16g Via in Lucina; Tel: 06-686 1068. Art-house movies are occasionally shown, as well as original-language films.

FESTIVALS

Over the past few years the number of cultural events and festivals in Rome has almost tripled, and many new buildings and museums have helped this process. The two most established festivals, which nevertheless grow every year, are the Romaeuropa Festival and the Estate Romana.

The **Romaeuropa Festival** (www.romaeuropa.net) is a cutting-edge event that takes place every year from mid-September to at least mid-November and

covers dance (usually modern), theatre, readings, cinema and music. Every year the festival has a different theme and the performers are a highly interesting mix of well-established international performers and emerging or avant-garde troupes.

The **Estate Romana** (literally, Roman Summer; www.estateromana.comune.roma.it) is the umbrella name for the huge programme of events sponsored by the local council. Running from June to September, it sees some of the city's most attractive parks and piazzas become venues for rock, ethnic and jazz concerts, theatre performances (in Villa Ada, Villa Celimontana, at the Fori Imperiali and in Piazza del Popolo, to cite but a few), outdoor cinema (for example, in Piazza Vittorio Emanuele II), dance lessons and other cultural events such as readings, book fairs and gastronomic evenings. Check the website or the local press and ask at the tourist information points for details.

Rome's **International Photography Festival** (www.fotografiafestival.it) puts on a wide range of photographic shows in the most diverse settings.

The **Rome Film Fest** (www.romacinemafest.it) is the city's official movie event. It takes place every October at the Audi-

torium with world premieres and celebrity guests.

ANNUAL EVENTS

Many festivals are linked to the Catholic Church. The tourist office (see page 308) can provide more details. Be aware that Romans throw firecrackers in the street on New Year's Eve.

January

1 January: **Tuffo nel Tevere**, *a long-standing popular tradition which sees daredevils take a 17-metre (56ft) plunge off Ponte Cavour bridge into the icy Tiber waters.*
6 January: culmination of Christmas fair in Piazza Navona (*see December*). Celebrating **Epiphany** (**Befana**), the traditional festival when good children receive presents and naughty children are given coal-shaped sweets.

February

February/March: **Carnevale**. Roman children put on fancy dress and take to the streets, and clubs organise themed fancy-dress events.

March

9 March: **Festa di Santa Francesca Romana**. Cars and mopeds are driven to the church of Santa Francesca Romana in the Foro Romano to be blessed by the patron saint of motorists.
La Festa della Primavera. The arrival of spring is marked by the decoration of the Spanish Steps with a sea of azaleas.
Maratona di Roma. City marathon; takes place end of March/beginning of April. www.maratonadiroma.it.
Late March/early April: **Giornate FAI**. The Fondo Ambiente Italiano (Environmental Fund of Italy; www.fondoambiente.it) organises a weekend when usu-

ally closed churches, monuments and gardens can be visited.

March/April: Easter week is huge, from the big Mass on Palm Sunday and the distribution of palm fronds to the mass pilgrimages for **Holy Week** (**Settimana Santa**) and concerts all over the city. The Pope leads an outdoor **Mass at the Colosseum on Good Friday**, followed by a procession passing the Stations of the Cross. The week culminates on Easter morning with the Pope's Urbi et Orbi speech. Call the Vatican tourist office for more info. (see page 308).

April

21 April: **Il Natale di Roma**. Rome celebrates its legendary founding with fireworks, music and other events. Festivities are centred around the Campidoglio.

25 April: **La Festa della Liberazione**. Public holiday commemorating liberation of Italy by Allied forces at the end of World War II.

Late April or May: **Settimana della Cultura**. Cultural Week throughout Italy, when entrance is free to all state-run museums

and historical sites, as well as many exhibitions, see www.beniculturali.it.

May

May Day is widely celebrated in Rome. A huge free concert is held in front of San Giovanni in Laterano.

Sporting Events. The Italian Open Tennis Championship is usually held in the first half of May, and the International Horse Show is at the end of the month in the Villa Borghese.

June

2 June: **Republic Day**. The Armed Forces parade on Via dei Fori Imperiali before the President and the state's most important personalities.

29 June: **San Pietro e San Paolo**. The founders of the Catholic Church are honoured with a public holiday. Special Masses are held in their basilicas.

Estate Romana begins in June (see Festivals, page 296).

July

Summer Opera. Opera and ballet in the open air at the Baths of Caracalla (continues in August).

Festa de' Noantri. A street festival in Trastevere that runs for two weeks from mid-July.

August

5 August: **La Festa della Madonna della Neve**. White rose petals fall onto the congregation of Santa Maria Maggiore to commemorate the miraculous summer snowfall on this day in the year AD 352.

October

Symphonic music season begins at the Auditorium, www.auditorium.com.

November

2 November: **Giornata dei Defunti**, or Day of the Dead, when the Pope celebrates Mass at the Verano cemetery.

December

8 December: **Immacolata Concezione**. The Immaculate Conception of the Virgin is celebrated around the statue of the Madonna in Piazza di Spagna.

Mercatino di Natale a Piazza Navona. Christmas arts and crafts fair with stalls selling food. Opens the second week of December, lasts until January.

Christmas. Major shopping streets are beautifully decorated and *presepi* (nativity scenes) are set up in churches around the city.

31 December: **San Silvestro**. Fireworks and free rock and pop concerts in Piazza del Popolo and other squares.

NIGHTLIFE

Roman nightlife tends to be fun rather than frenzied. The nightclub scene in Rome is far less adventurous than in Berlin, London or New York, apart from a few privileged or exclusive

DJs often play bars and restaurants as well as clubs.

TRANSPORT

ACTIVITIES

A – Z

LANGUAGE

clubs. In common with other capital cities, door policy determines whether you even get to cross the threshold of a club. As a general rule, it is safer to dress up rather than down.

You may be required to obtain temporary membership (a *tessera*, or membership card, should be available at the door). Entry price may include a free drink, but drinks are normally quite expensive. Groups of young men together are usually not welcome and, in some clubs, a man may be turned away unless accompanied by a woman.

Trastevere is still a reliable destination for Romans in search of a good time, while the slightly more alternative Testaccio is clubland central. A burgeoning gay, alternative and commercial scene is happening even further south in the industrial Ostiense quarter.

The historic quarters around Piazza Navona (around Via di Tor Millina), the Pantheon and Campo de' Fiori contain popular bars and clubs. The Via Veneto, scene of Fellini's *Dolce Vita*, is still home to certain elegant nightclubs and piano bars, which tend to be patronised by middle-aged, moneyed Americans and Russians.

Roma fans.

Most nightclubs don't get going until midnight; most close Monday night, some on Sunday too. Several of the better ones are around Via di Monte Testaccio. There's been an upsurge in so-called *discobar* and *ristodisco*, which as their names suggest mean bars and restaurants where there are also DJ sets and you can dance until late.

In summer, much young nightlife moves to the beach resorts south of the city. However, the glut of summer city festivals ensures that Rome remains lively.

Nightclubs

Akab
69 Via di Monte Testaccio Commercio (Testaccio)
Tel: 06-5725 0585
www.akabclub.com
A former carpenter's shop that hosts international DJs. One of Testaccio's best long-term fixtures.

Art Cafe
33 Viale del Galoppatoio (Villa Borghese)
Tel: 06-322 0994
www.art-cafe.it
This slick, trendy club, which plays mainly commercial dance, attracts a well-heeled, party-lov-

WHAT'S ON WHERE

English-language visitor magazine WHERE Rome, which can be picked up for free at the reception of all four- and five-star hotels, lists events and exhibits, and contains a number of month-specific recommendations. The Thursday edition of the national daily *La Repubblica* carries a supplement called *TrovaRoma* that contains full listings for the upcoming week, and the fortnightly English magazine *Wanted in Rome* (available at news-stands or online at www.wantedinrome.com) also has a listings section. The tourist information booths (see page 308) provide a multitude of leaflets, including the monthly guide *L'Evento* and a booklet called *Tourist's Passepartout*. Online, www.trovacinema.it lists all the films currently playing.

ing crowd whose aim is to see and be seen.

La Cabala
25 Via dei Soldati
Tel: 06-6830 1192
www.hdo.it
Paparazzi and cameras are not allowed in, and that's why celebrities love this place so much. Wear your most fashionable clothes.

Caruso Café de Oriente
36 Via di Monte Testaccio (Testaccio)
Tel: 06-574 5019
www.carusocafe.com
Latin American music is the order of the day at this cosy club, which bursts with enthusiastic salsa-dancing couples most nights. There's a pleasant roof terrace for a breath of fresh air in the summer months.

Goa
13 Via Libetta (Ostiense)
Tel: 06-574 8277
www.goaclub.com
One of the city's most popular clubs. Music ranges from house to electronica.

TRANSPORT

Fluid

46/47 Via del Governo Vecchio (Parione)
Tel: 06-683 2361
www.fluideventi.com
A popular, and often packed, wine and cocktail bar with stylish decor and hip music. Live DJ sets every night.

Micca Club

Nur Club, 19 Via del Teatro Valle (Parione)
Tel: 393-323 6244
www.miccaclub.com
The ex-oil cellar is now an alternative (and always crowded) cabaret and dance club where DJs spin tunes from the 1950s and '60s. Weekly burlesque shows.

Qube

212 Via di Portonaccio (Tiburtina)
Tel: 06-438 5445
www.qubedisco.com
Rock, eighties, swing and pop parties, plus the famous 'Muccassassina' gay night on Fridays.

Room 26

31 Piazzale Guglielmo Marconi
Tel: 339-611 9070
www.room26.it
Over 25s love this trendy EUR club where the DJs spin house and electronic music until the wee hours.

SPORT

Spectator Sports

You can find information on sporting events in two national papers devoted solely to sport: *Corriere dello Sport* and *Gazzetta dello Sport* – easy enough to understand even if you speak no Italian.

Football

Sporting life in Rome revolves around football *(calcio)*. Rome's Olympic Stadium is home to both the local clubs, SS Lazio and AS Roma, who play there from September to May. For fixtures, ticket information and official team paraphernalia, go to the Lazio Point, 34 Via Farini (near Termini) or the AS Roma Store, 360 Piazza Colonna.

Major Events

The three major sporting events that take place in Rome during the year and attract international stars and audiences are:

Concorso Ippico Internazionale (International Horse Show) at Piazza Siena in the gardens of the Villa Borghese in May (ask at a tourist information point or visit www.romatoday.it).

The **Italian Tennis Open** (www.internazionalibnlditalia.it), held at the Foro Italico, takes place in late April/early May.

Some of the matches of the **Six Nations Rugby** competition (www.rbs6nations.com) take place in Rome's Stadio Olimpico every February/March.

Participant Sports

Gyms

The sport Romans are most interested in is weight training at a local palestra (gym). **Farnese Fitness** (35 Vicolo delle Grotte; tel: 06-687 6931; www.farnese-fitness.com), near Campo de' Fiori, offers a decent range of classes in a 16th-century building.

Every summer, the Estate Romana festival organizes a giant outdoor gym space. Check www.estateromana.comune.roma. it for this year's location.

Swimming

For a hot city, Rome is decidedly under-provided with swimming pools, and most that do exist are privately run. The few city council pools are booked up with slot systems that are incomprehensible and inaccessible even for many Romans. Some luxury hotels (especially those outside the historic centre) offer access to their pools. If you choose this option be prepared tó pay for it.

Piscina Belle Arti (Flaminia), (158 Via Flaminia; tel: 06 324 1710; www.nuotobellearti.it) is a short tram ride (no. 2) from Plaza di Popolo. This is a

At the Villa Borghese zoo.

ACTIVITIES

pleasant and relatively uncrowded open-air pool open from end May until Sept. It is also one of the cheapest. **Hotel Parco dei Principi** (5 Via G. Frescobaldi; tel: 06-854 421; www.parcodeiprincipi.com), on the edge of the Villa Borghese, is a tranquil oasis (see page 185).

Radisson Blu es. Hotel, 171 Via Filippo Turati; tel: 06-444 841; www.radissonblu.com/eshotel-rome. A truly stunning rooftop pool with a unique view of Termini's train tracks and the city below.

Piscina delle Rose (20 Viale America; tel: 06-5422 1872; www.piscinadellerose.it). Take the metro (line B) to EUR Palasport. An Olympic-sized outdoor pool with rose gardens nearby. Open May to September only.

Hydromania (20 Vicolo del Casale Lumbroso; tel: 06-6618 3183; www.hydromania.it). The only water park near the capital, with wading pools, slides and water rides. Take the metro (line A) to Cornelia and then the 906 bus.

Other possibilities for swimming are the beaches (try Sperlonga or Santa Marinella beaches on Ostia Lido) and the lakes. The lakes are more pleasant than the beaches closest to Rome. Swimming is possible in

A – Z

LANGUAGE

Lago di Bracciano, Lago Martignano and in some of the lakes of the Castelli Romani.

Tennis

Most tennis courts belong to private clubs and are open to members and their guests only. Check with your hotel or tourist office for clubs that allow non-members to play.

CHILDREN'S ACTIVITIES

Explora – Il Museo dei Bambini (82 Via Flaminia; tel: 06-361 3776; www.mdbr.it; Tue–Sun 10am–6.45pm; visits by prior booking only on weekends, four slots daily) is Rome's only children's museum. With four sections dedicated to humans, the environment, communications and society, there are plenty of signs and material in English. Kids can star in their own TV show and have fun with the interactive displays. There's also a restaurant.

Time Elevator (20 Via SS Apostoli; tel: 06-6992 1823; www.time-elevator.it; daily screenings 10am–7.30pm) is touted as a multimedia experience that illustrates the history of Rome. You sit on a moving platform, wearing headphones, for a cinematic roller-coaster

ride through history with various protagonists (such as Nero and Michelangelo) playing major parts, and a narrator to help with the chronology. Quite cheesy, but a fun introduction to the Eternal City. Memorable moments include watching Rome burn.

The **Museo Criminologico** (29 Via del Gonfalone; tel: 06-6889 9441/2; www.museocriminologico.it; Tue–Sat 9am–1pm, also Tue and Thu 2.30– 6.30pm) may appeal to older children and teenagers. The Criminological Museum covers the history of the prison system in Italy, how criminal cases were solved and how criminals were punished over the centuries, but the part (older) children will enjoy best is the section with torture instruments and paintings depicting various and gruesome forms of punishment.

Capuchin Crypt (27 Via Veneto; tel: 06-8880 3695; www.cappucciniviaveneto.it; daily 9am–7pm). Children are always impressed and amused by this chapel, festively decorated with artfully arranged bones and skulls of dead Capuchin monks and their family members. Not recommended for young children or the overly timorous.

Casina di Raffaello (Piazza di Siena; tel 06 0608; www.casi-

nadiraffaello.it; Tue–Fri 9am–6pm, Sat–Sun 9am–7pm). A playhouse, kids' library and museum in the heart of Villa Borghese.

SIGHTSEEING TOURS

Walking and sightseeing tours are organised by a number of travel agencies and tour guides, both licensed and unlicensed. The quality of what's on offer varies wildly. Recommended is: **Enjoy Rome** (8a Via Marghera; tel: 06-445 1843; www.enjoyrome.com), a friendly English-speaking office near the station that organises walking tours. They range from the Vatican to the Jewish Ghetto and Trastevere, and also offer night tours. Day trips to the ruins of Pompeii are organised in the summer months, and they also offer a free accommodation booking service.

Context Rome (tel: 06-9672 7371; www.contextrome.com) is a network of architects, historians and art historians who lead walking seminars for discerning travellers in order to share their love of the city, its history and culture. Taking one of these tours (which should be booked in advance) is a great way of making contact with people who really know the city inside out.

Vatican sightseers.

TRANSPORT

A – Z

AN ALPHABETICAL SUMMARY OF PRACTICAL INFORMATION

ACTIVITIES

A

Accommodation

Traditionally Rome has always been an expensive city to stay in, with price often a poor reflection of quality. In recent years the accommodation options have begun to broaden, so that, while most hotels are still expensive, you can now choose to avoid the peeling pensione of old. Conventional facades now hide avant-garde interiors, while at the grander end of the scale, gracious, timeless hotels retain their cachet. But for those not on an imperial budget, there are plenty of welcoming guesthouses and family-run hotels, while self-catering apartments and bed and breakfasts are increasingly popular options.

In terms of location, the area around Piazza Navona, the Pantheon and Campo de' Fiori offers perhaps the best introduction to the city, since you are right in its medieval heart and within easy reach of most main sights. However, there are relatively few hotels in the area, and these tend to be booked up early, so try to plan ahead if possible.

The APT office publishes an annual list (Annuario Alberghi) showing star categories, facilities and prices of all Rome hotels. This may be obtained from the APT or through Italian national tourist offices; tel: 06-0608.

Admission Charges

Museum admission fees vary, but the major ones start at about €7 while the minor ones cost about €4. Most state or municipal museums offer free entrance to EU citizens under 18 or over 65. The entrance ticket to the Palatine (€12) can be used to visit the Colosseum and the Roman Forum. Entrance to the Pantheon and all basilicas and churches is free, as are the Vatican Museums on the last Sunday of the month (expect long queues).

B

Budgeting for Your Trip

Expect to pay at least €150 a night for a double room if you want to stay in the city centre somewhere decent. For a more elegant hotel the prices are well over €200 a night. The cost of eating out varies hugely; a three-course evening meal with wine costs about €40 a head, on average, at a decent restaurant in the Centro Storico, but it's also possible to pay as little as €15 if you're happy to settle for a no-frills meal (pizza being an ever-popular budget option). You will pay a little less at lunch time, or if you find a neighbourhood trattoria in the suburbs or something off the beaten track, but if you are in blatant tourist territory or in a modern minimalist restaurant with a "creative" menu, it is likely to be expensive. A birra media (medium beer) costs about €5 and a glass of wine starts at about €4.

One thing that remains very cheap is public transport. A single ticket costs €1.50 and can be used for 100 minutes, and a number of passes are available. There are one-day, three-day and seven-day passes, called Biglietto Integrato Giornaliero, Biglietto Turistico Integrato and Carta Integrata Settimanale respectively, which are good for unlimited metro, bus and local train or regional bus travel. They need to be validated only on first use. Month-long passes, Abbonamento Mensile, are also available. COTRAL, the regional bus company, offers a regional day-pass (BIRG), which covers your round trip and in-city travel. Taxis are also cheaper than in most other capital cities, with a trip from the station to the centre (Piazza Navona) costing

ACTIVITIES

A – Z

LANGUAGE

about €12–15 depending on the traffic; fares go up at night.

C

Children

Italians love *bambini*, and they will go out of their way to please them. Most restaurants will happily prepare half a portion of pasta with tomato sauce for their little guests. Children under six receive free entry in most museums, while at the zoo kids only pay if they are taller than 100cm.

Climate

Despite some very unusual weather in the past few years (exceptional winter snowfall, hail in July, heat waves in May), Rome can still be said to have a classic Mediterranean climate: mildish winters and very hot, long summers. July and August are the hottest and most humid months, when it is advisable to stay indoors or in the shade in the middle of the day.

When to Visit

April, May, September and October are the best months to visit as the weather is usually sunny and warm but devoid of that heavy, airless quality. In August many Romans go on holiday (especially around the Feast of the Assumption on 15 August), but for the past few years the city council has put on an incredible range of world-class outdoor concerts and other cultural events from June to September, and the city is less deserted than it used to be.

What to Wear

Light summer clothes are suitable from spring to autumn. The Roman heat is sometimes alleviated by a light breeze, which can produce cool evenings even in summer, so a cardigan or jacket is useful. Wear a hat in the summer if you burn easily. Sunglasses are essential.

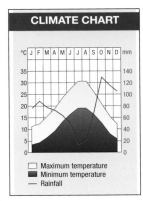

CLIMATE CHART

☐ Maximum temperature
■ Minimum temperature
— Rainfall

In summer, the likelihood of rain is slight: sometimes there is no rainfall in Rome for more than three months. If it does rain, it will probably be a downpour in a thunderstorm. There is little point in preparing for this: just run for cover. At other times of the year, some form of waterproofing is worth considering, but not worth a lot of weight in your luggage. The most likely times for rain are autumn and spring.

In winter, warmer clothes are needed, including a heavy overcoat, as it can be very cold. Indoors, you may find the heating levels are below your expectations. In response to the climate, Roman building design has always concentrated on keeping heat out, rather than creating cosy interiors.

If visiting churches, and particularly St Peter's, remember that bare arms or shorts (on men or women) and short skirts are not acceptable, and you will be refused admittance. If wearing a short-sleeved or sleeveless garment, carry a light shirt/blouse or scarf with you.

Romans, like most Italians, consider clothes important. Most will dress smartly for an evening out, a restaurant meal or a visit to the theatre. Rome is accustomed to casually dressed tourists, but you may wish to follow local habits.

Dress codes for clubs and bars vary enormously and change with the seasons and fashions. In general, however, dress is still likely to be slightly more formal than would be expected in much of Northern Europe or the US.

Crime and Safety

The main problem tourists experience in Rome is petty crime: pickpocketing and bag-snatching, together with theft from parked cars. Reduce the possibility of theft by taking elementary precautions. Leave money and valuables, including airline tickets, in the hotel safe. Carry your camera out of sight and always be discreet with your money or wallet.

If you are carrying a handbag, keep it on the side away from the road, and when sitting in a café, place it firmly on your lap – one Roman speciality is the motorbike snatch. Backpacks, while convenient, make easy targets, so take them off or sling them under your arm in crowds. Always keep a separate record of credit card and cheque numbers just in case. A photocopy of your passport is also a useful precaution.

On the streets and especially near the main tourist attractions, keep an eye on beggars, particularly the small children who crowd around you with boxes in their hands. Take extra care on crowded buses and the metro, and on bus routes frequented by tourists, such as the No. 40 Express and the No. 64.

Put a car with a foreign number plate in a garage overnight. Take your radio out, even if your insurance company will replace it, because fixing a broken windscreen means wasted time and trouble. Don't leave any items visible in the car.

If you are unlucky enough to have something stolen, report the theft *(furto)* to the police as soon as possible: you will need the police report for any insurance claim and to replace stolen documents. For information on the nearest police station call the central station, the Questura Centrale, 15 Via San Vitale; tel: 06-46861. Report the loss of travellers' cheques or credit cards to your credit card company, and of passports to your consulate or embassy.

Customs Regulations

Visitors from EU countries are not obliged to declare goods imported into or exported from Italy if they are for personal use, up to the following limits: 800 cigarettes, 200 cigars or 1 kg of tobacco; 10 litres of spirits (over 22 percent alcohol) or 90 litres of fortified wine (under 22 percent alcohol).

For US citizens, the duty-free allowance is 200 cigarettes or 50 cigars; 1 litre of spirits or 4 litres of wine; one 50ml bottle of perfume and duty-free gifts to the value of €430.

D

Disabled Travellers

Rome is a difficult city for people with disabilities, although facilities have improved in recent years. Most churches, museums and archaeological sites have steps; streets and pavements are often uneven or cobbled, and pavements in the medieval centre are frequently too narrow for a wheelchair or have cars parked on the access ramps. However, the following attractions have installed ramps and lifts: the Vatican Museums,

DISABILITY SERVICE

The public transportation company in Rome, ATAC, offers comprehensive information on transport services for people with disabilities. For information call toll-free: 800 154 451 or visit www.atac.roma.it.

The local polizia.

Galleria Doria Pamphilj, Castel Sant'Angelo, Palazzo Venezia, Palazzo delle Esposizioni, St Peter's, Galleria Borghese, Galleria Nazionale d'Arte Moderna, Vittoriano and the Bioparco (zoo). Ask at the tourist information points for other sites with facilities for disabled people.

Some trains have access for the disabled, but you will need to call the railway at least 24 hours before travelling as assistance staff and equipment need to be booked in advance. Train timetables have a wheelchair symbol next to accessible trains. Seats at the front of city buses are reserved for the disabled, and many have designated wheelchair areas in the centre. The newest trams and buses all have large central doors and access ramps. On the metro, most of the central stations on line A are now accessible, while all stations on line B have lifts, disabled toilets and designated parking spaces, except for Circo Massimo, Colosseo and Cavour, which are equipped with stairlifts. Follow the wheelchair symbol on the metro website (www. atac.roma.it) for information on wheelchair-accessible stations.

Restaurants are usually helpful, but call in advance to ask about access. A number of hotels claim to offer access to travellers with disabilities, but check with the individual hotel – be as precise as possible about your needs.

For more details, contact Roma Per Tutti (tel: 06-5717

7094; www.romapertutti.it), an English-speaking information line.

E

Electricity

Standard is 220 volts AC, 50 cycles. Sockets have either two or three round pins. For UK visitors, adaptors can be bought before you leave home, or at airports and main railway stations. Travellers from the US will need a transformer, though most laptops, phones and camcorders have it built in.

Embassies and Consulates

Consulates generally have answering machines on which you can leave a message in the event of a query or problem. If your passport is lost or stolen you will need to obtain a police report and give proof of your identity and suitable photos in order to get a new one.

Australia
5 Via Antonio Bosio
Tel: 06-852 721
www.italy.embassy.gov.au
Great Britain
80a Via XX Settembre
Tel: 06-4220 0001
Canada
30 Via Zara
Tel: 06-854 443 937
www.canada.it
Ireland
Via Giacomo Medici 1
Tel: 06-585 2381
www.ambasciata-irlanda.it
New Zealand
44 Via Clitunno
Tel: 06-853 7501
www.nzembassy.com/italy
South Africa
14 Via Tanaro
Tel: 06-852 541
www.sudafrica.it
United States of America
121 Via Veneto
Tel: 06-46741
http://italy.usembassy.gov

Etiquette

If you are invited for lunch or dinner in somebody's home, do not show up empty-handed. Bring a bottle of wine, flowers, pastries, or gelato. Food, travel, wine and football are good topics of discussion. When queuing, don't be too surprised if someone behind you is served before you: the queue concept is a bit blurry in Rome.

G

Gay and Lesbian Travellers

Rome has an active and vibrant gay community. For information on cultural events and news, contact:

Arci Gay/Arci Lesbica Roma: 14 Via Zabaglia; tel: 06-645 01102; www.arcigay.it. A group that runs a helpline and organises social get-togethers for the gay and lesbian communities.

Circolo di Cultura Mario Mieli, 2a Via Efeso; tel: 06-541 3985; www.mariomieli.org.

Alibi, 40–44 Via di Monte Testaccio; tel: 06-574 3448; www.lalibi.it. A predominantly gay disco.

Coming Out, 8 Via San Giovanni in Laterano (near the Colosseum); tel: 06-700 9871; www.

In Coming Out, near the Colosseum.

comingout.it. A mainstay of the Roman gay scene – it is often as crowded on the pavement outside as within.

Luna e L'altra, 1a Via San Francesco di Sales (in Trastevere); tel: 06-6889 2465; www.casainternazionaledelledonne.org; closed Sunday. A women-only evening restaurant run by the International House of Women.

H

Health and Medical Care

EU residents are entitled to the same medical treatment as an Italian citizen. Visitors will need to complete an EHIC form (see www.ehic.org.uk for information) before they go. This covers medical treatment and medicines, although it is still necessary to pay prescription charges and a percentage of the costs for medicines. Note that the EHIC does not give any cover for trip cancellations, nor does it provide repatriation in case of illness. For this, you will need to take out private insurance. US citizens are advised to take out private health insurance. Canadian citizens are also covered by a reciprocal arrangement between the Italian and Canadian governments.

EMERGENCIES

Carabinieri **112**
Police **113**
Fire **115**
Ambulance **118**

If you are covered by a reciprocal scheme and need to visit a doctor while in Italy, take the EHIC card (if an EU resident) or proof of citizenship and residence (eg passport) to the local health office (Unità Sanitaria Locale), which will direct you to a doctor covered by the state system and supply the necessary paperwork. Not all doctors work in the state scheme, and those who do are often busy, so be prepared to wait. A consultation with a private doctor may be quicker (and certainly requires less preparatory paperwork) but costs more, so private insurance is a good idea.

If you need emergency treatment, call 118 for an ambulance or to get information on the nearest hospital with an emergency department (*pronto soccorso*). The most central is Ospedale Fatebenefratelli (Isola Tiberina; tel: 06-68371; www.fatebenefratelli-isolatiberina.it). If your child is sick go to the Ospedale Pediatrico Bambino Gesù (4 Piazza Sant'Onofrio; tel: 06-68591; www.ospedalebambinogesu.it), on the Gianicolo hill.

Medical Services

The International Medical Center (tel: 06-488 2371; www.imc84.com) is a private referral service with English-speaking doctors who are on call for house visits 24 hours a day. The Rome American Hospital (69 Via Emilio Longoni; tel: 06-225 51; www.hcir.it), 30–40 minutes' journey out of the town centre by taxi, has English-speaking doctors and dentists. The George Eastman Hospital (287 Viale Regina Elena; tel: 06-7730 3232/3247) is Rome's only 24-hour dental hospital.

Chemists

Chemists *(farmacia)* can easily be identified by a green cross. Opening hours are usually Mon–Sat 8.30am–1pm and 4–8pm. A rotating system ensures there is always a chemist within walking distance that is open at night; a list outside every chemist indicates which it will be. Purchases at night may carry a surcharge.

Some chemists are also open 24 hours a day. A couple of the most central are Farmacia della Stazione (51 Piazza dei Cinquecento, corner of Via Cavour; tel: 06-488 0019), and Farmacia Piram Omeopatia (228 Via Nazionale; tel: 06-488 0754).

Catching up with the news in the Campo de'Fiori.

Internet

Many of the city's green spaces and piazzas are now public wireless hotspots (see www.romawireless.com for further information), and many bars and cafés offer free connection. There is no shortage of internet cafés in the Corso Vittorio Emanuele area, around Termini station and in the Esquiline neighbourhood.

Left Luggage

The leftluggage office in Termini Station (www.romatermini.com) is below ground level (level −1) at the side of platform 24 (open daily 6am–11pm). Fiumicino Airport has 24-hour left-luggage facilities in the international terminals.

Lost Property

For property lost on public transport (except trains), contact the Comune di Roma's lost property office, tel: 06-6769 3214. For objects lost on Metro A, tel: 06-4695 7068 (Mon, Wed and Fri 9.30am–12.30pm) and for things forgotten on Metro B,

tel: 06-4695 8165/4 (daily 8am–1pm).

M

Maps

Free city maps are available from the main tourist information offices dotted around town (see page 308). Free and comprehensive bus maps of the city centre are available from ATAC at 59 Via Volturno (Mon–Fri 9am–1pm, Tue and Thu also 2.30–5pm). Detailed transport maps of the city and outskirts called Roma Metro-Bus can be bought at any news-stand.

Most news-stands sell city maps, as do museum shops. At the latter ask for the Mondadori maps, which are available in various languages and are very durable.

Media

Newspapers and Magazines

Most important European dailies are available on the day of publication from street kiosks, as is the *International Herald Tribune*. The main Rome-based Italian newspapers are *La Repubblica* and *Il Messaggero*. Other Italian newspapers such as *Il Corriere della*

Sera publish Rome editions with local news and entertainment listings. *La Stampa* offers serious economics coverage.

TrovaRoma, La Repubblica's Thursday supplement, lists concerts, exhibits and events, but only in Italian.

Where Rome is a comprehensive monthly guide in English to everything in the city, from museums and art exhibitions, to shopping, eating and live music. *Wanted in Rome*, a fortnightly magazine in English, is another good source of information. The website (www.wantedinrome.com) is updated regularly.

Porta Portese (www.portaportese. it) comes out on Tuesday and Friday with thousands of classified ads, including a large accommodation section.

The American Magazine (www.theamericanmag.com) is a monthly magazine on Italian cultural life, available from news-stands in the centre.

Television

Italy has two main TV broadcasting organisations – state-owned RAI television (14 channels) and commercial Mediaset (12 channels), which are both owned by the Berlusconi family. Less popular broadcasters include Cairo Communication (La7 channel), Discovery Italia and Sky Italia. Most hotels also offer guests

TRANSPORT

ACTIVITIES

A – Z

LANGUAGE

LOST CREDIT CARDS

American Express
Telephone: 06-7290 0347
Bank Americard
Freephone: 800-207 167
Diner's Club
Freephone: 800-393 939
Visa and Mastercard
Freephone: 800-819 014

CNN, BBC World, and some French or German channels.

Radio

The three state-owned channels, RAI 1 (89.7 MHz FM), RAI 2 (91.7 MHz FM) and RAI 3 (93.7 MHz FM), offer popular music, classical music, chat shows and news (RAI 3 is the most serious); see www.rai.it for a list of programmes. The most popular music channels are Radio Capital (95.8 MHz FM; www.capital.it) and Radio Deejay (101 MHz FM; www.deejay.it). Isoradio (103.3 MHz FM) is the best for traffic news, also in English.
Vatican Radio One-O-Five Live (105 MHz FM; www.radiovaticana.va) offers news commentary and spiritual programmes in English.

Money

The unit of currency in Italy is the euro (€), which is divided into 100 cents. There are €5, 10, 20, 50, 100, 200 and 500 notes, coins worth €1 and €2, and 1, 2, 5, 10, 20 and 50-cent coins.

Changing Money

You need your passport or identification card when changing money, which can be a slow operation. Not all banks will provide cash against a credit card, and some may refuse to cash travellers' cheques in certain currencies. On the whole, the larger banks will be the best for tourist transactions.
Travellers' cheques are the safest way to carry money, but not the most economical, since banks charge a commission for

cashing them, and shops and restaurants give unfavourable exchange rates if they accept them at all. Using bureau de change counters at airports and railway stations can be expensive, as most offer fixed rates and charge up to 20 percent commission.

Credit Cards

Major credit cards are accepted by most hotels, shops and restaurants in Rome but are less easy to use in the countryside. Very few petrol stations accept travellers' cheques.
Automated cash dispensers (ATMs), called Bancomat, can be found throughout central Rome, and are linked with several international banking systems, including Cirrus. The transaction fee will depend on your home bank, but rates are generally the best. The daily withdrawal limit is €250, €350 in some banks (Intesa San Paolo is one of them).

Tipping

Service is not included in a restaurant bill unless noted on the menu. It is customary to leave a modest amount as a tip, but nothing like the 10–15 percent common in other countries. Romans usually leave between €1–5, depending on how satisfied they were with the service; tourists are expected to be slightly more generous.
By law, the old cover charge, called pane e coperto (bread and table linen), has been abolished, but still appears on many menus. Keep an eye out: in many cases it has turned into a charge for bread, which you may refuse if you wish.
Just round up the fare to the nearest euro when you take a taxi.

O

Opening Hours

Opening hours vary greatly, but in general shops open Mon–Sat

9am–1pm, 3.30–7.30pm. Many close on Monday morning. Recently, in the touristy areas and in the centre, many shops have started opening on Sunday and through lunch. Hairdressers and barbers are open all day but closed on Monday. In general the small food shops are open 8am–1.30pm, 5.30–8pm, and closed Saturday afternoon in summer and Thursday afternoon the rest of the year. Many shops and restaurants close for two weeks in August.
Churches generally open 7am–7pm with a three-hour lunch break; the four main basilicas open 7am–7pm with no lunch time closure.
Banks open Mon–Fri 8.30am–1.30pm and roughly between 2.30 and 4pm in the afternoon; a few in the city centre also open Saturday morning. Most currency exchange bureaux open until 7.30pm Mon–Sat, and even later in very touristy areas.
State and city museums are closed on Monday, but there are a few exceptions: the Colosseum, the Roman Forum and the Imperial Fora, the Vatican Museums and the Galleria Doria Pamphilj.

P

Postal Services

Post offices are generally open Mon–Fri 8.30am–1pm; central post offices are normally open in the afternoon too.
Stamps (francobolli) for postcards and standard-weight letters to most destinations can be bought at many tobacconists (tabacchi) and bars that sell tobacco products. Often you can buy stamps when you buy your postcards. You will only need a post office for more complicated transactions, such as sending a parcel, express letter or fax, or collecting poste restante.
Italian postboxes are red or yellow, but several blue boxes

specifically for foreign letters have been set up in the centre. Postboxes have two slots, *per la città* (for Rome) and *tutte le altre destinazioni* (everywhere else). The Italian postal system has improved considerably in recent years and now runs a pretty efficient service. If posting valuables or important documents, send them registered *(raccomandata)*. If sending an urgent parcel ask for *posta celere*, a courier-style service that is slightly slower, but far cheaper, than those run by private companies.

The Vatican runs its own postal service. When visiting St Peter's, buy Vatican-issued stamps for your postcards and post them immediately: they are only valid in the Vatican City's blue or yellow postboxes.

The main post office is in Piazza San Silvestro, just off Via del Corso (Mon – Sat 8am – 7pm). The post office at Stazione Termini is also open Mon – Sat 8am – 7pm. For more information visit www.poste.it or tel: 803 160; Mon – Sat 8am – 8pm. There are many other post offices, so ask at your hotel or in a local bar for the nearest – *Dov'è l'ufficio postale più vicino?*

PUBLIC HOLIDAYS

Banks and most shops are closed on the following holidays, and banks may close early on the preceding day. Practically everything, including most monuments, is closed on New Year's Day.

New Year's Day *(Capodanno)*: 1 January
Epiphany *(Befana)*: 6 January
Pasqua *(Pasqua)*: variable, March – April
Easter Monday *(Pasquetta)*: variable, March – April
Liberation Day *(Anniversario della Liberazione)*: 25 April
May Day *(Festa del Lavoro)*: 1 May
Republic Day *(Giorno della Repubblica)*: 2 June
Patron Saints of Rome *(San Pietro e San Paolo)*: 29 June
August Holiday *(Ferragosto)*: 15 August
All Saints' Day *(Ognissanti)*: 1 November
Immaculate Conception *(Immacolata Concezione)*: 8 December
Christmas Day *(Natale)*: 25 December
Boxing Day *(Santo Stefano)*: 26 December

R

Religious Services

Anglican
All Saints' Anglican Church
153b Via del Babuino
Tel: 06-3600 1881
www.allsaintsrome.org
Sunday Eucharist: 8.30 and 10.30am
Catholic
Santa Susanna (American)
15 Via XX Settembre
Tel: 06-4201 4554
www.santasusanna.org
Sunday Masses: 9am and 10.30am
San Silvestro (British)
1 Piazza S. Silvestro
Tel: 06-679 7121
Sunday Masses: 10am, 6.30pm
St Patrick's (Irish)
60 Via Boncompagni
Tel: 06-420 31201
www.stpatricksrome.com
Sunday Mass: 10am
Episcopal
St Paul's within the Walls
58 Via Napoli
Tel: 06-481 4549
www.stpaulsrome.it
Sunday services: 10.30am
Islamic
Moschea di Roma
(Centro Islamico)
Viale della Moschea (Parioli)
Tel: 06-808 2258
Jewish
Tempio Maggiore
(Comunità Ebraica)
Lungotevere Cenci
Tel: 06-684 00661

www.romaebraica.it
Presbyterian
St Andrew's Church of Scotland
163 Via delle Fontane
Tel: 06-482 7627
www.presbyterianchurchrome.org
Sunday service 11am.

S

Student Travellers

The Centro Turistico Studentesco (CTS) is a chain of travel agents designed to meet the needs of young and student travellers. One of their main branches is at 14 Piazza dell' Alberone (tel: 06-785 7906) and its website (http://associazione.cts.it) lists the others. It can provide you with student discount cards, hostel membership and bookings, cheap flights and language courses.

T

Telephones

The mobile phone revolution has resulted in a considerable decrease in payphone demand, and the few phone booths left are bound to disappear soon. You'll have better chances of finding public telephones at the train station or at the airport. The newest phones take coins and even credit cards (although rates can be outrageously expensive), while the older ones only take telephone cards *(schede telefoniche)*, available in several denominations from news-stands and tabacchi.

Additionally, there are a number of far cheaper international phonecards available from many news-stands, as well as call centres where you can make your call and pay later, particularly in the area around Stazione Termini. Landlines in Rome have an 06 area code that you must use whether calling from within Rome, from out-

TRANSPORT

ACTIVITIES

LANGUAGE

side Rome or from abroad. Numbers in Rome have four to eight digits. Toll-free numbers start with 800.

Mobile phone numbers begin with 3, for example 338, 340, 333, 348, and cost a lot more to call than landlines. If you bring your mobile phone with you, remember that if you are calling a local number you will need to dial the international access code as well as the country code before putting in the area code and subscriber number.

For a number outside Italy, first dial 00 (the international access code), then the country code, the area code (omitting the initial 0, if applicable) and then the subscriber number.

For international directory enquiries, tel: 892 412; for operator-assisted national and international calls, tel: 170.

Time Zone

Italy follows Central European Time (GMT+1). From the last Sunday in March to the last Sunday in September, clocks are advanced one hour (GMT+2). The following times apply in summer, when it is noon in Rome:
New York **6am**
London **11am**
Johannesburg **noon**
Paris **noon**
San Francisco **3am**
Sydney **8pm**

Toilets

Bars are obliged by law to let you use their toilets. This doesn't mean that they will do so with good grace; if you don't consume something at the bar first they may throw you a look. However, if you ask politely you should not have any problems. In many cases bar toilets are locked and you will need to ask for the key (*chiave*) at the till; once inside you may find out that there is no soap or toilet paper. In the past few years public and modern toilets have

been opened near most of the major sights and monuments, for which you may have to pay a small fee.

Tourist Information

The Hotel Reservation Service, in Stazione Termini opposite platform 24 (tel: 06-699 1000; www.romatermini.com; daily 7am–10pm), makes commission-free reservations.

PIT (*punto informativo turistico* or tourist information points) are open daily from 9am–6pm at:
Piazza Pia (Castel Sant'Angelo)
Piazza delle Cinque Lune (Piazza Navona)
Via Nazionale (Palazzo delle Esposizioni)
Piazza Sonnino (Trastevere)
Via dell'Olmata (Santa Maria Maggiore)
Via Marco Minghetti (Fontana di Trevi).

There is also an information point in Stazione Termini, in front of platform 24, which is open daily 8am–8.30pm.

The **Vatican tourist office** (Ufficio Pellegrini e Turisti) is in Braccio Carlo Magno, Piazza San Pietro (to the left of the basilica); tel: 06-6988 2350 (Mon–Sat 8.30am–6.30pm).

Useful Addresses

Italian Government's Tourist Board (ENIT)
Canada: 110 Yonge Street, Suite 503, Toronto M5C 1T4; tel: 416-925 4882.
UK: 1 Princes Street, London W1B 8AY; tel: 020-7408 1254.
US: 3, 686 Park Avenue, New York, NY 10065; tel: 212-245 5618.
Travel Agents in Rome
American Express, 15 Via Alexandre Gustave Eiffel; tel: 06-722 821.
Airline Contacts
Air Canada, Fiumicino Airport; tel: 06-8351 4955.

Air France, Fiumicino Airport, Terminal 1; tel: 892 057.
Alitalia, Fiumicino Airport; tel: 06-2222.
British Airways, Fiumicino Airport; tel: 06-6501 1575; call centre tel: 02-6963 3602 (no office in the city).
Delta Airlines, 02-3859 1451 (no office in the city).

Visas and Passports

EU passport holders do not require a visa; a valid passport or ID card is sufficient. Visitors from the US, Canada, Australia or New Zealand do not require visas for stays of up to three months; non-EU citizens need a full passport.

Nationals of most other countries do need a visa. This must be obtained in advance from the Italian Consulate. For addresses of embassies and consulates in Rome, see page 303.

W

Websites

www.turismoroma.it and www.060608.it (official Rome tourism sites)
www.comune.roma.it (Rome city council)
http://w2.vatican.va (Vatican)
www.trenitalia.com (train information)
www.adr.it (airport information)
www.atac.roma.it (public transport)
http://trovacinema.repubblica.it (cinema programmes for all Italy)
www.2night.it (regularly updated, hip nightlife and entertainment guide)
www.reidsitaly.com (exhaustive blog about Italy).

Weights and Measures

Italy uses the metric system.

VIETATO
SALIRE SUI RUDERI
CLIMBING
FORBIDDEN ON RUINS

LANGUAGE

UNDERSTANDING THE LANGUAGE

BASIC RULES

Here are a few basic rules of grammar and pronunciation: *c* before *e* or *i* is pronounced "ch" as in *ciao*. *Ch* before *i* or *e* is pronounced as "k", eg *la chiesa*. Likewise, *sci* or *sce* are pronounced as in "sheep" or "shed" respectively. *Gn* in Italian is rather like the sound in "onion", while *gl* is softened to resemble the sound in "bullion".

Nouns are either masculine (*il*, plural *i*) or feminine (*la*, plural *le*). Plurals of nouns are most often formed by changing an o to an i and an a to an e, e.g. *il panino, i panini; la chiesa, le chiese*.

Words are stressed on the penultimate syllable unless an accent indicates otherwise.

Italian has formal and informal words for "You". In the singular, *Tu* is informal while *Lei* is more polite. It is best to use the formal form unless invited to do otherwise.

BASIC PHRASES

Yes *Si*
No *No*
Thank you *Grazie*
Many thanks *Mille grazie/tante grazie/molte grazie*
You're welcome *Prego*
All right/That's fine *Va bene*
Please *Per favore/per cortesia*

Excuse me (to get attention) *Scusi* (singular), *Scusate* (plural); **(to attract attention from a waiter)** *Senta!* **(in a crowd)** *Permesso;* **(sorry)** *Mi scusi*
Can I help you? (formal) *Posso aiutarla?*
Can you help me? (informal) *Può aiutarmi, per cortesia?*
Could you help me? (formal) *Potrebbe aiutarmi?*
Certainly *Ma, certo*
I need… *Ho bisogno di…*
I'm lost *Mi sono perso/a*
I'm sorry *Mi dispiace*
I don't know *Non lo so*
I don't understand *Non capisco*
Do you speak English/French? *Parla inglese/francese?*
Could you speak more slowly? *Può parlare più lentamente, per favore?*
Could you repeat that please? *Può ripetere, per piacere?*
here/there *qui/là*
yesterday/today/tomorrow *ieri/oggi/domani*
now/early/late *adesso/presto/tardi*
What? *Quale/Come…?*
When/Why/Where? *Quando/Perché/Dove?*
Where is the lavatory? *Dov'è il bagno?*

Greetings

Hello (good morning) *Buon giorno*
Goodbye *Arrivederci*

Good afternoon/evening *Buona sera*
Goodnight *Buona notte*
Hello/Hi/Goodbye (familiar) *Ciao*
Mr/Mrs/Miss *Signor/Signora/Signorina*
Pleased to meet you (formal) *Piacere di conoscerla*
I am English/American/Irish/Scottish/Canadian/Australian *Sono inglese/americano(a)/irlandese/ scozzese/canadese/australiano(a)*
I'm here on holiday *Sono qui in vacanza*
Is it your first trip to Rome? *É il suo primo viaggio a Roma?*
Do you like it here? (formal) *Si trova bene qui?*
How are you (formal/informal)? *Come sta (come stai)?*
Fine, thanks *Bene, grazie*
See you later *A più tardi*
See you soon *A presto*
Take care (formal/informal) *Stia bene/Sta bene*
Do you like Italy/Florence/Rome/Venice? *Le piace Italia/ Firenze/Roma/Venezia?*
I like it a lot *Mi piace moltissimo*

Telephone Calls

I'd like to make a reverse-charge (collect) call *Vorrei fare una telefonata a carico del destinatario*
the area code *il prefisso telefonico*
May I use your telephone? *Posso usare il telefono?*

TRANSPORT

ACTIVITIES

A – Z

LANGUAGE

Hello (on the telephone) *Pronto*
My name is *Mi chiamo/Sono*
Could I speak to...? *Posso parlare con...?*
Sorry, he/she isn't in *Mi dispiace, è fuori*
Can he call you back? *Può richiamare?*
I'll try later *Riproverò piu tardi*
Can I leave a message? *Posso lasciare un messaggio?*
Please tell him I called *Gli dica, per favore, che ho telefonato*
Hold on *Un attimo, per favore*
a local call *una telefonata urbana*
Can you speak up please? *Può parlare più forte, per favore?*
Mobile phone: *il cellulare*

IN THE HOTEL

Do you have any vacant rooms? *Avete delle camere libere?*
I have a reservation *Ho fatto una prenotazione*
I'd like... *Vorrei...*
a single/double room *una camera singola/doppia*
a room with twin beds *una camera a due letti*
a room with a bath/shower *una camera con bagno/doccia*
for one night *per una notte*
for two nights *per due notti*
How much is it? *Quanto costa?*
On the first floor *Al primo piano*
Is breakfast included? *É compresa la prima colazione?*
Is everything included? *É tutto compreso?*
half/full board *mezza pensione/pensione completa*
It's expensive *É caro*
Do you have a room with a balcony/view of the sea? *C'è una camera con balcone/con vista mare?*
a room overlooking the park/the street/the back *una camera con vista sul parco/che dá sulla strada/sul retro*
Is it a quiet room? *É una stanza tranquilla?*
The room is too hot/cold/noisy/small *La camera è troppo calda/fredda/rumorosa/piccola*
with a double bed *una doppia/matrimoniale*

Could you show me another room please? *Potrebbe mostrarmi un'altra camera, per favore?*
Can I see the room? *Posso vedere la camera?*
What time does the hotel close? *A che ora chiude l'albergo?*
I'll take it *La prendo*
big/small *grande/piccola*
What time is breakfast? *A che ora è la prima colazione?*
Please give me a call at... *Mi può chiamare alle...*
Come in! *Avanti!*
Can I have the bill, please? *Posso avere il conto, per favore?*
Can you call me a taxi, please? *Può chiamarmi un taxi, per favore?*
dining room *la sala da pranzo*
key *la chiave*
lift *l'ascensore*
towel *un asciugamano*
toilet paper *la carta igienica*

AT A BAR

I'd like... *Vorrei...*
coffee: (small, strong and black) *un caffè espresso;* **(with hot, frothy milk)** *un cappuccino;* **(weak, served in tall glass)** *un caffè lungo;* **(with alcohol, usually brandy)** *un caffè corretto*
some cold milk in my coffee *del latte freddo nel caffè*
tea *un tè*
lemon tea *un tè al limone*
herbal tea *una tisana*
hot chocolate *una cioccolata calda*
(bottled) orange/lemon juice *un succo d'arancia/di limone*
orange squash *aranciata*
freshly squeezed orange/lemon juice *una spremuta di arancia/di limone*
mineral water (fizzy/still) *acqua minerale gassata/naturale*
with/without ice *con/senza ghiaccio*
red/white wine *vino rosso/bianco*
(draught) beer *una birra (alla spina)*
a bitter (Vermouth, etc) *un amaro*
milk *latte*
(half) a litre *un (mezzo) litro*
bottle *una bottiglia*
ice cream *un gelato*
cone *un cono*

pastry/brioche *una pasta*
sandwich *un tramezzino*
roll *un panino*
Anything else? *Desidera qualcos'altro?*
Cheers *Salute*

IN A RESTAURANT

I'd like to book a table *Vorrei prenotare un tavolo*
I have a reservation *Ho fatto una prenotazione*
lunch/supper *pranzo/cena*
we do not want a full meal *Non desideriamo un pasto completo*
Could we have another table? *Potremmo spostarci?*
I'm a vegetarian *Sono vegetariano/a*
Is there a vegetarian dish? *C'è un piatto vegetariano?*
May we have the menu? *Ci dia la carta*
wine list *la lista dei vini*
What would you recommend? *Che cosa ci consiglia?*
What would you like as a main course/dessert? *Che cosa prende di secondo/di dolce?*
What would you like to drink? *Che cosa desidera da bere?*
a carafe of red/white wine *una caraffa di vino rosso/bianco*
fixed-price menu *il menù a prezzo fisso*
dish of the day *il piatto del giorno*
home-made *fatto in casa*
cover charge *il coperto/pane e coperto*
that's enough/no more thanks *basta così, grazie*
the bill, please *il conto per favore*
Is service included? *Il servizio è incluso?*
Where is the lavatory? *Dov'è il bagno?*
Keep the change *Va bene così*
I've enjoyed the meal *Mi è piaciuto molto*

MENU DECODER

Antipasti – Starters

antipasto misto **mixed hors d'oeuvres: cold cuts, cheeses,**

roast vegetables (ask for details)
buffet freddo cold buffet
caponata aubergine, olives, tomatoes
insalata caprese tomato and mozzarella salad
insalata di mare seafood salad
insalata mista/verde mixed/ green salad
melanzane alla parmigiana fried or baked aubergine with parmesan and tomato
mortadella/salame similar to salami
pancetta bacon
proscuitto ham
peperonata grilled peppers drenched in olive oil

Primi – First Courses

gli asparagi asparagus (in season)
brodetto fish soup
brodo broth
crespolini savoury pancakes
gnocchi potato and dough dumplings
la minestra soup
il minestrone thick vegetable soup
pasta e fagioli pasta and bean soup
il prosciutto (cotto/crudo) (cooked/cured) ham
i supplì rice croquettes
i tartufi truffles (fresh in season, otherwise bottled or vacuum-packed)
la zuppa soup

Secondi – Main Courses

La Carne Meat
allo spiedo on the spit
arrosto roast meat
ai ferri grilled without oil
al forno baked
al girarrosto spit-roasted
alla griglia grilled
involtini skewered veal, ham, etc
stagionato hung, well aged
ben cotto well done (steak)
media cottura medium
al sangue rare
l'agnello lamb
la bresaola dried salted beef
la bistecca steak
il capriolo/cervo venison
il carpaccio wafer-thin beef

il cinghiale wild boar
il controfiletto sirloin steak
le cotolette cutlets
il fagiano pheasant
il fegato liver
il filetto fillet
la lepre hare
il maiale pork
il manzo beef
l'ossobuco shin of veal
il pollo chicken
le polpette meatballs
il polpettone meat loaf
la porchetta roast suckling pig
la salsiccia sausage
il saltimbocca (alla Romana) veal escalopes with ham
le scaloppine escalopes
lo stufato braised, stewed
il sugo sauce
la trippa tripe
il vitello veal
Frutti di Mare Seafood
affumicato smoked
alle brace charcoal-grilled
al ferro grilled without oil
fritto fried
alla griglia grilled
ripieno stuffed
al vapore steamed
acciughe anchovies
l'anguilla eel
l'aragosta lobster
il baccalà dried salted cod
i bianchetti whitebait
il branzino sea bass
i calamaretti baby squid
i calamari squid
la carpa carp
le cozze mussels
i crostacei shellfish
il fritto misto mixed fried fish
i gamberetti shrimps
i gamberi prawns
il granchio crab
il merluzzo cod
le ostriche oysters
il pesce fish
il pescespada swordfish
il polipo octopus
il risotto di mare seafood risotto
le sarde sardines
le seppie cuttlefish
la sogliola sole
surgelati frozen
il tonno tuna
la triglia red mullet
la trota trout
le vongole clams

I Legumi/La Verdura – Vegetables

a scelta of your choice
gli asparagi asparagus
la bietola (similar to spinach)
i carciofini artichoke hearts
il carciofo artichoke
le carote carrots
il cavolo cabbage
la cicoria chicory
la cipolla onion
i contorni side dishes
i fagioli beans
i fagiolini French beans
fave broad beans
il finocchio fennel
i funghi mushrooms
l'indivia endive/chicory
insalata mista mixed salad
insalata verde green salad
la melanzana aubergine/eggplant
le patate potatoes
le patatine fritte chips/fries
i peperoni peppers
i piselli peas
i pomodori tomatoes
le primizie spring vegetables
il radicchio red, bitter lettuce
i ravanelli radishes
ripieno stuffed
rughetta/rucola rocket
spinaci spinach
la verdura green vegetables
la zucca pumpkin/squash
zucchini courgettes

La Frutta – Fruit

le albicocche apricots
le arance oranges
le banane bananas
le ciliege cherries
il cocomero watermelon
i fichi figs
le fragole strawberries
frutti di bosco fruits of the forest
i lamponi raspberries
la mela apple
la pera pear
la pesca peach
le uve grapes

I Dolci – Desserts

al carrello desserts from the trolley

la cassata **Sicilian ice cream with candied peel**
il dolce **dessert/sweet**
le fritelle **fritters**
un gelato (di lampone/limone) **(raspberry/lemon) ice cream**
una granita **water ice**
una macedonia di frutta **fruit salad**
un semifreddo **semi-frozen dessert (many types)**
il tartufo (nero) **(chocolate) ice-cream dessert**
il tiramisù **cold, creamy rum and coffee dessert**
la torta **cake/tart**
zabaglione **sweet dessert made with eggs and Marsala**
zuccotto **ice-cream liqueur**
la zuppa inglese **trifle**

Basic Foods

aceto **vinegar**
aglio **garlic**
burro **butter**
formaggio **cheese**
frittata **omelette**
grissini **bread sticks**
marmellata **jam**
olio **oil**
pane **bread**
pane integrale **wholemeal bread**
parmigiano **parmesan cheese**
pepe **pepper**
riso **rice**
sale **salt**
senape **mustard**
uova **eggs**
zucchero **sugar**

SIGHTSEEING

abbazia (badia) **abbey**
basilica **church**
biblioteca **library**
castello **castle**
centro storico **old town/historic centre**
chiesa **church**
duomo/cattedrale **cathedral**
fiume **river**
giardino **garden**
lago **lake**
mercato **market**
monastero **monastery**
monumenti **monuments**

museo **museum**
parco **park**
pinacoteca **art gallery**
ponte **bridge**
ruderi **ruins**
scavi **excavations/ archaeological site**
spiaggia **beach**
torre **tower**
ufficio turistico **tourist office**
il custode **custodian**
il sacristano **sacristan**
Aperto/a **Open**
Chiuso/a **Closed**
Chiuso per la festa/per ferie/per restauro **Closed for the festival/ holidays/restoration**

AT THE SHOPS

What time do you open/close? *A che ora apre/chiude?*
Pull/Push (sign on doors) *Tirare/Spingere*
Entrance/Exit *Entrata/Uscita*
Can I help you? (formal) *Posso aiutarla?*
What would you like? *Che cosa desidera?*
I'm just looking *Sto soltanto guardando*
How much is this? *Quanto viene?*
Do you take credit cards? *Accettate le carte di credito?*
I'd like… *Vorrei…*
This one/that one *questo/ quello*
Have you got…? *Avete…?*
We haven't got (any) *Non (ne) abbiamo*
Can I try it on? *Posso provare?*
the size (for clothes) *la taglia*
What size do you take? *Qual è la sua taglia?*
the size (for shoes) *il numero*
Is there/do you have…? *C'è (un/ una)…?*
Yes, of course *Si, certo*
No, we haven't (there isn't) *No, non c'è*
That's too expensive *È troppo caro*
Please write it down for me *Me lo scriva, per favore*
cheap *economico/a buon prezzo*
Do you have anything cheaper?

Ha niente che costa di meno?
It's too small/big *È troppo piccolo/grande*
brown/blue/black *marrone/blu/ nero*
green/red/white/yellow *verde/ rosso/bianco/giallo*
pink/grey/gold/silver *rosa/ grigio/oro/argento*
No thank you, I don't like it *Grazie, ma non è di mio gusto*
I'll take it/I'll leave it *Lo prendo/ lo lascio*
This is faulty. May I have a replacement/refund? *C'è un difetto. Me lo potrebbe cambiare/ rimborsare?*
Anything else? *Altro?*
The cash desk is over there *Si accomodi alla cassa*
Give me some of those *Mi dia alcuni di quelli lì*
(half) a kilo *un (mezzo) kilo*
100 grams *un etto*
200 grams *due etti*
more/less *più/meno*
with/without *con/senza*
a little *un pochino*

Types of Shops

antique dealer *l'antiquario*
bakery/cake shop *il forno/la panetteria/pasticceria*
bank *la banca*
bookshop *la libreria*
boutique/clothes shop *il negozio di vestiti*
butcher *la macelleria*
chemist *la farmacia*
delicatessen *la salumeria*
dry cleaner *la tintoria*
fishmonger *la pescheria*
florist *il fioraio*
food shop *l'alimentari*
greengrocer *l'ortolano/il fruttivendolo*
grocer *l'alimentari*
hairdresser *il parucchiere*
ice-cream parlour *la gelateria*
jeweller *il gioiellere*
leather shop *la pelletteria*
market *il mercato*
news-stand *l'edicola*
post office *l'ufficio postale*
shoe shop *il negozio di scarpe*
stationer *la cartoleria*
tobacconist *il tabaccaio*
travel agency *l'agenzia di viaggi*

TRAVELLING

aeroplane *l'aereo*
airport *l'aeroporto*
arrivals/departures *arrivi/ partenze*
boarding card *la carta d'imbarco*
boat *la barca*
bus *l'autobus/il pullman*
bus station *l'autostazione*
coach *il pullman*
couchette *la cucetta*
connection *la coincidenza*
ferry *il traghetto*
ferry terminal *la stazione marittima*
first/second class *la prima/seconda classe*
flight *il volo*
left-luggage office *il deposito bagagli*
platform *il binario*
port *il porto*
porter *il facchino*
railway station *ferrovia (la stazione ferroviaria)*
return ticket *un biglietto andata e ritorno*
single ticket *un biglietto solo andata*
sleeping car *la carrozza letti/il vagone letto*
smokers/non-smokers *fumatori/non-fumatori*
station *la stazione*
stop *la fermata*
ticket office *la biglietteria*
train *il treno*
WC *il gabinetto*

At the Station

(trains, buses and ferries)
Can you help me please? *Mi può aiutare, per favore?*
Where can I buy tickets? *Dove posso fare i biglietti?*
at the ticket office/at the counter *alla biglietteria/allo sportello*
What time does the train leave/ arrive? *A che ora parte/arriva il treno?*
Can I book a seat? *Posso prenotare un posto?*
Are there any seats available? *Ci sono ancora posti liberi?*
Is this seat free/taken? *È libero/occupato questo posto?*

I'm afraid this is my seat *È il mio posto, mi dispiace*
You'll have to pay a supplement *Deve pagare un supplemento*
Do I have to change? *Devo cambiare?*
Where does it stop? *Dove si ferma?*
You need to change in Rome *Bisogna cambiare a Roma*
Which platform does the train leave from? *Da quale binario parte il treno?*
The train leaves from platform one *Il treno parte dal binario uno*
When is the next train/bus/ ferry for Naples? *Quando parte il prossimo treno/ pullman/ traghetto per Napoli?*
How long does the crossing take? *Quanto dura la traversata?*
What time does the bus leave for Siena? *Quando parte l'autobus per Siena?*
How long will it take to get there? *Quanto tempo ci vuole per arrivare?*
Next stop, please *La prossima fermata per favore*
Is this the right stop? *È la fermata giusta?*
The train is late *Il treno è in ritardo*
Can you tell me where to get off? *Mi può dire dove devo scendere?*

Directions

left/right *a sinistra/a destra*
first left/second right *la prima a sinistra/la seconda a destra*
Turn to the left/right *Gira a sinistra/destra*
Go straight on *Va sempre diritto*
Go straight on until the traffic lights *Va sempre diritto fino al semaforo*
Is it far away/nearby? *È lontano/vicino?*
It's 5 minutes' walk *Cinque minuti a piedi*
It's 10 minutes by car *Dieci minuti con la macchina*
opposite/next to *di fronte/ accanto a*
up/down *su/giù*
traffic lights *il semaforo*
junction *l'incrocio, il bivio*
building *il palazzo* **(could be a**

palace or a block of flats)
Where is...? *Dov'è...?*
Where are...? *Dove sono...?*
Where is the nearest bank/petrol station/bus stop/hotel/ garage? *Dov'è la banca/il benzinaio/la fermata di autobus/ l'albergo/ l'officina più vicino/a?*
How do I get there? *Come si arriva a...?*
How long does it take to get to...? *Quanto tempo ci vuole per andare a...?*
Can you show me where I am on the map? *Può indicarmi sulla cartina dove mi trovo?*
You're on the wrong road *Lei è sulla strada sbagliata*

HEALTH

Is there a chemist nearby? *C'è una farmacia qui vicino?*
Which chemist is open at night? *Quale farmacia fa il turno di notte?*
I feel ill *Sto male/Mi sento male*
Where does it hurt? *Dove le fa male?*
It hurts here *Ho dolore qui*
I suffer from... *Soffro di...*
I have a headache *Ho mal di testa*
I have a sore throat *Ho mal di gola*
I have a stomach ache *Ho mal di pancia*
Have you got something for air sickness? *Ha/Avete qualcosa contro il mal d'aria?*
Have you got something for sea sickness? *Ha/Avete qualcosa contro il mal di mare?*
It's nothing serious *Non è niente di grave*
Take me to the hospital/emergency room *Mi porti all'ospedale/ pronto soccorso*
Do I need a prescription? *Ci vuole la ricetta?*
antiseptic cream *la crema antisettica*
insect repellent *l'insettifugo*
sticking plaster *il cerotto*
sunburn *scottato dal sole*
sunscreen *la crema antisolare*
tissues *i fazzoletti di carta*
toothpaste *il dentifricio*
upset-stomach pills *le pillole anti-coliche*

FURTHER READING

HISTORY AND SOCIETY

The Early History of Rome, by Livy (Penguin Classics).
The Families who made Rome: a History and Guide by Anthony Majanlahti (Random House UK).
The History of the Decline and Fall of the Roman Empire, by Edward Gibbon (Dent and Penguin).
A History of Rome, by Michael Grant (Faber & Faber).
Rome: Biography of a City, by Christopher Hibbert (Penguin).
The Italians, by Luigi Barzini (Penguin).
La Bella Figura: A Field Guide to the Italian Mind, by Beppe Severgnini (Broadway Books).
The Dark Heart of Italy, by Tobias Jones (Faber & Faber).

ART AND LITERATURE

The Aeneid, by Virgil (Penguin).
Meditations, by Marcus Aurelius (Penguin).
Lives of the Artists, by Giorgio Vasari (Penguin).
The Life of Benvenuto Cellini, by Benvenuto Cellini (Phaidon).
Rome, by Emile Zola (The Echo Library).
The Woman of Rome and Roman Tales, by Alberto Moravia

(Oxford University Press).
A Violent Life, by Pier Paolo Pasolini (Carcanet).
I Claudius, Claudius the God by Rupert Graves (Penguin).

FOOD AND WINE

The Encyclopedia of Italian Wines, by Oz Clarke and Maureen Ashley (Prentice Hall and IBD).
Italian Food, by Elizabeth David (Penguin Cookery Library).
The Essentials of Classic Italian Cooking, by Marcella Hazan (Macmillan).
Jamie's Italy, by Jamie Oliver (Penguin).
Italy for the Gourmet Traveler, by Fred Plotkin (Kyle Books).

FAMOUS TRAVELLERS

Pictures from Italy, by Charles Dickens (Penguin Classics).
Italian Journey, by Johann Wolfgang von Goethe, translated by W.H. Auden & Elizabeth Mayer (Pantheon Books and Penguin).
Italian Hours, by Henry James (Penguin Classics).
A Traveller in Rome, by Henry V. Morton (Methuen).
With Byron in Italy: A Selection

of the Poems and Letters of Lord Byron Relating to His Life in Italy, by Anna Benneson McMahan (Nabu Press).

OTHER INSIGHT GUIDES

Insight Guide: Italy covers the whole country, with features on food and drink, culture and the arts. Other titles cover Northern Italy, Florence, the Italian Lakes, Tuscany, Venice, Sicily and Sardinia.
Insight Select Guide: Rome offers a collection of over 100 inspiring ideas for your stay in the city, with plenty of secret gems and offbeat haunts in the mix – all carefully selected by a local writer who knows Rome inside out.
Insight Explore Guides cover Florence, the Italian Lakes, Rome, Naples and the Amalfi Coast, Venice as well as Sicily. These books provide a number of timed itineraries, with recommended stops for lunch. The walks are plotted on an accompanying pull-out map.
Insight Fleximaps combine clear, detailed cartography with essential travel information. Italian maps include Lake Garda & Verona, Milan, Rome, Sicily, Tuscany, Umbria and Venice.

ROME STREET ATLAS

The key map shows the area of Rome covered by the atlas
section. An index of street names and places of interest
shown on the maps can be found on the following pages. For
each entry there is a page number and grid reference

Map Legend

▭▭▭	Autostrada with Junction
▭ ▭ ▭	Autostrada (under construction)
▭▭▭	Dual Carriageway
▭▭▭	Main Road
▭▭▭	Secondary Road
▭▭▭	Minor Road
▭▭▭	Track
▬▬ ▬ ▬	International Boundary
▭ ▭ ▭	Province/State Boundary
▭ ● ▭	National Park/Reserve
▭ ▭ ▭ ▭	Ferry Route

⊖	Border Crossing
✦✦	Airport
✝✝	Church (ruins)
✝	Monastery
▰⌂	Castle (ruins)
∴	Archaeological Site
๑	Cave
★	Place of Interest
⌂	Mansion/Stately Home
※	Viewpoint
⚑	Beach

▭▭▭	Autostrada
▭▭▭	Dual Carriageway
▭▭▭	Main Roads
▭▭▭	Minor Roads
▭▭▭	Footpath
▬ ▬ ▬	Railway
▭	Pedestrian Area
▭	Important Building
▭	Park

Ⓜ	Metro
🚌	Bus Station
❶	Tourist Information
✉	Post Office
✝	Cathedral/Church
☪	Mosque
✡	Synagogue
⚊	Statue/Monument
⎮	Tower
⌁	Lighthouse

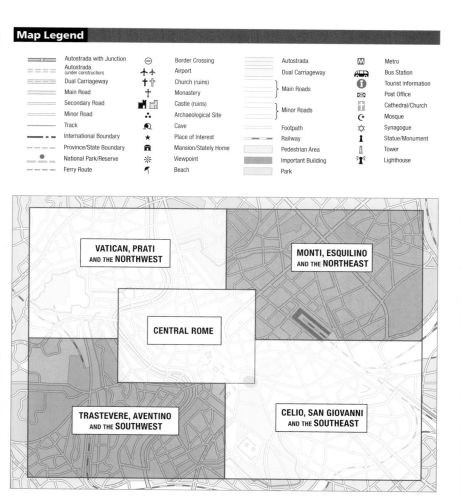

VATICAN, PRATI
AND THE NORTHWEST

MONTI, ESQUILINO
AND THE NORTHEAST

CENTRAL ROME

TRASTEVERE, AVENTINO
AND THE SOUTHWEST

CELIO, SAN GIOVANNI
AND THE SOUTHEAST

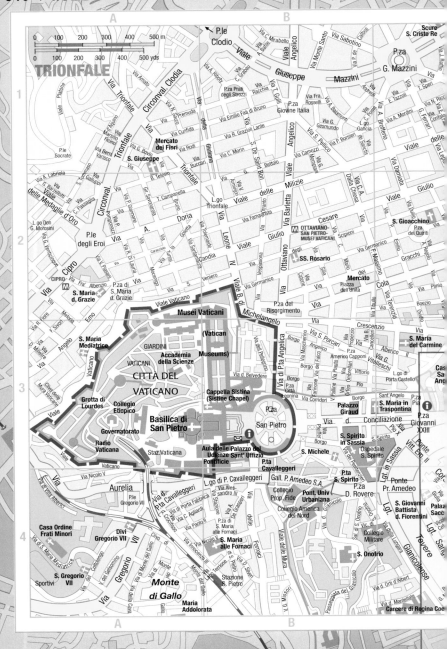

TRIONFALE

0 100 200 300 400 500 m
0 100 200 300 400 500 yds

P.le
Clodio

P.le
Socrate

P.le
degli Eroi

CIPRO

S. Maria
d. Grazie

S. Maria
Mediatrice

Grotta di
Lourdes

Collegio
Etiopico

Governatorato

Radio
Vaticana

Casa Ordine
Frati Minori

Divi
Gregorio
VII

S. Gregorio
VII

Sportivi

Monte
di Gallo

Maria
Addolorata

Aurelia

Staz.Vaticana

Basilica di
San Pietro

CITTÀ DEL
VATICANO

GIARDINI
VATICANI

Accademia
della Scienze

Musei Vaticani

(Vatican
Museums)

Cappella Sistina
(Sistine Chapel)

Aula delle
Udienze
Pontificie

Sant' Uffizio

Palazzo del
Pontificie

P.ta
Cavalleggeri

S. Michele

L.go di P. Cavalleggeri

Gall. P. Amedeo S.A.

Collegio
Prop. Fide

Collegio America
del Nord

Pont. Univ
Urbaniana

Collegio
Militare

S. Onofrio

S. Maria
alle Fornaci

Stazione
S. Pietro

P.za
San Pietro

Mercato
dei Fiori

S. Giuseppe

L.go
Trionfale

Doria

SS. Rosario

OTTAVIANO-
SAN PIETRO-
MUSEI VATICANI

Cesare

S. Gioacchino

P.za
del Quiriti

Mercato
Piazza
dell'Unità

P.za del
Risorgimento

Palazzo
Giraud

S. Maria in
Traspontina

S. Maria
del Carmine

Conciliazione

S. Spirito
in Sassia

Ospedale
S. Spirito

P.ta
S. Spirito

P.za
D. Rovere

Ponte
Pr. Amedeo

S. Giovanni
Battista
d. Fiorentini

Carcere di Regina Coe

P.za
G. Mazzini

Scure
S. Cristo Re

Giuseppe

Mazzini

P.za
Giovine Italia

P.za
Giovanni
XXIII

D | **E**

Accademia d. Romania
P.le Jose de S. Martin
P.za Cervantes
P.le Firdusi

Galleria Nazionale d'Arte Moderna e Contemporanea

Viale del Giardino Zoologico

VILLA STROHLFERN

Valle

Giulia

VILLA

Museo Canonica

Viale G. Filangieri
Via G. Mazzini
Via di Santa Maria

P.za della Marina
d. A. Azuni
Ministero Difesa Marina
Viale Madama

Viale del Giardino Zoologico

Via Flaminia
Via P.S. Mancini
Via Fortuny

Villa Ruffo

Viali degli Orti Giustiniani

Staz. Flaminio
P.le Flaminio

P.za del Fiocco

Tempio d. Esculapio

Viale P. Canonica
P.za di Siena

GIARDINO D. LAGO

P.le Lubin

Viale Washington

Museo Carlo Bilotti

Victor Hugo

P.za Canestre

VILLA BORGHESE

Tempio d. Diana

FLAMINIO PIAZZA DEL POPOLO

S. Maria d. Popolo

Monte

P.za del Popolo

Viale dell'obelisco

Pincio

Casina Valadier

VILLA MEDICI

GALOPPATOIO

Muro

Torto

S. Maria in Montesanto

S. Maria dei Mirac.

Via A. Brunetti

Casa di Goethe

Villa Medici

Accademia di Belle Arti

S. Giacomo

S. Cecilia

SPAGNA

PRATI

Teatro Adriano

Chiesa Valdese

P.za Cavour

Mausoleo di Augusto

Ara Pacis

S. Rocco

S. Carlo al Corso

Casa di Keats-Shelley

SS. Trinità dei Monti

S. Isodoro

Trinità dei Monti

Museo delle Anime del Purgatorio

Ponte Cavour

Palazzo Spagna

Ex Palazzo di Giustizia

Casa Madre d. Mutilati

Palazzo Borghese

Palazzo Ruspoli

Palazzo Bernini

Propaganda Fide

P.za Tribunali

Museo Napoleonico

Ponte Umberto I

Palazzo Fiano

S. Lorenzo in Lucina

S. Silvestro

S. Andrea d. Fratte

Castello

S. Antonio d. Portoghesi

Palazzo Altemps

S. Salvatore

S. Simeone

S. Agostino

Palazzo Montecitorio
Camera d. Deputati

Palazzo Chigi

S. Maria in Via

S. Claudio

Palazzo Poli

Fontana di Trevi

GIARDINO DEL QUIRINALE

S. Maria d. Pace

S. Maria d. Anima

S. Luigi d. Francesi

Galleria Alberto Sordi

Pal. del Quirinale

S. Agnese in Agone

Palazzo Madama (Senato)

S. Eustachio

Pantheon

Palazzo della Borsa

S. Macuto

S. Marcello

Scuderie del Quirinale

VILLA COLONNA

Chiesa Nuova

Palazzo Doria Pamphilj

S. Ivo

Archivio di Stato

S. Maria s. Minerva

S. Ignazio

Collegio Romano

SS. Apostoli

S. Silvestro

Palazzo del Gov. Vecchio

Palazzo Braschi

Teatro Argentina

Galleria Doria Pamphilj

Palazzo Odescalchi

Palazzo Colonna

Palazzo Taverna

Palazzo Massimo

Pal. della Cancelleria

P.za S. Andrea della Valle

Palazzo Altieri

Palazzo Bonaparte

Prefettura

S. Maria d. Monserrato

S. Andrea d. Valle

Palazzo Vidoni

Area Sacra dell'Argentina

Chiesa del Gesù

Palazzo Venezia

S. Marco

P.za Venezia

Col. Traiana

Foro di Traiano

S. Eligio

Teatro di Pompeo

Teatro d. Valle

V. Emanuele II

V.d. Plebiscito

D | **E**

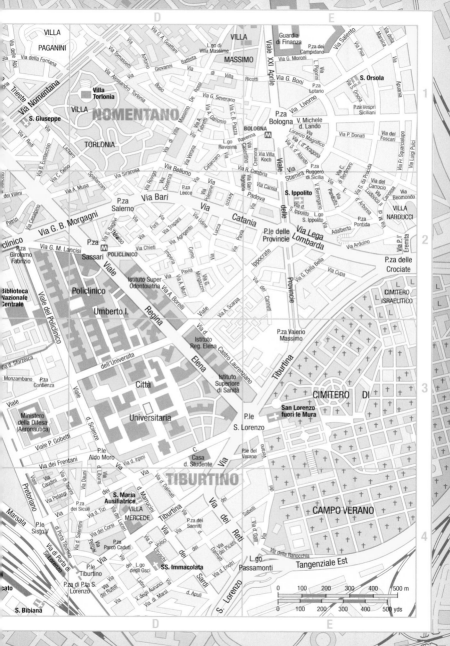

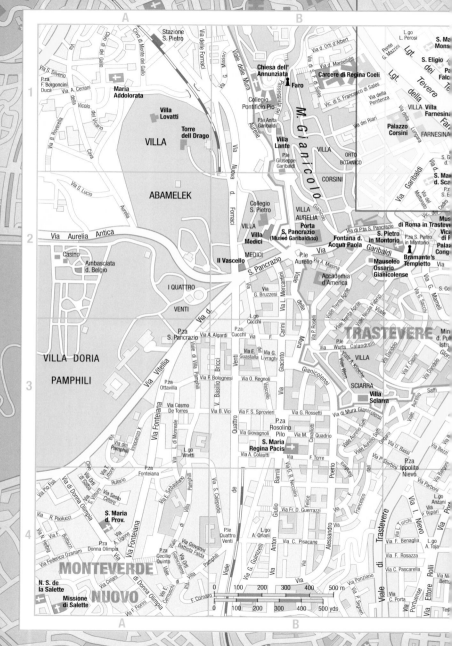

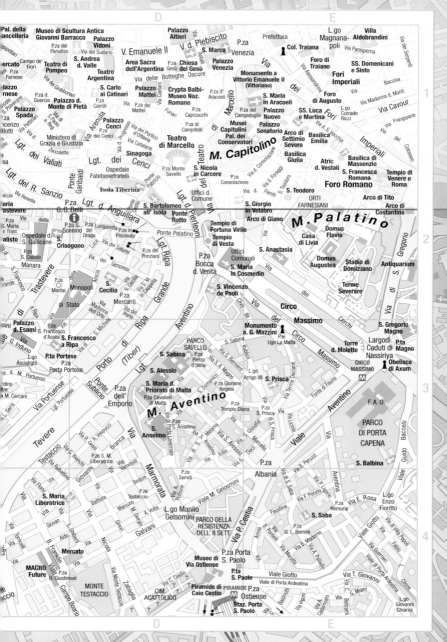

Pal. della ancelleria
Museo di Scultura Antica Giovanni Barracco
Palazzo Vidoni
Palazzo Altieri
V. d. Plebiscito
Prefettura
L.go Magnana-poli
Villa Aldobrandini

P.za del Paradiso
Via del Sudario
V. Emanuele II
P.za S. Marco
Via Panisperna

Campo de' Fiori
Teatro di Pompeo
S. Andrea d. Valle
Teatro Argentina
Area Sacra dell'Argentina
Chiesa Gesù del Gesù
Palazzo Venezia
Col. Traiana
Foro di Traiano
SS. Domenici e Sisto

Via delle Botteghe Oscure
Monumento a Vittorio Emanuele II (Vittoriano)
Via dei
Baccina

S. Carlo ai Catinari
Palazzo Mattei
Via Caetani
Crypta Balbi-Museo Naz. Romano
Foro di Augusto

P.za d. Quercia
Palazzo d. Monte di Pietà
P.za dei Cairoli
P.za d' Aracoeli
S. Maria in Aracoeli
SS. Luca e Martina

Palazzo Spada
Palazzo Cenci
Via d. Portico d'Ottavia
Teatro di Marcello
P.za del Campidoglio
Palazzo Nuovo
Arco di Settimio Severo
Basilica Emilia

Ministero di Grazia e Giustizia
Via Catalana
Sinagoga
Musei Capitolini Pal. dei Conservatori
Palazzo Senatorio
Basilica Giulia

LGT. dei Vallati
LGT. dei Cenci
Ospedale Fatebenefratelli
M. Capitolino
Arco di Tito

Isola Tiberina
S. Nicola in Carcere
Foro Romano
Tempio di Venere e Roma

S. Bartolomeo all'Isola
S. Giorgio in Velabro
M. Palatino
Arco di Costantino

Ponte Rotto
Tempio di Fortuna Virile
Arco di Giano
Domus Flavia

Ospedale d. S. Gallicano
S. Crisogono
Ponte Palatino
Tempio di Vesta
Casa di Livia

Trastevere
Monopoli di Stato
S. Cecilia
Uffici Comunali
S. Anastasia
Domus Augustea
Stadio di Domiziani
Antiquarium

S. Maria In Cosmedin
Terme Severare

Palazzo d. Esami
S. Francesco a Ripa
S. Vincenzo de Paoli
Circo
S. Gregorio Magno

Tevere
P.ta Portese
S. Sabina
Monumento a G. Mazzini
Massimo
Torre d. Molette
Largodi Caduti di Nassiriya

PARCO SAVELLO
S. Alessio
S. Maria d. Priorato di Malta
CIRCO MASSIMO
Obelisco di Axum

M. Aventino
S. Anselmo
PARCO DI PORTA CAPENA

F.A.O.

S. Maria Liberatrice
S. Balbina

Albania
Aventina
L.go Enzo Fioritto

Mercato
S. Maria Liberatrice
S. Saba

MACRO Future
PARCO DELLA RESISTENZA DELL' 8 SETT.

MONTE TESTACCIO
CIM. ACATTOLICO
Museo di Via Ostiense
P.za Porta S. Paolo
Piramide di Caio Cestio
PIRAMIDE Ostiense
Staz. Porta S. Paolo

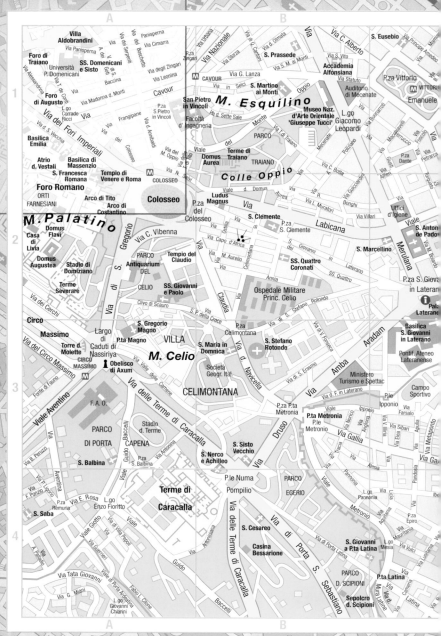

TUSCOLANO

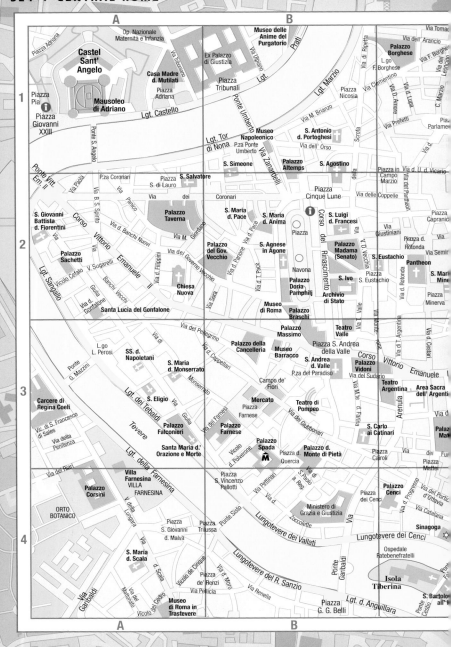

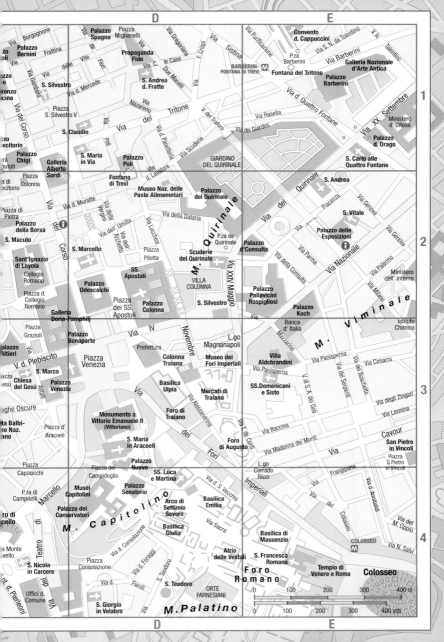

STREET INDEX

ART AND PHOTO CREDITS

Alamy 63B, 90ML, 110B, 170
**Alessandra Santarelli/Apa
Publications** 247
Apa Publications 9TR, 10/11, 20,
21, 25B, 28T, 29T, 28/29B, 38T,
38B, 40, 42, 42/43T, 44T, 48, 49,
51B, 53B, 52/53T, 56BR, 56/57T,
58, 64, 66, 72, 73, 74BR, 74MR,
74ML, 75ML, 75BR, 75TC, 84, 85,
86T, 86B, 86/87, 88T, 90MR,
91BR, 90/91T, 92/93M, 93BR,
92/93T, 95, 96B, 100B, 101B,
102TR, 102/103, 104B, 105B,
108, 110T, 116/117, 124/125B,
126/127B, 127T, 128T, 128B,
128/129, 134, 135, 136/137T,
138/139B, 138/139T, 140T, 140B,
144, 151, 153T, 154, 155B, 155T,
156/157B, 160, 161B, 164, 166,
167, 168B, 168T, 168/169,
170/171T, 172B, 173T, 176T,
177T, 178, 182, 183, 184/185,
186/187B, 188, 188/189B, 191,
194T, 194/195, 196, 197, 214,
215B, 214/215T, 216/217T, 218,
219T, 220/221B, 222, 226/227T,
230/231B, 232T, 238T, 244, 248B,
248/249, 250ML, 250/251M,
251BR, 251MR, 256, 258B, 258T,
258/259, 260/261, 263, 264B,
264T, 265T, 265B, 266B, 266T,
267, 268MR, 268BR, 268ML,
268/269M, 268/269T, 269TC,
269BR, 270, 272, 272/273T,
273BR, 273TR, 274T, 275T,
274/275B, 276T, 277, 280/281,
282T, 282B, 283B, 284/285
Bigstock 50/51T, 52, 60, 143B,
148/149M, 177B, 220, 255T, 257,
296
**Courtesy of the Archivio
Fotografico Soprintendenza
Speciale per il Polo Museale
Romano** 56ML
Corbis 24/25T, 44/45, 250MR
Dreamstime 10B, 148B,
148/149T, 149MC, 176B,
178/179, 186/187T, 206T,
206/207B, 298
Fondazione MAXXI 194B
Fotolia 57TR, 61, 102B, 104T,
123T, 199TR, 200, 271
Getty Images 62, 62/63T, 149B,
250MR, 252/253, 262, 276B, 278,
279, 280B, 280T
iStock 106/107B, 158B, 193B,
241, 254/255B, 260, 274B, 314
**Merian, M., Topographia
Germaniae, 1642.** 30T
**Ming Tang-Evans/Apa
Publications** 1, 6/7, 8ML, 8MR,
8B, 8/9T, 9MC, 8/9M, 9MR, 9BR,
8/9B, 10T, 11R, 12BR, 12BL, 12T,
12/13B, 14/15, 16/17, 18, 19T,
18/19B, 22, 22/23T, 23B, 24, 26B,
26T, 26/27, 28B, 36B, 38/39T,
46/47, 50, 54B, 54T, 56MR, 59,
65, 66/67T, 67B, 68T, 68B,
68/69T, 69B, 70, 70/71T, 71B,
74/75T, 76/77, 78/79, 80, 81T,
80/81B, 88B, 93TC, 94, 96T,
96/97, 99, 100T, 102TL, 105T,
106/107T, 108/109, 110/111,
111R, 112, 113, 114, 115T,
114/115B, 116, 118B, 118T, 120,
121, 122/123B, 124, 124/125T,
130/131, 142/143T, 146MR,
146/147T, 147TC, 150, 158T,
158/159T, 160/161T, 162B, 162T,
163, 171B, 172T, 172/173B, 174T,
174B, 174/175, 184, 186,
188/189T, 190, 201, 202,
202/203T, 203B, 204T, 204B,
204/205, 207T, 208, 208/209T,
212, 213, 216B, 216T, 216/217B,
218/219B, 220/221T, 223, 224,
225, 226/227B, 228, 229B,
228/229T, 230L, 232B, 232/233,
234, 235, 236, 237, 238B, 239B,
239T, 242/243, 245, 248T, 286,
288, 289T, 290, 291M, 290/291T,
300/301, 308/309
Photoshot 56/57B
Public domain 30B, 90/91M, 156
Rex Features 31
Scala Archives 32, 33, 34, 34/35T,
35B, 36/37, 39B, 40/41T, 43B,
44B, 54/55, 41B, 57BR, 90MR,
91MR, 92MR, 92ML, 122, 146ML,
146MR, 147BR, 148T, 156/157T,
159B, 192/193T, 198B, 198T,
198/199T, 198/199B, 199MR,
206B, 230/231T, 250/251T, 284
Shutterstock 126, 138, 282/283T
Susan Smart/Apa Publications
13T, 92MR, 100/101T, 130, 137B,
141, 146/147M, 152/153B,
208/209B, 230R, 294T, 303L, 305L

Cover Credits

Front cover: Spainish Steps
Shutterstock
Back cover: St. Peters *Ming Tang-
Evans/Apa Publications*
Front flap: (from top) Pincio terrace
Ming Tang-Evans/Apa Publications;
Terme di Diocleziano *Ming Tang-
Evans/Apa Publications*;
Gastronomia Volpetti *Ming Tang-
Evans/Apa Publications*; Santa
Bartolomeo all'Isola *Ming Tang-
Evans/Apa Publications*
Back flap: inside the Colosseum
Ming Tang-Evans/Apa Publications

INDEX

RESTAURANTS

BARS AND CAFÉS